George Eliot
and Community

George Eliot
and Community

A Study in Social Theory
and Fictional Form

◆

SUZANNE GRAVER

UNIVERSITY OF CALIFORNIA PRESS
Berkeley Los Angeles London

University of California Press
Berkeley and Los Angeles, California
University of California Press, Ltd.
London, England
© 1984 by
The Regents of the University of California

Library of Congress Cataloging in Publication Data
Graver, Suzanne.
    George Eliot and community.

    Bibliography: p.
    Includes index.
    1. Eliot, George, 1819–1880—Political and so-
cial views. 2. Eliot, George, 1819–1880—Criticism
and interpretation.   3. Social values in literature.
4. Community in literature.   5. Social history—
19th century.   I. Title.
PR4692.S58G7   1983   823′.8   82–13548
ISBN 0–520–04802–4

Printed in the United States of America
1 2 3 4 5 6 7 8 9

for Larry

Contents

vii

Acknowledgments

At the heart of this study is the idea of a community of interests created out of shared concerns and mutual endeavors. I think of my work on this book as engendering for me an analogous community. It includes a great many scholars and critics, but particularly Barbara Hardy, Gordon S. Haight, W. J. Harvey, U. C. Knoepflmacher, and David Carroll, whose writings opened George Eliot's novels to me long before I began this project. Beyond this imagined community, I have benefited greatly from the intellectual and emotional sustenance I have received from colleagues, friends, and family.

I am especially indebted to Michael Wolff of the University of Massachusetts at Amherst, an invaluable teacher, colleague, and friend. He has generously shared with me his matchless knowledge of Victorian England and its cultural complexities. He has contributed his time and expertise unstintingly, reading first and final drafts and cheering me on in between. Doris Kretschmer of the University of California Press similarly encouraged me to see the project through to completion, providing unfailing support. Amy Einsohn edited the manuscript with admirable intelligence and care.

I am grateful to the University of Massachusetts and Williams College for providing fellowship and research assistance. Sarah McFarland gave scrupulous attention to the index, and she and Lee Dalzell were valuable to me both as friends and expert reference librarians. Cheryl Martin and Rose Dinnerstein verified the text, and Nadene Lane typed the manuscript, with patience and good cheer. Other colleagues and friends provided information and support: Alex Zwerdling, Lee Edwards, Robert Keefe, Cynthia Griffin Wolff, and Thomas E. Foster. Susan P. Casteras of the Yale Center for British Art suggested the jacket illustration, and I also received assistance from her colleagues, Timothy Goodhue and

Laura Prete. To *Studies in the Novel* I owe thanks for permission to reprint material I first published there.

My greatest debt, however, is to my family. Within the context of this study, love and kinship emerge as the most positive, enduring forms of traditional community, and so have they proved to be for me. I am grateful to my parents, Sam and Rebecca Levy, whose fruitful lives testify to the strength of family ties. My writing of this book coincided with the years when my daughters, Ruth and Elizabeth, were growing up, and they responded with exceptional understanding and sympathy, sustaining me with their bright spirits. Lawrence Graver has been at once husband and colleague, ardent supporter and astute critic. The idea of sympathetic criticism is itself an important concept in this study. To my mind, no one exemplifies it better than he does, and I feel very fortunate to have had my best reader be also my spouse.

Short Titles

AB	George Eliot, *Adam Bede*, ed. John Paterson (Boston: Houghton Mifflin, 1968).
CH	*George Eliot: The Critical Heritage*, ed. David Carroll (London: Routledge & Kegan Paul, 1971).
DD	George Eliot, *Daniel Deronda*, ed. Barbara Hardy (Harmondsworth, England: Penguin Books, 1967).
Essays	*Essays of George Eliot*, ed. Thomas Pinney (New York: Columbia University Press, 1963).
FH	George Eliot, *Felix Holt, the Radical*, ed. Peter Coveney (Harmondsworth, England: Penguin Books, 1972).
G&G	Ferdinand Tönnies, *Community and Society (Gemeinschaft und Gesellschaft)*, ed. and trans. Charles P. Loomis (New York: Harper & Row, 1963).
Letters	*The George Eliot Letters*, 9 vols., ed. Gordon S. Haight (New Haven: Yale University Press, 1954–78).
M	George Eliot, *Middlemarch*, ed. Gordon S. Haight (Boston: Houghton Mifflin, 1956).
MF	George Eliot, *The Mill on the Floss*, ed. Gordon S. Haight (Boston: Houghton Mifflin, 1961).
R	George Eliot, *Romola*, Everyman's Library (London: Dent, 1968).
SCL	George Eliot, *Scenes of Clerical Life*, ed. David Lodge (Harmondsworth, England: Penguin Books, 1973).
SM	George Eliot, *Silas Marner*, ed. Q. D. Leavis (Harmondsworth, England: Penguin Books, 1967).
TS	George Eliot, *Impressions of Theophrastus Such*, Cabinet ed. (Edinburgh and London: William Blackwood & Sons, 1879).

ONE

❖

Introduction: Concepts of Community

Victorian social critics often described the loss of community and the need for its renewal to be one of the major problems of the age, and much of the century's fiction, poetry, drama, theology, history, and philosophy reflects this sense of loss. In England and in Europe, writers contemplated the presence of community in the Greek *polis*, among early Christians, and within the feudal arrangements of Anglo-Saxon, medieval, and postmedieval village life. By studying and describing earlier forms of social organization, they hoped to contribute substantially to understanding and changing their own. But these older forms of community, even when they offered perspectives that seemed corrective or admonitory, were at best only partially suited to a "modern age" frequently defined in terms of its differences from the past.

Broadly viewed, the preceding four centuries of European life seemed to be characterized by the growing prevalence of individualist values and the gradual decline of communal ones. The general historical trend was toward a steady advance in science and technology, the growth of highly developed commerce and large-scale industry, an increase in urban population and density, and a splintering of religious beliefs. Any effort to renew communal forms and values had to accommodate these new economic, social, and ideological conditions. Particularly in Britain, where industrialism had had its start, the loss was often located in the near past of the last half of the eighteenth century and the early decades of the nineteenth. This immediate past illustrated that the need for renewal was directly related to ongoing changes: to the new industrialism that was combining with an older system of agrarian capitalism to change not only the look of the land but also the nature of economic and social arrangements; and to the growth of egalitarian and religious movements that were contributing (for all

1

their differences) to the contract mentality and individualist ethos
upon which capitalism flourished. Those who desired a renewal of
community came increasingly to believe that as agrarian village
life was being replaced by modern urban society, communitarian
values were being undermined by individualistic ones whether
thoroughly worldly or narrowly religious. Among the writers to
be discussed in this study, that desire led above all to a strenuous
effort to integrate individualistic and communal values and to
transform religious ties into social ones.

To move beyond such generalizations, however, is to find almost
every claim about the idea of community in the nineteenth century open to question, not only because countries and individual
writers responded to modernization differently but also because
dilemmas first confronted by them remain unresolved. Perhaps
the most telling sign of this lack of resolution is our own inability,
despite persistent effort, to agree on a solid definition of community.[1] If the concept implies that a group of people have something
significant in common—family, neighborhood, property, ideas, beliefs, feelings—the range of categories is so broad as to preclude
useful definition. The traditional community, because it consisted
of a group of people living for generations in a given place and
regulating their lives according to set customs and beliefs, could
be described by a constellation of shared, concrete realities. But
when individuals become more mobile, these constellations of patterns fragment and disintegrate. Newer definitions of community
place less emphasis on concrete attributes, such as genealogy, locality, and custom, and more emphasis on less tangible elements,
such as affective ties, or the feelings, ideas, and interests that exist
apart from fixity of place and social role.[2] As a result, these modern
definitions lack solidity. Still, by describing a renewed mutuality

1. Among recent sociological studies of the historical development of the
word *community* and its shifting contexts are Jessie Bernard, *The Sociology
of Community*; Joseph R. Gusfield, *Community: A Critical Response*; Don
Martindale, *Community, Character and Civilization*; David W. Minar and
Scott Greer, eds., *The Concept of Community*; Robert A. Nisbet, *Social Change
and History, The Social Philosophers: Community and Conflict in Western
Thought,* and *The Sociological Tradition*; Raymond Plant, *Community and
Ideology*; Dennis E. Poplin, *Communities: A Survey of Theories and Methods
of Research*; and Neil J. Smelser, ed., *Sociology*.

2. See, for instance, Bernard, *Sociology of Community*; Gusfield, *Communi-
ty*; Minar and Greer, *Concept of Community*; Plant, *Community and Ideology*;
Nisbet, *Sociological Tradition*; and Thomas Bender, *Community and Social
Change*.

of concern independent of physical location and comparatively free of the pressure to agree and conform, they reshape traditional notions to accommodate the structures of a modern, diverse world and ensure a sense of freedom and individual choice. However, this liberal designation, no less than the conservative one, demonstrates another major problem of definition; namely, an evaluative dimension that blurs distinctions between community as fact and community as value and that encompasses an ideological range so wide as to make even the many descriptive meanings commonly assigned to community seem narrow and deficient.

Because George Eliot participated in a tradition of social thought that was preoccupied with the rediscovery of community, I wish to set this study of her fiction within such a framework of distinctive and problematic meanings. Despite many individual differences and internal contradictions, this intellectual tradition includes four principal elements alluded to earlier: the perception of a breakdown in traditional values, the belief in a need for social regeneration, the desire (virtually impossible to fulfill) to distinguish between fact and value so as to validate both, and the assumption that society could recover a sense of solidarity through a revolution of thought and feeling. The theoretical tradition of which I am speaking thus excludes Marx and all thinkers who put political revolution before a revolution in sensibility. But it does include a diverse group of social theorists who discussed most of the other major issues raised in modern debates about community, such as the place of traditional belief and custom; the relation of individualistic to social values; and the difficulty of creating new forms to counteract the fragmented, self-serving, and isolating tendencies of increasingly heterogeneous and complex societies. Moreover, the most distinctive and representative qualities of this tradition of social thought derive precisely from its commitment to social regeneration through a reshaping of thought and feeling. But this very goal suggests, in turn, how inadequate to the task social theory by itself was likely to be, and how absolutely central works of imaginative literature might be. George Eliot's fiction attained this kind of centrality, I believe, and in the chapters that follow I will define the nature of that achievement by relating her novels to nineteenth-century social theories and by analyzing how she and a group of theorists sought to influence the sensibilities of their contemporary readers.

The theorists include David Friedrich Strauss and Ludwig Feuerbach, the German biblical critics whom George Eliot translated and whose works help to clarify one problematical aspect of community: how it is both allied to Christianity and fundamentally at odds with it.[3] More important, however, are the French and English founders of sociology, Auguste Comte, Herbert Spencer, and John Stuart Mill, because they perceived themselves to be involved in a common enterprise and because George Eliot knew their work well and showed a continuing interest in it. George Henry Lewes is another key figure since he shared with George Eliot not only his knowledge and interests but also his life. Although the diverse nationalities even of this small group suggest the pervasiveness of the concern with social regeneration in nineteenth-century Europe, my own focus is on the problem of community in Victorian England. In turning to Strauss, Feuerbach, and Comte, I am simply following the lead provided by a good many Victorians. The biblical critics are important to this study, for example, because many Victorians—among them George Eliot, Lewes, Spencer, and Mill—came to share their conclusions about the way religion reflects and shapes social conditions.

Comte's significance is far too complex to be outlined here, but the intense interest in his work among the Victorian thinkers we are considering may be suggested simply by noting some of their writings of the 1850s and 1860s. During this time, Lewes and Mill both published essays as well as books on Comte, while Spencer wrote a long essay, "Reasons for Dissenting from the Philosophy of M. Comte," to counter the frequent associations made between them.[4] Lewes subsequently explained his own later divergence

3. For George Eliot, the work of local Coventry friends—Charles Christian Hennell and Charles Bray—was also important, having helped to make firm her rejection of Christian orthodoxy when she was in her early twenties. Hennell's conclusions were independent of those already reached by Strauss; George Eliot encountered them for the first time in 1842 when she read Hennell's *An Inquiry Concerning the Origins of Christianity*, 2d ed. Bray opposed (as did many of the theorists George Eliot was later to study) religious doctrines that place man's relation to his Creator above "the duties we owe to our fellow-creatures" (*The Philosophy of Necessity*, p. 371). Useful accounts of George Eliot's rejection of traditional Christianity are offered by Howard R. Murphy, "The Ethical Revolt Against Christian Orthodoxy in Early Victorian England," pp. 800–817; Basil Willey, *Nineteenth Century Studies*, pp. 204–44; and Gordon S. Haight, *George Eliot: A Biography*, pp. 39–69, 137–43, and passim.

4. Lewes, *Comte's Philosophy of the Sciences*, eighteen articles originally published in the *Leader*, April–August 1852, and revised in 1853 prior to book publication (for which George Eliot helped him to read proofs); "Auguste Comte"; "Comte and Mill." Mill, *Auguste Comte and Positivism*, two articles

from Comte and assessed Mill's increasing disagreement with Comte's ideas and methods in a piece entitled "Comte and Mill." The interest in Comte in Britain is also attested to by the number of his English translators—Harriet Martineau, Frederic Harrison, J. H. Bridges, and Richard Congreve; and by numerous periodical articles, among them a joint essay by John Chapman and W. M. W. Call in the *Westminster Review* and a debate between Huxley and Congreve conducted in the *Fortnightly Review* while Lewes was its editor.[5] Together these various writings reflect an interest in a tradition that extends well beyond Comte and that has at its center a preoccupation with social progress shared by other social evolutionists such as Henry Maine and E. B. Tylor. Within this tradition Spencer and Mill are no less significant than Comte, Spencer winning early fame as a philosopher of evolution for essays published in the *Leader* and *Westminster Review* when Lewes and Eliot were their respective editors, and Mill struggling throughout his career with "the great and vexed question of the progressiveness of man and society."[6]

George Eliot was not only versed in the work of these writers but also knew many of them. She and Lewes, of course, maintained a continuous union, and her friendships with Spencer and the Congreves spanned thirty and twenty years, respectively. She knew Harrison, Chapman, and Call well, and was acquainted with most of the other figures mentioned thus far: Martineau, Bridges, Huxley, Maine, and Tylor. She never actually met Mill and Comte, but the record of her reading reveals how closely she followed their work. Although it is difficult to determine when she first read Mill,

---

originally published in the *Westminster Review* 83 (April 1865) and 84 (July 1865), and subsequently in book editions. Changes within the various editions of Lewes's *Biographical History of Philosophy* and Mill's *Logic* offer further evidence of their continuous efforts to come to terms with Comte. Spencer, "Reasons for Dissenting from the Philosophy of M. Comte." The "maze of connections" between George Eliot and Lewes, Spencer, Comte, and Mill during the 1850s is discussed in detail by Michael Wolff, "Marian Evans to George Eliot: The Moral and Intellectual Foundations of Her Career," pp. 143–45 and passim.

5. [W.M.W. Call and John Chapman], "The Religion of Positivism," *Westminster Review*. In the *Fortnightly Review*: Huxley, "On the Physical Basis of Life"; Congreve, "Mr. Huxley on M. Comte"; Huxley, "The Scientific Aspects of Positivism."

6. *Leader*: "The Development Hypothesis" (20 March 1852), "The Use of Anthropomorphism" (5 November 1853); reprinted in Herbert Spencer, *Illustrations of Universal Progress*. *Westminster Review*: "A Theory of Population"; "The Universal Postulate"; "Manners and Fashion."

in 1849 and 1852 she lent her copy of *Logic* to friends (among them Herbert Spencer), and during the early 1850s, when she was editing the *Westminster Review*, she expressed admiration for Mill and considered both *Political Economy* and *Logic* to be authoritative reference texts. Later on, between 1865 and 1866, while reading for the first time *Auguste Comte and Positivism, Representative Government*, and *On Liberty*, and rereading *Political Economy* and *Logic*, she speaks of how frequently Mill's works have been "my companions of late" and of "going through many *actions de grâce* towards him."[7] In the case of Comte, from the early 1850s until the end of her life, she regularly studied his writings; and she was so often surrounded by people expounding and translating Comte or explaining their partial adherence to or disagreements with him that "her intellectual life," as one critic has recently put it, "was lived in an atmosphere saturated with Comte's influence."[8] That it was also saturated by Spencer's and Mill's, however, was clearer to her contemporary critics than it has been to us. In 1883, for instance, in one of the first books on George Eliot, George Willis Cooke opens the discussion by saying that we must

> know the nineteenth century in its scientific attainments, agnostic philosophy, realistic spirit and humanitarian aims, in order to know George Eliot. . . . As Goethe came after Lessing, Herder and Kant, so George Eliot came after Comte, Mill and Spencer. Her books are to be read in the light of their speculations, and she embodied in literary forms what they uttered as science or philosophy.[9]

7. Haight, *Biography*, pp. 115, 381; *Letters* 1: 310; 2: 47–49, 68, 145; 4: 196, 208, 232–33.

8. Thomas Pinney, "More Leaves from George Eliot's Notebook," p. 360; hereafter cited as "More Leaves." The most extensive argument for Comte's influence on George Eliot is made by Bernard J. Paris, *Experiments in Life*. He argues that George Eliot's personal, intellectual, and artistic development "recapitulated Comte's famous Law of the Three Stages" (theological, metaphysical, positivistic). However, the more usual estimate of George Eliot's selective appreciation of Comte, and of an adherence that was limited and skeptical, is far more accurate.

9. George Willis Cooke, *George Eliot: A Critical Study of Her Life, Writings and Philosophy*, pp. 1–2. By grouping together Comte, Mill, and Spencer, Cooke begins to suggest that what is at play in George Eliot's intellectual world is not one particular strand or another, necessarily attributable to this source or that influence, but rather what W. J. Harvey later calls a "nexus of ideas" ("Idea and Image in the Novels of George Eliot," p. 160). In the discussion that follows, I use the phrase "community of interest" to suggest something similar.

Because their science and philosophy, as well as George Eliot's novels, were guided by a belief that "the effort of the nineteenth century must be towards the reconstruction of society upon a new basis,"[10] these writers, together with less prominent members of their intellectual society, may be said to share a "community of interest." The phrase is one George Eliot uses in some notes titled "Birth of Tolerance" to make the claim that "community of interest is the root of justice," and it has important affinities with several related phrases that appear regularly in the theoretical writings of her contemporaries, as in Congreve's "community of purpose," Spencer's "fundamental community of opinion," Mill's "unity of interest," and Comte's "community of thought" and "community of principles."[11] Its fuller articulation may be illustrated by a passage from Comte that Mill took for his epigraph in the early editions of Book VI of his *Logic*, where his own reformist and theoretical interests lead him to attempt a new science of society.[12] Lewes later uses this same passage in the *Leader* articles he wrote to introduce English readers to Comte, and I quote from his translation:

> So long as individual minds do not adhere together from a unanimous agreement upon a certain number of general ideas, capable of forming a common social doctrine, the state of the nations will of necessity remain essentially revolutionary, in spite of all the political palliatives that can be adopted; and will not permit the establishing of any but *provisional* institutions. It is equally certain that, if this union of minds, from a community of principles, can once be obtained, institutions in harmony with it will neces-

10. The speaker in this instance is Lewes ("Auguste Comte," p. 388), but he is expressing an idea so common that Walter Houghton locates virtually the same words in Mill, Kingsley, and Huxley to point out an "assumption of the time" shared by others, including H. T. Buckle, John Morley, Frederic Harrison, W. K. Clifford (*The Victorian Frame of Mind, 1830–1870*, pp. 35–38). All the figures Houghton mentions were known to George Eliot. The group he assembles suggests, moreover, the "Philosophic Club" formed during the early 1860s to bring together "men who think variously, but have more hearty feelings in common than they give each other credit for" (*Letters* 4: 66). Its members included Lewes, Huxley, Kingsley, and Spencer.

11. "Leaves from a Note-Book," *Essays*, p. 449. Congreve, "Mr. Huxley on M. Comte," p. 417. Spencer, *First Principles*, pp. 10–11. Mill, *Principles of Political Economy, Collected Works of John Stuart Mill* 3: 896; *Autobiography*, p. 138. Comte, *System of Positive Polity* 4: 148–49; hereafter cited as *Polity*.

12. Mill, *System of Logic Ratiocinative and Inductive, Collected Works* 8: 832. The epigraph from Comte appears in the 1843 and 1846 editions.

sarily arise, without giving room for any serious shock,—that single fact of itself clearing away the greatest disorder.[13]

This passage is exemplary, but not because it calls for "unanimous agreement." Most of Comte's contemporaries recognized—and Mill, Lewes, and George Eliot above all—that they were far from attaining such unity of thought. What makes the passage characteristic is the underlying assumption, acknowledged even by the strictly scientific Huxley, of the need to "think deeply upon social problems and to strive nobly for social regeneration."[14] The concept of a community of interests, which is central to my argument, presupposes not agreement but a shared perception of problems among writers who approached the idea of community with a similar cast of mind. They wanted, for instance, to witness objectively the effects of ideology on past and present communities, but they often testified as well to a secular ideal that violated their empirical principles. They tried to find arguments for organic community in positivist laws of nature, but the increasingly complex and intricate social organism they perceived in the present often seemed to defy concepts of wholeness. Not only did they have to struggle with such self-contradictions, which at least they shared, but they had also to confront substantial disagreements among themselves as they brought uncertain answers or diverging conclusions to their common quest for community. But even in their differences of opinion they tried to see a community of spirit and purpose that was itself an essential basis of intellectual, moral, and social communion. As Lewes explains in the opening pages of *Problems of Life and Mind* (1: 2):

> The great desire of this age is for a Doctrine which may serve to condense our knowledge, guide our researches, and shape our lives, so that Conduct may really be the consequence of Belief. . . . In consequence of this desire, while thinking men appear, on a superficial view, to be daily separating wider and wider from each other, they are, on a deeper view, seen to be drawing closer together,—differing in opinion, they are approximating in spirit and purpose.

To include George Eliot in this community of interests is not to maintain that she was a systematic social theorist, but rather to suggest that she grappled with the problem of social renewal in different yet analogous ways. Many of the verbal devices and structural patterns characteristic of her fiction correspond to the inno-

13. Lewes, *Comte's Philosophy of the Sciences*, p. 14.
14. Huxley, "Scientific Aspects of Positivism," pp. 654, 670.

vative methods and ideas of the theorists. My major interest is the relationship between the concreteness her fictional communities attain and a tradition of social thought in which community becomes an abstraction, a qualitative ideal rather than a perceived reality—but an ideal that addresses an actual world, immediately present, dominated by individualist values and struggling to recover communal ones. Thus it is not my intention to chart "influences," but rather to show how certain nineteenth-century ideas about community informed George Eliot's sense of purpose as novelist and helped to shape her fiction.

The distinction between influence and shared affinities is an important one because it speaks to George Eliot's relation to the authors she read and to the effect she wished to have upon her readers. Writing about her rare qualities of mind, Spencer once described her as someone in whom "receptivity and originality . . . appear to have been equally great," confirming her own descriptions of her tendency to form "new combinations" out of the thoughts she found in others.[15] Taking her experience with Rousseau as exemplary, for instance, she argues in a letter written in 1849 that even were she to discover his views to be

> miserably erroneous . . . it would not be the less true that Rousseau's genius has sent that electric thrill through my intellectual and moral frame which has awakened me to new perceptions, which has made man and nature a fresh world of thought and feeling to me—and this not by teaching me any new belief. It is simply that the rushing mighty wind of his inspiration has so quickened my faculties that I have been able to shape more definitely for myself ideas which had previously dwelt as dim 'ahnungen' in my soul—the fire of his genius has so fused together old thoughts and prejudices that I have been ready to make new combinations.

> [*Letters* 1: 277

Over the years, she described her responses to other writers in similar ways, ascribing value to any teaching that arouses the reader to discovery, not by providing solutions, but by fostering an awareness of "the means by which endless solutions may be wrought" (*Essays*, p. 213). Thus, it is not surprising that while she thoroughly disclaims direct influences, she simultaneously affirms indebtedness —to Spencer "for much enlargement and clarifying of thought," to Comte for the "illumination" he "has contributed to my life," and

---

15. David Duncan, *Life and Letters of Herbert Spencer* 1: 395; *Letters* 2: 503.

to Mill for the great "benefit" she derived from his books (*Letters* 6: 163–64; 4: 333).

Speaking of the creative process at work in her own books, George Eliot also uses the phrase "new combinations" (*Letters* 2: 503). Furthermore, she adopts as one of her rules of authorship the standard she applies to others, to Rousseau, Ruskin, George Sand, and Carlyle:

> the most effective writer is not he who announces a particular discovery, who convinces men of a particular conclusion, who demonstrates that this measure is right and that measure wrong; but he who rouses in others the activities that must issue in discovery, who awakes men from their indifference to the right and the wrong, who nerves their energies to seek for the truth and live up to it at whatever cost.
>
> [*Essays*, p. 213

In her fiction, George Eliot applies this principle to challenge her readers into perceiving the necessity and difficulties of a gradual social transformation that would begin with a revolution in individual sensibilities.

Consequently, the concept of a "community of readers," both projected and actual, is as pertinent to George Eliot's writings as the community of interests that links her to the social philosophers. Indeed, her effort to further community by encouraging changes of consciousness is her distinctive contribution to the larger social revolution her fellow theorists contemplated. She defined her particular function as

> that of the *aesthetic*, not the doctrinal teacher—the rousing of the nobler emotions, which make mankind desire the social right, not the prescribing of special measures, concerning which the artistic mind, however strongly moved by social sympathy, is often not the best judge.
>
> [*Letters* 7: 44

The theorists similarly contrasted doctrinal and aesthetic teachings and assigned to the scientist and artist complementary yet distinctive functions. As an artist, George Eliot attempted to enlarge the experience of her readers and to alter their perceptions, in part by creating characters who experienced such changes as those she would ideally have her readers undergo, or such failings as might bring her readers to a fuller understanding of the human limitations and social conditions that inhibit the fellowship she wanted her readers to experience as a felt need.

The frequency, complexity, and modulation of her direct addresses to the reader offer still further evidence of her desire to foster a collaboration between author and reader. Again, the basis of interchange is not necessarily assent, but a serious and thorough engagement between text and reader. That her novels were "deliberately [and] carefully constructed" to affect changes in her readers George Eliot acknowledges when she speaks, for instance, of the "inspiring principle which alone gives me courage to write":

> that of so presenting our human life as to help my readers in getting a clearer conception and a more active admiration of those vital elements which bind men together and give a higher worthiness to their existence; and also to help them in gradually dissociating these elements from the more transient forms on which an outworn teaching tends to make them dependent.
>
> [*Letters* 4: 472

To judge from her readers' letters to her and contemporary reviews, she often evoked the kind of response she intended. The concept of a community of readers, then, presupposes an author whose avowed purpose is the nurturing of "those vital elements which bind men together"; a text that fosters a collaboration between author and reader; and a readership that brings to bear on the everyday world the demands made upon it by a fictional one.

Those demands are more complex than I can suggest here, but they are clearly related to the Victorian aesthetic of sympathy, which George Eliot not only participated in but also helped to create. This aesthetic, based on a belief in the power of art to enlarge the reader's capacities for sympathetic response, sought to effect so comprehensive a change of sensibility as ultimately to change society. Thus a community of readers is also a "community of feeling," a concept whose most obvious origins are in Wordsworth, the favorite poet of both George Eliot and Mill. The idea is related to Shelley's notion of the poet as unacknowledged legislator in "A Defense of Poetry." The publication of his "Defense" (written in 1821, first published in 1840) coincided with the growing belief that the sympathetic imagination is the greatest instrument of the moral good. Like these Romantics, many Victorians believed that poetry should quicken the noble emotions. But George Eliot, unlike many of her contemporaries, held that fiction could do so as well, thus providing for her readers an answer to the question Arnold asked upon Wordsworth's death: "But who, ah! who, will make us feel?"

The Victorian prejudice against fiction was shared by Arnold, who rarely read novels. It has its amusing side, as in Spencer's wish to exclude all novels except George Eliot's from the London Library, or Carlyle's dictum that readers of novels and the insane should be separated from the serious readers in the British Museum. George Eliot adds to the store of such anecdotes in commenting on the Carlyles' responses to *Adam Bede*:

> I reckon it among my best triumphs that she [Jane Carlyle] found herself "in charity with the whole human race" when she laid the book down. I want the philosopher himself to read it. . . . If he *could* be urged to read a novel!
>
> [*Letters* 3: 23

But other anecdotes reveal the serious side of this controversy. George Eliot prematurely terminated her first piece of fiction, *Scenes of Clerical Life*, when her publisher, John Blackwood, complained of a "Thackerayan cynicism" that worked against the "community of feeling" otherwise generated by the stories.[16] She had also to contend with the solemn distinction between poetry and fiction made by many Victorians, among them Mill. The everyday prosaic worlds depicted in the novel, they believed, preclude that lofty ennobling of emotion characteristic of poetry and essential to art that is to affirm the social enterprise as a spiritual whole. George Eliot was committed to both: to being truthful to the experience of the working-day world and to revealing the poetry in the commonplace. Thus, for her, community of feeling was to be created not only through the ennobling of experience, implicit in the argument Wordsworth makes in the Preface to the *Lyrical Ballads*, but also through the accurate portrayal of prosaic ordinariness. Together, they were to enlarge the reader's capacity to enter sympathetically into the human emotions, needs, experiences, and aspirations all people share.

Community of feeling neither precludes unity of thought nor makes of it an issue, and thus appears to avoid the grappling uncertainties and potential divisiveness of community of interests. As George Eliot often noted, because "agreement between intellects seems unattainable . . . we turn to the *truth of feeling* as the only universal bond of union" (*Letters* 1: 162). The social theorists also turned to the truths of feeling art might express and encourage, assigning to literature the task of affirming the secular values that might ideally sustain a social faith rendered fragile by many things,

16. *Letters* 2: 344, 347–49, 371, 409–10.

including the intellectual contradictions and disagreements that disturbed their systematic efforts to speak to the problem of community.

Community of feeling, however, is no more free of tension than are the other concepts of community we have noted. It does not escape the difficulties of intellectual disagreement since, as George Eliot notes in "Judgments on Authors," the extension of "moral sentiment" is dependent on an author's ability to impregnate "ideas with a fresh store of emotion" (*Essays*, p. 442). "Life and action are prior to theorizing, and have a prior logic in the conditions necessary to maintain them," she writes elsewhere, and "yet theory," she continues, "has entered into the formation of all individual and national character."[17] Furthermore, since community of feeling is realized through a community of readers, it is limited by the size of the reading public, which, even for novels, was small in number and restricted to the upper social classes. These limits constrained the effectiveness of community of feeling as an agent for overall social transformation.

In addition, community of feeling contains inherent tensions because it was to have been both a means and an end: a means employed by writers to control the readers' responses; and an end envisioned by artists who hoped to effect transformations in the individual and in society at large. George Eliot fully realized the difficulty of changing, yet not alienating, the reader. In her fiction her effort to enlarge the reader's sensibility often includes a criticism of conventional ways of thinking, acting, and responding. If the criticism is so sharp as to constitute an assault upon the reader, however, it threatens the very sense of community the author seeks to create. Yet to omit such criticism might also lead to failure, leaving the reader to rest comfortably instead of being aroused to transforming discovery. Throughout her career George Eliot struggled to bring into the aesthetic of sympathy both the assent required by community of feeling and the critical assessment and constructive dissent no less necessary to social regeneration.

As suggested by the phrase "community of interests, sympathies and sufferings" in G. W. Cooke's *George Eliot: A Critical Study* (1883), the various concepts of community we have noted *together* represent a mode of Victorian thought (p. 261). Moreover, these concepts and their internal paradoxes are central to the larger difficulties of achieving community in Victorian England. Thus by

17. "More Leaves," pp. 365–66.

concentrating on several related ideas—community of interests, readers, and feeling—I intend to explain why and how a particular group of nineteenth-century writers came to focus on certain aspects of community.

The methodological and scholarly advantages of particularity would soon be lost, however—neither the limits nor scope of this group of ideas adequately understood—were we not also to place these writers within a wider nineteenth- and twentieth-century theoretical tradition. Modern thinking about community has been dominated by a typology formulated by the German social theorist Ferdinand Tönnies in *Gemeinschaft und Gesellschaft,* published in 1887.[18] Tönnies's work seems to have fulfilled the need for a synthesis at once comprehensive and comprehensible. He uses *Gemeinschaft* to refer to local, organic, agricultural communities that are modeled on the family and rooted in the traditional and the sacred; and *Gesellschaft* to denote urban, heterogeneous, industrial societies that are culturally sophisticated and shaped by the rational pursuit of self-interest in a capitalistic and secular environment. The one signifies "community," the other "society." Together they constitute a typology, an ideal construct that boldly outlines prominent tendencies in a class of empirical cases. As ideal types, Gemeinschaft and Gesellschaft are not fully realized by any group; rather, the opposite poles they define are standards by which reality may be described and understood. Thus Tönnies's typology consolidates and lends coherence to a critical but confusing process of social change, and yet acknowledges that, given the irregular evolution and unstable complexity of actual social patterns, characteristics of both Gemeinschaft and Gesellschaft are likely to interpenetrate and coexist in actual social groups.

Although Tönnies was the first to compose this typology, the ideas it embodies were central to earlier nineteenth-century thinking about community. As we shall see, George Eliot and her contemporaries attested with great frequency to the same kinds of social patterns Tönnies defines. Thus his hypothetical construct establishes a polarity within which to comprehend their acute preoccupation with the historical transition from Gemeinschaft to

18. For example, Tönnies's influence on Emile Durkheim, Charles Horton Cooley, Robert Redfield, Howard Becker, and Max Weber has been pointed out by many sociologists, among them Charles P. Loomis and John C. McKinney in their Introduction to Ferdinand Tönnies, *Community and Society (Gemeinshaft und Gesellschaft),* ed. and trans. Charles P. Loomis, pp. 12–29.

Gesellschaft and their effort to promote in their world, which they perceived as Gesellschaft, the mutual ties and common interests associated with Gemeinschaft. In George Eliot's fiction, for instance, traditional and ancestral ties among family members and neighbors to the land they inhabit are vividly dramatized, but confrontations between Gemeinschaft and Gesellschaft principles, along with an urgent need to resolve them, are no less powerfully presented and are more persistently present. George Eliot, Feuerbach, Strauss, Comte, Mill, Spencer, Lewes—this diverse group often reached separate conclusions in their search for community, but each was concerned with the same kinds of dichotomies Tönnies later codified. Moreover, their individual efforts to find an alternative basis for the reintegration of society included a common solution. Assigning to public opinion in modern life the role that religion had played in traditional community, they proposed an interchange between scientists and artists. Their writings were to alter and shape public opinion, inducing widespread changes of perception. The end to be achieved was the reestablishment of common interests and shared feelings as the science and prose of Gesellschaft converged with a transformed poetry of Gemeinschaft to create the moral sanctions offered in the past by religion. Although this principle entails numerous practical difficulties, it nonetheless suggests how these thinkers perceived the cultural achievements of advanced societies to be associated not only with the disintegration of community but also with its recovery.

Two important points of divergence, however, differentiate Tönnies from the nineteenth-century thinkers known to George Eliot. First, Tönnies saw human nature as constant, or as essentially one and the same despite changes in the predominant types of social behavior over time.[19] Such changes, he maintained, were the result of shifting external conditions and differing social structures that elicited from individuals one of two fundamental tendencies, either the socially unifying temperamental traits, characteristics, and habits sanctioned by communal life in the village Gemeinschaft, or the self-interested, socially isolating behavior encouraged by the individualism of Gesellschaft.

The historical perspective Tönnies brings to changing social circumstances resembles that of the nineteenth-century social evolutionists George Eliot studied, a connection he himself acknowl-

19. For an analysis of Tönnies's theory of human nature, see Albert Salomon, "In Memoriam Ferdinand Tönnies," pp. 37–43.

edged by making clear his indebtedness to Comte, Spencer, and Maine.[20] But the absence of an evolutionary perspective from his theory of human nature separates him from these thinkers and shows him to be both more conservative and more radical than they were. For Tönnies, the personal habits characteristic of Gemeinschaft inevitably suffered destruction or became stunted in modern Gesellschaft society. Thus he frequently speaks of the past in terms of cohesiveness and social concord, and of the present in terms of decay, degeneration, and corruption. While George Eliot and Comte sometimes express a similar attitude, this kind of thinking does not predominate in their work, largely because they, like all the theorists central to this study, regarded human nature not as constant but as continuously developing, moving slowly but comprehensively toward the improvement of mankind. In fact, their unequivocal belief in the progressive malleability of man is one of the few ideas upon which they all agreed. Individual traits that were encouraged in the past by external rules, which had served to socialize human behavior, seemed to them still to be evolving and to be undergoing a process of internalization. They sought to further this process by encouraging changes in the individual that would correct the negative tendencies of Gesellschaft and by promoting the idea of an organic Gesellschaft that could accommodate the most positive values of Gemeinschaft.

For Tönnies, changes such as these seemed on the whole to be impossible so long as Gesellschaft remained the dominant social form. He turned to socialism, as a result, claiming Marx to be as important to his intellectual development as were Comte and Spencer.[21] Lewes and Mill had also been attracted to socialism, but they brought to it many more reservations. While they favored voluntarily arranged cooperative associations, they did not propose, as did Tönnies, "a new kind of *Gemeinschaft* based upon an organically developed combination of state and cooperative socialism."[22] Mill, in fact, repudiated state socialism; Lewes, though he looked favorably upon the *"doctrine"* of communism, rejected "socialist

20. See, for instance, "My Relation to Sociology" (1932), and Prefaces to the first and second editions of *Gemeinschaft und Gesellschaft* (1887 and 1912), reprinted in *On Sociology: Pure, Applied, and Empirical*, by Ferdinand Tönnies, pp. 3–4, 21–22, 29–35.

21. See sources cited in n. 20.

22. Rudolph Heberle, Introduction to *Custom: An Essay on Social Codes*, by Ferdinand Tönnies, p. 26. (Hereafter referred to as *Custom*.)

systems" as premature, arguing that "people begin at the wrong end of Communism, taking hold of the mere tail of *material arrangement* before securing the head of moral adaptation."[23]

But while Tönnies's advocacy of state socialism constitutes the second major difference between him and the nineteenth-century theorists known to George Eliot, he was also heir to their tradition by way of his points of difference with Marx: in the value he himself placed on traditional Gemeinschaft, in his own opposition to sudden revolution, and in his response to the Marxian division between economic base and social superstructure. Though Tönnies admired Marx for having exposed the economic law of development as the law of Gesellschaft, he found Marx's analysis too emphatically economic because it relegated to the social superstructure matters that Tönnies considered part of the basic foundation, among them intellectual activities and artistic creations.[24] Thus, while Tönnies's economic theories and advocacy of state socialism resemble Marx's work, the significance he attributes to mental and emotional attitudes places him in the non-Marxist tradition. Though it appears to be inconsistent with his theory of human nature, he believed that changes in human perception and feeling, such as might be encouraged by the art and science of Gesellschaft, are a precondition for reform. In fact, he identifies as the one truly positive characteristic of Gesellschaft its cultural brilliance, celebrating both the "contemplative, clear and sober consciousness in which scholars and cultured men now dare to approach things human and divine," and the "artistic intuition and creative will" that recreates through "spiritual friendship . . . a kind of invisible scene or meeting" capable of serving in the place of traditional ties (*G&G*, pp. 43, 202).

Tönnies's comprehensiveness, then, derives from his relationship to two nineteenth-century traditions of social thought. His work, furthermore, raises important methodological as well as substantive issues. The relation between social theory and empirical de-

23. [Lewes], "Socialism," p. 204; and "Sidney Smith's Mother Country," p. 663. See also Lewes, "Communism as an Ideal," pp. 733–34; John M. Robson, *The Improvement of Mankind*, pp. 245–71; and Hock Guan Tjoa, *George Henry Lewes*, pp. 44–49.

24. See, for instance, Tönnies, "Social Structures or Institutions: Effectiveness of Factors" (1931), in *On Sociology*, pp. 217–21, 229–31; Salomon, "In Memoriam," pp. 39–40; Heberle, "The Sociological System of Ferdinand Tönnies," pp. 62–66; and Cahnman, "Tönnies and Marx," pp. 219–38. See also Fritz Pappenheim, *The Alienation of Modern Man*, pp. 77–80.

scription is, of course, critical to any definition of community, whatever the historical context and however "objective" the declared method. Indeed, questions concerning a theorist's treatment of fact and value usually arise because disparities of method are noticed. Tönnies employs a shifting standard that alternates between the empirical and the ideal. His wavering is evident in the change of subtitle between the first and second editions of *Gemeinschaft and Gesellschaft*: the first edition (1887) is subtitled *A Treatise on Communism and Socialism as Empirical Forms of Culture*; the second (1912), *Basic Concepts of Pure Sociology*.

The same conflict of approach also characterizes the work of Mill, Comte, Spencer, and others—and not surprisingly, since for them the definition of community involves questions about the proper nature of social life. As a result, in their work (as in many modern discussions of community), an evaluative dimension often conditions and sometimes even determines altogether the descriptive meanings of community. Because Tönnies, for instance, values Gemeinschaft as unequivocally a good and Gesellschaft as predominantly negative, his descriptions of individualistic modes of behavior are relentlessly critical. Accordingly, the kind of social life he describes and the methods he adopts are each related to his ideology, since the effect of a typology, whatever its methodological function, is to emphasize extremes. Although Mill, Spencer, and their fellow thinkers adopted methods that allow for intricate adjustments, their efforts to describe, assess, and reshape various aspects of traditional Gemeinschaft and modern Gesellschaft are no less related to their judgments of the values implicit in each. Because they regarded neither in itself as an unequivocal good, they attempted both to transform and to create a convergence between those aspects of Gemeinschaft and Gesellschaft they most valued. My analysis approaches these prevalent though confusing links between fact and value in discussions of community by regarding them as givens and exploring how the definitions of each and their interrelation contribute to the concept of community.

This approach is equally applicable to recent literary criticism concerned with the concept of community in George Eliot's novels, the most important of which is the work of Raymond Williams. Williams relates George Eliot's fiction to the larger issue of community within an industrialized and "cultured" society, defining community as a "whole way of life"— political, economic, and social—as tested by its capacity to "sustain a general independence" within an egalitarian and classless social structure.[25] Kindness, cooperation, mutuality, and neighborliness continue to be givens, but Williams argues that such values are rendered essentially specious when a society and a literature, such as existed in nineteenth-century England, isolate "humanity and community into the idea of culture, against the real social pressures of the time" embodied in trade, industry, urban life, and the working classes. Exclusions of this sort were accompanied, he notes, by a tendency to locate value in a rural past and to give personal moral values and matters of individual psychology precedence over social issues. The result in the case of George Eliot "is withdrawal from any full response to an existing society. Value is in the past, as a general retrospective condition, and is in the present only as a particular and private sensibility, the individual moral action."

Though his focus is a good deal narrower, William Myers argues in a similar way. Sharing Williams's conception of a whole way of life, he criticizes George Eliot because she "habitually psychologizes social fact," fails to confront "concrete factors in social and economic life," and grasps human events only in personal terms.[26] In a related protest, Graham Martin takes her to task for the same kind of failure Marx assigned to Feuerbach, for interpreting the world when " 'the point . . . is to *change* it.' "[27]

Each of these critics correctly perceives that George Eliot's approach to social change is anti-Marxian, but their ideologies make primary her omissions or failures of confrontation: the working-class realities she places at a distance; the political acts she treats with skepticism; the educated sensibilities (her own and those given to her superior characters) she separates from the common life. At the same time, these critics often ignore how George Eliot's work includes a recognition of difficulties they claim she evades. They also fail to define *community* beyond appealing to a whole way of life inclusive of the working classes and dependent on a socialist state and direct political action.

Raymond Williams's frequent references to the "knowable" as opposed to the "known community," for instance, though rhetorically compelling, are finally unclear because he defines the terms so variously. Sometimes the two merge into the "knowable com-

25. The source cited is *The Country and the City*, p. 101, but the phrases are frequent in Williams's work. The two succeeding quotations in this paragraph are from *Country and the City*, pp. 79 and 180.
26. William Myers, "George Eliot: Politics and Personality."
27. Graham Martin, "*Daniel Deronda*: George Eliot and Political Change."

munity," which is based on perceptions both objective and subjective—on what is known, given the realities that exist, and on
what an observing consciousness, by nature limited, is able to
know, or chooses to know, or decides to communicate. At other
times, the inevitable disparities between these various kinds of perceptions cause Williams to identify the objective with the "known"
community and to oppose it to the "knowable community," now
defined as "a selected society in a selected point of view." Yet, as
Williams acknowledges, "all traditions are selective"; and for him,
finally, "known" and "knowable" are both measured by the inclusion or exclusion of working-class community.[28]

In the work of Ian Milner, another Marxist critic, the definition
of community in George Eliot's work is even more troublesome.
Milner uses the terms *community* and *society* indiscriminately,
sometimes regarding them as synonymous and sometimes as opposed. He assigns to the "structure of values" in George Eliot's
work a socialist ethic, taking the working-class community as his
standard, but applauds her for upholding it. Still his very faith in
her leads him to perceive what those who emphasize her anti-
socialist tendencies often overlook: George Eliot's belief in man
as a social being and her endorsement of characters who act beyond
merely personal interests to benefit the wider human community.[29]
His conclusions, then, counter the critics who attribute a personal
and individualistic orientation to George Eliot's responses to her
contemporary world. The insufficiency of both views is the subject
of chapters 4 and 5 of this study, but here we may note that the
impossibility of unequivocally establishing one or the other as
finally definitive is suggested by the varying assessments of George
Eliot even in Williams's own work. His recent emphasis in *The
Country and the City* on her "separated" individuals, for instance,
disturbs the poised balance between society and the individual he
applauds in *The Long Revolution*, and it simplifies the "profound
. . . tension" between the two he describes as a "creative disturbance" in *The English Novel*.[30]

As W. J. Harvey pointed out long ago, the disparate elements in
all of George Eliot's novels confront her readers with the problem

---

28. Raymond Williams, *The English Novel from Dickens to Lawrence*,
pp. 11–26, 80–92; *Country and the City*, pp. 18, 165–81.
29. Ian Milner, *The Structure of Values in George Eliot*, pp. 1–10.
30. *Country and the City*, pp. 174–76; *The Long Revolution*, pp. 278–80;
English Novel, pp. 85, 94.

of determining where to place "the main stress"—on the individual or on society.[31] This very difficulty, indeed impossibility, of identifying the main stress in her corpus has been and continues to be essential to her novelistic powers. The irresolutions force her readers to experience and confront the problem of community in the modern world, as is palpably evident from her Victorian readers' responses to her novels and modern critics' disagreements about whether her priorities lie with the individual or with community.

Thus far, except for Milner, the critics I mentioned emphasize the former and chastize George Eliot for denigrating the possibility of community. Several other critics offer the opposite emphasis, though the endorsements of community they perceive are a sore point for some and a delight to others. Thus C. B. Cox and Calvin Bedient speak of binding restrictions and of persecution and sacrifice, Cox by claiming that "the longing for a fuller way of life" dramatized in George Eliot's fiction "ends repeatedly with a return to traditional family and social duties"; and Bedient by maintaining that her worship at the "shrine" of society creates novels that "amount to little more than scriptures in the religion of home, community, and tradition."[32] But for Michael Squires and Henry Auster the affirmations of community in George Eliot's novels are cause for celebration. Squires praises her use of the pastoral, her evocation of a "happier time and place, where life is simpler and more meaningful and where an integrated community and a unified culture have not been displaced"; Auster commends her regionalism, the local rootedness that nurtures "community coherence," sympathy, wholeness, stability, and continuity.[33] Sandra Gilbert and Susan Gubar incorporate all these views by arguing that George Eliot gives primacy to her female characters because she believed women to be the preservers of community, but they find the conservatism of this position objectionable.[34]

Again, these critics have ideological biases that define their subject matter and direct their conclusions. Squires and Auster focus on George Eliot's early novels owing to, as each admits at one point,

31. W. J. Harvey, "George Eliot," p. 315.
32. C. B. Cox, *The Free Spirit*, p. 33; see also pp. 8, 37. Calvin Bedient, *Architects of the Self*, pp. 37, 81.
33. Michael Squires, *The Pastoral Novel*, p. 85 and passim. Henry Auster, *Local Habitations*, p. 103 and passim.
34. Sandra M. Gilbert and Susan Gubar, *The Madwoman in the Attic*, pp. 498–99, 528.

their nostalgia for what Auster calls "the 'charm,' cosiness, and satisfying vision of social coherence that mark her early books."[35] Bedient's credo is altogether opposite, based on individual self-fulfillment as the only good worth pursuing and on the "social self" as its enemy. Gilbert's and Gubar's feminism leads them to emphasize women's self-fulfillment. Finally, Cox's desire to restore community through Christianity causes him to censure George Eliot on all fronts—for political inaction, for isolating the individual, and for binding the individual to society. He condemns in her that duty to family and society which he himself affirms, because she denies what for him is essential: "a transcendental source of meaning by which alone confidence in the meaningfulness of action can be maintained" (p. 166).

These critics who agree that George Eliot places the main stress on community, then, rely on traditional standards of community: family or kinship, neighborhood or geographical locale, religious belief or common values. To compare them to those critics for whom the standard of value is a secular socialism is to see, furthermore, that both groups have something in common. Whether they develop concepts of community based on the working-class, a rural past, Christian belief, sexual equality, or even the bland "social self" Bedient deplores, each of these critics is a quester in search of a lost, a new, or a substitute vision. As such, many of them bring substantial insights to George Eliot's quest for community, but, even when informed by the knowledge and brilliance of a Raymond Williams, they are often limited or clouded by their partisan views. The connections, for instance, suggested by Squires and Auster, between the past of George Eliot's novels and the present she was addressing, are overlooked by Williams and Myers because they associate retrospection with an evasion or rejection of the present. At the same time, the nostalgia felt by Squires and Auster creates in their work a major contradiction between a past impossible to recover and a present it is to transform. Thus they neglect George Eliot's desire for progressive social change and thereby seem to validate the contention by Williams and other critics that her vision of community is unable to absorb Gesellschaft. So to argue is to suggest that she failed to nourish in her contemporaries and in future generations "the widespreading roots of social and personal good" which she took to be central to her mission as artist (*Letters* 6: 339). But the fact that critics so strenuously pursue through her fiction their own quests for community and selfhood, as indeed did many of her Victorian readers, is itself an indication of the opposite.

This analysis of opposing critical attitudes, and their relation to one another and to my own views, may easily be extended, but that is not to my purpose in this general survey of the concepts of community in recent criticism of George Eliot's fiction. Rather, it serves to introduce the themes I pursue throughout this study: a view of history that implicates past, present, and future in the recovery of community (chapters 2 and 3); a mode of story-telling that powerfully dramatizes but refuses ultimately to settle opposing claims (chapters 5 through 7). Furthermore, by acknowledging the work of these modern questers, I mean to express gratitude and indebtedness, since their writings have contributed greatly to my own understanding of community as both an issue and a problem in George Eliot's fiction. Finally, their disagreements bespeak the need for a study of George Eliot and community that focuses on the ideological issues she was attempting to confront and resolve. These issues are so intricate and contradictory as to require us to approach (as nearly as possible) the problem of community in her fiction by way of the concepts current within her intellectual world.

John Killham, in a recent essay, also argues for the need to study the concepts of community prevalent during the period in question; and he too finds Tönnies a useful starting point.[36] His essay is particularly valuable for calling attention to the centrality of Tönnies, yet his use of Tönnies to argue against Raymond Williams creates distortions. He wrongly ascribes to Tönnies an "historian's disinterestedness" in order to censure Williams's partisan views; and he minimizes the sociologist's emphasis on "intellectual affinity or friendship" so as to dismiss Williams's contention that community in the twentieth century becomes largely a matter of communication and language.[37]

Killham argues, then, for an approach such as the one I am taking; and Williams arrives eventually at a conclusion similar to mine. But I intend to prove what the one dismisses and the other displaces: that community as communication is not only a meaningful concept, but one generated by the nineteenth-century writers I am discussing. Steven Marcus makes a similar point by equating "society" and "communications," but his argument is peculiarly circumscribed because it is based primarily on the first stories

36. John Killham, "The Idea of Community in the English Novel."
37. Killham, "Idea of Community," pp. 380, 382, 394–96. See also Williams, *Long Revolution*, pp. 37–40, and *Culture and Society*, pp. 296–97.

George Eliot published. Furthermore, Marcus defines her participation in a tradition of social thought by way of Charles Horton Cooley, an American sociologist and social psychologist at best peripheral to the English Victorian tradition.[38] But Marcus's choice testifies again to the centrality of Tönnies, since Cooley, no less than the theorists George Eliot knew, essentially thought in terms of a Gemeinschaft-Gesellschaft typology.

This typology, moreover, may be brought to bear upon the work of George Eliot's critics, as in the Gemeinschaft evoked by Squires's pastoralism and Auster's regionalism, the Gesellschaft implicit in the industrialized worlds Williams, Myers, and Milner address, and the opposition between a female culture of community and a male world of politics and business identified by Gilbert and Gubar. Furthermore, within the work of a number of these critics is evidence for the convergence between Gemeinschaft and Gesellschaft principles that I take to be at the heart of George Eliot's efforts to redefine community for a present and future world. That convergence, we may recall, was to depend on changes of consciousness through a revolution essentially psychological, prompted by the art and science of Gesellschaft. This vision subsumes even Williams's argument, for despite his discomfort with culture as a positive regenerative force, when he turns to the twentieth century he grants that "the most deeply known human community is language itself."[39] Moreover, because Williams, Myers, and Martin adhere rigidly to Marx's contention that "the philosophers have only *interpreted* the world" when "the point is to *change* it,"[40] they reject or ignore the way George Eliot's "psychologizing of social fact" implicates a revolution of consciousness. But the very nature of their disagreements with George Eliot, nowhere clearer perhaps than in their suspicion of education as an active agent of social change, suggests how for George Eliot the point was to change the world by interpreting it.

At the same time, by drawing attention to George Eliot's emphasis on the psychology of individuals, these critics help to define the kind of crisis community was undergoing in the nineteenth century. In different ways, Auster and Milner contribute to its

38. Steven Marcus, "Literature and Social Theory: Starting In with George Eliot."

39. *English Novel*, p. 167.

40. Karl Marx and Frederick Engels, ["Theses on Feuerbach"], *Collected Works* 5: 5.

definition, albeit inadvertently. Auster, for instance, traces a movement in George Eliot's fiction away from local roots and "particularity" of time and place, towards "potentialities" increasingly universal, general, and psychological.[41] Milner offers an analogous point when, in his discussion of *The Mill on the Floss*, he opposes "Society," as represented by the conventional Tom, to "the voice of a community true to its own moral law," as represented by the outcast Maggie (p. 31). In Gilbert and Gubar the sense of crisis is overt, for they point out how George Eliot "associates women with precisely the traits she felt industrial urbanized England in danger of losing" (p. 499). Each of these critics, then, provides evidence of George Eliot's participation in the movement away from fixed social realities we have noted throughout this chapter. In addition, while such evidence undermines the regionalism, which is Auster's subject, and speaks inconsistently to the "structure of values" at issue in Milner, the very unsteadiness that marks their definitions of "regionalism," "society," and "community" is a sign of the crisis in community George Eliot confronted in her fiction. Thus the critics' blurring of definition ironically suggests how the concept of community suffers an instability when it is resurrected on a basis essentially psychological or when community as concrete place yields to community as spirit or ideal. Just as the shifts in the definition of community both reflect and respond to concrete changes in social life, so the corresponding movement in George Eliot's fiction and in the social theorists toward individual psychology and even toward idealizing abstraction is most accurately seen not as a withdrawal from social fact and action but as a prolonged, troubled, and conflicted confrontation between community as fact and community as consciousness.

This confrontation is the subject of this book, but I will first conclude my opening discussion by once again locating in Tönnies a vantage point. Tönnies defines *Gemeinschaft* in terms of "three pillars" that *together* provide "the real foundation of unity": "blood, place (land), and mind"; or "kinship, neighborhood, and friendship" (*G&G*, pp. 47–48; 192). During the course of his argument, the third pillar (signified by "mind" or "friendship") is described as including common beliefs, ideas, interests, feelings, sentiments—precisely those aspects of community that lack fixity and therefore lend themselves to transmutation. Since Tönnies's time,

41. Auster, *Local Habitations*, pp. 29, 62, 178–79, 195, 205.

continuing shifts in the nature of social life have led us to define Gemeinschaft primarily in terms of this third pillar.

The 1973 edition of *The Random House Dictionary* defines *Gemeinschaft* simply as "an association of individuals having sentiments, tastes, and attitudes in common; fellowship." Along with the disappearance of blood ties and fixed locale, even the attributes of mind and spirit are now absent. In the more formal definition of the *International Encyclopedia of the Social Sciences* (1968), the idea of intellectual affinity appears, but the emphasis again is on community of feeling. The entry establishes that while "*Gemeinschaft* cannot be accurately translated . . . it refers to the 'community of feeling' (a kind of associative unity of ideas and emotions) that results from likeness and from shared life-experience."[42] Stipulations against limiting the concept to "formal kinship" appear as well: "for neighborhood and collective proprietorship produce a similar unity, and friendship expresses a kind of Gemeinschaft that is tied to neither blood nor locality" (3: 175). A similar process of excision and expansion is at play in the introduction to the most recent edition of Tönnies's writings. Of Gemeinschaft, the editors state:

> By "community," the reader must not understand a territorial or administrative entity, but what is held in common, what makes for cohesion, what provides bonds among men. . . . Of course, initially the local community, the community of blood and the community of minds and hearts were one and the same thing, but this unity has been lost.[43]

Tönnies's *three* pillars help to clarify how this gradual transformation of meaning developed from a disposition of thought about community which originated in the nineteenth century and reached its fullest early articulation in the work of the writers who are the subject of this study.

While many Romantic and Victorian writers assigned to art the task of social regeneration through the creation of unifying sentiments, a new fullness of scale was achieved and a different evaluative dimension was created when social theory and imaginative literature, the science of the time and also its art, became together self-consciously implicated in the recovery of community. As I ex-

---

42. *International Encyclopedia of the Social Sciences*, 1968 ed., s. v. "Community-Society Continua," by Horace M. Miner.

43. Cahnman and Heberle, Introduction to *On Sociology*, by Ferdinand Tönnies, p. xx.

plain in the chapters that follow, the successes and failures of this process reveal a tradition of social thought in which community in its concrete sense confronts an abstract or imaginary vision, or becomes a matter of spiritual, emotional, and intellectual affinities. To clarify the nature of that tradition is to provide, I believe, some new ways of understanding George Eliot's intentions and the kind of success she achieved. If the efforts to reconcile opposites often ended in deadlock, nevertheless for George Eliot and for her readers they were the source of powerful, energizing tensions. Through her fiction, moreover, these tensions achieved something of a resolution by way of the interests and feelings aroused within her community of readers. In essence, through her art she attempted to create new and vital substitutions for the face-to-face encounters of traditional community.

The chapters are organized in pairs: in each case, the first of the two is devoted to theoretical social issues, the second to George Eliot's fiction. Thus the discussion of the problems with which the social theorists were grappling are succeeded by an analysis of their counterparts in the formal composition of George Eliot's novels. The first such pair (chapters 2 and 3) concerns the troublesome history of social life as shaped by philosophical empiricism and fictional realism alike, and the effort of both the social theorists and George Eliot to transcend the limits of their methods, she by turning to a poetic, and they to a metaphysical ideal. Just as the theorists were discovering in social evolutionary patterns ways of explaining the shift from Gemeinschaft to Gesellschaft, and of exploring new possibilities for Gemeinschaft, so major patterns of imagery vital to the creation of scene and character in George Eliot's fiction illustrate similar efforts and concerns. The second pair of chapters (4 and 5) focus on the structure of the social organism in the existing present. These chapters demonstrate how the dilemmas inherent in revisionary social organicism are embodied in the structure of *The Mill on the Floss, Middlemarch,* and *Daniel Deronda,* the novels which most strenuously confront the present. The concern in the closing pair of chapters is George Eliot's relation to her contemporary audience. Chapter 6 discusses reviews of her novels, particularly the correspondence they suggest between fictional style and social value. Chapter 7 analyzes patterns of reader address in George Eliot's novels in terms of their communalizing function. Both chapters argue that the idea of community achieved its fullest realization in the intricacy and intensity of response she aroused in her Victorian readers.

◆

TWO

Natural History and the Recovery of Community

George Eliot and W. H. Riehl: Modeling Natural History

For readers of George Eliot, the term *natural history* is most likely to bring to mind a review she wrote in 1856, "The Natural History of German Life." But though among the best known of her essays, the significance it has acquired has had little to do with the subject of its title, its importance having been understood instead largely in terms of the credo of realism it begins to define.[1] This interpretation is altogether understandable: the piece was written just a few months before George Eliot began writing fiction, and the review offered her the occasion to set down some thoughts on the value of realism in art. Furthermore, her aesthetic observations are predicated on social concerns, and the realism she came to practice is committed to a renewal of community. But the more immediate subject of this particular essay—the nature and uses of natural history—relates even more extensively to the theme of community in George Eliot's work, because it includes matters more comprehensive than an aesthetic of realism is able to address. Thus we may begin by considering both the essay's overall shape and its general contents.

In "The Natural History of German Life," George Eliot reviews two books by Wilhelm Heinrich von Riehl, the German pioneer of *Kulturgeschichte* who has come to be regarded as one of the founders of sociology in Germany. George Eliot wrote about Riehl because she wanted his work to serve "as a model for some future

1. A notable exception is A. J. Sambrook's "The Natural History of Our Social Classes." The "natural history" Sambrook defines is synonymous with "social history," and with "observing and relating the creature to its surroundings" (p. 131).

or actual student of our own people."[2] But because she so immediately became that student, the model has been lately understood
in ways too singularly literary. The natural history George Eliot
actually had in mind was to serve the social theorist no less than the
artist; and the alliance between the two was to lead toward a renewal of community based on a more accurate and complex understanding of social life in both the past and the present. As we shall
see, George Eliot's interpretation of Riehl embodies in embryonic
form a set of premises as important to her as they were to the social
theorists she addresses in her argument. Before turning to these
matters, however, we must consider briefly the nature of the highly
selective material George Eliot chose to include in the review and
the shape of the piece, for both reveal that she was already beginning
to model anew the natural history she found in Riehl.

The essay falls into four parts: an introduction that includes the
famous remarks on realism (pp. 267–73); an account of German
peasant life as described by Riehl (pp. 273–86); an interpretative
definition of natural history (pp. 286–90); and an overall summary
of Riehl's two-volume *Die Naturgeschichte des Volkes* (pp. 291–
99). George Eliot devotes most of her attention to the first of the
volumes, *Die bürgerliche Gesellschaft*, which, like her essay, has a
four-part structure, but of a very different sort. Riehl proceeds by
devoting one section to each of the four social classes he discusses:
the peasantry, the aristocracy, the bourgeoisie, and a composite
fourth estate that includes an intellectual proletariat as well as
manual laborers. He had originally planned to call the volume
"Vier Stände," or *The Four Estates*, but as he explains in the
preface to *Die bürgerliche Gesellschaft*, the more he studied his
subject the more he became convinced that the "forces of social
movement" are controlled and motivated by the bourgeoisie. Thus
they are at the center of his book, the subject of its third section,
while the "forces of persistence and endurance," as represented by
the peasantry and the aristocracy, are the subject of its first two
parts.

In her essay on Riehl, George Eliot proceeds in an altogether
different way, though her points are similar. At the start, she takes
a "cultivated and town-bred" reader and places before him the associations the word *railways* is likely to call up for two different
but distinctly modern men. One of them knows everything about
the subject, having had "successively the experience of a 'navvy', an

2. George Eliot, "The Natural History of German Life," *Westminster
Review* 66 (1856); reprinted in *Essays*, p. 273.

engineer, a traveller, a railway director and shareholder, and a landed proprietor in treaty with a railway company"; the other knows only of a vague stretch of track, the railway guide timetable, and the one station he regards as "his" (pp. 267–69). The succeeding discussion of Riehl turns us in other directions, introducing first the traditional life of the German peasantry and then suggesting how various and concurrent the stages of social development can be. But at the close of the essay, the narrow gentleman of its opening reappears, this time through the image of a *"Philister* (Philistine)." After noting that this epithet is one "for which we have no equivalent [in English], not at all, however, for want of the object it represents," she explains:

> the *Philister* is one who is indifferent to all social interests, all public life, as distinguished from selfish and private interests; he has no sympathy with political and social events except as they affect his own comfort and prosperity, as they offer him material for amusement or opportunity for gratifying his vanity. He has no social or political creed, but is always of the opinion which is most convenient for the moment. He is always in the majority, and is the main element of unreason and stupidity in the judgment of a "discerning public."
>
> [pp. 296–97

George Eliot here begins to mold a technique that became a signature of the fiction she would soon start to write: the piece begins and ends in a Gesellschaft world of the present, yet the body of the work moves the reader into the past while simultaneously using a variety of devices to remind him of the present. This intricacy of movement serves a crucial purpose. Directed toward the predominantly middle-class reader, its function is to turn the Philistine into a person of wide understanding, one whose experience and knowledge "would include all the essential facts in the existence and relations of the *thing*" (p. 267). Instead of railways, however, the "thing" at issue was to become nothing less than the nature of social life past and present, and the intricate relation between the two.

At the same time, however, that George Eliot was creating her own particular structures to shape the materials of natural history, she also shared with many of her contemporaries a sense of its general contours. As she interprets Riehl, we can easily perceive exact equivalents for the Gemeinschaft-Gesellschaft dichotomy Tönnies later codified. The *Philister* is Gesellschaft man essentially "by himself and isolated," affirming "the actions of others only in so far as and as long as they can further his interest," and "separated in spite of all uniting factors."[3] Similarly, the picture of German peasant life provides ample evidence of Tönnies's three pillars of Gemeinschaft, based on the "obligation of family-ties," the strength of "settled existence," and the rule of "sacred *custom*" and tradition (*Essays*, pp. 275–86). The material drawn from the second of Riehl's volumes, *Land und Leute*, anticipates and confirms moreover Tönnies's contention that the actual patterns of social life reveal "the continuous sequence and interrelation of fluctuating concepts" (*G&G*, p. 222). That such fundamental correspondences exist is only to be expected. Tönnies (no less than George Eliot) knew and valued Riehl's work, and Comte and Spencer were even more vital figures for Tönnies than for her. Yet, if facts such as these are significant, they are also in one way beside the point. Tönnies was above all a model-maker, a synthesizer who took the historical forms of common life, as defined by a variety of writers, and used them to create ideal and representative constructs that might in turn sharpen our understanding of the spectrum of social forms. Thus, the Gesellschaft-Gemeinschaft dichotomy may be applied to the individualism of the modern town-dweller and to the peasant's strict adherence to custom mentioned by George Eliot in her comments on Riehl. It helps also to illuminate the more complex claim she puts forth when she says: "though our English life is in its core intensely traditional, Protestantism and commerce have modernized the face of the land" (p. 288). This description combines the traditionalism associated with Gemeinschaft, the commerce that is the distinctive mark of Gesellschaft, and the Protestantism which contains elements of each by fostering values at once religious and individualistic. Throughout "The Natural History of German Life," George Eliot's illustrations of Riehl include both theoretical types and examples of contemporary amalgams. Despite some serious incompatibilities between the two approaches, which arise from principles that are both ideal and empirical, together they help to create "natural history." Let us now turn to a preliminary survey of some of its major premises, continuing for the time being, however, to restrict the discussion to George Eliot's essay on Riehl.

We have seen how its opening images (evoked by the word *railways*) serve a rhetorical purpose. In addition, the man of wide experience, whose response might bring to bear "all the essential facts in the existence and relations of the *thing*," exemplifies one of the most important premises of "natural history": that all knowledge

3. *G&G*, pp. 65, 77.

is a knowledge of relations. At the close of the long introduction, George Eliot returns to this point, giving it full elaboration at the very moment when she first calls for a "natural history of our social classes" (p. 272). She then establishes the extraordinary "moral and intellectual breadth" such a task demands. It requires a cast of mind so tolerant and comprehensive as to make even the widely experienced gentleman of the opening vignette seem narrow. One must have not only a complex sense of relations in the present, though that would be formidable enough, but also a thoroughly integrated perception of the past, because natural history teaches that the present condition of things results from changes in the past. This premise is everywhere at work in the essay, fusing together the natural and the historical, since *natural* itself signifies "roots deep in the historical structure of society . . . [which] are still, in the present, showing vitality above ground" (p. 294).

In the more general discussion of natural history to follow, we will return to both premises to consider how the emphasis they place on "relations" and "conditions" serves to measure community as fact and value. For now, let us simply note George Eliot's repeated use of the word *conditions* in her essay and the particular concept of change it conveys. In the interpretative third section, George Eliot speaks of "the complexity of vital conditions" and assigns to "Natural History" (now capitalized) the task of embracing "the conditions of social life in all their complexity." Urging upon the reader Comte's classification of the sciences, she calls attention to "conditions" as she distinguishes Biology, which deals with the "laws . . . and conditions of life in general," from Natural History, which takes as its subject man's "special [i.e., social] conditions" (p. 290). Like Riehl, she "sees in European society *incarnate history*" that is created through "the gradual operation of necessary laws":

> The external conditions which society has inherited from the past are but the manifestation of inherited internal conditions in the human beings who compose it; the internal conditions and the external are related to each other as the organism and its medium, and development can take place only by the gradual consentaneous development of both.
>
> [p. 287

Repeating this point, she speaks of the "delicate union . . . between the moral tendencies of men and the social conditions they have inherited" (p. 288).

As the essay makes clear, by *conditions* George Eliot means geographical locale, language and custom, "mental culture and habit," ideas and motives, beliefs and institutions. Such topics, though variously modeled, were for many writers in the eighteenth and nineteenth centuries the materials of natural history. But during the nineteenth century, as we shall see shortly, a dominant pattern begins to emerge: natural history becomes joined to evolutionary theory, as that which is "natural"—in the sense that it emanates from the very nature of the thing when left undisturbed—is assigned a place according to specified "laws" of development. The passages quoted earlier reflect this change: "conditions" culminate in "development"; "the gradual operation of necessary laws" regulates the relation between "external" and "internal." This process of development applies to the individual no less than to society, and the crucial correspondence between the two makes these connections the most vital of all for George Eliot. As a result the natural history of our social life finds its complement in what she later called a "natural history of mind," with *mind* signifying the psychological evolution of individuals, but especially their developing capacity for moral growth.[4]

Each of the four premises just outlined has essential bearings on the theme of community. The concept that all knowledge is a knowledge of relations makes everything and everyone mutually dependent. The emphasis on "conditions" links the healthy life of the community to the nature of its past, to its knowledge of that past, and to the degrees of continuity and change within the present. The idea of development holds the promise of progress. As applied to society in general, however, for George Eliot it was the least certain premise in the group. Thus, in her essay on Riehl, her illustrations and interpretations of matters related to this issue contain both a wavering movement and moments of assurance. In the interpretative third section, for instance, she calls attention to "those grand and simple generalizations which trace out the inevitable march of the human race as a whole" (p. 290); and in the essay's closing paragraph, she looks forward to the "grander evolution of things to which all social forms are but temporarily subservient" (p. 299). Nevertheless, during her exposition of Riehl's work she seems to give her assent to his picture of peasant life as an embodiment of Gemeinschaft now almost eclipsed, and also to share at times his perception of a "decomposition . . . commencing in the organic constitution of society" (p. 295).

Yet, though she allows for a process of degeneration, which may

4. "Notes on Form in Art" (1868); reprinted in *Essays*, p. 435.

be signaling the destruction of community, she is careful to suggest
a vital source of renewal, which derives, moreover, from the very
individualism characteristic of Gesellschaft. The strict adherence
to custom in Gemeinschaft, she points out, although creating a uniformity of thought and habit that contrasts markedly with the individualistic behavior of "cultured man," tends to exclude intense
"emotional susceptibility" and "tender affection." Custom encourages one kind of solidarity, but it discourages the fellowship
that has its origins not in the group response but in "individual feeling" (pp. 274, 280). The sympathetic fellowship that acknowledges individual differences, in contrast, posits a reshaping
of Gemeinschaft compatible with the characteristics of Gesellschaft, yet open to tolerance, acceptance, and understanding of
others. Because it has its origins in individual not social development, the principle of fellow-feeling, moreover, was one George
Eliot could trust. Thus the last of the premises mentioned earlier—
the concept of development as applied to the psychological and
moral evolution of individuals—becomes for her the cornerstone
of modern community.

Returning now to the statements about art in the introductory
portion of the essay on Riehl, we can see a direct correspondence
between this last supposition and the aesthetic principles George
Eliot begins to set down. Assigning to art an educative function
allied to the growth and development of the moral imagination in
the individual, she writes:

> The greatest benefit we owe to the artist, whether painter, poet or
> novelist, is the extension of our sympathies. . . . Art is the nearest
> thing to life; it is a mode of amplifying experience and extending
> our contact with our fellowmen beyond the bounds of our personal
> lot.
>
> [pp. 270–71

The overall shape of the essay suggests, moreover, that the person
most in need of such "benefit" is none other than the *Philister* defined at its close. As defined by Riehl, he is already the very incar-
nation of the individual bound entirely within his own person.
Bringing additional emphasis to the point, George Eliot expands
Riehl's definition:

> We imagine the *Philister* is the personification of the spirit which
> judges everything from a lower point of view than the subject de-
> mands—which judges the affairs of the parish from the egotistic or

purely personal point of view—which judges the affairs of the nation from the parochial point of view, and does not hesitate to measure the merits of the universe from the human point of view.

[p. 297

But art has the power, George Eliot tells us, to surprise "even the trivial and the selfish into that attention to what is apart from themselves, which may be called the raw material of moral sentiment" (p. 270). Art has the power then, she implies, to create the raw material of renewed community, since moral sentiment is as fundamental and indispensable to the regeneration of community in Gesellschaft as is the rule of tradition (by nature social and public) in Gemeinschaft.

The aesthetic credo George Eliot here announces refers in other ways, too, to the premises of natural history. The changes in human perception and feeling that begin in the individual relate to the general concept of development by preparing the way for widespread social change. The adjustment of value away from the center of an isolated and circumscribed single self encourages the sense of "relative proportions" central to the premise that all knowledge is a knowledge of relations (p. 297). The extension of contact "beyond the bounds of our personal lot" inevitably subsumes the past and the future as well as the present, and so contributes to an awareness of fundamental continuities between present conditions, future possibilities, and changes in the past.

While George Eliot's first concern was the function and nature of art, she incorporated into her thinking principles deeply embedded in social theory. Moreover, she wished for the work of the artist and the social scientist to be complementary. In their effort to achieve reform both were ideally to be involved in a common enterprise, the artist forcefully awakening, through the power and accuracy of his representations, the social sympathies without which the dry "generalizations and statistics" of the theorists would die still-born (p. 270). Yet, in the essay on Riehl (and in George Eliot's other writings) there is if not hostility to theory, certainly a decided uneasiness with it. In part, this attitude is less a denigration of theory than a criticism of its misuse, for George Eliot applies the argument about natural history to both the artist and the social theorist, neither of whom has "sufficiently disclosed" a thorough knowledge and understanding of "our social classes" (pp. 268–72). Because the issue is the accuracy and fullness of the facts as presented by the theorist or as represented by the artist, the attack is twofold, directed against inaccuracy or misrepresentation in art and social theory. The one misleads by a false particularity based on literary convention not life; the other distorts or renders itself ineffectual by inattentiveness to detail and excessive abstraction. As applied to social theory, the corrective is empiricism and the "inductive process" (p. 287); as applied to art, the corrective is the realism that teaches us "to feel, not for the heroic artisan or the sentimental peasant, but for the peasant in all his coarse apathy, and the artisan in all his suspicious selfishness" (p. 271).

Though we may find these principles ironic in light of the heroic artisans George Eliot created in characters such as Adam Bede and Felix Holt, nevertheless the point she makes here holds firm. We need true conceptions of natural history, she argues, "to guide . . . rightly" the sympathies brought into activity by art, and "equally to check our theories, and direct us in their application" (p. 272). We need artists and theorists who are free from the "prejudice" of "party prepossessions" and "the partisanship of a class" to shape a natural history that is based on a "real knowledge of the People" and "a thorough study of their habits, their ideas, their motives" (pp. 286, 299, 272).

But despite this sense of a common enterprise, analogous shortcomings, and similar correctives, there remains nonetheless in George Eliot's attitude toward theory a residual discomfort difficult to explain. We cannot reduce it to the familiar and predictable opposition between the theoretician's search for unifying patterns and the artist's wariness of artificially ordering the particular, circumstantial, and extremely various nature of individual experience. In George Eliot the two tendencies existed together—the craving for unity and the apprehension of multiplicity—and in her fiction she struggled to accommodate both without sacrificing one to the other. Another explanation, again partial and embodying dual tendencies, is suggested by George Eliot's personal history— her early years in Warwickshire and her later ones in London. As critics have often noted, George Eliot's attachment to the countryside of her youth remained with her throughout her life and was a regular source of nostalgic, Gemeinschaft-like associations. Such feelings are reflected in George Eliot's defense of the peasant in the essay on Riehl and in her mockery of the "educated townsmen" whom she equates with "abstract theorizing," "algebraic signs," and "over-wrought nerves" (pp. 284, 288, 280). Yet her own acutely educated consciousness came to have as much in common with their world as it had once had with rural life; and to such a degree as even to suggest certain resemblances between George Eliot and those literary "day-labourers with the quill" whom Riehl associates with "the decomposition which is commencing in the organic constitution of society." The similarities are partial, of course, and George Eliot would have thoroughly resisted numbering herself among this "literary proletariat." According to Riehl, they are "the deserters of historical society" because they have broken rank with the "mental character . . . habits . . . [and] mode of life" of their family upbringing (pp. 294–95). Like them, George Eliot too breaks rank, but she continues nevertheless to affirm the sacredness of her feelings for the past, while turning ironically enough to "novel theory" to confirm the principle of historical continuity. As J. W. Cross explains in *George Eliot's Life*:

> Her roots were down in the pre-railroad, pre-telegraphic period . . . but the fruit was formed during an era of extraordinary activity in scientific and mechanical discovery. Her genius was the outcome of these conditions.

[1: 7–8

Yet this picture too is incomplete, since Cross avoids the ambivalence, self-division, and unsteadiness of feeling George Eliot brought to these opposing "conditions." We see them reflected in the essay on Riehl when, after having argued for pages against sentimentalizing the peasant, she submits to the error herself in advising that "a return to the habits of peasant life is the best remedy for many moral as well as physical diseases induced by perverted civilization" (pp. 280–81). But this, too, is overturned by a tough-minded dismissal of attempts to turn back the clock, or to "restore the 'good old times' by a sort of idyllic masquerading, and to grow feudal fidelity and veneration as we grow prize turnips, by an artificial system of culture" (p. 272). There is in George Eliot, then (as in Riehl and Tönnies), a nostalgia evoking at its most extreme and least controlled an overly simplified Gemeinschaft world, but leading at its best to a careful assessment of the past and its relation to the present. She speaks, for instance, of the "sweet and bitter prejudices of hereditary affection and antipathy" (p. 287), and her negative portrait of Gesellschaft incorporates the belief that renewal in the present is to be grounded in the modern culture that contributed to the disintegration of traditional Gemeinschaft.

But George Eliot's uneasiness with "modern generalization"

continues, nevertheless, and extends even to theory at its best—when it establishes significant laws or principles and yet remains free from the falsifications that distort facts to fit a hypothesis or endorse a stereotype. Consequently, while she praises Riehl for avoiding faults such as these, she abstains from pointing out how theoretical are the principles at work in his *Natural History of German Life*, despite the fact that Riehl took as his main task a formulation of "the laws of society."[5] Even more significantly, she calls no attention to her own dependence on theory, though her proclivity for the theoretical is everywhere evident in the essay, not only in her discussion of his ideas but also in statements of her own thoughts. In the most generalized and abstract paragraph of the essay, she presents with some urgency her argument for "Natural History," based now not on Riehl but on Comte. "It has not been sufficiently insisted on," she writes, "that in the various branches of Social Science there is an advance from the general to the special, from the simple to the complex, analogous with that which is found in the series of the sciences, from Mathematics to Biology" (pp. 289–90). She does not insist on the theoretical foundations of her aesthetic credo, but they are nonetheless substantial.

By way of explaining further the disquietude in George Eliot's attitude toward theory, we may consider an uneasiness resulting from her strong dependence on principles that threaten constantly to be undependable. To discuss this matter requires us to move beyond the essay on Riehl, as we shall be doing shortly, but a number of the contradictory points already noted suggest that underlying the tension between fact and theory is a more troublesome and intractable problem. Though often described by George Eliot as an opposition between observable fact and individual experience, on the one hand, and the shifting and unstable nature of theory, on the other, the more fundamental opposition is not between theory and fact, but between fact and value. George Eliot would like to be able to trust facts allied to theoretical principles derived through a process of induction. Such an empirical base promises dependability in a variety of ways—through the objectivity of fact, the solidity of concrete observation, and the capacity to do justice to peculiarities, anomalies, and idiosyncrasies. But consistently structured and rigorously applied, the positivist principles of observation,

5. G. P. Gooch, *History and Historians in the Nineteenth Century*, p. 575. See also Riehl's 1853 Preface to *Land und Leute*; reprinted in 8th ed., p. vii. I am indebted to Bruce Kieffer, Department of German, Williams College, for help with translating Riehl.

description, and comparison work to separate fact from value. George Eliot applauds Riehl for proceeding according to them; yet her descriptions of his work reveal that he often makes value judgments, particularly when class differences are at issue. Similarly, value judgments intrude when George Eliot puts forth her own ideas, particularly when the social function of art is at stake. At one critical point, for instance, she writes:

> The thing for mankind to know is, not what are the motives and influences which the moralist thinks *ought* to act on the labourer or the artisan, but what are the motives and influences which *do* act on him.

> [p. 271

The context of this sentence makes clear, however, the critical importance of simultaneously establishing a center of value.

As a result, the distinction she makes between *ought* and *is*, prescription and description, does not reject the normative but functions instead to create value. The reason we are to know the truths of rustic life, however harsh and disagreeable, is so we may learn to feel "sympathy with the perennial joys and struggles, the toil, the tragedy, and the humour in the life of our more heavily-laden fellow-men." No less at stake than the accuracy of the representation, she feels, is the "perversion" of feeling created by a misrepresentation that turns the reader "towards a false object instead of the true one." But this attempt to bring fact and value together tends to overturn the empirical and objective theoretical base George Eliot wants to establish, and it threatens to undermine the very congruence between fact and value that was to justify nothing less than the nature of her art and her commitment to it. The terms of the "sacred" task George Eliot assigns to the artist demand the renewal of community through "the awakening of social sympathies": to this end she denounces "falsification" by calling it "pernicious" (p. 271). Yet an account of the actual conditions of working-class life, or an exposure of the real motives and influences at work in bourgeois society, might just as easily arouse antagonism as compassion in the predominantly middle-class reader, encouraging not sympathy and fellow-feeling but hostile defensiveness and a sense of division and difference. Thus, even the facts of natural history carry a dangerous as well as a salutary potential, threatening to split fact from value, although the theoretical separation was intended to create a solid foundation for the renewal of value.

Natural History and
Social Evolutionary Theory

Because the phrase *natural history*, as commonly used today, suggests the study of natural objects (animal, vegetable, and mineral)
and the display of them in museums, the broader significance
George Eliot attaches to the term may strike us as idiosyncratic, but
she was actually participating in a debate already well underway.
Two of the premises incorporated in the essay on Riehl, those concerning the conditions of social life and relations within them, are
fundamental to a concept of natural history whose origins lie in
the eighteenth century. As defined by Frederick J. Teggart and by
Robert A. Nisbet, it is essentially a developmental theory, with the
word *natural* denoting an entity's intrinsic essence, which manifests itself unless corrupting or interfering circumstances deflect it
from its course of development.[6] Since the theory holds that the
undeflected process of growth and development itself reveals the
true nature of an entity or thing, an equally fundamental concept
is that natural causes account for change. Such causes were often
located in the evolving conditions of social life internal and external. To study history, therefore, is to focus on changes in the
nature of society and in the nature of man that have caused civilization to develop to its present stage, and to discover (if possible) how
best to aid the process of development in the interest of a more
perfect society. Through its great emphasis on the power of conditions in preceding epochs to shape those that follow, the theory
of natural history embraced by many eighteenth-century social
philosophers includes as well the basic presupposition that "all
knowledge is knowledge of relations."[7]

As recent scholarship has demonstrated, the theory of social evolution that gained such predominance during the third quarter of
the nineteenth century incorporates such principles and introduces
new ones.[8] These include the two other premises that inform

6. Frederick J. Teggart, *Theory and Processes of History*, pp. 77–127. Robert
A. Nisbet, *Social Change and History*, pp. 139–58. As Teggart points out, the
terms *theoretical, philosophic, conjectural, hypothetical,* and *natural,* as
applied to the kind of history we are discussing, are for the most part interchangeable.

7. Gladys Bryson, *Man and Society*, p. 91. See also pp. 87–90.

8. Nisbet, *Social Change*, pp. 160–65. Nisbet's work develops from Teggart's,
as does Bryson's, though her study is narrower, focusing only on the eighteenth
century. J. W. Burrow, *Evolution and Society*, pp. 111–12 and passim. As

George Eliot's essay on Riehl, those concerning the laws of evolutionary change in society and in the individual. The nineteenth-century debate continues the call for a new subject matter, at the same time that it questions the conjectural, hypothetical, and deductive foundations of eighteenth-century natural history, and tries to establish empirically, by way of social evolutionary theory, a natural history at once speculative and factual.

During the eighteenth and early nineteenth centuries, dozens of natural histories were written, taking for their subject matter not only "the planets, the earth, [and] organic life," but also "man's psychological being, his moral sentiments, along with his polity, economy, social classes, religion and kinship."[9] Among them were David Hume's *Natural History of Religion*, an interpretative account of the origins and changing nature of religious practices and beliefs, and Adam Ferguson's *Essay on the History of Civil Society*, a study so wide-ranging as to have suggested to later scholars "Tönnies's idea of *Gesellschaft in nuce*."[10] In contrast to the customary emphasis on politics, rulers, and war, these "new" histories stress the importance of customs, manners, ideas, and institutions. This redirection of subject matter was continued by the nineteenth-century writers with whom we are concerned. Thus Lewes writes: "Popes, kings and emperors—courts, camps and dungeons—these have filled the 'swelling scene' to the exclusion of all that was important, vital—all that produced *them* and much else." "History, therefore, in its highest form," he argues in another essay,

> is not the chronicle of events—not the gazette of camps and courts, of diplomatic intrigues or royal misfortunes—it is the *Life of Humanity as evolved by human beings.* . . . History is, so to speak, the Geology of Humanity. Its records are the annals of the growth and development of Humanity through the ages. . . . [But] no one has reached the high standard required; no one has understood like a philosopher, and painted like an artist, the section of Humanity selected.

Nisbet and Burrow make clear, although evolutionary social theory received considerable support from Darwinian evolutionary theory during the third quarter of the nineteenth century, it nevertheless predates it and is in some fundamental respects at odds with it. Maurice Mandelbaum, *History, Man, & Reason*, explains how developmental and evolutionary concepts were joined to the definition of historicism to create a distinctive mode of nineteenth-century thought.

9. Nisbet, *Social Change*, p. 154.
10. Heberle, "Sociological System of Ferdinand Tönnies," p. 52.

In several essays he discusses what he would have history include: "literature, art, law, religion, customs and manners, and commerce," as well as the "beliefs, opinions, institutions, etc." that have created them; but his arguments for including "all the elements of social life" have a distinctively nineteenth-century flavor in their demand for a "science of history" capable of discovering "the laws of the evolution of humanity."[11]

T. H. Huxley very much doubted the science of society the others were trying to create, yet he too expresses the wish to have history treated "not as a succession of battles and dynasties; not as a series of biographies . . . but as the development of man in times past, and in other conditions than our own."[12] Spencer's expression of this same basic idea combines social evolutionary doctrines and organic notions to establish interrelationships far more comprehensive than those imagined by eighteenth-century natural historians:

> That societies are not artificially put together, is a truth so manifest, that it seems wonderful men should have ever overlooked it. Perhaps nothing more clearly shows the small value of historical studies as they have been commonly pursued. You need but to look at the changes going on around, or observe social organization in its leading peculiarities, to see that these are neither supernatural, nor are determined by the wills of individual men, as by implication historians commonly teach; but are consequent on general natural causes.

This passage from "The Social Organism" (p. 51) suggests what the rest of the essay makes explicit: changes in social life are comparable to the growth of a living thing; and the various aspects of social life are by nature related to one another and to the organism as a whole.

Taken together these various illustrations begin to suggest a philosophy of history, one that is intricately connected to "sociology" and to "historicism" as modes of inquiry initiated in the nineteenth century. Particularly relevant to our discussion is the accompanying shift in subject matter—away from a preoccupation with politics, wars, or battles, and toward a concern with the social evolution of manners, institutions, customs, and beliefs. In George Eliot's essay on Riehl, for instance, traditional historical facts ap-

11. [G. H. Lewes], "The State of Historical Science in France," p. 74; "History by Modern Frenchmen," pp. 405–6; "Buchez and Daunou on the Science of History," pp. 176–77, 186. See also Lewes "The Thirty Years' Peace," pp. 360, 370; and "The Art of History—Macaulay," pp. 298–300, 306–7.

12. Thomas Henry Huxley, "A Liberal Education," p. 59.

pear rarely and then only as evidence of the habits, ideas, or motives of a social group. Thus, while history as traditionally conceived emphasizes actions and deeds, situations and happenings, outstanding events and exceptional personages, the developmental perspective common to natural history and evolutionary social theory focuses on the growth of ideas, institutions, customs, and art, and on the average person's participation in the life of the culture. George Eliot puts the matter succinctly when she locates "the natural history of the race" in "the study of men, as they have appeared in different ages, and under various social conditions" (*Essays*, p. 336).

This shift in subject matter invites a particular approach to the present, regarding it not so much as the latest "situation" emerging from previous deeds and events, but rather as a "condition" of things resulting from gradual changes in and among the many forms of social life in the past and present.[13] The nineteenth-century appeal for a broader-based history includes, beyond this, "a middle-class revolt against the treatment of history as a chronicle of the deeds of an aristocratic and military caste, and a demand instead for history which shall concern itself with the man in the street, his opinions, conditions of life and the factors which have made for his happiness and unhappiness."[14] Changes such as these bring to the forefront materials vitally related to the contents of the realistic novel, and they reveal at the same time a way of thinking perceived to be essential to the renewal of community by virtually all the nineteenth-century writers we are considering.

At stake in this natural history was nothing less than a major redefinition of social values. A social theory that combined sociology and a philosophy of history in a matrix of evolutionary social theory was being asked to provide a great deal more than explanations of how society works or how it changes. It was to acknowledge that religious and philosophical doctrines had once satisfied the need for a coherent social faith, but it was also to expose their current inadequacies. Further, in order to rescue social life from randomness and arbitrariness, it was to provide a scientific foundation for individual and social ethics. This sense of pressing need is conveyed by the appeal to "History" in Comte's elevation of "Social Feeling" and in the epigraph Lewes chose for the *Leader*, a passage from Humboldt's *Cosmos*:

13. See Teggart, *Theory*, pp. 77–81, on distinction between historical and evolutionary inquiry.
14. Burrow, *Evolution*, p. 67.

The one Idea which History exhibits as evermore developing itself into greater distinctness is the Idea of Humanity—the noble endeavour to throw down all the barriers erected between men by prejudices and one-sided views; and by setting aside the distinctions of Religion, Country, and Colour, to treat the whole Human race as one brotherhood, having one great object—the free development of our spiritual nature.

How passionately George Eliot was committed to this idea of history, may be illustrated by a passage from *The Mill on the Floss* in which the narrator pities Maggie and many another girl in the "civilised world of that day" who had

> come out of her school-life with a soul untrained for inevitable struggles—with no other part of her inherited share in the hard-won treasures of thought, which generations of painful toil have laid up for the race of men, than shreds and patches of feeble literature and false history—with much futile information about Saxon and other kings of doubtful example—but unhappily quite without that knowledge of the irreversible laws within and without her, which, governing the habits, becomes morality, and, developing the feelings of submission and dependence, becomes religion.
>
> [*MF*, ch. 32, pp. 252–53

In the opening pages of Lewes's *Problems of Life and Mind*, the lamentations of "an age clamorous for faith" become a rallying call for a "Religion" expressing "the highest thought of the time, as that thought widens with the ever-growing experience" (1: 1–3). What both Lewes and Eliot had in mind, of course, was a "transformed Religion," based not on conventional forms, but on certain modern principles to be found in natural history and social evolutionary theory. It was to have the prestige and authority of science, and the spiritual force of religion.

To this end, the nineteenth-century social theorists, whose work George Eliot closely followed, attempted to create a science of society at once theoretical and factual. Though the eighteenth-century natural history they inherited had redirected the subject matter of history in a vitally needed way, it seemed to them too abstract, hypothetical, and speculative. Metaphysical and deductive, this legacy exemplified an impatience with the multiple facts of social life, regarding them as inessential obstructions that obscured the essential universal laws of nature. The new effort, in contrast, would employ deductions only in combination with inductions and would discover in the very particularity of facts the laws of social development. The method was now to be empirical so as to validate objectively a social vision otherwise to be regarded as a mere creation of the mind. "The object of our philosophy is to direct the spiritual reorganisation of the civilised world," Comte announces, while insisting that his admittedly "abstract" history is founded on the positivist rules of observation, description, and comparison (*Polity* 1: 30–35). In the work of George Eliot, Lewes, and Spencer, as well, the craving for new forms of moral and social community repeatedly includes arguments for uniting "theory and observation," and for supporting "abstract definitions" with "series of facts." This desire to create a working relation between theoretical reflection and empirical methodology is evident also in the religious theorists: in Strauss's contention that his *Life of Jesus* is both "critical and speculative"; in Hennell's acknowledgment of having to proceed conjecturally to fill in the gaps between facts; in Feuerbach's insistence that his "faith in the historical future, in the triumph of truth and virtue," is based on a philosophy "in the highest degree positive and real."[15]

All of them sought a method that would both validate their means of knowing and unify consciousness by establishing the "Idea of Humanity" as a conceptual and a social "whole." This effort to unite theory and fact in order to establish, through a philosophy of history, an inseparable and palpable link between science and social ethics reaches its most comprehensive articulation in what Comte, Spencer, Mill, Lewes, and George Eliot called *Social Dynamics* and *Social Statics*, terms that mirror the scientific and social nature of their originators' mission. Defining the hypothesis of "Dynamical study" in his *Positive Philosophy*, Comte establishes that its "master-thought" is "continuous progress, or rather . . . the gradual development of humanity." In explaining its "suitability to the needs of a modern society," he writes:

> The true general spirit of social dynamics then consists in conceiving of each of these consecutive social states as the necessary result of the preceding, and the indispensable mover of the following, according to the axiom of Leibnitz—*the present is big with the*

15. David Friedrich Strauss, *The Life of Jesus, Critically Examined*, trans. [George Eliot], 3: 432–42. Ludwig Feuerbach, *The Essence of Christianity*, trans. George Eliot, pp. xxxiv–xxxv. George Eliot's great appreciation of Hennell's *Inquiry* included a recognition that he had often to construct "probabilities" (*Letters* 5: 96); Basil Willey describes the book as a "conjectural natural history of Christianity" (*Nineteenth Century Studies*, p. 213).

future. In this view, the object of science is to discover the laws
which govern this continuity, and the aggregate of which determines the course of human development. In short, social dynamics
studies the laws of succession.[16]

The key word in the definition of Social Dynamics (whether in
Comte and his disciples, or in Spencer, Mill, Lewes, and George
Eliot) is *progress,* so that *Social Dynamics* and the *science of progress* become equivalent terms, explained by way of the laws of
"continuity," "succession," and "gradual evolution." Such laws had
always existed, it was argued, but they had long been ignored, and
were only now, through the study of history as applied to human
and social development, being discovered.

George Eliot acknowledges their importance in her notes on
"Historic Guidance" by stating that *"Continuity* (in human history)" must be taken first as a fact "quite apart from . . . [its] entrance into the human consciousness," and by establishing how
vitally important it is for continuity to pass "from a mere fact into
a motive." To confirm continuity as a fact, she summons the principle everywhere to be found in natural history, saying: "it is clear
that the conditions of an age are determined by the conditions of
the age that went before it." To establish "the dependence of one
generation on the preceding," not only as a fact but as a motive
guiding thought and action, she goes several steps further. Raising
a question her contemporaries also asked, she writes: " 'how can
we so determine things during our existence as to determine bene-
ficently the existence of our posterity?' " And shaping an answer
in terms particularly important to her, she replies:

> We study the preparation made for us by previous ages, & discern-
> ing how laborious devoted lives or grand jets of noble resolution
> have made currents of good effect reaching to ourselves, grateful
> admiring love is more or less stimulated by our contemplation; &
> this sentiment reinforces our desire to exert some corresponding
> influence over the destiny of our own successors.
>
> ["More Leaves," p. 371

Both the question and her answer reflect another hypothesis
vital to the concept of Social Dynamics: the theory of "modification." A distinctly nineteenth-century idea, this theory posits that
natural phenomena, though subject to laws, are modifiable by man's

16. Auguste Comte, *The Positive Philosophy,* freely trans. and condensed
by Harriet Martineau, pp. 463–64. Comte admired this version of his *Cours
de philosophie positive.*

intervention; and that of all such phenomena the conditions of social and psychological life are the most modifiable. Their very complexity, it was argued, make them especially susceptible to social influences and to human desires and actions. The laws of natural phenomena could not be overturned, but the process of change inherent in the nature of man and society could be quickened and intensified through modifications in individual and social life acting upon one another.

Because the concept of modification is so central to George Eliot's creation of character and to the effect she wished her novels to have upon her readers, we give it separate consideration in the section that follows. The Comparative Method, another matter related to Social Dynamics, is also discussed in this next section, not because George Eliot adopted the idea, but because she so intricately and variously adapted it to shape new techniques particularly suited to the purposes of her fiction. The Comparative Method was introduced by eighteenth-century natural historians and developed fully by nineteenth-century social evolutionists. For the latter, it served to substantiate and verify their theories of progressive change, enabling them to classify the stages of human and social development by comparing present-day "civilized" societies and contemporary less-advanced cultures. For George Eliot the Comparative Method served many purposes, enabling her readers, for instance, to perceive contrasts and similarities between social life in the past and present, to make connections between their own lives and the ones portrayed in her novels, and to apprehend how they themselves might contribute to what George Eliot in the Finale to *Middlemarch* calls "the growing good of the world."

This brief introduction to Social Dynamics must also note one other matter to be discussed at length in later chapters. Discussions of Social Dynamics in the nineteenth century invariably included at least some mention of Social Statics, since the two are coordinate concepts: while the one is concerned with progress, succession, and continuous historical change, the other deals with order, coexistence, and with people living in the same period within a given culture. In Lewes's definition of Social Statics as "the state of the Social Organism at the time being," we see, furthermore, that its fundamental principle is *organic* coexistence (*Problems* 1: 160). Thus Social Statics serves to complement the historical and evolutionary perspective provided by Social Dynamics; the former's emphasis on "solidarity," "consensus," and the "interdependence" of all coexisting social elements provides direct counterparts to continuity, modification, and the successive phases of development. Consequently, Social Statics is no less vitally connected to the theme of community than is Social Dynamics, but the issues it raises are different enough and sufficiently complex that chapters 4 and 5 are devoted exclusively to organicism as a social theory and a fictional mode.

Community as Fact and Value

George Eliot and the social theorists wanted to witness objectively the facts of social life, and they wanted also to testify to the renewal of community; but however committed they were to observation and description, their evaluative bias determined the conditions on which they chose to focus. Custom and social convention, religious practice and belief—these were the established conditions to which they paid special attention. In addition, they attempted through their science of society to bring new definition to the forms of social life by expanding the meaning of conditions, introducing the concept of modifications, and employing the Comparative Method. The natural histories they were shaping culminate in what Tönnies later called the third pillar of community, created out of intellectual and emotional affinities, mutual toleration, and common concerns. But although they looked to similar sources of renewal, contradictions repeatedly undermine the solutions they proposed, creating instabilities between fact and value, and suggesting within the community of interests they shared a number of intractable dilemmas.

CUSTOM, TOLERANCE, AND CONVENTION

The Victorian social philosophers adopted the principle "that the past rules the present, lives in it, and that we are but the growth and outcome of the past" (*Letters* 3: 320), but they were also keenly aware of discontinuities within what they took to be their own age of transition. Thus they turned to those areas of experience least dependent on fixity of locale and family ties to explore how common interests and feelings might continue to exist quite apart from the traditional three pillars of community. Similarly, in studying the Gemeinschafts of the past, they focused on conditions arising out of beliefs and ideas. They hypothesized that inherited patterns were likely to exert a lingering influence despite the demographic changes caused by industrialization; yet, unlike the lines established by kinship and geography, patterns of thought and behavior are malleable. They studied the conditions arising out of beliefs and ideas in the Gemeinschafts of the past, then, in order to understand and participate in the present. Spencer and Comte, for instance, devote major portions of their sociologies to describing the effects of custom and ceremony on communal life, while George Eliot explores in one novel after another the force of tradition and hereditary habit; but their concern with the binding power of customary usages includes significant attempts to recreate value within their own society. Along with others, they sought to account for the habitual practices and ceremonial observances that serve as socializing agents, to comprehend the formative influences of historical conditions on societies and individuals, and to assess the present vitality and worth of inherited social forms. They also struggled to define "outmoded forms" while contributing to the growth of new ones, by acknowledging and accepting cultural diversity, and by evaluating with an open mind the customs they were studying.

Thus from the very intolerance custom engenders they created the alternate value of tolerance. Its importance to community in Gesellschaft is signaled in some jottings George Eliot made on the "Birth of Tolerance":

> Community of interest is the root of justice; community of suffering, the root of pity; community of joy, the root of love.

[*Essays*, p. 449

Her stress on tolerance as a corrective to prejudice, dogmatism, ignorance, and insensitivity, as well as the emphasis noticeable here on community as idea and feeling, is evident in letters written near the start and close of her novelistic career. In 1857, she writes of her "growing conviction that we may measure true moral and intellectual culture by the comprehension and veneration given to all forms of thought and feeling which have influenced large masses of mankind" (*Letters* 2: 301); and in 1876 she tells a fellow novelist, Harriet Beecher Stowe, "There is nothing I should care more to do, if it were possible, than to rouse the imagination of men and women to a vision of human claims in those races of their fellow-men who most differ from them in customs and beliefs" (*Letters* 6: 301). That these remarks should have been made to Stowe is particularly fitting, since Eliot had some ten years earlier said to her:

> I think your way of presenting the religious convictions which are not your own except by indirect fellowship, is a triumph of in-

sight and true tolerance. A thorough comprehension of the mixed
moral influence shed on society by dogmatic systems is rare even
among writers, and one misses it altogether in English drawing-
room talk.

[*Letters* 5: 48

Great value was placed on tolerance by all the nineteenth-century
writers we are considering, even if their comprehension was at times
limited. This effort to be flexible and widely sympathetic distinguishes them from many eighteenth-century natural historians,
but both groups serve to illustrate how comprehensively matters
of value determine the descriptive materials of natural history. During the earlier period, a cosmopolitan point of view brought to the
subject matter of history the study of diverse cultures, but the aban-
donment of provincialism was often accompanied by a tendency to
ridicule ways of life thought to be less "civilized." The values of
the Enlightenment often caused eighteenth-century natural historians to regard customs as artificial interferences or as deviations
from nature that had to be cleared away or penetrated before the
essential and rational order of things could be uncovered.[17] In contrast, the nineteenth-century social evolutionists generally treated
communal traditions with reverence, because they were thought
to be at the very heart of social life, revealing both its origins and
progressive development. George Eliot's awareness of these differences is apparent in the first major essay she published. After re-
marking that Mackay's " 'Progress of the Intellect' [1850], is, perhaps, the nearest approach in our language to a satisfactory natural
history of religion," she criticizes the "tone of ridicule adopted by
many authors of the eighteenth century," presumably including in
her indictment *The Natural History of Religion* published by
Hume a hundred years earlier (*Essays*, pp. 35–36).

Within these patterns there are of course variations, but the exceptions also demonstrate the close connection between matters of
fact and value. Mill, for instance, argues for the artificiality of laws
and customs, but for reasons different from those put forward in
the eighteenth century; not simply because custom conceals what
is natural (as yet an unknown, according to Mill), but because in
contemporary society custom is so despotic that "unnatural generally means only uncustomary."[18] At the same time, whatever his

17. Mandelbaum, *History, Man, & Reason*, pp. 234–35; Nisbet, *Social
Change*, pp. 141–43.
18. John Stuart Mill, *The Subjection of Women*, p. 138.

doubts about social evolutionary theory, Mill maintains, along with other nineteenth-century theorists, but unlike eighteenth-century natural historians, that custom is basic to the historical social order and that it has contributed greatly to social development by inculcating and furthering the social principle. His argument, then, is that given the present advanced stage of development custom exerts too powerful a rule. In this respect he is not fundamentally at odds with the other figures we are considering, once we recognize an underlying distinction they each make between custom in traditional and modern societies.

It seemed to them that in turning from Gemeinschaft to Gesellschaft, society had become mechanical and artificial, ruled by convention and contract rather than by ceremony and tradition. A formal distinction between the two—between societies based primarily on tradition and ascribed status, and those based on contract and achieved status—is first expressed by Henry Maine in *Ancient Law* (1861) and is later extensively developed by Tönnies through his contrast between custom in Gemeinschaft and convention in Gesellschaft.[19] Whereas custom is equated with folkways, concord, and community, convention is equated with social climbing, class rivalry, and the rule of etiquette and fashion. Accordingly, convention is seen as a corruption of custom, resulting from changes that have substituted for the intrinsic, communal, and nonmaterial customs of traditional community, practices that are superficial, self-serving, and artificial.

While developing these concepts, Tönnies frequently expresses his indebtedness to Maine and mentions as well the work of Riehl and Spencer.[20] More significant for our purposes, however, is that Tönnies's distinction helps to clarify a separation—sometimes explicit but more often implicit—made regularly by all these writers. Whereas they treat custom in Gemeinschaft if not always with reverence at least with tolerance, they treat convention in Gesellschaft skeptically and critically, as at best an unsatisfactory transitional phase, but more often as a serious debasement of custom. Spencer is to some extent an exception, but only because his radically individualist bias and thorough belief in progress cause him to favor the movement from status and custom to contract and convention. For Comte, in contrast, the losses accompanying the dis-

---

19. Nisbet, *The Sociological Tradition*, pp. 72–73.
20. Tönnies credits his indebtedness to Maine in both *G&G* and *Custom*. In the latter, he cites in addition work done by Riehl and Spencer (pp. 105, 103–10).

integration of custom in modern society seem so great that in order to "revive the sense of Solidarity . . . and inspire the sense of historical Continuity" he devises an entire structure of ceremonial observances, creating for his positivist calendar no fewer than eighty-one festivals (*Polity* 1: 274). But while Comte's efforts in this direction were so extreme as generally to be a subject for ridicule, they nevertheless spoke to George Eliot's wish to give lasting emphasis to the inspirational character of rites and ceremonies, and on at least one occasion she attempted to draw up a "Saints of Humanity" calendar.

These various attitudes toward custom, tolerance, and convention illustrate that prior customs, no matter what the specific beliefs, generally suggest community and elicit a tolerant response, while contemporary customs connote social convention and often provoke a critical response. But even within these areas of agreement, serious tensions exist. While the theorists agreed that all social phenomena are "right" in their historical context, nevertheless they found it difficult to refrain from negative judgments of contemporary usages, in part because they were afraid of encouraging moral relativism. If careful discriminations offered a possible compromise, a clearly balanced response was often hard to achieve because those same social forms that seemed to have outlived their usefulness seemed also to "carry in solution precious sentiments & habits of mind," while those most predominant in the present seemed to diminish community as a value ("More Leaves," p. 373). Equally troublesome was a tendency to respond nostalgically to the nature of custom in the past for, as Raymond Williams demonstrates in *The Country and the City*, nostalgia turns "protest into retrospect" (p. 83). The nineteenth-century preoccupation with community is retrospective in that it often includes a nostalgic response to the dissolution of the old; yet the passionate concern with advancing new forms of social life conducive to community in Gesellschaft makes it simultaneously progressive and innovative. Pulled in both directions, George Eliot on one occasion writes, "tradition is really the basis of our best life," and on another that "unreflecting obedience to custom and routine" subverts true morality (*Essays*, p. 409; *TS*, p. 111).

RELIGION, THE "HIGHER CRITICISM," AND "LOVING ONE'S NEIGHBOR"

As applied to a particular system of belief, or to Christianity as a condition of social existence, the preceding analysis of custom and convention continues to hold, while important nineteenth-century reinterpretations of Christian doctrines on historical and scientific grounds bring additional facts and values to bear on the problem of community.[21] George Eliot's encounters with the "higher criticism"—which she first read in Hennell and later made the subject of her first published books, her translations of Strauss and Feuerbach—are too familiar to need retelling. What is pertinent here is that these analyses of the forms of belief include arguments for the renewal of community through the substitution of social ties for religious ones. These studies of Christianity reinforce a number of principles common to natural history and social evolutionary theory. But while they contribute to the restructuring of the third pillar of Gemeinschaft, they also perpetuate the tension between actual social conditions and humanistic ideals.

Though not social evolutionists, Hennell, Strauss, and Feuerbach brought a developmental hypothesis to their study of the origins and essence of Christianity, and their writings added substantially to the natural history of religion. Thus it is not surprising that several of the most basic principles informing their work are present also in Comte, Spencer, Mill, Lewes, and George Eliot. They each regarded Christianity as a stage in the religious development of the race, saw its origins and growth in terms of "natural" causes, and attributed to religious dogma "the operation of human motives and feelings, acted upon by the particular circumstances of the age and country."[22] There are some differences among them: Feuerbach and Mill emphasize the psychological nature of religious belief, while Comte resists psychological explanations and promotes social evolutionary concepts foreign to Feuerbach and suspicious to Mill. For Lewes, Spencer, and George Eliot, however, the natural history of self augments and regularly finds its complement in the natural history of social life: beliefs of all kinds are viewed as projections of inward feeling and reflectors of outward conditions.

21. Spinoza, though a seventeenth-century philosopher, was in some respects so ahead of his time as to be pertinent to the intellectual climate I am defining. His *Tractatus Theologico-Politicus*, which George Eliot translated in 1843, discusses the social usefulness of convention, custom, and sacred rites. Like the *Ethics*, which she also translated (1854–56), it anticipated the nineteenth-century "higher criticism" and religion of humanity. Still, though it is important to note these affinities, Spinoza's basic philosophical principles are so different from those at play in the tradition we are considering as finally to exclude him.

22. The passage quoted is from Hennell's *Inquiry*, p. iv, but he is expressing ideas the others shared.

In addition to reinforcing common perspectives such as these, the higher criticism contributed to the view that the subject matter of history, at its most significant, is to be found in the secular and the ordinary. The extraordinary events in the life of Christ, as reported in the Gospels, provided a perfect test case, allowing the claims of natural history to be validated through the argument that "the soul of Christianity," as George Eliot puts it, "lies not at all in the facts of an individual life, but in the ideas of which that life was the meeting-point and the new starting-point" (*Letters* 4: 95). Accordingly, the Gospels came to be regarded as poetry, or as fictions and myths corresponding to "the metaphysics of that time," and expressing the culture of the community, its needs and longings as well as the actual knowledge and experience of its members. Thus the originating conditions of Christianity, as Hennell, Feuerbach, Strauss, and George Eliot emphasize, are to be taken as having been caused by "ordinary events" and "common everyday things," while Christ is to be seen not as the "God-man," but as *one* of the great human teachers, and neither the first nor the last.[23]

At the same time, his own education and his role as a teacher made Jesus something of a model for the ideal human hero, exemplary because he " 'first taught fraternity to men' " (*Letters* 1: 253). He was, furthermore, the teacher they each aspired to be. In a passage George Eliot singled out for special approval (*Letters* 1: 237), Hennell speaks of Christ as a man "fully conversant with the notions of his age and country, but yet able to modify or add to them" from his own resources. In an analogous passage, Strauss describes Christ's "comprehensive faculty of reception" to be "as with great men ever the reverse side of their powerful originality." While Hennell discusses Christ's role as a reformer working to establish a regenerated Israel in *this* world, Strauss qualifies his admiration for Jesus by saying that though he stands among "improvers of the ideal of humanity . . . in the first class," nevertheless he represents an ideal which is incomplete because it excludes "trade and art," and active participation in the "body politic."[24]

23. The sources of the phrases quoted in this paragraph are: Hennell, *Inquiry*, pp. 294–95, 250; Feuerbach, *Essence of Christianity*, p. 276; Strauss, *A New Life of Jesus* 2: 438–39 (a new edition written for general public, whereas earlier ones were addressed primarily to theologians). See also George Eliot, "More Leaves," p. 356.

24. Quotations from Hennell are from *Inquiry*, p. 440; for his discussion of Christ as reformer see pp. 413–31. Quotations from Strauss are from *Life of Jesus* 1: 295 and *New Life of Jesus* 2: 437–38.

Assuming themselves the roles of teacher and citizen, both the religious and social critics came to argue that the essence of religion suffered a deflection through the development of Christian doctrines that either neglected or narrowed truly human concerns by encouraging a preoccupation with individual salvation and by preaching an exclusive faith. Tracing the origins of Christianity, and making clear his own "devotion to the cause of happiness on this earth," Hennell discovers a source of Christian exclusiveness even in one of the Gospels, and accordingly censures John for leaving "the impression that belief in Jesus as the Christ . . . is the chief obligation laid upon man":

> The commandment to love one another is certainly enforced with much strength and pathos; but the commandment partakes too much of an exclusive spirit; it is for the Christian sect alone; it is not the language of wide philanthropy, "love all men;" but, "I pray not for the world, but for these whom thou hast given me out of the world."

[p. 302

Feuerbach, moreover, argues that the forms of Christianity, by setting God above all else, had developed so as to separate matters of faith from the love that alone constitutes the essence of religion. Conceiving of a love at once "particular and limited, *i.e.*, directed to one's neighbour," but "in its nature universal, since it loves man for man's sake, in the name of the race," he contrasts his own ideal with the narrowness, intolerance, and exclusiveness of Christian doctrine (p. 269). "Faith," he declares, "is essentially a spirit of partisanship" (p. 255). A Christian loves men for the sake of Christ and loves them egotistically because he would ensure his own salvation through the return of love he expects from God. Feuerbach would "change 'the friends of God into friends of man, believers into thinkers, worshippers into workers, candidates for the other world into . . . free, self-reliant citizens of earth.' "[25]

During her own early religious struggles, George Eliot experienced that alienation from self and from one's fellowmen which Feuerbach attributes to the evolution of Christian belief. But by the middle 1850s, when she was translating Feuerbach and writing essays for the *Westminster Review* on the preacher Dr. Cumming and the poet Young, she was attacking "Christians" for being too self-serving, and Evangelicals for teaching "the love of the *clan*,

25. Feuerbach, *Das Wesen der Religion*, p. 14; quoted by Karl Barth, Introduction to *The Essence of Christianity*, p. xi.

which is the correlative of antagonism to the rest of mankind. It is not sympathy and helpfulness towards men as men, but towards men as Christians" *(Essays,* p. 179).

Similar conclusions are offered by the social critics: Comte, for instance, argues that the promise of eternal reward unavoidably taints "our benevolent affections" with "calculations of self-interest"; and Mill maintains that Christian morality, by failing to offer an ideal of public obligation, disconnects "each man's feelings of duty from the interests of his fellow-creatures."[26] In writing about the negative aspects of Christian doctrine, then, quite apart from lamenting inevitable disparities between theory and practice, several of the most important religious and social theorists attacked it as anticommunal for having transferred to God the love we owe to our fellow creatures, and for having encouraged through its doctrine of compensation a selfish concern with personal salvation.

At the same time, in writing about past and present communities, they kept returning to that ideal unity of feeling embodied in the traditional precept of loving one's neighbor. While Hennell and Strauss were distressed to think that their critical inquiries into the origins of Christianity might undermine morality, George Eliot, along with Feuerbach, Comte, Mill, Spencer, and Lewes, rejected Christian dogma partly because it seemed to contain a repudiation of its most valuable moral precept: to love our neighbors as ourselves. This phrase and related ones concerning brotherhood and fellowship appear so regularly in their work as to constitute a leitmotif whose dominant theme may be heard in these words from Comte: "When the morality of an advanced society bids us love our neighbors as ourselves, it embodies in the best way the deepest truth" *(Positive Philosophy,* p. 501). From this "sublime precept" it was a short step to the altruism they were all committed to furthering. Indeed, the French word *altruisme,* which opposes against selfishness and egoism an ideal of living for others, was coined by Comte, and the word *altruism* was introduced into English in the early 1850s by his translators and expounders, among them Lewes. In his 1852 *Leader* articles on Comte, Lewes explains that the normative tags of "good" and "bad" are commonly applied to people depending on whether the altruistic or egotistic impulse predominates.[27]

While the complex of ideas conveyed by altruism and related

26. Comte, *A General View of Positivism,* p. 246; Mill, *On Liberty, Collected Works* 18: 255.
27. Lewes, *Comte's Philosophy of the Sciences,* pp. 217–24.

phrases was explicitly designated a "Religion of Humanity" by Strauss and by Comte, this way of thinking was common among other figures especially important to George Eliot, among them Lewes, Feuerbach, and her close friend Charles Bray.[28] They held that the object of religious feeling should be transferred from God and Christian orthodoxy to humanity and secular community. The natural history of social life was not only to replace the authority of scripture but also to validate the idea of humanity and the concept of brotherhood. Lewes's identification of "Humanity" with a "vast chain of Existence which encompasseth us and all men, past, present, and to come, in one real vital brotherhood"; Strauss's call for a "carrying forward of the Religion of Christ to the Religion of Humanity"; Comte's elaborate efforts to dictate the shape of that religion; Feuerbach's declaration "that only community constitutes humanity"; George Eliot's invocation of "one comprehensive Church whose fellowship consists in the desire to purify and ennoble human life, and where the best members of all narrower churches may call themselves brother and sister in spite of differences"—all these reaffirmations of community are based on secular friendship of spirit.[29]

Thus we find repeated the pattern identified in our discussion of custom and tradition: the recreating of value through the third pillar of community and the reshaping of solidarity through the force of ideas and sentiments available to the generality of mankind. Tolerance, which remains a value, is joined by brotherhood, now given predominance over the concrete ties of kinship; love of one's neighbor transcends particularity of neighborhood. Spencer, for instance, establishes as one of the criteria of progress a decrease in the influence of the external physical environment and an increase in man's capacity for internal change. Comte, too, finds in the modern positivist phase a movement away from the kinship in the realm of the moral, accompanied by a movement toward the industrial in the sphere of activity and the scientific in the realm of the intellectual. The traditional primacy of kinship seemed also to Lewes to be in decline, a development he regards as auspicious be-

28. The groundwork in this area has been laid by P. Bourl'honne, *George Eliot: Essai de biographie intellectuelle et morale, 1819–1854*; Basil Willey, *Nineteenth Century Studies*; U. C. Knoepflmacher, *Religious Humanism and the Victorian Novel*; and Bernard J. Paris, *Experiments in Life*.

29. Lewes, "History by Modern Frenchmen," p. 410; Strauss, *New Life of Jesus* 2: 436; Comte, *Polity* 1: 257–73, 2: 53–70, 4: 24–37; Feuerbach, *Essence of Christianity*, p. 158; George Eliot, *Letters* 6: 89.

cause it bolsters the human capacity for change. Furthermore, in much of the major fiction of the century, one finds a "growing consciousness of the impossibility of the biological family."[30]

Given George Eliot's feelings about the importance of rootedness in the life of an individual, attitudes such as these may seem to be at odds with her cast of mind, but while she valued greatly the "fixed local habitation" that "renders fellowship real," she experienced within her own life and in the conditions of Victorian England the distancing and disappearance of such places. Her responses to these conditions were various, but even in one of her most nostalgic pieces, the "Looking Backward" section of *Theophrastus Such*, the portrait of her father's England and the celebration of the countryside of her childhood culminate in the present and spiritualize place by affirming "something not visibly, tangibly existent, but a spiritual product of our visible tangible selves" (p. 51). This tension between that which is actually present and the idea or sentiment presented inhabits each of the themes discussed earlier —the elevation of the commonplace, the ideal role of the teacher, and the reconstitution of community through the substitution of social ties for religious ones. These further efforts to recreate value, moreover, are disturbed by the unresolved conflicts surrounding custom, tolerance, and convention.

Victorian religious practices again required tolerance to contend with convention. The degeneration of custom into etiquette and fashion made churchgoing a matter of the parishioner's stylishness of dress and the minister's manners. The rule of convention in religious as well as secular matters turned salvation into a contract with God and competition with one's neighbors. Thus, while George Eliot and the others did indeed believe that "all the great religions of the world historically considered, are rightly the objects of deep reverence and sympathy—they are the record of spiritual struggles which are the types of our own" (*Letters* 5: 447–48), still the battle against convention caused them to censure sharply many of the social practices common among "Christians." Their implicit target was the divisive contract mentality predominant in Gesellschaft. Lewes, for instance, prints in the pages of the *Leader* a "curse" from the hand of a "Christian priest," in the form of a letter from Charles Kingsley damning the "wolfish competition" that "is the custom of selfish and unorganized mankind." Elsewhere in the *Leader*, Lewes argues for the honest and open debate necessary to

---

30. Alan Mintz, *George Eliot and the Novel of Vocation*, p. 82.

social renewal by attacking Mrs. Grundy and John Bull, symbols of a "religion" grounded in " 'respectability' " and " 'customers.' "[31] Even Mill's tolerance was tried by the intolerance he found all around him, whether rooted in the customs that sanctioned self-interest in nation and class, or in the Evangelicalism that contributed to the dogmatic atmosphere in nineteenth-century England. Both seemed to him irreligious, the one by adopting a compromising worldly standard while claiming to respect the precepts of the New Testament, and the other by following a doctrine so narrow as to render "what is boasted of at the present time as the revival of religion . . . at least as much the revival of bigotry" (*On Liberty, Collected Works* 18: 240).

In George Eliot's case, though her tolerance for sincere Christians came to be so thorough and convincing that her early fiction was thought by many to have been written by a clergyman, when it came to the "irrationalities of social habits . . . daily displayed by men," her own tolerance too was severely tested. Spencer, for instance, reports that for both George Eliot and Lewes "reverence for humanity in the abstract seemed . . . to go along with irreverence for it in the concrete."[32] His remark was undoubtedly prompted in part by his own lack of generosity, but it speaks nonetheless both to the antagonism George Eliot sometimes expressed toward many of the conventions prevalent in Victorian England and to her frequently avowed wish to improve social existence.

Even within the community of interests we are describing, then, the difficulties of tolerance were such as to cause high-minded arguments to verge on intolerance or to be accompanied by personal antagonisms of various sorts. Sometimes they grew out of inner self-divisions, arising out of what George Eliot once called "the attitude of antagonism which belongs to the renunciation of *any* belief" (*Letters* 3: 230), as in Strauss's relentless dissection of beliefs he professed to venerate, or in George Eliot's initial hostility to the religious beliefs she had renounced. But they also included conflicts between individuals such as were caused, for instance, by Comte's tyrannical insistence on total adherence to the sacerdotal system he had imposed upon what was to have been a science of society.

As the center of value is enlarged beyond matters related to tolerance, the tensions between ideals or principles and resistant realities increase. They are evident in Strauss's and Hennell's efforts to

31. Charles Kingsley, "Robert Owen's First Principle," letter to *Leader*; [G. H. Lewes], "Mrs. Grundy and the Public Press."
32. Herbert Spencer, *An Autobiography* 2: 237–38.

treat the Gospels as fiction or myth, thereby retaining the poetry that fosters the ideal, though neither was able to resolve the problem of restoring the ethical substance of Christianity after having destroyed critically its historic and doctrinal forms. Joseph Wiesenfarth argues that George Eliot's fiction addresses this problem by replacing Christian mythology with the myth of fellow-feeling.[33] But while his argument is persuasive, still we are left with the unalterable fact that reality, not myth, was her object. For the social theorists as well, a commitment to the actual and not always salutary forms of social life accompanied a need to testify simultaneously to those secular values that would ideally contribute to the renewal of community. This dual commitment to being both witness and advocate often yielded vital connections between past and present, as in the reaffirmation of loving one's neighbor or in the negative assessments of convention as a corruption of custom; but the double role also severed past from present in that forms which had once sustained social faith were isolated from the continuing need to affirm social unity as a value. Their own troubled awareness of this problem is everywhere evident: in the struggle to reconcile form and belief noticeable in revisions made by Hennell and Strauss; in Feuerbach's declaration that "while reducing theology to anthropology, [I] exalt anthropology into theology"; in the embattled and troubled responses so many of them had toward Comte for having delivered theology when he had promised sociology; in George Eliot's conviction that while "the conditions of an age are determined by the conditions of the age that went before," nevertheless "for succeeding ages to dream of retaining the spirit along with the forms of the past, is as futile as the embalming of the dead body in the hope that it may one day be resumed by the living soul."[34] All these thinkers felt a similar tension between inherited social conditions and an imagined ideal. Attempting to bring the two together, both the religious and social critics found it necessary to move beyond the familiar, or beyond custom, convention, and religion, to locate new sanctions for tolerance, brotherhood, and

33. Joseph Wiesenfarth, *George Eliot's Mythmaking*; see pp. 26, 40–41, and 237, among others.

34. Compare prefaces to 1st and 2d editions of Hennell's *Inquiry*, and conclusions to Strauss's 1840 *Life of Jesus* and 1867 *New Life*. Passages quoted are from Feuerbach, *Essence of Christianity*, p. xxxviii; George Eliot, "More Leaves," p. 371, and *Essays*, p. 29. To suggest how long-standing a conviction this was for George Eliot, I have quoted from a review she wrote in 1850 and a notebook entry from the middle 1870s.

the love of one's neighbor in the science of Gesellschaft society, and to look to its art for a means of achieving a modern community of interest and feeling.

PROGRESSIVE CHANGE AND
THE DYNAMICS OF MODIFICATION

Essential to the concept of Social Dynamics was the principle of modification, or the idea that the developing conditions of social life and the courses of human action are accessible to influences capable of profoundly affecting the rate and degree of evolutionary change. Such influences were located in society and in individuals. Accordingly, it was argued, a person's opinions, feelings, and habits may be significantly modified by social influences that are themselves largely related to the modifications experienced by the individuals who both compose and create society. Whether external social conditions or internal psychological factors exert the greater motivation was a matter for disagreement among several of the most important theorists, and a source of contradiction within individual writers. Spencer and Comte tend to emphasize external social conditions, and Mill internal psychological ones, though evidence to the contrary is also found in each. Lewes and George Eliot attempt to balance the two and yet also veer at times to one side or the other.[35]

These instabilities may explain the different assessments made by scholars who discuss the subject of evolutionary change in the work of these writers. W. J. Harvey presents an excellent analysis of the idea that we are "the sum of our origins and development" based on "the dictum that Freud transferred from biology to psychology, 'Ontogeny recapitulates phylogeny.'" But Harvey renders the "nexus" of evolutionary ideas too static, by stressing "continuity" as "sameness beneath change" and neglecting the concept of modification. K. M. Newton brings a Darwinian rather than a psychological perspective to the idea of evolution. Arguing that Lewes and Eliot neither completely accepted nor rejected Darwin's theories, he shows how their attention to language and the social medium led them to distinguish between human and animal evolution. Newton's argument is illuminating, yet Darwinism by itself excludes matters important to the nexus of evolutionary ideas.

35. See, for instance, Comte, *Polity* 2: 348, 371; 3: 39. Spencer, "Progress, Its Law and Cause," pp. 244–67. Mill, *Logic, Collected Works* 8: 911–30, and *Subjection of Women*, p. 149. Lewes, *Problems* 1: 148; 4: 5–6, 78, 165–66 (publication of vol. 4 of *Problems* supervised by George Eliot).

"Acquired modifications," for instance, go unnoticed in his discussion, even though they appear as one of the "three regulative
laws of life" in a passage from Lewes that Newton cites. Because
acquired modifications offset the selfish impulses associated with
the law of adaptation, they help to explain why evolutionary *social*
theory is free from many of the terrors associated with Darwinian
cosmology. U. C. Knoepflmacher makes the evolutionary ideas current in George Eliot's world seem bleaker than they are by emphasizing the latter, and in so doing enforces an opposition between
science and religion that runs counter to the effort to create a new
religion through science.[36]

That effort makes the differences of assessment in modern scholarship, as well as the instabilities in the work of the social theorists,
less important than the agreement among the latter that human
nature is extraordinarily susceptible to external influences; that
individual and social modifications are closely related and essentially similar; that the more complex the society the greater the
possibilities for modification; and that "the progress of the world"
is critically dependent on "the modified action of the individual
beings who compose the world" (*Letters* 6: 99).

The social theorists looked to education as the key to the kinds
of modifications that would best further progressive change, particularly within the Gesellschaft world in which they perceived
themselves to be living. However much they disagreed about other
things, a belief in the power of education to transform the lives of
individuals, and through them the life of society, is central to
Comte's "positive polity," to Mill's arguments for the "improvement of mankind," and to Lewes's conception of a social medium
"constituted by the education of the race and of the individual;
so that the state of social evolution which has been reached at any
given time in any given place, will be one of the necessary determi-
nants in every individual mind" (*Problems* 1: 148). In accordance
with the principles of natural history and social evolutionary theory,
education was to address both the future and the past. As individuals were transformed through knowledge and heightened sensibility, the external conditions of social life would be altered to effect
changes in other individuals in both current and successive genera-

36. The scholarly studies referred to in this paragraph are: W. J. Harvey,
"Idea and Image in the Novels of George Eliot," pp. 153–60, 169; K. M. Newton, "George Eliot, George Henry Lewes, and Darwinism"; U. C. Knoepflmacher, *Religious Humanism*, pp. 18–19, 29–31, and passim.

tions. Yet at the same time that education was to help shape a new future, it was also to honor the beliefs and observances of the past, since "in their beginnings they were also reformatory changes, representing efforts after a more complete social condition, a more thorough union through obedience to ideas." These words are George Eliot's on the occasion, significantly enough, of a self-debate on conformity; but the social theorists also argued that the past no less than the present and future must be viewed dynamically. In this way, they tried to resolve the conflict between what George Eliot terms "the advance of knowledge" and the "benefits of the existing order," but for a fuller reconciliation between the two they looked to the transformations education would bring. Thus, in the debate on conformity, George Eliot no sooner acknowledges the conflict than she says: "If you ask how, then, are the reformatory changes to be brought about? I answer, by the gradual spread of advanced knowledge over such a majority in the community as would make the changes an imperious demand" ("More Leaves," pp. 367–68).

This "answer" has particular significance for George Eliot because it speaks not only to the ideal of education but also to the educative power she hoped her fiction would have. Such a commitment to education incorporated ideals of social change that were dependent in several ways on the theory of modification. Allowing for the gradual spread of successive changes through whole communities, it made for a "safe revolution," as George Eliot puts it, "arising . . . with individuals, as with nations . . . out of the wants which their *own progress* has generated" (*Letters* 1: 162). Flourishing at the same time as Darwinian evolutionary theory, it drew authority from the growing prestige of science, as in George Eliot's appeal to "physical science" when she proclaims "the great conception of universal regular sequence . . . the most potent force at work in the modification of our faith, and of the practical form given to our sentiments" (*Essays*, p. 413). The principle of modification had also the advantages of particularity, as Lewes points out when he speaks of how successive modifications create individual "mental diversities" (*Problems* 1: 150). This attention to the changing character and motives of individuals, when extended to the modifications they may cause as well as experience, serves also to counter the deterministic thrust of evolutionary theory. Moreover, because the dynamics of modification suggest a way of "extending the bounds of sympathetic, altruistic action," it could be used to address what many nineteenth-century thinkers took to be the "chief moral problem" of the age.[37]

Having the authority of science and the appeal of religion, the theory of modification seemed ideally suited to furthering the natural history of the race. As Lewes explains in a statement that again testifies to a reshaping of the third pillar of community, "manifold and far-reaching modifications of opinion, of feeling, and of practice, will necessarily produce" profound alterations in the conditions of society.[38] But while the theory of modification is freer from internal conflicts than were the attempts to create new values by transforming old ones, nevertheless this effort to redefine the changes possible within social life also poses the difficulties of creating a solid foundation upon which to structure a modern community of mind and spirit. In addition to the continued threat of relativism, the scientific validity of the concept would require a psychology that could adequately justify the theory. Two of the foremost biologists, Darwin and Huxley, repudiated as unscientific both the physiological and psychological bases the social philosophers were attempting to create. One of the foremost psychologists, Alexander Bain, was so untheoretical (at least according to Spencer's assessment) as to have provided only the "raw material" for the "natural history of the mind" he had hoped to write. Even more troublesome were the uncertainties demonstrated by the theorists who believed in the social dynamics of modification. Mill separated psychology from biology to emphasize the former in matters related to social life. Comte, Spencer, and Lewes located a biological basis for the concept of modification in the Lamarckian principle of acquired characteristics, genetically transmitted, but differed about the degree to which the overall foundation was to be physiological or psychological, with Comte arguing for the first, and Lewes and Spencer proposing a combination of the two, yet not agreeing altogether with one another.[39]

37. Mandelbaum, *History, Man, & Reason*, p. 35. Mandelbaum analyzes the many strands of thought that contributed to the nineteenth-century belief in the "malleability of man," and he links them to the "almost unlimited faith which the nineteenth century placed in education" (p. 141). His fine study has contributed to my understanding of the way the concept of modification includes an expression of both beliefs.

38. Lewes, "Communism as an Ideal," p. 733.

39. Herbert Spencer, "Bain on the Emotions and the Will," pp. 288–313. Lewes devotes nearly an entire chapter to contrasting the views toward psychology held by Comte, Mill, Spencer, and himself (*Problems* 4: 54–70).

The social implications of these instabilities are significant. Spencer, for instance, in endorsing the adaptations central to Lamarckian theory, places great emphasis on the ability of an organism to adjust to its environment. Comte, Lewes, and George Eliot place an equally important value on an individual's ability to transform his environment, thus moving closer to Mill, whose entire commitment to man as a progressive being was based on his belief in the ability of individuals to transform themselves and consequently the nature of social life. But even more telling than these shifting, and as a result insecure, perspectives is the acute awareness expressed by both Mill and George Eliot of the difficulties of knowing whether a given tendency can or should be modified. Thus Mill warns of the obstacles that prevent us from knowing "what are the practical contingencies which require a modification of the rule[s governing society]," and George Eliot speaks of the impossibility of determining with certainty "what is an inherent quality or characteristic or need of the human being (i.e. the social man who is alone really human), & what is modifiable."[40] In her fiction, she was often able to turn this uncertainty into an advantage by creating characters who are at critical moments suspended between submission and revolt. But for a novelist committed to creating community of feeling in her readers, there was the related, but in this case inescapable, difficulty of determining when, how, and whether to adapt herself to the needs of an audience she desired both to win and to transform. In addition, both the theorists and George Eliot had to face the suspicions aroused by the irony of their having arrived, through their individualistic heterodoxies, at an altruistic ethic founded on principles of social unity.

Still, the unstable alliances between theory, fact, and value arising from the concept of modification produced oppositions which for George Eliot were on the whole fruitful, paradoxically accommodating both adaptation and transformation, and thereby reconciling theory and value despite the uncertainty of the factual underpinnings. Consequently, the concept of modification and the

George Eliot's Lamarckian views are discussed by Neil Roberts, *George Eliot: Her Beliefs and Her Art*, pp. 46–49.

40. Mill, *Logic, Collected Works* 8: 945–46. George Eliot, "More Leaves," p. 373. See also *DD*, ch. 42, p. 585 (Deronda speaks here of the difficulty of knowing with certainty when to hasten or retard a given social tendency; and he worries about the " 'danger of mistaking a tendency which should be resisted for an inevitable law that we must adjust ourselves to' ").

conflicts surrounding it suggest more clearly than do other themes how the impulse to conserve and reform, which George Eliot recognized in herself and which we recognize as a characteristic of her century, was to be a vital factor in her creation of a community of readers. They were to be engaged by tensions in her work that they had themselves experienced, and they were to be aroused by George Eliot's benevolent but imperious demand that her readers contribute to "the growing good of the world." Thus she invokes at the close of *Middlemarch* the "unhistoric acts" that both give shape to her fictional world and have the power to alter the shape of natural history in the world her readers inhabit.

THE COMPARATIVE METHOD

Simultaneously, the social evolutionists were defining the shapes already assumed by natural history by bringing the Comparative Method to bear on their observations and descriptions of social life. They compared and classified societies of different types, as well as different stages of the same society, by studying cultures within the present that were taken to represent various stages of evolutionary development ranging from the primitive to the civilized, and they used direct and indirect "evidence" to postulate broad sequential laws of historical change. Comte's famous law of the three stages (theological, metaphysical, positivist), and Spencer's militant-industrial progression offer examples of social evolutionary laws arrived at by the Comparative Method, as does Tönnies's Gemeinschaft-Gesellschaft formulation when taken as an empirical concept. Each of these theorists held that complex mixtures exist and various stages coexist, but that during any given historical epoch a particular stage is predominant. Though the Comparative Method pointed to the ascendancy of positivistic Gesellschafts in present-day Europe, by uncovering their relation to the earlier cultures from which they evolved, it had also the virtue of correcting, as Sir Henry Maine describes it, the tendency "to consider ourselves as exclusively children of the age of free trade and scientific discovery."[41] Commenting on the value of a work written by another important social evolutionist, Sir John Lubbock, George Eliot makes a similar point when she says: "I am reading about savages and semi-savages, and think that our religious oracles would do well to study savage ideas by a method of comparison with their own" (*Letters* 4: 424). Still another benefit to be derived from the Comparative Method,

41. Sir Henry Maine, *The Effects of Observation in India on Modern European Thought* (1875), quoted by Burrow, *Evolution and Society*, p. 155.

and one that embraces all the others, is expressed by Comte when he speaks of how it helps "to develop the social sentiment, by giving us an immediate interest in even the earliest experiences of our race."[42]

As noted throughout this discussion of natural history, the controlling point of view is the condition of present social life, but if the advantages of the Comparative Method consist in the order it brought to the processes of history from the vantage point of the present, this very mode of approach was also responsible for its limitations. Its proponents were seeking a method that was at once factual and speculative, allowing them to classify elements from many different social traditions and to generalize from them, while also presupposing that successive modifications follow a single and uniform pattern despite differences in the rate of change. But the universal laws derived from this method were unable to stand the tests of either a rigorously scrutinized methodology or an acutely felt sense of the particularities and anomalies of individual and social development. The latter suggested not the linear historical sequence established by the Comparative Method but complex sets of social circumstances intricately woven into a vast network or web immensely difficult to untangle despite individual strands of continuity. Among those who doubted the laws associated with the Comparative Method were Mill and George Eliot, and each responded in characteristic ways, Mill by attempting to shape a more complex and logically consistent methodology, and George Eliot by imaginatively employing constructs appropriated from science and adapted to extend the boundaries of art.[43]

Thus for George Eliot the Comparative Method became part of the elaborate analogical network that, as many of her critics have noted, functions in her fiction as a vitally important internal structural device.[44] Equally significant, as we shall see later (particularly in chapters 3 and 7), is the way she would have the Comparative Method function externally as well by making her readers party to

42. Comte, *Positive Philosophy*, p. 482. For further discussion of the Comparative Method, see also *Positive Philosophy*, pp. 478–84; Spencer, *Principles of Sociology* 2: 190; Bryson, *Man and Society*, pp. 91–92; Burrow, *Evolution and Society*, p. 11 and passim; Mandelbaum, *History, Man, & Reason*, pp. 95–100; Nisbet, *Social Change*, pp. 189–208.

43. K. K. Collins, in "Questions of Method: Some Unpublished Late Essays," discusses how George Eliot's late essays challenge the Comparative Method and the laws of progress to which it was allied. As noted at the beginning of this chapter, her skepticism about progress as applied to society in general is evident even in her early work.

44. David Carroll's "Unity Through Analogy" is especially illuminating.

the creation of natural history. The close alliance in her own mind between "comparison" and "natural history" may be illustrated by a passage from *Theophrastus Such*:

It is my way when I observe any instance of folly, any queer habit, any absurd illusion, straightway to look for something of the same type in myself, feeling sure that amid all differences there will be a certain correspondence; just as there is more or less correspondence in the natural history even of continents widely apart, and of islands in opposite zones. No doubt men's minds differ in what we may call their climate or share of solar energy, and a feeling or tendency which is comparable to a panther in one may have no more imposing aspect than that of a weasel in another. . . . Still, . . . our precious guide Comparison would teach us in the first place by likeness, and our clue to further knowledge would be resemblance to what we already know. Hence, having a keen interest in the natural history of my inward self, I pursue this plan I have mentioned of using my observation as a clue or lantern by which I detect small herbage or lurking life; or I take my neighbour in his least becoming tricks or efforts as an opportunity for luminous deduction concerning the figure the human genus makes in the specimen which I myself furnish.

[ch. 13, pp. 225–26

In her fiction, George Eliot calls upon her readers to enter into this process of extending the "inward self," and of learning to tolerate and understand the complexities of human nature by bringing the power of comparison to bear on the fictional worlds she has created and on their own internal and external worlds. Proceeding in this way, she avoids the split between theory, fact, and value endemic to the social theorists, shaping the Comparative Method to her own purposes by exercising the novelist's right to control the facts presented and by employing rhetorical strategies to enforce particular values.

Two passages from *Middlemarch* serve to illustrate this point. In both George Eliot employs the most prosaic of activities—social climbing and financial extravagance—to prompt her readers to comparisons important precisely because they involve commonplace experiences. Describing the relation between Rosamond's infatuation with "good birth" and her falling in love with Lydgate, the narrator tells the reader:

If you think it incredible that to imagine Lydgate as a man of family could cause thrills of satisfaction which had anything to do with the sense that she was in love with him, I will ask you to use your power of comparison a little more effectively, and consider whether red cloth and epaulets have never had an influence of that sort. Our passions do not live apart in locked chambers, but, dressed in their small wardrobe of notions, bring their provisions to a common table and mess together, feeding out of the common store according to their appetite.

[ch. 16, pp. 123–24

Commenting later on the "vulgar hateful trials" Lydgate experiences after their marriage, in part because his upper-class "appetite" puts him deeply into debt, George Eliot writes:

It is true Lydgate was constantly visiting the homes of the poor and adjusting his prescriptions of diet to their small means; but, dear me! has it not by this time ceased to be remarkable—is it not rather what we expect in men, that they should have numerous strands of experience lying side by side and never compare them with each other? Expenditure—like ugliness and errors—becomes a totally new thing when we attach our own personality to it, and measure it by that wide difference which is manifest (in our own sensations) between ourselves and others.

[ch. 58, p. 429

In each of these examples, the reader is asked to corroborate commonplace experiences by comparing them with what he or she has felt and known, and also to perceive how the "power of comparison" may yield correctives able to diminish that sense of "wide difference . . . between ourselves and others" encouraged by upper-class attitudes and middle-class aspirations. Thus, what the characters take to be desirable marks of social difference become for the reader signs of a damaging conventionality, enforcing a separateness ironically rooted in conformity.

Two illustrations from *Daniel Deronda* serve also to demonstrate how George Eliot would bring a wide-ranging social criticism to the "knowledge [that] continues to grow by its alternating processes of distinction & combination" (*Essays*, p. 433). Each example warns the reader to "beware of arriving at conclusions without comparison," the first by leading him to realize that a far worse version of Gwendolen's unusual dominion over her family is only too ordinary among "a very common sort of men" (ch. 4, p. 71); and the second by showing through Deronda how even a "little comparison" can work to counter the "unfairness and ridiculous exaggeration" characteristic of racial stereotyping (ch. 32, p. 415).

Thus one of the most important uses to which George Eliot puts comparison is to correct the conventional responses that inhibit tolerance and fellow-feeling in areas likely to be among the most sensitive to middle-class readers. Social class itself is frequently at issue in the comparisons she would have them make, as are matters related to sexual and racial prejudices. Education, too, is often a topic of comparison, in part because it is a typically middle-class mode of advancement, but the narrative asides (many of them ironical) that contrast education in the past and present are intended to further not material advancement but rather an enlargement of thought and feeling conducive to social and personal good.

As these examples suggest, George Eliot's use of the Comparative Method is innovative in focusing the reader's attention on convention and its roots in custom and habit, and in emphasizing education as a means of understanding the past and bringing about modifications in the future. Her employment of the method testifies nonetheless to her participation in the community of interests she shared with the social theorists. In the following passage from *The Mill on the Floss*, she even establishes a direct link between the uses of the Comparative Method and its origins in "science" and evolutionary theory. Explaining the conflict between Maggie and the "emmet-like Dodsons and Tullivers" in terms of a collision between the "young natures in many generations, that in the onward tendency of human things have risen above the mental level of the generation before them," she writes:

> The suffering, whether of martyr or victim, which belongs to every historical advance of mankind, is represented in this way in every town, and by hundreds of obscure hearths; and we need not shrink from this comparison of small things with great; for does not science tell us that its highest striving is after the ascertainment of a unity which shall bind the smallest things with the greatest? In natural science, I have understood, there is nothing petty to the mind that has a large vision of relations, and to which every single object suggests a vast sum of conditions. It is surely the same with the observation of human life.
>
> [*MF*, ch. 30, pp. 238–39

The idea of progressive advance evident in this passage is reinforced by the placement, subject matter, and title of the chapter in which it appears. Locating it precisely in the middle of the novel, George Eliot invites the reader to compare the fictional events throughout the story with "details" from "our own vulgar era," and to connect both to the "large vision of relations" newly provided by science (ch. 30, p. 237). In addition, by calling the chapter "A Variation of Protestantism Unknown to Bossuet," she calls attention to those transcendent visions by which religious historians of the past, such as Bossuet, once described the order of things.[45] In this way she creates still a further comparison—between traditional ways of bringing coherence to the "vast sum of conditions" and modern ones, or between a belief in Providence and a belief in Progress.

However, as seen even in the above quotation, the language George Eliot uses suggests but does not proclaim Progress. In addition, the subject matter of the chapter makes the reader question whether the advances she describes have indeed been beneficial. At the same time, the chapter emphatically enforces, through language that moves from the universal to the particular, and from the "grand historic life of humanity" to the lives of individuals, the "relations" that both sever and link succeeding generations, at once disturbing the traditional foundations of community and confirming the need to reformulate them. Thus for George Eliot instructing "the imagination in true comparison" means encouraging an expansion of sensibility based not on a singular philosophy of history but on a multiple apprehension of "conditions" and "relations," rendered concrete through the failures and successes experienced by individuals, and rendered salutary through the community of interests and feelings she hoped to encourage in her readers.[46]

Scientists and Artists

The social evolutionists' commitment to the Comparative Method, like their other conceptual positions, was threatened by tensions and instabilities. Recognizing the dual needs they were trying to satisfy, Spencer and Lewes each came to define their approaches in terms that are themselves paradoxical, the one arguing for a "Transfigured Realism" capable of mediating between "realism and idealism" and "empiricism and apriorism"; and the other proposing

45. The description of Casaubon as a "living Bossuet" is also to the point, since it suggests how his system is of the past not the present, and is therefore not truly "luminous with the reflected light of correspondences," a criticism Ladislaw later makes explicit (*M*, ch. 3, p. 18, and ch. 22, pp. 164–65).

46. See "Historic Imagination," *Essays*, p. 447.

in his later work an "empirical metaphysics" capable of reconciling tendencies he had earlier thought were opposed.[47] Lewes, especially, was eager to achieve a synthesis that could mediate the severe and unacknowledged split in Comte between scientific method and social mission. Like Lewes, Mill most valued Comte for the scientific methodology put forth in the *Cours de philosophie positive* (1830–1842), and was distressed by Comte's turning away from it in the *Système de politique positive* (1851–1854); but Mill responded by regretting that Comte, Spencer, and Lewes alike had succumbed to "the metaphysical mode of thought," and by continuing rigorously to explore methods of inquiry he discovered in Comte.[48] Thus, through the "Historical Method" termed the "Inverse Deductive," he studies how "empirical generalizations are raised into positive laws" by reversing "the method of the deductive physical sciences: for while, in these, specific experience commonly serves to verify laws arrived at by deduction, in sociology it is specific experience which suggests the laws, and deduction which verifies them." However, the intricate "inversion of the ordinary relation between Deduction and Induction," by which he would have deductions based on universal laws of human nature verify "the direction actually taken by the developments and changes of human society," is itself so convoluted as again to suggest the strain of reconciling opposites.

Each of these efforts to extend empirical principles using a speculative philosophy earlier repudiated was motivated by the urgent need to create values through a new kind of natural history. It was to have the empirical and national qualities of history and the abstract and universal attributes of social theory, so as to bear witness to actual social conditions in the past and present while testifying to a secular ideal of community. However, the history of ideas in this period, whether focused on individual figures or on patterns of nineteenth-century thought, reveals the difficulties if not the impossibilities of combining philosophical speculations, empirical methods, and social imperatives in a system of thought both logically sound and ethically compelling. As various modern critiques of "historicism" as a philosophy of history show, teleological and idealist presuppositions are closely interwoven with a

47. Spencer, *Principles of Psychology* 2: 489–503; Lewes, *Problems* 1: 5–80; see also H. G. Tjoa, *George Henry Lewes*, pp. 104–34.

48. Mill, *Auguste Comte and Positivism*, pp. 72–73. Succeeding quotations are from the same volume, pp. 85–86; see also *Logic, Collected Works* 8: 911–929.

scientific empiricism in the work of many nineteenth-century writers, among them the social evolutionists we are discussing.[49] Focusing on the latter, J. W. Burrow speaks of "the contortions of an intellectual tradition, predominantly secular and hence deprived of transcendental sanction for its values, trying to escape an absolute moral and political relativism" (p. 102). Tjoa's study of Lewes as a representative "Victorian mind," explains in a similar way his "advocacy of a combination of the scientific method and a secularized religious concern." "A difficult blend," to be sure; yet as Tjoa further acknowledges "one preferred by a significant section of the Victorian intellectual community" (p. 134).

In part because a scientist could not easily reconcile a commitment to the empirical method with the dual roles of witness and advocate, the nineteenth-century social critics familiar to George Eliot looked to the artist to serve as the advocate. Comte assigns to art an idealizing power that positivism denies to science, arguing in his later work that "the true object of Art . . . is to charm and elevate human life" so as "to strengthen our sympathies" and "cultivate our sense of perfection." But while art "should surpass realities so as to stimulate us to amend them," he insists that "the ideal must always be subordinate to the real" in accordance with the "objective dogma of Philosophy, that Humanity is subject to the order of the external world." Comte claims that "Art may be defined as an ideal representation of Fact," but its effect is to blur what he would blend.[50]

Like Comte, Mill too speaks of the artist in the widest sense of the word, newly acknowledging as it were Shelley's "legislators of the world," or Carlyle's "Hero as Poet" or "Man of Letters," and granting to the artist the right to make the normative judgments prohibited by a strictly applied positivism. The artist's task is to bring new currents of morality into the community by developing man's affective and imaginative powers, increasing his capacity for sympathy, and cultivating his instinct for perfection. But unlike Comte, Mill tries to delineate precisely the terms of the collaboration between artists and scientists. He assigns to the artist the task of defining the end to be pursued and to the scientist the job of discovering the various means by which that end might be achieved. The artist is then again to step in, this time to examine the means,

49. For examples of such critiques, see Karl R. Popper, *The Poverty of Historicism*; Isaiah Berlin, *Historical Inevitability*; Mandelbaum, *History, Man, & Reason*, part II.

50. Comte, *General View of Positivism*, pp. 310–16.

decide which are the most practicable and moral, and persuade society to adopt them. However, the very intricacy of procedure suggests forced reconciliations, particularly in relation to arguments Mill makes elsewhere. Though he insists in *Logic*, for instance, that art be based on the "laws of nature disclosed by science," in his writings on literature the standard he establishes of an inspiring idealism causes him to condemn that immersion in mere "outward things" characteristic of the novel and of those "addicted to novel-reading."[51]

Though Comte and Mill generally speak as social scientists rather than literary theorists, George Eliot's susceptibility to their way of thinking about art is evident enough. Of all Comte's work she preferred *A General View of Positivism* (later to become the introduction to *System of Positive Polity*). Written to vindicate positivism from the charge of being hostile to imagination and feeling, it contains Comte's celebration of art, imagination, and affection in a Positive Polity. That George Eliot was also attracted to Mill's formulation of the relation between scientist and artist is suggested by a passage from *Daniel Deronda*. Comparing scientists and artists, while looking (as Mill does) to the artist to envision ends and engender belief, she writes:

> And since the unemotional intellect may carry us into a mathematical dreamland where nothing is but what is not, perhaps an emotional intellect may have absorbed into its passionate vision of possibilities some truth of what will be—the more comprehensive massive life feeding theory with new material, as the sensibility of the artist seizes combinations which science explains and justifies.
>
> [ch. 41, p. 572

Similar attitudes underlie the "idealism of conception" Lewes regards as essential to great art, and they also inform the "metaphysics" of his revised empiricism. The idealism he advocates requires "realism of presentation" as its complement; together they are to portray the "highest forms of reality" as well as the "forms of ordinary life," the one communicating a knowledge of ordinary experience and creating believable characters, and the other compelling us to "sympathize in their struggles." But the highly equivocal nature of a great deal of Lewes's literary criticism speaks to the

---

51. Mill, *Logic, Collected Works* 8: 949–50; "Thoughts on Poetry and Its Varieties," *Dissertations and Discussions* 1: 92. See also Robson, *Improvement of Mankind*, pp. 121–22, 160–62, 173–74.

difficulty of the fusion. Assigning "first place to Realism" or "truth of presentation," he would exclude the "Falsism" that is "removed from or opposed to realities," but include the "Idealism" that conveys "a vision of realities in their highest and most affecting forms." However, his frequent contrasts between the "simply realistic" or "prosaic" and the "ennobling beauty that transfigures the commonplace" suggest a displacement of the real by the ideal. Attempting to heal this disparity, he extends the boundaries of realism to include whatever is real to the imagination, while nevertheless maintaining that the "merit of each representation" continues to depend on its fidelity and accuracy.[52]

This compromise is an important one because it incorporates a vision of social renewal and captures objectively the "natural history of social life." But the compromise discomforted Lewes, as demonstrated by his ambivalent judgment of Dickens. While granting that Dickens sets in motion "the secret springs of sympathy," stirring the "universal heart," and touching "common life . . . to 'fine issues,' " Lewes nonetheless objects to the excessive flights of fancy and imagination that caused this "seer of visions" to portray "human character and ordinary events . . . with a mingled verisimilitude and falsity altogether unexampled."[53] In *The Principles of Success in Literature*, furthermore, Lewes no sooner grants that a poetical mind can fulfill the "necessity of verification" through images that "have at least subjective truth" than he concludes that:

> In truth, the imagination is most tasked when it has to paint pictures which shall withstand the silent criticism of general experience, and to frame hypotheses which shall withstand the confrontation with facts.

> [*Fortnightly Review* 1: 577–79

Thus Lewes's argument reveals that the artist was actually no freer than the social theorist from the tensions generated by a commitment to realism and a need to idealize. Whether allied to philosophic or aesthetic principles, the two were similarly implicated in trying to mediate the disparities between observed social realities and an ideal of communal wholeness.

52. [G. H. Lewes], "Realism in Art: Recent German Fiction," pp. 273–77; G. H. Lewes, *The Principles of Success in Literature*, *Fortnightly Review* 1: 588. These points are repeated often in the six chapters (published serially) of *Success in Literature*. In an 1856 review of Ruskin, George Eliot makes similar distinctions between a "True" and "False Ideal" in art: "Art and Belles Lettres," *Westminster Review* 65: 344–46.
53. Lewes, "Dickens in Relation to Criticism," pp. 144–51.

Given the close alliance between philosophic and aesthetic principles, one is not surprised to find that George Eliot's statements about art incorporate a major "scientific" hypothesis and contain paradoxes, contradictions, and adjustments akin to those present in the work of the social theorists. But while intellectual historians have recently scrutinized the opposing tendencies within this tradition of social thought, and though George Eliot's critics have clarified considerably the nature of both her realism and idealism, still we have only begun to explore the relationship between an intellectual tradition understood to be self-conflicted and an aesthetic containing analogous opposites as well as a drive for fusions extremely difficult to achieve.[54]

How vital this relationship was to a renewed conception of community is illustrated by the terms George Eliot uses when, in a letter written in 1874, she links the "main bearing" of her books to

a conclusion without which I could not have cared to write any representation of human life—namely, that the fellowship between man and man which has been the principle of development, social and moral, is not dependent on conceptions of what is not man: and that the idea of God, so far as it has been a high spiritual influence, is the ideal of a goodness entirely human (i.e., an exaltation of the human).

[*Letters* 6: 98

Echoing a variety of nineteenth-century efforts to reconstitute community through a Religion of Humanity, the idealism expressed at the close of the passage is familiar enough, having often been related to Strauss's humanistic mythmaking, Feuerbach's exaltation of anthropology, and Comte's deification of society. But equally significant, though less apparent until examined from the perspectives afforded by eighteenth-century natural history and nineteenth-century social evolutionary theory, is the scientific hypothesis to which this idealism is allied. Leading to an affirmation

54. The first major study of the tension between realism and idealism in George Eliot's fiction is U. C. Knoepflmacher's *George Eliot's Early Novels* (1968). Recent important studies include George Levine's "George Eliot's Hypothesis of Reality" and *The Realistic Imagination*. Levine illuminates the relation between George Eliot's attempts to fuse science, poetry, and morality in her later fiction and scientific and philosophical efforts to reconcile empiricism and metaphysics. But the successful resolution of opposites for which he argues seems to me doubtful, as does the internal coherence he attributes to the "philosophico-scientific community" in which she participated.

of community based on values at once secular and spiritual, scientific and aesthetic, the hypothesis at issue is none other than that "principle of development, social and moral" summoned by George Eliot in defense of her art. Creating a fusion between scientific principle and aesthetic credo, it joins together scientist and artist, fulfilling not only Wordsworth's prophecy of a time when the poet will "follow the steps of the man of science . . . carrying sensation into the midst of the objects of the science itself," but also foreshadowing the position Tönnies later adopted. Like the men of science, George Eliot tried to locate new sources of renewal within the very Gesellschaft responsible for undermining traditional community. The nature of the remedy bespeaks the malady: modern scientific and aesthetic culture was to modify the Philistinism that afflicted the middle classes as a result of the material progress conferred by Gesellschaft.

Turning the remedy into a warning, George Eliot writes in her last book: "We have been severely enough taught (if we were willing to learn) that our civilisation, considered as a splendid material fabric, is helplessly in peril without the spiritual police of sentiments or ideal feelings" (*TS*, ch. 10, p. 185). The demands she would place on aesthetic culture are also evident in her somewhat earlier statement that "the art which leaves the soul in despair is laming to the soul, and is denounced by the healthy sentiment of an active community" (*Life* 3: 35). The argument begun here, in her "Notes on *The Spanish Gypsy*" (1868), carries over as well into some comments on authorship she made during the 1870s:

> It is for art to present images of a lovelier order than the actual, gently winning the affections, and so determining the taste. But in any rational criticism of the time which is meant to guide a practical reform, it is idle to insist that action ought to be this or that, without considering how far the outward conditions of such change are present, even supposing the inward disposition towards it. Practically, we must be satisfied to aim at something short of perfection.
>
> [*Essays*, p. 437–38

In contrast, the essay on Riehl (1856) applies the forceful strictures against prescription to artist and social theorist alike. Arguing in this early essay that "Art is the nearest thing to life," she committed the artist to what Lewes called "realism of presentation," or to what has more recently been called formal realism. As defined by Ian Watt, *formal realism* is the narrative embodiment of a premise . . . implicit in the novel form in general: the premise, or primary convention, that the novel is a full and authentic report of human experience, and is therefore under an obligation to satisfy its reader with such details of the story as the individuality of the actors concerned, the particulars of the times and places of their actions, details which are presented through a more largely referential use of language than is common in other literary forms.[55]

Bringing similar standards to bear in the criticism she wrote during the 1850s, George Eliot applauds Goethe for following "the stream of fact and of life" in *Wilhelm Meister*, and Charles Kingsley for his "genuine description of external nature," and insists in her many reviews on "truthfulness of close observation," "genuine observation," "natural combinations of character and circumstance," and "close, genuine presentations of life."[56] Later, bringing these same standards to bear on her own work, she explains in chapter 5 of "Amos Barton," in her correspondence with Blackwood over *Scenes of Clerical Life*, and in chapter 17 of *Adam Bede* that the highest vocation of the novelist is to represent things as they have been or are. Indeed, she pledges her narrator to speak "as if . . . in the witness-box narrating my experience on oath" (*AB*, ch. 17, p. 150), a metaphor that corresponds to Watt's comparison of the expectations of a "jury in a court of law" and those of the novel reader: "both want to know 'all the particulars' of a given case—the time and place of the occurrence; both must be satisfied as to the identities of the parties concerned, . . . and they also expect the witnesses to tell the story" (p. 31).

Other correspondences between George Eliot's aesthetic and Watt's concept of formal realism are apparent. His contention that formal realism is an ethically neutral mode of presentation, for instance, parallels George Eliot's admiration of writers free from the "partisan" spirit, and her objections to "characters and incidents . . . selected with a view to the enforcement of a principle."[57] But the inadequacies of formal realism, given the wider purposes she assigned to her fiction, are inadvertently suggested by Watt's argument, which associates the "rise of the novel" with a larger movement in Western thought, away from a unified world vision and toward a belief in the individual apprehension of reality within a

55. Ian Watt, *The Rise of the Novel*, p. 32.
56. *Essays*, pp. 146, 125, 133, 324; "Belles Lettres," *Westminster Review* 64: 319–20.
57. "Memoirs of the Court of Austria," p. 159; *Essays*, pp. 126–30, 134, 299.

society consisting of an "unplanned aggregate of particular individuals." The philosophical system Watt describes cannot be ethically neutral when in fact it supports the individualist ethos of Gesellschaft—the ideology George Eliot and the social theorists were attempting to correct though they were themselves heirs to the tradition from which it was derived. Like the social and religious philosophers to whom she turned, George Eliot's quest for community forced her beyond the logic of the method she initially espoused, beyond the credo of realism she announced early in her career toward the idealism of conception she later openly advocated.

These nineteenth-century thinkers hoped to achieve a natural history capable of fusing the speculative and the concrete, through the union of idealism and realism in art, and of hypothesis and fact in science and philosophy. Together they were to foster fellow-feeling by dealing with the conditions, conflicts, ideas, aspirations, and feelings common to us all. Validating the significance of the ordinary through the emphasis on "conditions," and allowing for a vision of communal wholeness by attending to "relations," natural history indeed proved to be an inspiring conception. It compelled George Eliot, moreover, to discover new forms in fiction, ones capable of addressing the split between fact and value while incorporating the narrative rejected by the social theorists as the trappings of a history based on outstanding figures and events. Arguing in her notes on "Historic Imagination" for "freedom from the vulgar coercion of conventional plot," and struggling in her own fiction to dramatize the "unhistoric acts" neglected by conventional historians, she would return to the particularity of narrative while doing justice to the subject matter of natural history (*Essays*, p. 446; *M*, Finale, p. 613).

Still, the fusion between fact and value they all wanted to achieve was threatened by instabilities in every area, as we have seen—ones that could not be resolved simply by allowing to the artist what was prohibited to the scientist. Thus, however much George Eliot wanted to escape from the demands of philosophical consistency by writing fiction, she could not free herself from a fundamentally related problem: how to write novels that would allow her to be both witness and advocate, not by idealizing and diminishing actual commonplace reality, but by showing how the real and the ideal might inform one another.

◆

THREE

Workaday Worlds and the Poetry
of Community

Holiday and Workaday Worlds

In George Eliot's novels, ideals and formal techniques are not always harmoniously integrated, yet the two are nonetheless inseparable. Most of the concerns she shared with the social theorists are reflected in choices about form in her fiction. Even the unsuccessful fusions can be explained by analogous irresolutions, as in the conflict between empiricism and metaphysics in social thought and between realism and idealism in art. Therefore, our discussion of how George Eliot's novels are implicated in the task of social regeneration focuses on the way certain forms in her fiction—image patterns, framing devices, setting, scene, and aspects of characterization—embody matters significantly at issue in the natural history defined in the previous chapter. As we have seen, they include a belief in an evolutionary progression from Gemeinschaft to Gesellschaft, and an attention to the everyday and the unhistoric, or to conditions in the present as they relate to changing customs, institutions, ideas, and art forms. They include as well an effort to incorporate into modern society those positive values of Gemeinschaft capable of being transferred or transformed, and to discover within Gesellschaft new possibilities for community. Striving to achieve these ends, the social theorists evaluated the social role of custom and convention, and encouraged within individuals modifications conducive to beneficial and widespread changes. They posited a sense of relatedness so overarching and comprehensive as to make knowledge synonymous with an awareness of relations ever in need of extension, thus making education essential to the renewal of community.

As important to George Eliot as to the social theorists, such matters greatly affected the fictional forms she created. She believed that form in art has its genesis in rhythms and images initially spontaneous and private and then consciously selected and ordered. As she explains it:

> Form begins in the choice of rhythms & images as signs of a mental state, for this is a process of grouping or association of a less spontaneous & more conscious order than the grouping or association which constitutes the very growth & natural history of mind. *Poetry* begins when passion weds thought by finding expression in an image; but *poetic form* begins with a choice of elements, however meagre, as the accordant expression of emotional states.
>
> [*Essays*, p. 435

Her early letters continually reveal that, long before she began to write novels, her own "emotional states" included a passionate response to the evils of Gesellschaft, first expressed in a frenzy of images. In 1841, she writes:

> The prevalence of misery and want in this boasted nation of prosperity and glory is appalling, and really seems to call us away from mental luxury. O to be doing some little toward the regeneration of this groaning travailing creation! I am supine and stupid, overfed with favours, while the haggard looks and piercing glance of want and conscious hopelessness are to be seen in the streets.
>
> [*Letters* 1: 116

In 1848, still having done "little," she compares "society" to

> a face one half of which—the side of profession, of lip-faith—is fair and god-like, the other half—the side of deeds and institutions—with a hard old wrinkled skin puckered into the sneer of a Mephistopheles. . . . You will wonder what has wrought me up into this fury—it is the loathsome fawning, the transparent hypocrisy, the systematic giving as little as possible for as much as possible that one meets with here at every turn. I feel that society is training men and women for hell.
>
> [*Letters* 1: 267

The extravagant emotions make it easy to charge the first of these letters to youth, and the second to temporary revolutionary fervor induced by the times. Yet elsewhere in her work images so persistent and so highly ordered as to constitute a fundamental cluster confirm what is already noticeable here: how for George Eliot the poetic form that begins in spontaneous rhythms and images makes "consentaneous" with the "growth & natural history of mind," the natural history of social life (*Essays*, pp. 287, 435). In contrast to the thrashing about from one image to another in the passages above, the persistent cluster establishes a central metaphor, projecting a "working-day world" rhythmically related (whether in tonal harmony or in discord) to a "holiday" one. Vitally connected to both kinds of natural history, this workaday-holiday metaphor was for George Eliot a starting point that gradually became part of the "process of grouping or association" she deemed vital to form in art. Accordingly, it is also our starting point here.

The phrase " 'This working day world,' "—adopted from *As You Like It* (1. 3. 12) and referred to as her "favorite little epithet" as early as 1840—and "holiday," its shorthand obverse, appear to have haunted her imagination (*Letters* 1: 44). Among the things *workaday* by itself signifies is that sense of "ordinary humdrum everyday life" so prevalent in her fiction that a quotation from *Middlemarch* (ch. 56, p. 406) serves to gloss its definition in the *OED*. In the passage cited, "the working-day world" is associated specifically with "capital" and with skill in business affairs, but they are clearly part of that larger reality which regularly in George Eliot's fiction denotes "common" practices, "ordinary" causes, "prosaic" experiences, or the many "details," "objects," and "concerns" characteristic of "everyday" life. Appearing with great frequency in her novels, such words establish a standard of "things as they are," and one so thoroughly associated in George Eliot's mind with the "working day" that the phrase becomes "a key term in George Eliot's conception of realism."[1]

At the same time, other groupings and associations reveal that her continued concern with "working day" realities has as much to do with her desire to fuse or connect the prosaic everyday world to a poeticized, ideal holiday world. Her use of the phrase, for instance, as well as the highly mediated realism characteristic of her novels, often carries figurative meanings—ones which serve to modulate "the daily struggle with the petty details, perhaps with the sordid cares" associated with a literal "working-day world" (*Essays,*

1. Thomas Pinney, *Essays*, p. 302, n. 6. The phrase appears regularly in George Eliot's essays and fiction: *Essays*, pp. 92, 161, 302. *SCL*: "Amos Barton," ch. 9, p. 110, and "Janet's Repentance," ch. 5, p. 286. *AB*, ch. 19 (titled "Adam on a Working Day"); ch. 20, p. 182; ch. 27, p. 249; ch. 50, p. 407. *FH*, Introduction, p. 79. M, ch. 25, p. 190; ch. 56, p. 406. See also *Letters* 1: 66. Specific references to the "working day" are augmented by countless phrases of the sort quoted earlier in the paragraph. Similarly, many phrases contribute to the contrast between the "workaday" and "holiday"; in *AB*, ch. 50, p. 407, and *M*, ch. 25, p. 190, the counterpointing is direct.

p. 92). The phrase's figurative significance for her is evident even in her first documented use of it:

> Our house is . . . miserably noisy and disorderly with the musical operations of masons carpenters and painters. You know how abhorrent all this is to my tastes and feelings, taking all the spice out of my favorite little epithet "This working day world": I can no longer use it figuratively.
>
> [*Letters* 1: 44

But the real complications are yet to come. She would try in her fiction not simply to cast aside her favorite little epithet when reality intrudes, but to create a working-day world that grows to great constancy by taking on literal and metaphoric significance:

> And I would not, even if I had the choice, be the clever novelist who could create a world so much better than this, in which we get up in the morning to do our daily work, that you would be likely to turn a harder, colder eye on the dusty streets and the common green fields—on the real breathing men and women, who can be chilled by your indifference or injured by your prejudice; who can be cheered and helped onward by your fellow-feeling. . . .
>
> Therefore let Art always remind us of them; therefore let us always have men ready to give the loving pains of a life to the faithful representing of commonplace things—men who see beauty in these commonplace things, and delight in showing how kindly the light of heaven falls on them.
>
> [*AB*, ch. 17, pp. 151–53

The literal is to be conveyed through a "faithful" representation, and the figurative through an illumination of the everyday that uncovers the "secret of deep human sympathy" (p. 153). This "beauty" or "light," then, is allied to that idealism of conception which has at its center the selfsame vision of fellowship, tolerance, and sympathy thought crucial to the renewal of community.

Nonetheless, the development of George Eliot's fiction reveals a growing uncertainty about whether realism of presentation and idealism of conception could together lead toward this end. The nature of the problem is illustrated in a passage from *Daniel Deronda*. Markedly different from the passage from *Adam Bede* quoted above, it expresses the narrator's concern that Deronda,

> notwithstanding all his sense of poetry in common things, . . . could not, more than the rest of us, continuously escape suffering

from the pressure of that hard unaccommodating Actual, which has never consulted our taste and is entirely unselect. . . . The fervour of sympathy with which we contemplate a grandiose martyrdom is feeble compared with the enthusiasm that keeps unslacked where there is no danger, no challenge—nothing but impartial mid-day falling on commonplace, perhaps half-repulsive, objects which are really the beloved ideas made flesh. Here undoubtedly lies the chief poetic energy:—in the force of imagination that pierces or exalts the solid fact.

[ch. 33, pp. 430–31

Behind both the early proclamation and the later lament (that yet ends in an affirmation) is the author's desire to connect the reader with "the broad life of mankind" (*DD*, ch. 33, p. 431). However, the unequivocal celebration of prosaic reality in her first novel gives way to a resurgent fear in the last that the commonplace may be too circumscribing. The response here and elsewhere is an unsteady and shifting balance between the prosaic and the poetic that sometimes veers so entirely towards an imaginative ideal of "love and reverence . . . for my everyday fellow-men" as to displace the actual (*AB*, ch. 17, p. 153).

Still, she struggles throughout her fiction to fuse fact and value by connecting the poetic to the prosaic. Crucial to this process is her use of holiday, holy-day images. Intensely personal at first, the Sunday-holiday metaphors also become a shaping element in her fiction, eventually bodying forth far more than the "holiday foolery" of the *As You Like It* passage. When in 1848, for instance (in a letter now famous), she angrily opposes the "hard angular world of chairs and tables and looking-glasses . . . in all its naked prose" to the "poetry or religion" of life, it is the invocation of "this 'good Sunday morning' " that puts a stop to her "grumblings" (*Letters* 1: 264). In her fiction, the holiday images, like the workaday ones, mirror the nature of social life and the values of the individuals who participate in it. Attending more directly to the nonmaterial, however, they bring to the forefront what the workaday tends to put aside or obscure—the importance to secular community of spiritual values.

In George Eliot's portraits of traditional community, a holiday world is most obviously and characteristically associated with the ceremonials of village life, and especially with the harmonious alternation between a literal Sunday or holiday world and the working-day one. In her portraits of Gesellschaft, however, the positive holiday images, instead of depicting actual social rituals, tend to be metaphorical. Often they refer to art and to its role in advanced societies, as in the following comment by Dorothea:

"When I enter a room where the walls are covered with frescoes, or with rare pictures, I feel a kind of awe—like a child present at great ceremonies where there are grand robes and processions; I feel myself in the presence of some higher life than my own."

[*M*, ch. 21, p. 153

In the one case, the holiday images reflect and evaluate communal activities in Gemeinschaft, and in the other they present art (music, literature, sculpture, and painting) as a positive force in Gesellschaft. Both therefore complement the workaday, but the first creates a visible poetry of community embodied in concrete social rituals, and the second an invisible poetry created by the effect of a work of art on the beholder.

Another group of holiday images complements the workaday in a different way, converging with it in both traditional and modern societies. Tied to love relationships and to vocational calling, they celebrate the widening connections and social sympathies initiated by commitments that originate in the private self but lead to the individual's participation in a larger life. Beginning with her first novel, *Adam Bede*, love and devotion to work are associated with the creation and continuity of community. The chapter "Adam on a Working Day" ends with a ceremonial tribute to those workmen whose

lives have no discernible echo beyond the neighbourhood where they dwelt, but you are almost sure to find there some good piece of road, some building, some application of mineral produce, some improvement in farming practice, some reform of parish abuses, with which their names are associated by one or two generations after them. Their employers were the richer for them, the work of their hands has worn well, and the work of their brains has guided well the hands of other men.

[ch. 19, p. 182

Just as George Eliot pictures the benefit they bring to both the immediate and the ongoing community, so she confers on these workers a tribute that extends far beyond the local "place of honour" they are awarded "at church and at market."[2] It therefore

2. *AB*, ch. 19, p. 182. Other examples of this sort of tribute may be found in *AB*, ch. 24, p. 227; *R*, ch. 39, p. 331; *FH*, ch. 16, pp. 276–77; *M*, ch. 24, pp. 185–86, and ch. 40, p. 295.

seems appropriate that this first of several such tributes identifies
the artisan with the artist:

> The sound of tools to a clever workman who loves his work is like
> the tentative sounds of the orchestra to the violinist who has to bear
> his part in the overture: the strong fibres begin their accustomed
> thrill, and what was a moment before joy, vexation, or ambition,
> begins its change into energy. All passion becomes strength when
> it has an outlet from the narrow limits of our personal lot in the
> labour of our right arm, the cunning of our right hand, or the still,
> creative activity of our thought.
>
> [*AB*, ch. 19, p. 180

Still, it is the "passion that becomes strength" through love for a
person that far more frequently forms a "holiday-time in the working-day world" of George Eliot's fiction. The latter phrase is first
used to disclose what is missing from Adam's world when the destruction of his dream of Hetty carries away all pleasure, even the
joy to be had from the work that "had always been part of his religion." At the same time, the very sorrows initiated by love develop
"new sensibilities" in Adam and lead to a growing perception of
"visible and invisible relations beyond any of which either our
present or prospective self is the centre" (ch. 50, p. 407). In the
closing scenes of *Adam Bede*, George Eliot attempts to convey
imagistically "this sense of enlarged being," renewing the poetry
in his life in chapters in which the stages of a new love are marked
by successive Sundays and suffused by images of "Sunday sunshine,"
Sunday churchgoing, and Sunday reading in "a holiday book."[3]

Whether allied to the ceremonies of traditional community, the
culture of advanced society, vocational calling, or a self-transcend-
ing love, this group of holiday images reveals how George Eliot
would bring to her natural history a poetry of community created
from unifying social rituals, vocational calling, and expansive human commitments. In addition, many holiday-workaday images
reveal a false poetry destructive to community. Associated primarily
with Gesellschaft, these images expose hypocrisy in religion, falsity
in art, and artificiality in social convention. Their poetry is false
because it creates a counterfeit world that entices; and it is destruc-

3. The proliferation of Sunday images is greatest in ch. 51 (itself called
"Sunday Morning"), but they are also important in the other chapters (52
and 54) dealing with Adam's and Dinah's love. In the last of them, the "sense
of enlarged being" associated with Adam's suffering in the workaday world
unites with the holiday images surrounding his courtship with Dinah (ch. 54,
pp. 441–43).

tive to community because those forms it renders specious—custom, art, religion—have the capacity to contribute greatly to the creation of solidarity. This theme is also evident in her earliest work. In an 1855 essay, "Evangelical Teaching: Dr. Cumming," the Sunday preaching that should hallow the everyday is revealed to be at best no better than the "working-day interests and lay splendours" it attempts to outdo (*Essays*, p. 161). In an essay written a year later, falseness in art and in society are together impugned in the "silly novels by lady novelists" who neglect "the working-day business of the world," rarely introducing "us into any other than very lofty and fashionable society," and failing even here to achieve "verisimilitude in their representations" (*Essays*, pp. 302–4). In her own fiction, notions of what is fashionable are employed from the start, but they are used to satirize social conventions.

George Eliot's career as a novelist demonstrates how a set of personal images, derived from a "favorite little epithet," comes to play a major role in a body of fiction designed to engage the reader in the process of bearing witness to the prosaic in human life and learning where and how to discover its poetry. These images participate in George Eliot's realism of presentation and idealism of conception, and in her creation of a natural history at once factual and speculative. The prosaic and the poetic themselves become figurative in her fiction—emblems of the prose and poetry of community—and the resonances they acquire carry over into the images that define and evaluate Gemeinschaft and Gesellschaft.

Moreover, each of the elements in each pairing is connected in a great many ways to its obverse. Just as idealism of conception, holiday worlds, and the poetry of community are not to be understood apart from realism of presentation, workaday worlds, and the prosaic, neither can Gemeinschaft be understood apart from Gesellschaft. The pairs themselves, furthermore, are intricately related to one another. Though Gemeinschaft in the figurative sense always signifies the poetry of community, some of the working-day realities dramatized in George Eliot's natural history of old-fashioned village life do not. Similarly, while her realism of presentation reveals Gesellschaft as threatening to social unity, her idealism of conception creates transformations that imaginatively renew community by redefining Gemeinschaft. Together, then, the intricate crossings within this cluster of images speak not only to the historical conditions of life in Gemeinschaft and Gesellschaft and their interrelated evolution, but also to the liabilities and virtues particular to each.

These pairings and crossings required the endless adjustment of opposite claims, a process that often led to new disjunctions. The difficulties involved were for George Eliot at once private and public, aesthetic and ideological. She writes to a "fellow-worker," the novelist Elizabeth Stuart Phelps, of how difficult it is "to believe, until the germ of some new work grows into imperious activity within one, that it is possible to make a really needed contribution to the poetry of the world" (*Letters* 5: 388). While she wished to paint for her readers things "which are easy to discern . . . on the large canvas of poetic story," she also felt compelled to dramatize the often alarming and "pressing details of actual experience," and they confuse and obscure the poetry of the world (*FH*, ch. 42, p. 520). Her remarks about contributing to such a poetry are consequently surrounded by expressions of doubt:

> I must tell you that I never believe in future books of my own, and always after finishing any work I have a period of despair that I can ever produce anything else worth giving to the world. The responsibility of the writer becomes heavier and heavier—does it not?
>
> [*Letters* 5: 388

Juxtaposing "poetic story" and "pressing details," while striving for a convergence between them, she repeatedly calls attention to the twisted conditions in the workaday world that entangle an ideal of fellowship—class privilege, self-centered demands, false ideals, cold conventions—and she tries as well to capture and to create a poetry that affirms community. The result is continual division and fusion as each side (itself complex) extends or inverts, integrates or violates, ennobles or diminishes the other. How the form and content of George Eliot's fiction participate in this process, and through it shape a natural history of social life that extends into the present and implicates the future, is the subject of this chapter.

First, we will examine how George Eliot frequently uses framing devices, depicting the present and its relationships to the past and future, to complement her canvases, which are retrospective histories. Then we will return to the controlling images of Gemeinschaft and Gesellschaft, observing how images crucial to the creation of scene and character radically divide traditional Gemeinschaft from modern Gesellschaft and markedly separate one group of novels from another. Finally, we will examine certain fusions in her novels that dramatize the presence of Gemeinschaft *in*

Gesellschaft. However, most of these fusions—whether effected by a genuine poetry embodied in characters who share some ideal outside of self, or by a failed poetry uncovered in scenes that reveal harmful separations or a severe debasement of the traditional pillars of community—include inescapable difficulties. These difficulties are most successfully resolved in those novels whose characters struggle to evaluate anew the working-day world they had once misprized, while searching within it and within themselves for genuine mutuality of feeling. Since the discriminations and connections George Eliot would have her characters discover are in essence the same as those she would encourage in the reader, the fusions they struggle to achieve become both subject and object, or ends and means. The education her characters experience serves as a model for the education of her readers.

Framing the Present

George Eliot's great concern with the present may seem incongruous with the historical setting of almost all her novels, but in natural history, as we have seen, existing conditions prompt the investigation of change during the course of time. How this preoccupation with the present helps to determine the shape and content of her fiction may be seen in the way she frames the openings and closings of many novels. In the early pages of the three stories in *Scenes of Clerical Life*, *The Mill on the Floss*, and *Felix Holt*, time is measured in phrases that refer to the present: "five-and-twenty years ago," "more than a quarter of a century" ago, "thirty years ago," "five-and-thirty years ago." Although the intervals are longer, *Silas Marner* and *Romola* open with similar markers: "early years of this century" and "more than three centuries and a half ago." In *Middlemarch*, this pattern is complicated by a Prelude that speaks first of a "Spanish woman who lived three hundred years ago," and then of an indefinite present characterized by "no coherent social faith and order." Thus close to each novel's start, and often in the very first sentence, time is measured according to its distance from the immediate present of her contemporary readers, and it is exemplified through ordinary events, responses, conditions: the remodeling of a local church; a newcomer's insensibility to traditional customs; a stranger's fascination with communal village life; the lot of women at a particular time, and the needs of human nature in all times; the shape of the landscape and the way it reflects continuities and changes in economic, social, and political life.[4]

These temporal markers immediately force comparisons between the fictional world and the contemporary world of the reader. While the requisite countback encourages at least a glance at the intervening years, a host of images evoking the present establish the reader as an inhabitant of a Gesellschaft world created (for good and for ill) by change. "Efficiency," "endless diagrams," "a well-regulated mind," "scientific certitude," "people accustomed to reason," "art and science," "ships" and "wharves," "railway," "gold-fields," "manufacturing town," "trades-union meetings," "modern bankrupts," "brilliant gas light," and "dull, gas-poisoned absorption"— these phrases and images are drawn from the early pages of George Eliots novels, excluding only *Adam Bede* where Gemeinschaft predominates.[5] Yet even there, the sense of a reader who lives in Gesellschaft is not altogether absent. The opening act of magic that brings to the reader "far-reaching visions of the past," along with the stranger who appears at the close of the first chapter, indicate that old-fashioned village life is a thing set apart; just as the road the stranger travels and Dinah's preaching in the second chapter suggest the Stonyshire world of cotton mills lying beyond.

Not only the openings, but also the closings of many of George Eliot's novels, evoke the present. Amos, Janet, Philip and Lucy and Stephen, Felix and Esther, Deronda and Gwendolen and Mirah are still alive when their histories are brought to a close. So are Rosamond, Fred and Mary, Sir James and Celia, Ladislaw and Dorothea. The ending of *Middlemarch*, like its beginning, again complicates the pattern by striving for universality as well as particularity, as the direct address with its "we," "you," and "me" extends the present and blurs the line between it and the past. At the same time, in *Middlemarch* and elsewhere, as the historical framework is completed, roughly half of the characters alive in the present are located in new places, having moved not merely from one provincial town to another, but from Shepperton to a "large manufacturing town,"

4. George Eliot marked time in the same way in her essay on Riehl: "nearly fifty years ago" and "no longer ago than the beginning of the present century" (*Essays*, pp. 274, 278).

5. Unless otherwise noted, the phrases quoted appear in the opening chapters. In the case of "Janet's Repentance," the relevant chapter is the second not the first, because the story begins with a dramatized scene. "Modern bankrupts" appears in the chapter from *Romola* that establishes Florence as a great commercial power comparable to England in the present (ch. 5, pp. 43–44).

from Middlemarch to London and the Continent, from London to Palestine. Suggesting the uprootings common in Gesellschaft and a corresponding shift toward the urban, the national, and the international, such changes of habitation disturb the local ties of traditional community. Changes of occupation are noted as well through children who take up typically Gesellschaft work and become engineers or scientists.

In addition, although the images of Gemeinschaft and Gesell-schaft are regularly made to touch on one another, the novels' openings emphasize the differences between them, while the closings portray a coalescence. Most of the characters mentioned above are pictured with at least some members of their families in final scenes that often include a memorial ritual: Amos and his daughter visit Mrs. Barton's grave; Philip and Stephen visit the tomb of Tom and Maggie; the narrator laments and honors the many Dorotheas who "rest in unvisited tombs"; Mordecai dies in the arms of his sister and Deronda. In each case, the Gesellschaft perspective of the novel's closing scenes incorporates into the picture of modern society positive images of Gemeinschaft. The effect is to establish continuities that offset the omnipresence of an isolating or hostile society. The "respectable selfishness," "griping worldliness," and "oppresive narrowness" we know to exist in Milby, St. Ogg's, and Middlemarch, along with countless images of a pervasive Philistinism in English society, are thus to a certain extent altered by images of kinship, continuity, and spiritual affinity.[6]

As these openings and closings suggest, the focal point in all these novels (as in natural history) is the present, perceived as an existing condition of things resulting from the everyday continuities and changes that together create a way of life. Although the novels' frames differ in emphasis and strategy, they all serve the same rhetorical purpose of directing attention to the nature and potential of social life in the present. The emphasis in the openings upon a Gesellschaft world resulting from and in need of change is as necessary, for instance, as the emphasis on both continuity and change at the close, or on leaving the reader with a poetry of community created out of still vital old forms and beneficial new ones.

6. Though the framework is different in *AB*, it too participates in this pattern by way of the stranger. Appearing again late in the novel, he is the magistrate who admits Dinah to the prison in Stoniton where Hetty awaits trial, having remembered from her preaching in Hayslope her ability "to unlock hearts" (ch. 45, p. 372–73).

At the same time, the images of Gemeinschaft and Gesellschaft that compose the opening and closing frames reflect thematic progressions correlative to the changing nature of community within the corpus of her work. To compare the opening pages of *Felix Holt* and *Daniel Deronda*, for instance, is to find in the later novel a far more hostile social milieu. In the former, the genial Sampson tells stories from atop his coach as it travels through the rapidly changing countryside of the English Midlands; in the latter, a cold, automatic, and disembodied voice calls the game at an international gambling hall. Similarly, even though the closing images embody positive values, the nature of those images changes considerably over the course of George Eliot's work. In *Scenes of Clerical Life* kinship ties predominate, and they continue to provide an important base; but between the first and last of the *Scenes* a change that is to become increasingly more important appears. The local and concrete poetry of community begins to become more expansive and abstract, progressing from Amos's ties to his wife and daughter to the family Janet creates by adoption and the spiritual kinship she finds in the Reverend Mr. Tryan. This widening in the image of community is present too in *The Mill on the Floss* as the closing memorial renders the secular spiritual.

Middlemarch characteristically complicates the pattern, rendering it equivocal through closing images that simultaneously narrow and enlarge the image of community. It is narrowed through Lydgate, whose death is noted but not really commemorated, because his own sense of failure makes his later life a living death. But while the disintegration of his public and private lives erodes all the fundamental bases of community, turning his family into a bondage, his residence into a seasonal place, and his vocation into a profitable practice, still his dream of contributing to the good of the world is echoed in the greatly enlarged vision of the close. An opposite but similarly counterpointed movement characterizes the truly commemorative memorial Dorothea receives, as the summary preceding the final benediction brings to the forefront severely circumscribed realities, associated in her case with the "neighbourhood of Middlemarch" (from which she too has departed) and with "the conditions of an imperfect social state." Still, the counterpointing includes the progression we have been noting. In the *Scenes*, closing images of a "grave" or "gravestone" mark the local burying place of characters known to us. In *The Mill on the Floss*, kinship ties, a regional landscape, and a "tomb" bearing "the names of Tom and Maggie Tulliver" dominate the closing.

In *Middlemarch*, the "tombs" of the ending invoke the family of humankind.[7]

This movement in George Eliot's fiction from the territorial to the relational, or from *the* community to community, anticipates subsequent changes in the very definition of the word. If it threatens to reify the term, it also speaks to the real difficulty of creating community in the modern world. The form of her fiction embodies this difficulty, for the attempt to join realism of presentation and idealism of conception reflects the striving to unite that which had been severed by incorporating into Gesellschaft everyday realities that had once supported and continue to be essential to community. The endings of George Eliot's novels depict the increasing intensity of this pressure. As though attempting to bring Savonarola's "great feelings" down to earth, the final ceremony in *Romola* (organized around the decoration of an altar to the Frate in Romola's house) emphasizes concrete ties to religion, family, place, and friends. The start of the Finale to *Middlemarch* has a similar emphasis: family, place, and occupation are celebrated through Fred and Mary, who furthermore bring to them (by way of the books they write) the art and science of Gesellschaft. In addition, the references to Dorothea's substantial family ties, and to the sacred feelings she engenders even in Rosamond, also carry a reminder of traditional community and a glimmer of modern Gemeinschaft. But such images form only a part of the closing picture, and by the end of the Finale we see the disparity between them and the wide vision of social good imagined by Lydgate, Dorothea, and their creator.

As if addressing that disparity, the closing scene of *Daniel Deronda* is an attempt to make the poetry of community visibly concrete and ideal. The kinship ties that unite Mordecai, Deronda, and Mirah are literal and spiritual, joining brother and sister, husband and wife, an individual and his race, a people with the " 'families of man.' " Deronda's " 'lasting habitation,' " too, is at once concrete and invisible, based on his setting out for Israel, but also on a " 'spirit . . . carried from generation to generation' " and " 'lasting because movable.' "[8] But if the closing image of *Daniel*

7. Corresponding to this movement is Quentin Anderson's point that the "immediacies" in the later novels "are not things seen but things felt and believed," "George Eliot in *Middlemarch*," *The Pelican Guide to English Literature* 6: 280. Auster makes a similar point, *Local Habitations*, pp. 54–57.

8. The phrases quoted appear earlier in the novel (ch. 42, pp. 587–88, 591), where they are spoken by Mordecai, as Deronda has not yet taken over his

Deronda brings together the traditional and the modern—kinship, fixed locale, and a shared tradition, on the one hand, and a fluid communion of thought, spirit, or feeling, on the other—nevertheless the union remains to be confirmed and tested.

Gemeinschaft and Gesellschaft

A GEMEINSCHAFT PAST

As one might expect, the images of traditional Gemeinschaft are most frequent and pristine in the novels of English life set furthest back in time. George Eliot worked most often from two historical centers, one focused on the years near the turn of the century, and the other on the period surrounding the Reform Bill of 1832. She considered the latter to have immediacy for her readers, as the Gesellschaft frames characteristic of the novels depicting this period indicate. During the 1870s, she comments that "changes such as the first Reform Bill" took place "within lives still vigorous" ("More Leaves," p. 372). Responses of contemporary readers to the Reform-era novels and to recent histories of those times confirm this sense of immediacy. The period is described as "modern," "striking and immediate" precisely because readers saw in it "the moving currents of our own life" and "the story of our own day—the history we ourselves have acted."[9] The England of the Reform era was "an England moving quickly toward a new dispensation": religion was hardening into habit or splitting into sect; old social structures were being threatened by industrialism and new political faiths.[10] It is this England—one in which Gemeinschaft was giving way to Gesellschaft—that George Eliot dramatizes in "Amos Barton," "Janet's Repentance," *The Mill on the Floss, Felix Holt,* and *Middlemarch.*

mission. For a discussion of Judaism in *Daniel Deronda* as emblematic of the " 'ultimate unity of mankind,' " see Wiesenfarth, *George Eliot's Mythmaking*, pp. 222–24.

9. For descriptions of George Eliot's novels as "modern," see Cooke, *George Eliot*, pp. 325, 329; [Richard Holt Hutton], *British Quarterly Review*, American ed., 57 (1873): 218; see also my conclusion to this section and nn. 30–33. Other passages quoted are from Lewes's review of Harriet Martineau's *The History of England during the Thirty Years' Peace 1815–1845, British Quarterly Review* 11 (1850): 355–56.

10. Claude Bissell, "Social Analysis in the Novels of George Eliot," p. 229. Many historians have made this point and critics have noted its relevance to George Eliot's fiction, but Bissell is perhaps the first modern critic to write about the connection between the two, and to define the "historical centres" of her novels accordingly.

Gesellschaft is also unquestionably present in *Daniel Deronda*—the novel set after the Reform era, in the 1860s—and in *Romola*, though its Italian Renaissance setting places it literally furthest back. *Romola* does not so much change as widen the historical perspective. The controlling point of view becomes Western rather than English, as though locating the most essential roots of Gesellschaft in the movement from the communalism of medieval life to the individualism of the Renaissance. The implication is that Victorian England, as the leading commercial power of the day, was now what Renaissance Florence had once been, and in neither could traditional Gemeinschaft flourish.

In contrast, we do find traditional Gemeinschaft in the pastoral, rural, local, and preindustrialized worlds of the stories set at the end of the eighteenth and the beginning of the nineteenth century—"Gilfil's Love Story," *Adam Bede*, and *Silas Marner*. As we have seen, their openings—incorporating the present—attest to the differences between present and past. But unlike the other works, a coalescence does not occur at the close of these. Ending in the past, their closings convey images of traditional community: a "dear old Vicar" respected and loved by all his parishioners; a thriving and extended family so settled and secure as to be able to welcome back an outcast; a bridal group, a communal feast, and "four united people" approaching the garden and old home they plan always to be near. These closing images, moreover, reaffirm the essential pictures of community presented within. Hayslope is a village where people live a "simple family life of common need and common industry." Raveloe is a place "where many of the old echoes lingered, undrowned by new voices . . . never reached by the vibrations of the coach-horn, or of public opinion," "aloof from the currents of industrial energy and Puritan earnestness." They are also beautifully situated villages: Hayslope is located in a "rich undulating district" and Raveloe in a "snug well-wooded hollow" where nature contributes to neighborhood.[11]

The social rituals of the old-fashioned village life depicted in *Adam Bede* and *Silas Marner* reveal, in addition, how custom contributes to community. The holidays and holy days, the celebrations and the ceremonies, in these novels either alternate harmoniously with or participate in the everyday world. Chapter 17 of *Adam Bede* promises us "beauty in . . . commonplace things" and chapter 18 ("Church") commemorates the Sunday rituals that alternate

11. Passages quoted in order of citation are from: *AB*, ch. 19, p. 181; *SM*, ch. 1, p. 53; ch. 3, p. 71; *AB*, ch. 2, p. 16; *SM*, ch. 1, p. 53.

naturally and harmoniously with the weekday rhythms in turn evoked in chapter 19 ("Adam on a Working Day"). In the "Church" chapter, the usual Sunday practice of "neighbourly talk" and "simple civilities" is augmented by a funeral service that begins with "the friendly sympathetic nods of . . . fellow-parishioners." We see the Reverend Mr. Irwine "looking benignly round on that simple congregation," and Mrs. Poyser extending an invitation to tea, "for she would have held it a deep disgrace not to make her neighbours welcome to her house: personal likes and dislikes must not interfere with that sacred custom."

In *Silas Marner*, social rituals and ceremonial events again signify the "common custom and common belief" that do not guarantee but are essential to the "unity and peace of life of a people."[12] The distinction is from Tönnies, but its applicability to *Silas Marner* is clear. Though a miscarriage of custom causes Silas's eviction from the community of Lantern Yard, nonetheless his adoption of "the forms of custom and belief which were the mould of Raveloe life" is essential to his living in unity and peace among its people (ch. 16, p. 201). Furthermore, those very ceremonies by which "the charter of Raveloe seemed to be renewed" serve also to mark Silas's integration into the life of the community (ch. 11, p. 158). Its early stages coincide with Christmas time, the annual New Year's Eve dance, and the simple act of noticing "when Sunday came round" in Part One of the novel (chaps. 10–13); and its completion takes place in the holiday world of Part Two, as the literal Sunday of chapters 16 through 20 extends figuratively into the ones that follow, first through the Sunday clothes Silas and Eppie put on for their commemorative visit to Lantern Yard, and then through the closing wedding festivities.

Finally, just as in *Silas Marner* the movement from alienation to integration is marked by Gemeinschaft images of a holiday world, so the structure of *Adam Bede*, from peace to disturbance to peace, is reflected in its images of a holiday world. Here, the opening and closing books echo one another, as ceremony presides again in the last chapters to reaffirm a "holiday-time in the working-day world" (chap. 50). The two converge in the ritualistic celebration of "The Harvest Supper" (chap. 53), while a holiday world is evoked in the other four concluding chapters, three of them taking place on a Sunday (chaps. 51, 52, 54), and all echoing earlier motifs. The walk to church for a burial, for instance, becomes at the close

12. Tönnies, *G&G*, p. 49; *Custom*, pp. 93–98.

a walk from church leading to still another return, this time for the marriage ceremony of the last chapter.

In "Mr. Gilfil's Love Story," the predominating images differ from those previously mentioned, but they too offer perfect illustrations of the traits Tönnies later ascribed to Gemeinschaft. For him the father's role in the family is the model for the influence of the priest over his parishioners, "of the master over his people, of the landlord over his copyholders," just as in George Eliot's *Scenes* Gilfil is father to the flock, and Sir Christopher patriarchal lord of Cheverel Manor.[13] This extension of kinship into the "sacerdotal" and "feudal" is also seen in the portraits of the Reverend Mr. Irwine, and of the Donnithornes and the Casses at The Chase and The Red House in *Adam Bede* and *Silas Marner*. The Squires fall far short of the feudal ideal they should represent; still, the central role they play in the life of the community contrasts sharply with the peripheral function of the great houses in the fiction set nearer to the present. In those novels, the priests too suffer displacements as their parishes become divided into opposing sects, and custom suffers as well, though more through corruption than dispersion.

Despite the many Gemeinschaft images of unity and peace in the stories set in an earlier, rural England, the discordant notes are more than occasional. In addition to generating the conflicts required by the plot, the discordancies reveal how workaday realities disrupt the ideal unity associated with Gemeinschaft. Some of the disturbances are external, arising in industrial England or revolution-beset France, places outside the stories' main loci. When disturbances of this kind affect the action, it is usually by way of eliminating the intrusion: Dinah gives up preaching in the bleak cotton-mill town of Snowfield to marry and live in Hayslope; Silas moves from a manufacturing district to rural Raveloe. Far more often, however, the disharmonies are not external to the Gemeinschaft. They have their origins in Hayslope or Raveloe, not in industrial Snowfield or Leeds or the other manufacturing towns that lie at the periphery of these novels. Caused for the most part by abuses of rank and privilege among the rural gentry, and by the fixity of peasant ways, their source lies at the very essence of Gemeinschaft.

In George Eliot's fiction, disturbances of the first sort most

13. *G&G*, pp. 42–59. Auster, *Local Habitations*, has a fine discussion of Sir Christopher's "enlightened feudalism," and of his enthusiasm for Gothic architecture (pp. 88–89).

characteristically involve substantial landowners who fail in their
obligations to tenant, neighbor, and land (Squires Donnithorne
and Cass), and young gentlemen who abuse the privilege of rank
by entering into secret and injurious liaisons with women below
them in station (Captain Wybrow and Tina, Arthur Donnithorne
and Hetty, Godfrey Cass and Molly). Far more prevalent than Sir
Christopher's protective treatment of the widow Hartopp are the
unjust advantages taken by Squires Donnithorne and Cass. Critics
sometimes read into these portraits of mean-spirited landlords and
mismatched lovers a severe and even radical social criticism, but
while George Eliot does suggest that we need not regret the passing
of a system so liable to abuse, it is the failure to fulfill mutual
obligations, themselves supported by the feudal code, that she most
openly and severely censures. As Tönnies explains, "the essence of
the Gemeinschaft" is "the unity of unequal beings" bound together
through "rights and duties . . . authority and service" (G&G, p.
46). Arthur's dream embodies this kind of unity. Regarding his
" 'position, not merely as one of power and pleasure for myself
but as a means of benefiting my neighbours,' " he wishes to be a
" 'model landlord . . . able to respect every man on the estate, and
to be respected by him in return,' " thereby sharing "a joy that is
general and not merely personal."[14] The dream of course evapo-
rates, but primarily because Arthur fails to live up to his principles.
Though his grandfather, Squire Donnithorne, is so far from fancying himself a model landlord as to seem an opposite extreme, even
he recognizes mutuality to be a ruling principle, as his tactic with
the Poysers is to claim an " 'arrangement . . . which will be to our
mutual advantage.' " When Mrs. Poyser responds by "fly[ing] in
the face of the catechism," the code described by Tönnies is still
at play, for her landlord's flagrant failure to fulfill his share of
their mutual obligations clearly prompts and justifies her famous
"say out" (AB, ch. 32).

At the same time, the disparity between principles and action
suggests that in practice the code is unworkable. The easy abuse
of the semi-feudal system, however, instead of emphasizing a problem actually works to clear one away. Feudalism was becoming an
outmoded form, and in the best tradition of natural history, George
Eliot was assessing its virtues and liabilities while putting the system to rest. She dramatizes a current condition—"in the nineteenth
century Gemeinschaft was not yet divorced from distinctions of

14. AB, ch. 16, pp. 139, 145; ch. 24, p. 225.

rank, wealth, and authority"—and even establishes that such distinctions are in principle allied to the mutuality she values; but she also calls this particular code into question by frequently dramatizing its failures.[15]

Simultaneously, certain kinds of plot resolutions propose a democratic ideal. Though Adam is "very susceptible to the influence of rank," he declares himself Arthur's equal at the moment of discovering his patron's irresponsible behavior to Hetty (ch. 16, p. 139; ch. 28, p. 260). Similarly, though Adam would never put " 'worldly interest' " before his sense of what is " 'honourable,' " he begins as a foreman but ends up owning a flourishing building business (ch. 43, p. 394). In *Silas Marner*, too, a sense of natural equality vies with prescriptive respectability and wins, so that Godfrey Cass, the most substantially landed parishioner, must give up his claims to the daughter who has been adopted by Silas, a working man. And in general in George Eliot's fiction, the curtailment of upper-class dominance, whether in Gemeinschaft where it rules, or in Gesellschaft where it lingers, is shown to be far more a gain than a loss. Thus these novels exemplify Tönnies's theory that the "essence of the Gemeinschaft" is "the unity of unequal beings," but they fail to explore its corollary that "the greater . . . the freedom" the less cohesive the Gemeinschaft (*G&G*, pp. 46–47). George Eliot later confronts this corollary, of course, when Gesellschaft is her actual as well as her rhetorical subject.

In these studies of an earlier time, she does however explore how the fixity of ways in Gemeinschaft can deny individuality. The traditional superstition, for instance, that works to hallow custom also renders the uncustomary suspect. It makes Silas an outcast and ensures his long years of isolation; it also fosters an intolerance towards "furriners" and outsiders whenever they appear. Furthermore, as seen in Martin Poyser's hardness toward Hetty, or Godfrey's and Nancy's insensitivity to the ties between Silas and Eppie, "the yoke of traditional impressions" makes the irregular intolerable and creates an insensibility to suffering in even the kindest of people (*SM*, ch. 40, p. 347). Such impressions also reinforce "that insulation by class" which, as Q.D. Leavis points out, "destroys the powers of imaginative sympathy in everyone."[16] To find correctives to the narrowing effects of the fixed responses dictated by old-fashioned Gemeinschaft, one must look elsewhere, as George Eliot does by advocating "the flexibility, the ready sympathy, or the

15. John Killham, "Idea of Community," p. 391.
16. Introduction to *SM*, p. 37.

tolerance, which characterizes a truly philosophic culture" (*Essays*, p. 29). In her novels such virtues are often the signature of a narrator who persistently strives to encourage in the reader, by way of the culture of Gesellschaft, values essential to the creation of modern Gemeinschaft.

Nevertheless, though these novels no more depict a lost Eden than a degenerate social order, they present an integral world where the unifying forces far outnumber the isolating ones, and where tradition, because it contributes to solidarity, is more often a blessing than a yoke. The result is a workaday world in many ways infused with the poetry of community. This poetry consists of themes noted earlier—communal celebrations, rural peacefulness and plenitude, kinship ties, dignifying work, love and social sympathy, mutuality of obligation and concern—and of varied and broad amplifications of these themes. There is the unanimity of opinion and common sentiment evident at Hetty's trial in the "one sob" that metaphorically expresses the great sympathy everyone feels for the shame Martin Poyser must endure because of his niece's crime, and in the "sublime" silence signifying "that sudden pause of a great multitude, which tells that one soul moves in them all" in the moments before the expected verdict is announced (*AB*, ch. 43, pp. 358, 365). There is the nourishing tie to the land among people who have lived for generations in the same place; and there is the sense of honor and integrity that places respect above "worldly interests" among people "who derived dignity from their functions rather than from their pocket" (*AB*, ch. 23, p. 220).

But above all there is the manifold power of love, in the form of marriage, filial piety, and the "centre of common feeling" generated by children, and in the shared trouble that makes " 'us kin,' " and the sympathy that transforms pain into "all our best insight and our best love." [17] This loving kinship, literal and metaphoric, is the most centrally binding of all the forces that contribute to George Eliot's poetry of community. Encompassing "a positive attitude toward fellow beings which is rooted in sentiment, mind, and conscience," and based on an ideal of "mutual sympathy and interdependence," it both integrates social existence and creates social sympathy.[18] Furthermore, since it can survive the particularities of custom, time, and place, it possesses what many other features of

17. *SCL*, "Janet's Repentance," ch. 8, p. 306; *AB*, ch. 48, p. 387; ch. 50, p. 407; see also *SM*, ch. 14, p. 190.
18. *G&G*, p. 129; Salomon, "In Memoriam," p. 34.

traditional community lack—the potential to contribute to community in the present.

The mutual interdependence and "positive attitude" stipulated above are part of Tönnies's definition of Gemeinschaft, as is the idea that the attendant relationships are "natural and emotional," but apart from a difference in the meaning assigned to *natural*, such concepts correspond closely to George Eliot's fundamental ideal of community. She described her intention in *Silas Marner* as "to set . . . in a strong light the remedial influences of pure, natural human relations," and here, as in Tönnies, *natural* means precisely what it does in *natural history*: the essence within the nature of a thing that manifests itself so long as no corrupting or interfering circumstances deflect it from its course of development.[19] But in her statement *remedial* significantly qualifies *natural*, suggesting not Tönnies's static identities but the concept of progressive change essential to the complex of evolutionary ideas espoused by the social theorists known to her. Such changes are to take place in her readers as well as in her fictional characters; but whereas for Silas (to take perhaps the least complicated example) the change requires the replacement of one traditional community by another, for the reader the "remedial influences" depend on the discovery of essential values deflected by the predominance of Gesellschaft, and on progressive modifications that can both reflect and alter the "onward tendency of human things" (*MF*, ch. 30, p. 239).

Feudalistic order, fixity of place in a rural world, social rituals and traditions conducive to solidarity: the continuity of bonds such as these had indeed been interrupted. But their deficiencies and the course of historical development made their recovery undesirable and unlikely, for not only were they becoming outdated, but their constitution was such as to survive few modifications of outward form. The rural landscape perhaps suggests an exception. Though it had changed over the years, the countryside was still very much in evidence, and even when its immediate presence was not felt, memories of its beauty and attraction could exert a compelling imaginative or spiritual force in true Wordsworthian fashion. Throughout George Eliot's fiction, the countryside exercises this power, even in *Adam Bede* and *Silas Marner*, where the spatial distance between the landscape and the narrator contributes greatly

19. *G&G*, Part Two (pp. 103–170); Salomon, "In Memoriam," p. 34; *Letters* 3: 382; see also chapter 2, "Natural History and Social Evolutionary Theory."

to the pastoral effect and its appeal to the urban reader.[20] But this very spiritualization of the landscape, though poetic, also suggests a turning away from community, for once the countryside is separated from the realities of people, work, and everyday life, it ceases to be a social force except in so far as the pastoralism functions as a critique of urban and industrial life. Thus, what U. C. Knoepflmacher refers to as "the asocial Wordsworth" displaces Riehl's emphasis on land *and* people.[21] As a result the rural landscape, instead of affirming the continuation of Gemeinschaft, comes to suggest the disappearance from the modern workaday world of a traditional prose and poetry of community.

Therefore, for readers living in the present, the overriding emphasis must be, as it is, on the human values George Eliot wished to have transposed to Gesellschaft, or on the loving kinship and on the mutuality of concern, feeling, and interest that are both essential to Gemeinschaft and amenable to modifications and development. Henry Auster illuminates the first of these, or the natural essence, by pointing out how George Eliot "repeatedly contrasts the atmosphere of her stories with the life of her urban, intellectual readers only to call attention to the essential uniformity of human nature and the continuity between the simple past and the increasingly complex present" (p. 46). But, as noted in chapter 1, while both Squires and Auster reveal how George Eliot's pastoralism and regionalism serve as a criticism of the modern world, Squires portrays an author attempting to escape into the past, and Auster one who is responding statically to the present. The effect in both cases is to lend credence to Raymond Williams's contention that George Eliot's sense of community is itself arrested, and to come to the conclusion (though they avoid it) that she defeated her own best purposes by urging a retreat to what was no longer possible. I am arguing, instead, that the continuities she wishes her readers to discover take their elemental essence from natural human relations and that the forms these relations take are by nature not static but dynamic or developing.

A GESELLSCHAFT PRESENT

Perceived as an absolute, Gesellschaft seems at first glance to preclude such natural human relations almost as much as the ideal

20. See Michael Squires, *Pastoral Novel*, pp. 68–78, 93.

21. U. C. Knoepflmacher, "George Eliot," p. 250. George Eliot's tendency to find sustenance in a rural, unsocialized landscape is frequently noticeable in the *Letters* (e.g., 1: 70–71; 2: 367–69; 3: 14; 6: 46; 8: 171, 468).

of Gemeinschaft includes them. Competition replaces cooperation, negotiated contracts supplant relationships based on recognized status, rational calculation subverts spontaneous emotional ties, and common values become merely a provisional fiction created to further a business transaction calculated exclusively in terms of profit and loss. Instead of the mutual familiar relationships between kinsman, neighbor, and friend that help to define the Gemeinschaft typology, the materialistic ties associated with trade, and later with commerce and industry, determine Gesellschaft models of social organization. Accompanying changes in human values render the proposition " 'Everyone a Merchant' " metaphorically true even if it is not literally applicable. The result is a world where self-interest rules as "every person strives for that which is to his own advantage and . . . affirms the actions of others only in so far as and as long as they can further his interest." Though other people are kept constantly in mind, it is only because they furnish "means and tools" to be used for one's own "ends or purposes" within an individualist ethos directed entirely toward self-advantage.[22]

This typology of Gesellschaft, given abstract formulation by Tönnies, is visible in the representation of ordinary social reality in all of George Eliot's novels except *Adam Bede* and *Silas Marner*. It is manifest, for instance, in the delineation of a host of major and minor characters, in the alteration of kinship and neighborhood ties resulting from their behavior, and in the opposition between their values and those associated with traditional community. For the Dodson sisters of *The Mill on the Floss*, "the great fundamental fact of blood" (ch. 13, p. 116) becomes so thoroughly infused with material interests as to make the two generally inseparable, or worse, as to favor a good business investment over family sentiment when the two are at odds. The inversion of value that results is noticeable even in the victims, so that for the bankrupt Dodson-Tullivers "community of feeling" is generated only by the "hateful incubus of debt" (ch. 31, p. 244). Still, while the Dodsons treat their relatives badly, they do not disavow them. Their "community of feeling" is not nearly so macabre as the "fellowship in hostility" exhibited by the relatives, or "Christian Carnivora," who watch over Featherstone's death in *Middlemarch* (ch.

22. *G&G*, pp. 76–78, 165; see also Cahnman, "Tönnies and Social Change," pp. 112–14. For an excellent discussion of this same general point from a different but related perspective, see Mintz's application of Weber's "new economic man" to Eliot's fiction (*Novel of Vocation*, pp. 61–64).

35, p. 242). That the bad blood becomes thicker, so to speak, in the
later novels is seen as well in the perjuries committed by Tito in
Romola, Jermyn in *Felix Holt*, Bulstrode in *Middlemarch*, and
Grandcourt in *Daniel Deronda*. Violating promises made to father,
wives, lovers, and children, their acts of self-interest lead to out-
right and even criminal denials of kinship.

In addition, in all the novels except *Adam Bede* and *Silas Marner*,
marketplace marriages and love relationships calculated in terms
of profit and loss regularly infect the generating source of all family
relations, as in Mr. Glegg's "money-getting, money-keeping . . .
conjugal" calculations; Tito's and Jermyn's attempts to turn " 'love
into a good bargain' "; Mrs. Arrowpoint's efforts to prevent Cath-
erine from marrying Klesmer; and Gwendolen's decision to marry
Grandcourt despite Mrs. Glasher's warning against making one's
" 'gain out of another's loss.' "[23] In each case, the negative force is
allied to what Gwendolen's uncle calls a "well-regulated mind"
(*DD*, ch. 13, p. 177).

Within Tönnies's Gesellschaft typology, too, "the gain of one is
the loss of the other"; and in his work and George Eliot's the
phenomenon is seen in business and marital arrangements, and
in the "general competition which takes place in so many other
spheres" (*G&G*, pp. 77, 80). In *Middlemarch*, for instance, class
rivalry, social power, kinship, and political reform are reduced
to matters of profit and loss even in a single scene, as when Mawmsey ("a chief representative in Middlemarch of that great social
power, the retail trader") and Brooke argue the issue of Reform.
Both agree to " 'put it in a family light,' " but when Brooke adds
" 'but public spirit, now. We're all one family, you know, it's all
one cupboard,' " he is thoroughly bested by Mawmsey, who answers: " 'But as to one family, there's debtor and creditor' " (ch.
51, pp. 366–67).

In this scene, the many spheres of interest also include neighborhood ties. Just as Brooke's empty cupboard points to the absence
of "one family," so does his real relationship to the surrounding
community speak to his severance from it. Thus when Brooke says
during his election campaign, " 'I like this, now—this kind of public made up of one's own neighbours,' " the narrator is quick to

23. *MF*, ch. 12, p. 108; *FH*, ch. 42, p. 518; *DD*, ch. 22, pp. 289–91; ch. 36,
p. 500; ch. 56, p. 757. See also the bribing merchant epigraph in *DD*, ch. 26,
and the discussion of Gwendolen's "marriage" as "a contract" (ch. 54, p. 732).
As such, it corresponds closely to Tönnies's definition of marriage in Gesellschaft (*G&G*, pp. 192–93).

point out that "the weavers and tanners of Middlemarch, unlike Mr Mawmsey, had never thought of Mr Brooke as a neighbour, and were not more attached to him than if he had been sent in a box from London" (ch. 51, p. 368). Elsewhere in the novel, many of the attachments that do exist also fail to be genuinely neighborly. " 'Contented to be no worse than my neighbours,' " Mr. Vincy, the mayor of Middlemarch and one of its leading manufacturers, not only cheats his customers by using cheap dyes that rot the silk he sells, but even worse he " 'suck[s] the life out of the wretched handloom weavers' " he employs.[24] Featherstone too victimizes those around him, in his case by the vengeful pleasure he derives from making his family compete for the land he values above all else. The irony of course is that he leaves the land to a secret, illegitimate son, "almost more calculating . . . than himself," who promptly sells it in order to become "a money-changer" in a distant port.[25]

In other novels as well, the breakup of neighborhood ties is a sign of ascendant commercial values. Both are evident, for instance, in the various contractual arrangements that separate the Tulliver family from the mill they have owned for generations, as well as in the "detached, disjointed" attitude Stephen Guest has toward "the neighbourhood," for though " 'he's seen nothing of business,' " his "supercilious indifference" toward his neighbors is the result of his family's owning "the largest oil-mill and the most extensive wharf in St Ogg's."[26] In a different way, a detachment from neighborhood informs the characterizations of Tito and Bulstrode, for each comes to wield public power by moving to a new place while making a secret of his past.

In Tito's case especially, the parallels to the typology of Gesellschaft man are so striking that one of Tönnies's descriptions reads like an abstract of his character. Again, the image of a merchant provides the model for the typical member of society:

> He is without home, a traveler, a connoisseur of foreign customs and arts without love or piety for those of any one country, a linguist speaking several languages, flippant and double-tongued, adroit, adaptable, and one who always keeps his eye on the end or purpose he plans to attain. He moves about quickly and smoothly, changes his character and intellectual attitude (beliefs or opinions) as if they were fashions of dress, one to be worn here, another

24. *M*, ch. 13, p. 97; ch. 34, p. 239.
25. *M*, ch. 41, p. 302; ch. 53, p. 381.
26. *MF*, ch. 40, pp. 316–18; ch. 43, p. 345.

there. He is a mixer and smooth fellow who uses either the old or
the new, whichever is to his advantage. In all these respects he is
the absolute opposite of the peasant who lives and clings close to
the soil.

Even the link between merchants and strangers is to the point, for
since all men are essentially strangers in Gesellschaft the difference
between them and native inhabitants becomes irrelevant. George
Eliot's Tito rejoices in "his position as an alien," and in the "power
. . . possible to talent without traditional ties." He uses his considerable powers of mind to pursue a "rational course," defined by
him as making others "subservient to his own interest."[27]

This pervasive sense of the "real business of life" being a matter
of "monetary affairs" carried on by people who care little about genuine "public spirit" is compounded by a great many characters
whose "favourite key of life" is "doing as one likes." A common
enough catch phrase (note the attention it receives in *Culture and
Anarchy*), in George Eliot's fiction it defines a number of characters, women as well as men, Rosamond and Gwendolen as well as
Tom Tulliver, Harold Transome, Tito, Featherstone, Bulstrode,
and Grandcourt. In addition, the values it represents are regularly
given dramatic representation in a host of characters whose "desire
for predominance" and "determination to mastery" prompt each
to get a "handle" on others and use them as "tools" so as to push
"one's own way forward in the world."[28] The result, at times, is an
inversion of values so complete as to inspire this chapter heading in
Felix Holt:

> Your fellow-man?—Divide the epithet:
> Say rather, you're the fellow, he the man.
>
> [ch. 25, p. 347

The "fellow" in this case is a man named Christian, come from afar.
A "sober calculator," he measures the "market value" of every-

27. Passages quoted from *G&G*, p. 168; R, ch. 39, p. 340; ch. 46, p. 391.
J. B. Bullen argues that Tito represents the first of Comte's Law of Three
Stages—the "primitive 'polytheistic,' undeveloped stage of man's moral nature"
—but Tito's deliberate assessment of his every move argues against this view
of him as an "emblem of uninhibited naturalism" ("George Eliot's *Romola*
as a Positivist Allegory," pp. 429–30).

28. The phrases are quoted from the following places, but they appear with
great frequency elsewhere: *MF*, ch. 12, p. 107; ch. 14, p. 118; ch. 47, p. 375;
R, ch. 39, p. 340; ch. 48, p. 400; *FH*, ch. 8, p. 196; ch. 17, p. 278; ch. 29, p. 384;
M, ch. 33, p. 235; ch. 58, p. 427; ch. 65, p. 487; ch. 71, p. 534; *DD*, ch. 13, pp.
168, 173; ch. 25 epigraph; ch. 36, p. 501; ch. 48, p. 659.

thing, including himself, and treats his neighbors with scorn not love.[29] No less ironical is the word *Christian* as applied to the townspeople's assessment of Felix, who according to "Trebian report" is

> a young man with so little of the ordinary Christian motives as to making an appearance and getting on in the world, that he presented no handle to any judicious and respectable person who might be willing to make use of him.

[ch. 17, p. 278

Such images of Gesellschaft are no less a part of George Eliot's natural history than are her portraits of Gemeinschaft. There was in the nineteenth century a widely felt sense of changes caused by "the transition from general home (or household) economy to general trade economy, or the transition from the predominance of agriculture to the predominance of industry" (*G&G*, p. 78); and George Eliot explores in her fiction both the earlier way of life and the origins and development of subsequent changes. As though confirming the correlation in natural history between the individual life and outward social conditions, the compositional chronology of her novels reveals how her efforts to respond to a world in which Gesellschaft was becoming increasingly predominant implicate her own private natural history. She "gradually synthesizes," as Michael Squires points out, "her provincial experience, her knowledge of urban culture, and her awareness of historical change" (pp. 20–21). In the early fiction, the historical perspective shifts back and forth: "Gilfil" comes between "Amos" and "Janet"; *The Mill on the Floss* comes between *Adam Bede* and *Silas Marner*. But thereafter the sense of a dissolving Gemeinschaft and a burgeoning Gesellschaft is constant.

At the same time, the body of her fiction reflects her attempts to confront her readers with a natural history of social life that would reveal how conditions were once different, how they came to be what they are, and how this process—for good and for bad—still continues. Thus in the very chapter of *The Mill on the Floss* that relates the history of the town and the legends that surround it, the narrator notes: "the mind of St Ogg's did not look extensively before or after." Its inhabitants had indeed "inherited a long past," but being thoroughly preoccupied with business and having "no

---

29. *FH*, ch. 25, p. 347; ch. 12, p. 233. In his introduction to *FH*, Coveney points out how Felix's "values of an 'unmarketable' kind" constitute a "negative commentary on the values of Victorian society" (p. 63).

eyes for the spirits that walk the streets," they give its history not the least bit of thought. In addition, she establishes in the reader's present—referred to as "these days of rapid money-getting"—a pretension to knowledge, a susceptibility to "new-fashioned smartness," and a proliferation of material interests so great that "even Mrs Glegg's day seems far back in the past now, separated from us by changes that widen the years." But though the narrator speaks of "widely-sundered generations," separated by immediate changes and by long tracts of historical time, the narration, by enabling the reader to look before or after, actually works to relate one generation to another (ch. 12, pp. 104–9). Finally, though a sense of positive change is missing from this chapter, the conditions established here are essential to understanding the novel's later treatment of the "young natures in many generations, that in the onward tendency of human things have risen above the mental level of the generation before them" (ch. 30, pp. 238–39).

For many of George Eliot's Victorian readers, the natural history she was writing had all the immediacy she hoped it would have. Taking both the older and the younger generations of the Dodsons and Tullivers to be their contemporaries, readers discovered in Maggie "the restless spirit of the nineteenth century," and thought the Dodsons' "sordid life of vulgar respectability" to be "typical"— "a picture in little of nine-tenths of the world we live in" as one critic put it, or according to another "the sort of life which thousands upon thousands of our countrymen lead."[30] In response to other novels as well, readers spoke of the portraits of "modern society," the criticisms of "modern social life," and the author's attentiveness to "the most serious problems of the age" and "of the day."[31] Of course, her readers included those who responded to and those who resisted the "deliberate challenge to Society as at present constituted" they found in her books.[32] Many, for instance,

30. Cooke, *George Eliot*, p. 300. *CH*, p. 135 ([E. S. Dallas], *Times*, 19 May 1860); *CH*, p. 142 ([John Chapman, prob.], *Westminster Review*, July 1860). For reviews of George Eliot's novels reprinted in *CH*, author (if known), journal, and date are noted in parentheses.

31. [Rev. Robert Laing], *Quarterly Review*, American ed., 134 (1873): 193; authorship identified *Wellesley Index to Victorian Periodicals, 1824–1900*, 1: 755, ed. Walter Houghton. Cooke, pp. 325, 329, 353. *Standard* (24 December 1880), p. 3. *Academy* 18 (1880): 460. Even *Romola* was felt to be contemporary in its preoccupations: *CH*, pp. 200–203 ([Richard Holt Hutton], *Spectator*, July 1863); *CH*, p. 217 [(Justin McCarthy], *Westminster Review*, October 1863).

32. *CH*, p. 320 (*Saturday Review*, 7 December 1872).

objected to the harsh, workaday realities she depicted, not because they were untrue, but because they were not a fit subject for art. Equally challenging, as readers on both sides recognized, was her never-ending effort to integrate into modern life the social sympathies that were to correct, but seemed also incompatible with, the fiercely competitive spirit of the age. But whatever their reaction to the challenges they found in her work, and however hard put they would have been to define "historic guidance" as she did—in terms of "present conditions . . . determined by the conditions of the age that went before"—they understood that she was speaking to and about the existing generation and revealing to them "the tangled threads of our consciousness and of our new conditions." [33]

Gemeinschaft in Gesellschaft

The two major historical centers George Eliot chose as the settings for her fiction embody a contrast between Gemeinschaft and Gesellschaft, and make the new conditions a function of the latter. But George Eliot hoped to reveal as well, within those new conditions, Gemeinschaft continuities worthy of survival and Gesellschaft tendencies capable of altering modern life for the better. Reestablishing solidarity as a value, the two were to contribute to a modern poetry of community by sustaining or newly creating Gemeinschaft *in* Gesellschaft. The intricate blendings that result are of course far more "natural" to history than are the strict oppositions characteristic of a typology. Even Tönnies is careful to point out that "in the [actual] social and historical life of mankind there is partly close interrelation, partly juxtaposition and opposition" of Gemeinschaft and Gesellschaft (*G&G*, p. 225). In George Eliot's natural histories, each is unquestionably at play, and "close interrelation" above all. "It was easy . . . to conceive that town and country had no pulse in common," she writes in the introduction to *Felix Holt* (p. 80); but so to conceive, the majority of her novels makes clear, is far less apposite to the natural history of social life than is a "mixed condition of things" (*R*, ch. 57, p. 462). Still more needful, as a result, but far less easy to conceive was a common pulse existing within the very conditions responsible for the

33. George Barnett Smith, "George Eliot," *Saint Paul's Magazine* 12 (1873): 593. Statements similar to those documented in nn. 30–33 often appear elsewhere. The immediacy of Eliot's fiction is also very much in evidence in the sources cited by James Wayne Geibel, "An Annotated Bibliography of British Criticism of George Eliot, 1858–1900," pp. 57–58.

"tangled threads of our consciousness." When she writes in *Middlemarch* of how "municipal town and rural parish gradually made fresh threads of connection," she first locates the threads in the very "vicissitudes which are constantly shifting the boundaries of social intercourse," and then speaks of the movement as "begetting" a "new consciousness of interdependence" (*M*, ch. 11, pp. 70–71). But however much she wished the "mixed condition of things" to be a "sign, not of hopeless confusion, but of struggling order," the constant tensions within her work between a workaday world inimical to community and a way of life conducive to solidarity attest above all to the fragility of the order and the strenuousness of the struggle.

A CONTINUING POETRY OF COMMUNITY

Various in form and in force, George Eliot's efforts to reveal a continuing poetry of community within Gesellschaft testify both to the comprehensiveness of the effort and to the limited strengths of the result. She often, for instance, creates a character whose best self contrasts markedly with his Gesellschaft self. To take an early example, in "Janet's Repentance" the lawyer Dempster's loving tenderness toward his mother exists in antithesis to his otherwise "hard, astute, domineering" behavior (*SCL*, ch. 7, p. 296). Wakem's treatment of his son creates a similar contrast in *The Mill on the Floss*, as does the behavior of a number of other characters. In Mr. Tulliver and Tom, the strong attachment to the mill, which has been in the family for five generations, exists alongside the opposing wish to turn Tom into "good commercial stuff" (*MF*, ch. 34, p. 270). Even playful Bob Jakin is both peddling merchant out to cheat his customers and chivalrous protector of Maggie. In all the later novels, as well, George Eliot includes characters motivated by dual tendencies. This same kind of disparity exists in *Daniel Deronda*, for instance, in the difference between the Cohens in the pawnshop and at their Sabbath dinner. But wherever they appear, the affirmations embodied in characters in whom Gemeinschaft and Gesellschaft traits coexist in isolation from one another are tenuous at best and presented as such, surrounded as they are by harsh and constant ironies, or else made light of through comic treatment.

At the opposite extreme are characters who remain essentially untouched by the Gesellschaft world that surrounds them. Among them is Sir James Chettam, whose "simple and comprehensive programme for social well-being" requires only that "people would behave like gentlemen"; and Caleb Garth, who "gave himself up entirely to the many kinds of work which he could do without handling capital." At the same time, and in contrast to the split characters, the surrounding contexts lend a certain strength to the affirmations made through these integral characters. Helping to make "the family . . . whole again," the gentlemanly Chettam is an agent of reconciliation at the close of *Middlemarch*; and Caleb is presented throughout as "one of those precious men within his own district whom everybody would choose to work for them, because he did his work well, charged very little, and often declined to charge at all."[34]

Yet, these portraits too participate in the struggle for positive value, and bring to it the added difficulties of the author's having to persuade the reader of viable Gemeinschaft continuities and having to control in herself a nostalgia that would defeat her purposes by affirming what seems merely to be anachronistic. With regard to Chettam, the problem is not nostalgia, but continuities revealed to be suspect, since the irony that controls the nostalgia also exposes the character's limitations. With Caleb, a character modeled on George Eliot's father, the reverse seems at first to be true. Nostalgia figures so largely in the creation of Caleb's character as to make even his limitations seem like virtues:

> He could not manage finance: he knew values well, but he had no keenness of imagination for monetary results in the shape of profit and loss: and having ascertained this to his cost, he determined to give up all forms of his beloved "business" which required that talent.
>
> [ch. 24, p. 185

But while George Eliot returns to Caleb the "veneration" and "poetry" she has him ascribe to the "myriad-headed, myriad-handed labour by which the social body is fed, clothed, and housed," she also continues to pose a challenge to the reader through him. The regular reminders that "by 'business' Caleb never meant money transactions, but the skilful application of labour," though they create a character who is unworldly, come from a narrator who is worldly-wise.[35] As Alan Mintz explains:

> George Eliot puts "business" in quotation marks, because her use of the word is a conscious transvaluation of its meaning. Caleb's work exemplifies the kind of transactions a man should have with the world: direct, selfless, moneyless. "Business," as it came to be

34. *M*, ch. 24, pp. 185–86; ch. 38, p. 280; Finale, p. 611.
35. *M*, ch. 24, p. 185; ch. 56, pp. 402, 409.

used in the nineteenth century, described the commercial activity
of merchants who bought and sold commodities through the medium of money for the purposes of profit in money.

[*Novel of Vocation,* p. 138

Through Caleb, then, the struggle for positive value takes still
another form by challenging the reader to consider standards of
value far different from those that predominate.

Still, Caleb's devotion to labor entirely divorced from monetary
results makes him too idiosyncratic a figure. Caleb's attitude toward
work (like Adam Bede's) is "deeply religious" (*M*, ch. 56, p. 409),
but because his world is more commercial than Adam's, his affirmation of value seems to require a thorough repudiation of economic
gain. Such poetry is weakened not only by its rarity but also by
excluding the very workaday world it supposedly celebrates.

Far more persuasive than either of these extremes, and also far
more pervasive in George Eliot's fiction, are Gemeinschaft continuities enmeshed within and without the life of a character living
in Gesellschaft. Most often, they are rooted in kinship ties, which
are everywhere in George Eliot's fiction the most substantial of the
pillars of community. Being so rooted, they have the advantage of
exerting their force on the reader through memories and experiences familiar to many. Dramatizing the "loves and sanctities of
our life" that memory honors and preserves, George Eliot keeps the
past alive in the present for both character and reader, and also reveals how such memories and the continuing attachments they foster can check or call into question the modern mania for "striving."
"Heaven knows where that striving might lead us," she writes in
The Mill on the Floss, "if our affections had not a trick of twining
round those old inferior things—if the loves and sanctities of our
life had no deep immovable roots in memory" (ch. 14, p. 135). That
such roots encourage avowals of kinship is repeatedly dramatized
in her fiction, as in Mr. Tulliver's enduring love for his sister,
Maggie's unbreakable attachment to her brother, and Mrs. Glegg's
principled loyalty to her niece, as well as in Romola's efforts to
honor her father's wishes, Esther's feeling for Lyon, Mrs. Bulstrode's
support for her husband, and Gwendolen's attachment to her
mother.

Just as immediate family ties are linked by George Eliot to the
"primitive mortal needs" that make us "all one," so extensions of
kinship within the larger community are regularly linked to a sim-

plicity that makes for "universal kinship."[36] "Loving one's neighbor," as well as honoring those close to one, is an essential base to which George Eliot returns the reader in every novel. As Thomas Pinney has shown, "the authority of the past" in George Eliot's novels is "inseparable from the affections that grow out of personal experience," but it is not, as Pinney also argues, for the most part limited to them.[37] The immediacy of personal experience for both characters and readers makes it a necessary and vital starting point, but George Eliot attempts regularly to go beyond its boundaries by creating a human history that links the private and public in the lives of the characters and amplifies the sense of the past she brings to the reader (whatever the character's awareness). Maggie's " 'prompting to go to your nearest friends—to remain where all the ties of your life have been formed' " is brought into direct relation with the " 'human needs' " prompting the " 'original constitution' " of the Church (supposed " 'to represent the feeling of the community so that every parish should be a family knit together by Christian brotherhood' "). Savonarola's dream is likewise both private and public, as his own "hunger" is not to be separated from his vision of "a pure community, worthy to lead the way in the renovation of the Church and the world."[38]

Religious ideals such as these, held by characters who are men of the Church, by bearing witness to an idea of community once vigorous but no longer so, purposefully dramatize discontinuity. At the same time, however, in all of George Eliot's fiction, a basic or root continuity of fellowship is also affirmed. As though reminding the reader of fundamental but often ignored or forgotten truths, it demonstrates the continuing force of the "primitive," the "simple," and of the kinship that survives all change. Romola's drift towards death is arrested by a "new baptism" that affirms "the simpler relations of the human being to his fellow-men" (ch. 69, p. 545). Felix Holt goes free because Esther's "incongruously simple" testimony and "inspired ignorance" transform the disagreement and hostility of the townspeople into cooperation and sympathy (chaps. 46–47). "Simple inspiration" is also the force that moves Dorothea "to show her human fellowship" to Lydgate and Rosamond in *Middlemarch* (chaps. 76, 77, 81). In *Daniel Deronda*, as

36. *MF*, ch. 58, p. 453; *DD*, ch. 11, p. 159.
37. "The Authority of the Past in George Eliot's Novels," p. 143.
38. *MF*, ch. 55, pp. 432–33; *R*, ch. 35, p. 308.

well, we are shown the "way our brother may be in the stead of God to us" (ch. 64, p. 833). Because the dramatized needs are in each case so elemental as to be irrefutable, they result in a poetry powerful in its appeal. Yet within the fuller context of the growth of an individual, it tends also to be a flawed poetry, as we will discuss in this chapter's concluding section. For now, we merely note what George Eliot points out and what her fiction often reveals—that a poetry based on a primitive simplicity of wants can meet only in a limited way the needs of people living in a complex society.

A NEW POETRY OF COMMUNITY

As early as 1856, or shortly before she began to write fiction, George Eliot was calling attention to a fundamental difference in the culture of early as opposed to late, or simple as opposed to complex, societies. Reviewing Longfellow's *Hiawatha* and Browning's *Men and Women*, she contrasts the "simplicity" of "primitive feelings and primitive forms of imagination" with the "complex questions and the complex forms of life" that belong to advanced civilizations.[39] Her own art was to move back and forth between the two in a great many ways, for while its cultural center shifts entirely to complex societies after *Silas Marner*, her efforts to dramatize how "we are all one with each other in primitive mortal needs" are constant (*MF*, ch. 58, p. 453). But simultaneously, and in the later fiction especially, she was also attempting to create a poetry of community that would take into account "mortal needs" far too complex to be met by the "primitive rough simplicity of wants" she associates with the "poetry" of "peasant life" (*MF*, ch. 30, p. 238). Requiring far more than inherited ties, sacred memories, and a simple work ethic, this new poetry entails deliberate and complicated adult choices. The "labour of choice" it requires from author, character, and reader is already evident in the movement from immediate family bonds in the earlier novels to the more spiritualized and generalized affirmations of kinship predominant in the later ones.[40] In addition to transforming Gemeinschaft continuities, such

39. [George Eliot], "Belles Lettres," *Westminster Review* 65: 164. See also "Belles Lettres," *Westminster Review* 66: 312.

40. The phrase "labour of choice" appears in *Mill on the Floss*, ch. 14, p. 135, where it is associated with the painful growing into consciousness that comes after the comforting, unquestioning acceptances of youth. A comparable phrase, "burden of choice," appears in *Romola* (ch. 68, p. 540). Both examples depict a simultaneous confrontation with and retreat from the complexities of the outer world.

choices give new definition to community by locating its poetry, as well as its prose, in the nature of Gesellschaft.

Within Tönnies's typology, a defining characteristic of Gesellschaft man is the constant exercise of choice, or of *Kürwille*. Translated as "rational" or "arbitrary will," and derived from " 'küren,' an ancient Germanic word for choosing," it requires deliberation, discrimination, calculation, and consciousness. Its opposite is *Wesenwille*, or the "natural," "integral," "essential will" associated with the habit, memory, and instinctive or inherited feelings encouraged by Gemeinschaft.[41] *Kürwille* is further distinguished from *Wesenwille* in its emphasis on ends over means. Whereas man in modern society regularly calculates his actions in terms of the end he wishes to achieve, in traditional society, where work is synonymous with a way of life, ends and means are likely to be one. "The fields, soil, and livestock of the peasant are in and of themselves ends," according to Tönnies, "whereas the means to the profits of the trader are sharply differentiated from the ends. . . . The more the actions of man are controlled by love, understanding, custom, religion, folkways, and mores, the less people, animals, and things are thought of as mere means to ends."[42] As we have seen, contrasts such as these abound in the images of Gemeinschaft and Gesellschaft present in George Eliot's fiction. At the same time, however, the conscious decisions she too associates with living in complex and advanced (as opposed to simple and primitive) societies are essential to her delineation of characters who purposefully choose to repudiate the Gesellschaft of the marketplace and to devote their lives to a social good they must themselves define.

For Felix, " 'to determine for myself' " is synonymous with the " 'great aims' " that define his private life and his social calling. Justifying both he refers constantly to what he has voluntarily chosen:

> "I would never choose to withdraw myself from the labour and common burthen of the world; but I do choose to withdraw myself from the push and scramble for money and position."
>
> [ch. 27, p. 362

> "It is just because I'm a very ambitious fellow, with very hungry passions, wanting a great deal to satisfy me, that I have chosen

---

41. Heberle, "Sociological System of Ferdinand Tönnies," p. 52; *G&G*, p. 105; Loomis and McKinney, Introduction to *G&G*, p. 5.
42. Loomis and McKinney, Introduction to *G&G*, pp. 5–6.

to give up what people call worldly good. At least that has been
one determining reason. It all depends upon what a man gets into
his consciousness. . . . There are two things I've got present in that
way: one of them is the picture of what I should hate to be. I'm
determined never to go about . . . telling professional lies for profit;
or to get tangled in affairs where I must wink at dishonesty and
pocket the proceeds, and justify that knavery as part of a system
that I can't alter."

[ch. 27, p. 363

"I am a man of this generation; I will try to make life less bitter
for a few within my reach. It is held reasonable enough to toil for
the fortunes of a family, though it may turn to imbecility in the
third generation. I choose a family with more chances in it."

[ch. 27, p. 367

In addition to declaring himself " 'a man of this generation,' "
Felix also affirms his heritage, but while he speaks of having " 'the
blood of a line of handicraftsmen in my veins,' " the continuation
of that line is for him a matter of deliberate choice (ch. 27, pp.
366–67).

To realize his " 'inward vocation,' " furthermore, Felix turns to
forces distinctive to Gesellschaft. In the same way that public opinion in modern society is for Tönnies equivalent to belief, faith, or
creed in traditional society, so " 'public opinion—the ruling belief
in society about what is right and what is wrong, what is honourable and what is shameful' " is for Felix " 'the greatest power under
heaven.' "[43] Felix, of course, is defining public opinion, not as it
is, but as it should be. Not only here, but also in *The Mill on the
Floss* and *Middlemarch*, George Eliot exposes how the voices of
public opinion lend themselves to subterfuge—to people making
"their consciences perfectly easy in doing what satisfied their
own egoism" while pretending to be making "a neighbour unhappy for her good" or "for the preservation of Society."[44] But another force "evolved by man's consciousness"—the force of education—holds out the possibility of making public opinion what it
should be (*G&G*, p. 231). Thus Felix's plan " 'to be a demagogue
of a new sort' " is in essence a plan to educate public opinion (ch.
27, p. 366). By teaching people not " 'to make public questions
which concern the welfare of millions a mere screen for their own
petty private ends,' " he would turn public opinion into " 'the

43. *G&G*, pp. 220–22, 231, 268–69; *FH*, ch. 30, p. 401.
44. *MF*, ch. 55, pp. 429–30; ch. 57, p. 442; *M*, ch. 74, p. 543.

steam that is to work the engines' " of genuine social reform (ch. 30, p. 401).

In Lydgate and Klesmer, as well, the commitment to vocation is distinctively Gesellschaft, rooted in science for the one and in art for the other, or in the culture thought to be as characteristic of advanced societies as the marketplace mentality it opposes. Lydgate's aspirations, as James F. Scott points out, ally him with Comte's "would-be agents of social reconstruction," men " 'of the new world with complete scientific and moral cultivation.' "[45] Lydgate's great flaw is that in choosing to dedicate himself to science, he does not simultaneously choose consciously enough to repudiate conventional material wants, and they finally overtake him. Thus the scientist in Lydgate is defeated by the incomplete moral cultivation of the man; but his chosen vocation demands nonetheless high ambition, original thought, and public contribution.

Klesmer too combines aspirations at once personal, professional, and social; but instead of being compromised by material needs, they are fueled by his opposition to them. As with Felix, both what he opposes and what he affirms participate in the nature of Gesellschaft. Arguing with a politician, Klesmer denounces all those who rally round the banner of " 'Buy cheap, sell dear,' " as well as that "lack of idealism in English politics, which left all mutuality between distant races to be determined simply by the need of a market." The " 'cosmopolitan ideas' " he advances posit "mutuality" through " 'a fusion of races,' " and give equality of place to art and politics. The one, no less than the other, he argues, contributes to the running of nations and the shaping of an age. Defining the role of the " 'creative artist,' " and declaring himself to be " 'no more a mere musician than a great statesman is a mere politician,' " he says:

> "We help to rule the nations and make the age as much as any other public men. We count ourselves on level benches with legislators. And a man who speaks effectively through music is compelled to something more difficult than parliamentary eloquence."
>
> [*DD*, ch. 22, pp. 283–84

---

45. James F. Scott, "George Eliot, Positivism, and the Social Vision of *Middlemarch*," p. 62. Scott offers a lucid analysis of George Eliot's ambivalence toward positivism. His assessment of Lydgate, however, differs from mine, since he believes Lydgate fully "conforms to Comte's specifications" (p. 70).

Within the overall structure of *Daniel Deronda*, furthermore, Klesmer serves to measure the many artists, artistes, and *artistes man-
qués* depicted in the novel. As Douglas Fricke points out, in contrast to "the self-absorbed artist, who uses art as either a social
stepping-stone, a means to financial gain, or a means to escape or
reject duty and responsibility in the real world of human problems," Klesmer is "the dedicated artist who pursues beauty within
the realm of social and moral responsibility."[46]

For Felix, Lydgate, and Klesmer, then, work is synonymous, as
it is in Gemeinschaft, with "a way of life" (*G&G*, p. 5). Their way
is distinctly Gesellschaft, however, democratic rather than aristocratic, equalitarian rather than hierarchical. Their work, furthermore, involves those forces of Gesellschaft—public opinion, science,
and art—most responsible for social regeneration within the nineteenth-century tradition of social thought shared by Tönnies and
George Eliot. For her, art was most important, but not only because it was her chosen vocation. Art has also an inclusiveness
missing from the other two. The power of public opinion is not to
be separated, after all, from the power of language, a point George
Eliot makes while considering the relation between "public opinion" and "social duty" during a discussion of authorship (*Essays*,
p. 438). The link between public opinion and a workaday world
in need of reform (implicit in Felix's references to lies, or in Klesmer's mockery of the "Buy cheap, sell dear" slogan) is, furthermore,
directly related to the corruption of language in Gesellschaft. Language unifies ends and means by expressing and uncovering feelings, meanings, and significances; but "traders and designing, am-
bitious persons" subvert its original purpose by using it as "a tool
. . . to deceive, to advertise, to exaggerate" (*G&G*, p. 5). In order
for public opinion, then, to be a positive force, art has first to restore language to its original purpose. While science, as well, was
to contribute to the shaping of a new public opinion, its role was
secondary. Unlike art, which is both intellectual and emotional,
the appeal of science seemed to be primarily rational. Art, because
it had originated in Gemeinschaft, had also the advantage of continuity.

At the same time, the inclusiveness of George Eliot's art is related to her effort to turn her back neither to science nor to the task
of educating public opinion. Her own ideal remained "the continual intercommunication of sensibility and thought" (*Essays*, p.
436). Like Piero di Cosimo (the artist in *Romola*), she sought to

46. Douglas Fricke, "Art and Artists in *Daniel Deronda*," p. 220.

unite "empirical observation and spiritual intuition," discovering truths by way of a penetrative imagination that ponders the surfaces it would get beyond.[47] The portrait of Cosimo, furthermore, greatly resembles the poet in Browning's "How It Strikes a Contemporary," part of which she quotes in the 1856 review. Fancying that Browning's "description of a poet applies to himself," she applauds his "freshness, originality," and "subtle, penetrating spirit," along with his "clear eye, . . . vigorous grasp, and courage to utter what he sees and handles":

> His keen glance pierces into all the secrets of human character, but, being as thoroughly alive to the outward as to the inward, he reveals those secrets, not by a process of dissection, but by dramatic painting.

> ["Belles Lettres," *Westminster Review* 65: 161

Like Browning's poet, in her art George Eliot sought to neglect neither the outward material world nor the "underground stream," though to do so included the risk of being thought too analytical and scientific.

Although fully aware of how difficult it is to change public opinion, her efforts to educate the reader were nonetheless constant. Because they were also comprehensive—purposefully excluding nothing that might help to convey the "vast sum of conditions" and the "wide relations" that connect them—the process of inclusion is one to which we must continually return.[48] At this point, I want simply to note how her way of putting characters to the test of perceiving the "sum of conditions" and relations that connect them calls attention to the inadequacies of customary modes of education and incorporates an alternate standard.

Whether one turns to the first of the Gesellschaft novels or to the last, to *The Mill on the Floss* or to *Daniel Deronda*, the ability of a character to make "a wide comparison of facts," or a "wide kind of inference," involves judgments based not only on the sensibility of the character but also on the education he or she has received.[49] Sometimes the focus of the criticism is formal schooling, as in the satirical treatment of the "method of education" Tom is made to suffer at Mr. Stelling's in *The Mill on the Floss*, or in the attack on

47. Hugh Witemeyer, *George Eliot and the Visual Arts*, p. 58; see also p. 172.
48. The phrase "wide relations" appears in all the Gesellschaft novels; "vast sum . . ." is from *MF*, ch. 30, p. 239.
49. Passages quoted from *MF*, ch. 14, pp. 119, 122, but the same point is made in *DD*, ch. 4, p. 71; ch. 32, p. 415.

the inadequacies of the "university methods" Deronda experiences at Cambridge—the one found faulty for "uniformity of method and independence of circumstances," and the other for failing to provide "any insight into the principles which form the vital connections of knowledge."[50] At other times, and particularly for female characters, the emphasis is on the absence of schooling. Although Maggie, for instance, longs to be educated, the instruction she receives is so haphazard as to cause her mind to remain "not active in questioning premises, but only in drawing wide inferences" (*MF*, ch. 6, p. 40, n. 6).

George Eliot would have her readers do both. The standard of judgment she applies to education, as these examples reveal, incorporates the most basic premises of natural history. At certain moments, natural history is even summoned directly. "Mental inability," as well as thoughtless class prejudices inherited from Gemeinschaft, blind Mrs. Transome to a great many things, including the unconventional Mr. Lyon—"not from studied haughtiness, but from sheer mental inability to consider him—as a person ignorant of natural history is unable to consider a fresh-water polype otherwise than as a sort of animated weed, certainly not fit for table" (*FH*, ch. 38, p. 478). A "knowledge of natural history," in contrast, makes her son Harold "acquainted with many strange animals, together with the ways of catching and taming them"; but having been acquired solely for the purposes of electioneering, it too is severely limited (*FH*, ch. 16, p. 267). Used to turn people into tools, his knowledge of history exemplifies its corruption in Gesellschaft. No less ironical is the pretension to learning satirized in *Daniel Deronda* as in the "astonished questioning from minds to which the idea of live Jews, out of a book, suggested a difference deep enough to be almost zoological, as of a strange race in Pliny's Natural History that might sleep under the shade of its own ears" (ch. 58, p. 775).

Although natural history, in each of these examples, is measured according to its absence or subversion, George Eliot continues to incorporate its premises into her judgments by attending to the conditions of a character's life and time. Those conditions, she makes clear, always constitute a sort of education, but one likely to be severely limited. How she would take the very deficiencies of customary education—whether located in formal or informal education, in the self, or in social conditions—and turn them into a

50. *MF*, ch. 14, pp. 122–25; *DD*, ch. 16, p. 220.

strategy for educating the reader, is illustrated by the following passage from *The Mill on the Floss*:

> Tom, like every one of us, was imprisoned within the limits of his own nature, and his education had simply glided over him, leaving a slight deposit of polish: if you are inclined to be severe on his severity, remember that the responsibility of tolerance lies with those who have the wider vision.
>
> [*MF*, ch. 56, p. 437

The narrator here, like Lydgate, Felix, or Klesmer elsewhere, simultaneously opposes and affirms qualities exemplary of Gesellschaft: self-enclosure marks its prose, and "the wider vision" its poetry.

As we have seen, this poetry of Gesellschaft is new in that it requires deliberate, wisely educated choices and encourages tolerance and regard for other people, in contrast to the prejudice characteristic of traditional Gemeinschaft. Unlike the poetry of traditional community, which like the nature of Gemeinschaft itself is directed "inwardly toward the center of the locality," the poetry of Gesellschaft is directed outward (*G&G*, p. 79). Instead of mirroring a whole that is integral and self-contained, and instead of embodying intrinsic and inherited connections that by nature orient the individual toward the community, this new poetry must create, not merely reflect, fellow-feeling. The connections to be perceived are in theory no less intrinsic, but because they are far more complex and wide-reaching, they are far less obvious. This knowledge, then, that is exclusive to the culture of Gesellschaft and essential to its poetry is hard to achieve.

For other reasons, as well, the regeneration of community by way of the wider vision is fraught with difficulties. While the choices made by characters such as Felix, Lydgate, and Klesmer—or by George Eliot herself in choosing to become a novelist—are prompted by the desire to address and redress complex Gesellschaft realities, still their decisions are marked by an individualism that threatens the very unities they were struggling to create. Though their individualism is directed against selfishness and isolation, the traits that separate them (and such characters as Maggie, Romola, and Dorothea) from the majority who choose material ends lend to them a singularity that enables the reader to dismiss them as extremes. What is more, their idealistic beliefs and the originality of their ideas place them in the position of antagonists and create estrangements between them and the community. Even in Dorothea, the exercise of the belief that " 'people are almost always better than their neighbours think they are,' " requires "an active force of antagonism within her," and causes her to be regarded "as the dangerous part of the family machinery."[51]

In other ways, too, the individualism that is a defining mark of Gesellschaft, even when it serves to generate "the wider vision," raises a good many questions about the possibility of renewing community in the modern world. No less problematic, for instance, is the emphasis on rational choice. George Eliot was acutely aware of the ease and the frequency with which such choices are entirely self-serving. As though loathe to see in Raffles's cunning a sign of his "intellect," she hedges and yet connects the two: "And if the cunning which calculates on the meanest feelings in men could be called intellect, he had his share" (*M*, ch. 53, p. 388). Similarly though she believed the capacity for modification to be essential to the process of positive change within individuals, in characters such as Tito and Christian she reveals adaptability to be far more destructive to solidarity than is "brutish unmodifiableness" (*DD*, ch. 58, p. 778).

At the same time, her wish to shape characters, who though they are "men of the world" yet consciously *choose* the right, is evident in her response to an analysis of Harold Transome written by John Crombie Brown, her proofreader at Blackwood. Though she rarely endorsed a reader's interpretation, she writes in this instance of how "pleased" she is "with his fine sense of the points in Harold Transome and his history" (*Letters* 7: 180). Taking Harold to be "one of the most difficult and one of the most strikingly wrought out conceptions, not only in the works of George Eliot, but in modern fiction," Brown first establishes how "clear-headed, hard, shrewd," and "greatly alive to his own interests and importance" Harold is, and then asks this question:

> How comes it that this "well-tanned man of the world" thus always chooses the higher and more difficult right; and does this in no excitement or enthusiasm, but coolly, calculatingly, with clear forecasting of all the consequences, and fairly entitled to assume that these shall be to his own peril or detriment?[52]

51. *M*, ch. 72, p. 537; ch. 77, p. 566; ch. 84, p. 596.
52. John Crombie Brown, *The Ethics of George Eliot's Works*, pp. 28–29.

His answer is not nearly so well-pointed as his question, since it confirms what he had hoped to explain, the split between Harold's Gesellschaft self and his true essence:

> We see that, howsoever overlaid by temperament and restrained by circumstance, the noblest capability in man still survives and is active in him. He *can* choose the right which imperils his own interests, because it *is* the right; he *can* set his back on the wrong which would advantage himself, because it *is* the wrong. That he does this coolly, temperately, without enthusiasm, with full, clear forecasting of all the consequences, is only saying that he is Harold Transome still. That he does so choose when the forecast probabilities are all against those objects which the mere man of the world most desires, proves that under that hard external crust dwells as essential a nobleness as any we recognise in Felix Holt.
>
> [pp. 30–31

Brown's difficulties, moreover, in explaining Harold's contradictory behavior lie within the character George Eliot created, and relate to contradictions she herself felt. While she would have the reader believe that all choice requires an effort of independent thought, she creates in Harold a character whose "noble" decisions seem to be made in spite of, rather than by virtue of, his intellectual capacities. Here and elsewhere George Eliot's skepticism about intellect as a unifying force leads to a paradox, for while reason makes possible self-serving calculations altogether inimical to solidarity, it discloses as well the complex interdependencies on which all notions of modern community depend.

Still an additional problem is posed by the integration of feeling and thought required by a comprehensive knowledge of relations. Although George Eliot frequently tells the reader that it is futile to "seek wisdom apart from the human sympathies," and that it is essential for the affections to be " 'clad with knowledge,' " few characters embody such a synthesis.[53] Similarly, though the appeals to "the wider vision" are constant in her fiction, its actual nature is left vague. As though redressing this problem, Deronda's sense of "universal kinship" is made to complete itself in his Jewish heritage. In most other respects, however, Deronda participates in the pattern noted in Felix, Lydgate, and Klesmer. Like them, he chooses to reject "motives . . . of a more pushing sort," and to separate himself from "the commonplace calculators of the market,"

53. *R*, ch. 15, p. 159; *DD*, ch. 36, p. 508.

while seeking to connect himself instead with a social good. In
Deronda too, then, the secular urge for community remains powerful, but it is no more fulfilled in him than in them, for his "social
captainship" is grounded finally in an ancient and exclusive religion.[54]

SEPARATING PILLARS

For different reasons, both the new and the continuing poetry in
George Eliot's fiction, as we have seen, are brought into question
by the natural histories in which they are embedded, making simplicity impossible but desirable, individualism estranging when
liberating, intellect expansive and restrictive, modifications salutary and damaging, the integration of thought and feeling necessary
but absent. For these reasons, and others, there is a continual tension within the rhetoric of George Eliot's fiction between actual
separateness or fragmentariness, on the one hand, and a vision of
unity, on the other. Its formal counterpart is the tension between
her idealism of conception and her realism of presentation, one aspect of which is the relation between the workaday worlds of her
fiction and the poetry she brings to them. Its sociological counterpart is the Gemeinschaft-Gesellschaft typology; and not only
because it opposes communitarian values, emotional ties, and affective habits and traditions to individualistic values, conscious
choice, and rational calculation. Even more to the point are
Gemeinschaft and Gesellschaft tendencies coexisting in number-
less ways. A mixture of the two, in addition to being far more characteristic of George Eliot's natural histories and of modern social
life than is the one or the other by itself, is also essential to her
creation of a modern poetry of community, which depends ultimately on her readers' ability to discover and comprehend, within
the workaday world of Gesellschaft, connections bound to be un-
even, complex, and various. Such blendings of Gemeinschaft and
Gesellschaft elements, no less than the separations between them,
contribute amply to the tensions within George Eliot's fiction and
participate in the struggle to affirm community. As we have seen,
such difficulties arise even when the Gemeinschaft continuities
are positive, or when the characters are committed to reforming
Gesellschaft. Intensifying this struggle, and yet engaging positively
in it by educating the reader, are a great many scenes in which the
Gemeinschaft-Gesellschaft mix works to deny fellow-feeling.

54. DD, ch. 11, p. 159; ch. 16, p. 219; ch. 38, p. 527; ch. 63, p. 819.

In traditional community, the three pillars of kinship, neighborhood, and common practices and beliefs are mutually supporting, together creating a cohesive society. But in George Eliot's depictions of Gesellschaft, they are for the most part separate forces, and their negative aspects render them either mutually perverting or mutually exclusive. In "Amos Barton" and "Janet's Repentance," for instance, while many scenes depict "a neighbourhood where people are well acquainted with each other's private affairs," finding "your neighbour . . . good for nothing" tends to be the general rule.[55] Similarly, the religion that is supposed to be a unifying force is so divided against itself as to make Christian fellowship as uncommon as true neighborliness. Both are denied in the resounding " 'No!' " that opens "Janet's Repentance":

> "No!" said lawyer Dempster, . . . "as long as my Maker grants me power of voice and power of intellect, I will take every legal means to resist the introduction of demoralizing, methodistical doctrine into this parish."
>
> [ch. 1, p. 247

Likewise, the kinship ties dramatized in the family gatherings of *The Mill on the Floss* suggest not brotherly and sisterly love, but exclusive, intolerant, and unloving clannishness:

> There was in this family a peculiar tradition as to what was the right thing in household management and social demeanour, and . . . a painful inability to approve the condiments or the conduct of families ungoverned by the Dodson tradition. . . . There were some Dodsons less like the family than others—that was admitted; but in so far as they were "kin," they were of necessity better than those who were "no kin." And it is remarkable that while no individual Dodson was satisfied with any other individual Dodson, each was satisfied, not only with him or her self, but with the Dodsons collectively.
>
> [ch. 6, pp. 39–40

In Tom, this "family feeling" that has "the character of clanship" ends in a thoroughly isolating "personal pride" detaching him from all but Dorlcote Mill (ch. 56, p. 437). In the other Dodsons, the adherence to custom is itself a separating force because it is above all a mark of their clanship.

55. Passages quoted are from *SCL*, "Amos Barton," ch. 4, pp. 76, 79; but the same sentiments are expressed in "Janet's Repentance," ch. 1, p. 251; ch. 2, pp. 257–58, 263–64.

As in her early portraits of Gesellschaft, in her later novels George Eliot continues to uncover traditional Gemeinschaft continuities that divide rather than unify a community. Indeed, the sense of family and religious ties turned inward and clannish, and of neighborhood ties exclusive of true neighborliness, intensifies. Kinship relations take on wide but negative political ramifications in *Romola* as the Medicis' plot "to save our Medicean skins" (ch. 23, p. 216). "Blood and family" and the absence of ties beyond them so isolate Mrs. Transome in *Felix Holt* as even to separate her from family (ch. 40, p. 494). " 'Worldly-spiritual cliqueism' "—the religious counterpart of family clannishness—lies behind Bulstrode's private "tribunal" and the public tribunals that expel him from Middlemarch, both of them marked by "the use of wide phrases for narrow motives," and each in its own way subversive of fellow-feeling.[56]

Perhaps the most extreme example of a Gemeinschaft attribute become a force of radical separation and ironic connection is that of Grandcourt in *Daniel Deronda*. His "importance as a subject of this realm," we are told, "was of the grandly passive kind which consists in the inheritance of land." Detached from everything save the land he has inherited, Grandcourt repeatedly uses his residences—in scenes set at Diplow, Gadsmere, Ryelands, and the Abbey at Topping slated to be his—to exercise "within his own sphere of interest" a ruthless dominion. Its appalling connection to a far larger world is more briefly, but no less brilliantly, established as George Eliot links his "qualities" and "ability" to "triumphal diplomacy of the widest continental sort," and to colonial rule of the foulest kind (*DD*, ch. 48, pp. 644–45, 655).

In each case, the cause and effect of the separation or corruption is the material, the mechanical, or the contractual. Behind the lack of genuine friendship in the *Scenes* is "the main line of self-interest" ("Janet's Repentance," ch. 10, p. 317). Behind the effort to stamp out religious revivalism are the related Gesellschaft forces of intellect and legal proceedings. In Bulstrode, sectarianism, which at its best "gets some warmth of brotherhood by walling in the sacred fire," is subverted by material interests.[57] "Worldly notions and habits" similarly effect the debasement of custom among the Dodsons and the displacement of social sentiment in the Medicean

56. *M*, ch. 17, p. 130; ch. 61, pp. 453–54; see also ch. 71, pp. 532–36; ch. 74, p. 543.

57. The qualified defense of sectarianism is from *MF*, ch. 31, p. 245, but the sentiment is expressed elsewhere as well.

"commercial nobility."[58] Such notions and habits infect even the aristocratic Grandcourt, for not unlike the breed of "commercial men" he dismisses as " 'brutes,' " he is "touched" by "political and social movements . . . only through the wire of his rental" (*DD*, ch. 48, pp. 644–45).

The corruption of the third pillar of community, through the erosion of a spiritual (though not necessarily religious) base, always attends those Gemeinschaft continuities that exert a strong negative force, the most comprehensive of which concern habit and custom. As Tönnies explains, in traditional Gemeinschaft shared habits beget customs, and "custom ever signifies community" (*Custom*, p. 98). The "ever," of course, applies only to Gemeinschaft; yet custom continues to exert a powerful, though debased, force in Gesellschaft. Instead of expressing such sentiments as "mutual affection and love," and of being "directed towards fraternal fellowship, cooperation and mutual aid," customs become "mere forms," or "empty forms," existing quite apart from the "moral sense which demands sincerity," and followed whether or not the corresponding sentiment exists.[59]

Custom, in this sense—for Tönnies, George Eliot, and many of the theorists known to them—signifies not community but society. Affecting religious and social practices alike, the debasement of custom in Gesellschaft implicates the third pillar of community through what Tönnies calls the "conventionalization of custom." Taking "to a large degree the place of the folkways, mores, and religion," but not like them "kept as sacred inheritance of the ancestors," convention strips custom of "piety" and renders it "cold," "superficial," or "refined." Custom become conventional, then, is custom become "soulless."[60] George Eliot has something very similar in mind when she equates "conventional worldly notions and habits" with "the most prosaic form of human life," for she means by *prosaic* what Tönnies means by *soulless*, namely "the absence of anything suggesting the ideal, the higher life."[61]

In George Eliot's fiction, this absence is frequently alluded to by the failure of social rituals and ceremonies to create a balanced rhythm between the everyday world and the special occasion, or to affirm the significance of certain events by endowing them with an importance at once individual and communal. Among the most

58. *MF*, ch. 30, p. 238; *R*, ch. 1, p. 13.
59. Tönnies, *Custom*, pp. 103–9, 116.
60. Tönnies, *Custom*, pp. 103–4, 116, 123, 125, 128; *G&G*, pp. 76, 229.
61. *MF*, ch. 30, p. 238; *Letters* 8: 466.

universal of such ceremonies are the funeral rites that prescribe, according to custom, the reverence to be shown to the dead. Such practices serve traditionally, as they do also in George Eliot's Gemeinschaft fictions, to link the dead and the living, the past and the present, the commonplace and the sacrosanct. For example, the prosaic and the poetic harmonize within the "beautifully rendered communion and ritual" of Thias's burial service in *Adam Bede*.[62] In the Gesellschaft fictions, however, the ceremony of funeral is either overly poeticized or made utterly prosaic.

In the *Scenes*, both Milly's death and Tryan's create a "hallowed precinct," but one so radically differentiated from the surrounding workaday life as to render their deaths too sacrosanct. Acknowledging the "hallowed precinct" to be "shut out from the world," George Eliot attempts to adjust the relation ("Amos Barton," ch. 9, p. 110). Yet, here and elsewhere, when complex societies are at issue, the poetic often displaces the prosaic or heightens the incongruity between the two. Attempting to counterbalance them, she follows Dempster's funeral with Tryan's:

> The faces looked very hard and unmoved that surrounded Dempster's grave.... The pallbearers were ... men whom Dempster had called his friends while he was in life; and worldly faces never look so worldly as at a funeral. They have the same effect of grating incongruity as the sound of a coarse voice breaking the solemn silence of night.
>
> ["Janet's Repentance," ch. 25, pp. 388–89

> He [Tryan] was followed by a long procession of mourning friends. ... Slowly, amid deep silence, the dark stream passed along Orchard Street, where eighteen months before the Evangelical curate had been saluted with hooting and hisses. ... The faces were not hard at this funeral; the burial-service was not a hollow form. Every heart there was filled with the memory of a man who, through a self-sacrificing life and in a painful death, had been sustained by the faith which fills that form with breath and substance.
>
> ["Janet's Repentence," ch. 28, p. 411

Clearly, the second scene is meant to offset the first, just as George Eliot always offers the poetry that affirms solidarity to place in perspective a realism of presentation that often suggests the absence of love; but the extreme idealization of the Tryan scene makes for

---

62. See Barbara Hardy's excellent discussion of Thias's funeral in *Rituals and Feeling in the Novels of George Eliot*, pp. 6–8.

its own imbalance, and consequently contributes to the incongruities it would correct.

Though many deaths take place in George Eliot's novels, after *Adam Bede* she dramatizes only one other burial service, perhaps because the ceremony of funeral seemed to her no longer to be "sustained by the faith which fills that form with breath and substance." Instead, the "form," as *The Mill on the Floss* makes clear, is dictated by propriety or respectability, and money or wills. In the one funeral she does dramatize—Featherstone's in *Middlemarch*—the full extent of its hollowness is laid bare. " 'This funeral,' " says Dorothea, seems " 'the most dismal thing I ever saw. It is a blot on the morning. I cannot bear to think that any one should die and leave no love behind' " (ch. 34, p. 240). Rather, Featherstone leaves behind a will and a great many relatives hoping to feed off a "limited store which each would have liked to get the most of." When they join together for his funeral procession, the "rites and ceremonies" they perform, instead of signifying reverence, barely disguise their rapaciousness. Only the reading of the will, because it concerns Featherstone's "demise" or the "merely legal aspect" of his death, is not a hollow form, but the substance is undisguisedly prosaic and quintessentially Gesellschaft.[63]

This emptying or darkening of ritual in the fiction set in modern times equally degrades ceremonies that are by nature festive and celebratory. To compare even briefly, for instance, the scenes describing the Christmas holidays in *Silas Marner* with those in *The Mill on the Floss*, *Middlemarch*, and *Daniel Deronda*, is to see again how the rituals that had once lifted events "above the level of common days" and strengthened "the primitive fellowship of kindred" no longer do so (*MF*, ch. 15, p. 136). Some festivities offer a momentary heightening, as in the opening paragraphs of the chapter in the *Mill* called "The Christmas Holidays," but the cheering image of old Father Christmas is soon dispelled by all the talk of "going to law," an action analogous to a "cockfight, in which it was the business of injured honesty to get a game bird with the best pluck and the strongest spurs" (p. 138). And in *Middlemarch* Christmas dinner and New Year's Day parties alike serve merely as ironic background for Lydgate's fierce estrangement from himself and from his wife because of financial difficulties. Making his already miserable situation even worse,

63. *M*, ch. 31, p. 223; ch. 35.

the merry Christmas bringing the happy New Year, when fellow-citizens expect to be paid for the trouble and goods they have smilingly bestowed on their neighbours, had so tightened the pressure of sordid cares on Lydgate's mind that it was hardly possible for him to think unbrokenly of any other subject.

[*M*, ch. 64, p. 473

At first glance, the New Year's Eve dance at the Mallinger estate in *Daniel Deronda* sounds festive and restorative:

It was always a beautiful scene, this dance on New Year's Eve, which had been kept up by family tradition as nearly in the old fashion as inexorable change would allow.

[ch. 36, p. 495

But despite its opulent grandeur, this scene too functions ironically, serving primarily as the mordant setting for the terrifying fears that alienate the newly married Gwendolen from her husband and herself, and attract her to Deronda. As bride and prospective mistress of the Abbey, she is guest of honor at the New Year's ball; yet she sits "in her splendid attire, like a white image of helplessness," her bitter feelings making empty both the celebration of her three-week-old marriage and "this festival in honour of the family estate" (ch. 36, pp. 495, 503–4). The traditional New Year's dance dramatized in *Silas Marner*, in contrast, is indeed a celebration or a "renewal by ceremony." As Michael Squires points out, "unlike the similar dance in *Daniel Deronda*," and despite the disturbing revelation that occurs in the middle, it confers "stability and meaning" on the community by revitalizing "orderly patterns of human life" (p. 96). In *Silas Marner* the holiday season further serves as background to the coming of love and the putting away of avarice, while in the novels set in the nineteenth century it brings to the foreground the absence of love and the pressure of material wants.

In such scenes the poetry of ceremony is absent because the attendant emotions make it impossible for ritual to lift events above the dead level of everyday existence. Elsewhere, custom and ceremony contribute to a specious poetry. For example, unity of spirit and disruptive deviation are brought together in Arthur's birthday celebration in *Adam Bede*, and in the many processional and holiday scenes in *Romola*. The entire community assembles for Arthur's coming-of-age party, and the dominant note is one of festive celebration, but "the dangerous divisions of class and rank" make for a "false harmony."[64] The treatment of ritual in *Romola* is often satirical: a "mimic" St. John the Baptist crowns the processional car of the Zecca (Mint) (ch. 8, p. 89); "spiritual pelting" at the "new Carnival, which was a sort of sacred parody of the old," forces people to surrender items they treasure to the Burning of Vanities bonfire (ch. 49, pp. 408–9). Yet the novel includes a defense of the " 'ancient symbols' " that give " 'rise to the sense of community in religion and law' " (ch. 8, p. 90).

In the fiction set in the nineteenth century, however, the treatment of public ritual is scarcely anything but ironical. The deviations become the norm, and they establish an increasingly counterfeit holiday world in which the negative qualities, rather than the positive ones, of the everyday world are intensified. In both *Adam Bede* and *Felix Holt*, for instance, the Benefit Clubs display a similar motto, but in the former the banner with the words " 'Let brotherly love continue' " is innocently carried by the members who play at Arthur's feast, while in the latter it is Chubb, the self-serving and relentlessly calculating publican, who declares: " 'Love an' 'armony's the word on our club's flag, an' love an' 'armony's the meaning of "The Sugar Loaf, William Chubb." ' " Making doubly negative the corruption of custom into customer, Chubb is unctuous toward the miners who make a habit of coming to his "public," and complicitous with Johnson, the corrupt electioneering agent from London, who would bribe the miners he calls his "neighbours" into disturbing the Nomination and Election Day events by treating them to drinks and "a day's holiday."[65]

Between *Felix Holt* and *Daniel Deronda*, the connections between customary practices and moral corruption intensify. In *Daniel Deronda*, the tone at the start is set not by a genial coachman, but by "the automatic voice . . . of the croupier" calling " '*Faites votre jeu, mesdames et messieurs.*' " The setting—"one of those splendid resorts which the enlightenment of ages has prepared for the . . . pleasure [of gambling] at a heavy cost of gilt mouldings, dark-toned colour and chubby nudities"—suggests a blatantly false poetry, and one clearly not restricted to the world of pleasure. Deliberately pairing "winning money in business" and "winning money in play," the opening scene in *Daniel Deronda*, as Ian Milner has shown, brilliantly anticipates the dangerous game of life Gwendolen begins to play when the failure of the joint-stock concern of Grapnell & Co. (announced in the very next chapter) leaves

64. Hardy, *Rituals and Feeling*, p. 10.
65. *AB*, ch. 22, p. 214; *FH*, ch. 11, pp. 215, 224, 228.

her moneyless.[66] So close to Tönnies's conception of Gesellschaft are these connections between "personal gambling" and the "wider world of business operations" that he uses the same analogy: "For commerce is by nature akin to gambling (le commerce est un jeu)" (G&G, p. 91).

While gambling plays an important role in other of George Eliot's novels, the associations created in *Daniel Deronda*, through scene and echoing metaphors, are unequaled elsewhere. Another kind of scene, however, equally rich in its metaphorical extensions and widely at play in the novels set in the nineteenth century, depicts with great regularity how holiday practices, instead of giving symbolic expression to unity of spirit, reveal a self-centered vying for attention and predominance. Their subject matter at its most direct deals with custom as costume. Because the habitual practices associated with fashion are at once perhaps the most rapidly changing in their particulars, and among the most obstinately persistent in their continuing social power, they represent the conventional at its most trivial and commonplace. "Fashion, like custom, invades every province of life," Tönnies explains, but "it is custom-become-fluid . . . casual and superficial. Therefore it is custom which has become perverted into its contrary" (*Custom*, pp. 122–23). For George Eliot, the most serious effect of this contrariety, which she too locates in the identity between "custom & fashion," is that while together they "doubtless, represent a great social power . . . it is not the power of love."[67]

The world of fashion represents, instead, the power of rank and status, class and wealth. It intrudes into religious practices, displacing spirituality and Christian brotherhood. Already in "Janet's Repentance," the customs of churchgoing, of dressing well for church, and of mocking the unfashionably dressed, are shown to be one and the same. "Few places could present a more brilliant show of outdoor toilettes than might be seen issuing from Milby church," George Eliot writes, but "the respect for the Sabbath, manifested in this attention to costume, was unhappily counterbalanced by considerable levity of behavior during the prayers and sermon," especially toward "persons inferior in dress and demeanour" (ch. 2, pp. 254–55). The confirmation scene likewise reveals "Sunday sensations" to be so "chiefly referable" to wearing one's "best frocks" and having "hair particularly well dressed" that even the

---

66. *DD*, ch. 1, pp. 35–40; Milner, *Structure of Values*, p. 112.
67. "More Leaves," p. 369; *MF*, ch. 17, p. 155.

bishop is measured by the costume he wears. "Sensations" of this sort are shown to be entirely prosaic not only for the values they embody but also for their total neglect of the "working-day look" the world wears for those who labor in the fields and at the hand-looms (ch. 5, p. 286). Devoting an entire chapter to "Charity in Full-Dress," George Eliot in *The Mill on the Floss* again turns a church activity into a fashion show and reveals how far removed from true charity it is (ch. 48). That fashion is also far more power-ful than charity is later punctuated by the metaphor that describes Dr. Kenn's failed efforts to elicit from his parishioners kindness toward Maggie. "He suddenly found himself as powerless," George Eliot writes, "as he was aware he would have been if he had at-tempted to influence the shape of bonnets" (ch. 57, p. 441).

Costume is also used by George Eliot to reveal within the purely secular sphere of kinship the perversion of custom into its con-trary of unlovingness. In *The Mill on the Floss*, for instance, rituals of dress help to reveal both the paganism that unifies the Dodson kin and the economic rivalry that inspires their reverence for "whatever was customary and respectable" (ch. 30, p. 239). Each of the Dodson sisters is introduced and differentiated by her way of dressing; and each of the ceremonial family gatherings is marked by rivalries reflected in modes of dress. Sister Pullet, who "had married a gentleman farmer, and had leisure and money to carry her crying and everything else to the highest pitch of respecta-bility," appears at the first gathering wearing a costume matched in extravagance only by her tears (ch. 7, p. 53). Mocking both, the narrator links them to the debasement of custom and displacement of emotion in so-called civilized society:

> It is a pathetic sight and a striking example of the complexity in-troduced into the emotions by a high state of civilisation—the sight of a fashionably drest female in grief. From the sorrow of a Hotten-tot to that of a woman in large buckram sleeves, with several brace-lets on each arm, an architectural bonnet, and delicate ribbon-strings—what a long series of gradations! In the enlightened child of civilisation the abandonment characteristic of grief is checked and varied in the subtlest manner.
>
> [ch. 7, p. 51

Weeping for the death of an acquaintance, Mrs. Pullet wears her grief as she wears her bonnet—for adornment—and as the passage continues she begins to prepare her ornaments for a return to "a calm and healthy state." In contrast, the genuine emotions that

emerge during this family gathering are quarrelsome from beginning to end, whether the subject be Tom's education, Maggie's
hair, funerals, millinery, or money. The overriding importance of
the last, moreover, turns the feast into a disastrous feud.

Even when the metamorphosis of custom into costume seems
relatively innocent, it is marked by an inversion of value. In another chapter of *The Mill on the Floss*, for instance, a "procession"
leads merely to a shrouded "best room" where an expensive new
bonnet that is the pride of one sister and the envy of the other is
unveiled with "funereal solemnity" (ch. 9, pp. 80–81). At the opposite extreme, though no more generous, is the shabby "costume"
("selected with the high moral purpose of instilling perfect hu-
mility into Bessy and her children") Sister Glegg puts on for the
family council (ch. 23, p. 183). At this meeting, the refusal of aid
to the bankrupt Tullivers is so absolute as to suggest to Maggie
"a world where people behaved the best to those they did not pretend to love, and that did not belong to them" (ch. 25, p. 208).
The novel reveals, furthermore, how even Maggie thinks elegant
and expensive dress essential to producing "any effect with her
person"—"Girls are so accustomed," the narrator explains, "to
think of dress as the main ground of vanity" (ch. 33, p. 263). At
the same time, the narrative strategy of moving from Maggie to
"girls" renders costume, however clannish or idiosyncratic in its
particulars, emblematic of the great difference between custom as
a great social force and custom as a force of social goodness.

Good society, of course, is defined by a great deal more than
costume. It has to do with manners as well, but as Tönnies points
out and as George Eliot regularly dramatizes, "manners are 'dictated' by fashion, because the *good* society shows them off in order
to indicate its 'refinement' " (*Custom*, pp. 123–24). Maggie's manners and dress, for instance, not only mirror her "tender and affectionate" nature but also serve as foil to the "artificial airs," "pre-
tentious etiquette," and "petty contrivances other women have,"
especially women wanting to assert their position in "good society."[68] This identity of manners and fashion—nowhere more apparent than in the equation of "good society" and "fashionable
society"—continues in George Eliot's late novels to uncover social
and moral corruption, and to sanction unconventional behavior.
Sometimes the identity functions metaphorically, as in the rejection
of fashion that accompanies Felix's avowal of loyalty to the working

68. *MF*, ch. 44, p. 349; ch. 47, p. 375; ch. 48, p. 376; ch. 49, p. 385.

class, or in the allusions to "costume and horsemanship," " 'high door-step and a brass knocker' " that convey his contempt for " 'clerkly gentility' " (ch. 5, pp. 144–45; ch. 11, p. 219).

In addition, here and elsewhere, whether through scene or image, all the accouterments of good society testify in George Eliot's Gesellschaft fictions to fashion's invasive power and to a corresponding conventionalization of custom. "Marriage," in *Middlemarch*, "according to custom," depends greatly on "good looks, vanity, and merely canine affection"; and "genteel visiting" on "suitable furniture and complete dinner-service," not "esteem" (ch. 1, pp. 6–7; ch. 23, p. 170). Tönnies writes that "fashion is always a phase and a symptom of the dissolution of custom" (*Custom*, p. 129). George Eliot dramatizes a good many of the phases, ranging from the relatively innocent to the sophisticatedly corrupt, and renders them symptomatic of the dissolution of custom. In the first and most transitional of her Gesellschaft novels, she puts to rout at the close "all the artificial vesture of our life" (*MF*, ch. 58, p. 453). In the last and most contemporary of her novels, she makes the world of "highest fashion," complete with "bedizened child," entirely one with the gambler's world depicted throughout (*DD*, ch. 1, pp. 35–36).

In a great many ways, then, the Gemeinschaft continuities present in the Gesellschaft worlds of George Eliot's fiction reveal the disintegration of community. Each of the three pillars, as we have seen, suffers a corruption, but the degradation of custom and ceremony—because it is related to the third pillar, or to those forces which by virtue of their adaptability were to play a crucial role in the regeneration of community—is in the last analysis more serious than the fragmentation of neighborhood and kinship ties. George Eliot's realism of presentation particularizes the ways in which custom in Gesellschaft is corrupted into fashion and convention, and thus subverts community. Tönnies later documents this same development, but he ends his argument once he establishes that "the morality of custom has . . . become inadequate" and needs to be "purified" and supplemented by a "conscious ethic." As a result, he fails to demonstrate how custom might be transformed to achieve within modern society "the joyous creation of *Gemeinschaft*" (*Custom*, p. 146). Because George Eliot's realism of presentation captures only too vividly the disintegration of positive communal values, her treatment of custom in Gesellschaft is also unsettling. Using the novelist's tools, however, she dramatizes not only the negative transformations the social theorists were noting, but positive ones as well.[69] At the same time that she reveals the poetry of ritual and public ceremony to be either utterly prosaic or delusively poetic, she also reveals how this process may begin to be reversed, as we shall now see.

A FALSE POETIC CORRECTED:
ROMOLA, LYDGATE, ESTHER, AND GWENDOLEN

Just as the holiday-workaday images uncover in the customary practices of Gesellschaft a false poetic detrimental to community, they also reveal the importance and value of discriminating between the true and false notions that sustain and subvert social existence. As though returning this complex of images to its origins, while endowing it with new life by giving it fictional form, George Eliot attempts to reestablish that harmonious alternation or convergence between the poetic and the prosaic that signifies the spirit of Gemeinschaft, to be located now not in custom, but in self-aware-ness, conscious fellow-feeling, and social understanding. Thus in her later work, the intricate process of discerning between the prose and poetry of community is dramatized primarily through individual characters struggling to make the same kinds of dis-criminations toward which George Eliot would lead her reader. The transformations occur on the whole "without the aid of sacred ceremony or costume" (DD, ch. 35, p. 485); they depend, instead, on changes of perception, which lead in turn to individual modi-fications and eventually to social change.

Rituals are not absent from the later novels, and darkened cere-mony has an important function within them, but the poetry of community comes to depend on the inward revolutions experi-enced by individual characters. Positive rituals are also dramatized, but the ceremonies that accompany them are for the most part individual and personal.[70] At the same time, the sphere of the

69. Feuerbach is an exception in that he too was proposing positive trans-formations. The connection between "Feuerbach's revaluation of the main ceremonies of the Christian religion" and the poetry George Eliot would bring to her fiction is elucidated by U. C. Knoepflmacher, but only in terms of "the poetry of the old faith" (Religious Humanism, pp. 55–59).

70. Barbara Hardy offers a fine discussion of the "growing secularity and individuality of ritual" in M and DD, as illustrated by symbolic changes of dress in Dorothea, Mrs. Bulstrode, and Gwendolen. But "this personal creation of ritual" is better explained, I think, by the growing emphasis on conscious-ness in the later novels than by "the need for support from tradition" (Rituals and Feeling, pp. 5, 12–13).

private becomes public in a new way, as the psychological dramas experienced by certain characters both counter and measure innumerable "small social drama[s]" marked by a failure of "consciousness" and insensitivity to "wider relations" (*DD*, ch. 14, pp. 185–86). The emphasis in the psychological drama, consequently, is on learning how to discern between the prosaic and the truly poetic, and on the need to create fine adjustments between them. That this should be so is altogether fitting, for George Eliot took "the human task . . . to be the discerning and adjustment of opposite claims" (*TS*, p. 348). The adjustments required, however, are so difficult to attain as often to be only partially realized. Still, the very irresolutions speak forcefully to the problem of community in the modern world, for they both affirm and call into doubt the possibility of achieving Gemeinschaft among complicated individuals living in complex societies.

One character from each of the last four novels can serve to illustrate how George Eliot's use of workaday-holiday images helps to define what her narrator aptly calls an "uneasy, transforming process" (*DD*, ch. 35, p. 477). The characters to be considered— Romola, Esther, Lydgate, and Gwendolen—all start out with a false sense of the poetry in life, but finally arrive at some understanding of their own participation in the common life they once rejected. Through a difficult process of discovery, they adjust or even revise their initial sense of the prosaic and the poetic in individual and social life. This theme, as the differences between these characters illustrate, is limited, amplified, and complicated within George Eliot's later fiction. Romola and Lydgate, for example, are opposites in the sense that for Lydgate everyday life destroys the ideal purpose that ennobles common experience for Romola. Through Lydgate, moreover, George Eliot leads the reader to a successful adjustment of opposites. The continual pressure this task of adjustment exerted on George Eliot is apparent in her treatment of Esther and Gwendolen. Like Lydgate (whom the one precedes and the other follows), Esther and Gwendolen value at the start a poetry rendered false by its bondage to social convention. Like Romola before them, they grow to perceive an ideal related to the poetry of community. Although each character locates a different source for this poetry—Romola finds it in "simple human fellowship," Esther in conjugal love and creating in others a "state of sympathetic ardour," and Gwendolen in self-awareness and a consciousness of "wide-stretching purposes"—these forms of

poetry are alike in failing to accommodate sufficiently the workaday.[71] The very tensions between the prose and the poetry, however,
make the reader party to the education the characters receive.[72]

George Eliot's treatment of Romola is representative of the educative process at play in all the later novels in that the character's
evolving perception of workaday-holiday reality allows the reader
to perceive disparities and connections between the two. The pattern of Romola's development relates as well to the earlier novels,
for it demonstrates the kind of adjustment U. C. Knoepflmacher
defines when he speaks of George Eliot's effort to reconcile the
ideal and the actual by ennobling everyday experience.[73] Knoepflmacher's illuminating thesis is also relevant to the later novels, but
in them the ennobling of experience is often only a point of departure, and one that includes at times even a reversal of direction.

"Brought up in learned seclusion from the interests of actual
life, and . . . accustomed to think of heroic deeds and great principles as something antithetic to the vulgar present," Romola at
the start lives "aloof from the life of the streets on holidays as well
as on common days."[74] This sense of separateness, of finding poetry
in books and in a romanticized past rather than in life and an
actual present, is ironically reinforced by her marriage to Tito.
The world of books does not in itself suggest a false poetic, of
course; but a romanticizing of the past through books does involve
a falsification of history and of the present it excludes. In addition,
Tito represents a thoroughly false holiday world, one that mirrors
and measures Romola's delusion as well as the corruption in Florence. While the shrewd trader, Bratti, instantly recognizes that Tito
is too sharp to have been " 'born of a Sunday,' " for almost everyone

71. *R*, ch. 40, p. 349; *FH*, ch. 47, p. 576; *DD*, ch. 69, p. 875.
72. George Eliot's efforts to educate her readers, through the education her
characters experience, are analyzed by Barbara Hardy, Reva Stump, and
Bernard Paris, each from a different but rewarding perspective. Hardy in
The Novels of George Eliot focuses on tragic form; Stump in *Movement and
Vision in George Eliot's Novels* on the imagery of "vision" in *Adam Bede*,
Mill on the Floss, and *Middlemarch*; and Paris in *Experiments in Life* on a
progression from egoism to altruism based on Comte's Law of the Three Stages.
Hardy's stress on tragedy is different from the emphasis on adjustment in this
discussion, and Stump's analysis of Eliot's figurative language does not deal
with the workaday-holiday imagery, whose patterns suggest that Eliot's preoccupations are at once more personal, assimilative, original, and conflicted
than Paris takes them to be.
73. Knoepflmacher, *George Eliot's Early Novels*.
74. *R*, ch. 11, p. 112; ch. 27, pp. 239–40.

else, and especially for Romola and her father, "that bright face, that easy smile, that liquid voice, seemed to give life a holiday aspect," like a "strain of gay music and the hoisting of colours" (ch. 1, p. 12; ch. 9, p. 95). In George Eliot's novels, music and ceremony regularly signify the poetry of community or its perversion, now represented by Tito and later by the macabre Carnival mummers. Chanting something that sounds like "a *Miserere*," the mummers disturb the brightness of the Betrothal Day "ceremony," and remind us of what Tito's " 'pretty symbols' " hide (ch. 20, pp. 197–99). Romola discovers the truth about Tito quickly enough, but it takes longer for her to apprehend any connection between her world and the life of Florence. She is first pressed to this discovery, significantly enough, through Tito's betrayal of her father's last wishes. At this point she learns as well that to ignore the "vulgar present" is to court delusion; but at the same time Romola's initial recognition of a working-day world strips away all the poetry in her life and brings her to a point of despair.

Positive value is restored to her through Savonarola. She goes to hear him preach in order to understand his powerful influence in public affairs, but comes away affected by "a strange sympathy . . . not altogether unlike the thrill which had accompanied certain rare heroic touches in history and poetry" (ch. 27, p. 241). His vision of great purpose ennobles Romola's endurance, exalting the common deeds and "daily labours" she assumes by tending the sick in plague-ridden Florence and in a remote village. She becomes Madonna Romola, "the blessed Lady."[75]

Savonarola's influence on her, however, is portrayed in such a way as to reveal both the character and her creator confusedly resisting and succumbing to his enthusiasm—at one moment fearful of being drawn "into fellowship with some wretched superstition," and at the next finding "exquisite poetry" in the imagined " 'glow of a common life' " and in the "simple human fellowship" the priest seems to offer.[76] At the same time, the truly difficult task turns out to be not the discerning of opposite claims but the adjustment between them. Far more significant than the claims of a supernatural as opposed to a humanistic religion is the fragility of the secular one. The poetry in Savonarola's voice holds out a selfless ideal of "pure human fellowship," but it threatens regularly to be

75. *R*, ch. 52, p. 429; ch. 44 (titled "The Visible Madonna"); ch. 68, p. 544.
76. *R*, ch. 37, p. 320; ch. 40, pp. 349, 352. Complimenting Frederic Leighton for his illustrations of *Romola*, George Eliot speaks of the "exquisite poetry" in his drawing for ch. 40 (*Letters* 4: 63).

"eclipsed . . . by the sense of a confusion in human things which made all effort a mere dragging at tangled threads; all fellowship, either for resistance or advocacy, mere unfairness and exclusiveness." It is this "tangle of egoistic demands, false ideas, and difficult outward conditions" that George Eliot's art most convincingly dramatizes.[77] Still, a counter impulse, as she was the first to admit, "forced" an "idealization" in *Romola*, particularly in the concluding chapters (*Letters* 4: 104, 301). Though the body of the novel reveals "simplicity" to be "impossible," Romola's "new baptism" affirms in the end "the simpler relations of the human being to his fellow-men" (ch. 59, p. 478; ch. 69, p. 545). Elsewhere in *Romola*, too, the realism of presentation and idealism of conception regularly eclipse the opposite claims implicit in each. The effect is severely to limit the adjustments between them.

In *Middlemarch*, in contrast, the convergence of the workaday and holiday is so various as to be played out differently in the lives of more than half-a-dozen major characters. Some of the patterns are familiar enough. Through Dorothea, for instance, George Eliot again scrutinizes the ideal that ennobles the commonplace. In addition, through Lydgate she explores in detail for the first time how within a single individual an ideal may be diminished or subverted by commonplace notions. Through this reversal, still other discriminations are made between a true and false poetic in individual and social life. While Lydgate's "spots of commonness" make impossible the valid convergence he seeks, George Eliot's treatment of him powerfully demonstrates the kinds of adjustments that are necessary—adjustments that depend on recognizing one's own immersion in the everyday, responding with imaginative sympathy to the ordinary difficulties others experience, and discovering community in the relationship between prosaic experience and high aspiration.

Lydgate's initial vocational ideal is genuine enough; wishing "to do good small work for Middlemarch, and great work for the world," he thinks "the medical profession as it might be . . . the finest in the world; presenting the most perfect interchange between science and art; [and] offering the most direct alliance between intellectual conquest and the social good" (ch. 15, pp. 107–10). His passion for scientific discovery, moreover, seems so fervent and comprehensive as even to include the powers George Eliot wished to bring to her art:

77. *R*, ch. 59, pp. 473, 478; ch. 61, pp. 487–88.

He was enamoured of that arduous invention which is the very eye of research, provisionally framing its object and correcting it to more and more exactness of relation; he wanted to pierce the obscurity of those minute processes which prepare human misery and joy, those invisible thoroughfares which are the first lurking-places of anguish, mania, and crime, that delicate poise and transition which determine the growth of happy or unhappy consciousness.

[ch. 16, p. 122

Once the novel begins to test Lydgate's dream, however, the inexactness of relation he brings to his own intellectual and social life becomes increasingly more apparent. The "perfect interchange between science and art" he imagines is insufficient because he would reserve to science both the stringent facts of life and all genuinely inspired imaginative activity; and "the direct alliance between intellectual conquest and the social good" he desires is nullified altogether by the false poetry his "spots of commonness" create. Derived from "hereditary habit," they are responsible for the prejudices that cause Lydgate to separate himself from his fellow men, whether by viewing their "petty obstacles" and "trivial" business with aristocratic disdain, or by feeling humiliated when anxieties of an "everyday" sort force him to solicit "men with whom he had been proud to have no aims in common."[78] Reflexive attitudes engender the entirely false poetry he imagines in Rosamond. Wishing for " 'exquisite music,' " "holiday freedom," and "perfect womanhood," he would have her "create order in the home and accounts with still magic, yet keep her fingers ready to touch the lute and transform life into romance at any moment."[79] Again he thinks to unify the prosaic and the poetic, but this thoroughly conventional and false poetic cannot but debase the life it transforms.

As Lydgate comes gradually to understand how entirely the workaday world possesses him, he learns to "modify his opinion as to the most excellent things in woman" and a great deal else as well (ch. 10, p. 69). The self-contempt he comes to feel is so great as to be relieved only during that moment when "simple inspiration" moves Dorothea to "show her human fellowship" to him.[80] Thus his discerning of opposite claims reveals to him both the unfulfilled glory of the genuine dream he brought to his vocational call-

78. *M*, ch. 13, p. 92; ch. 18, p. 132; ch. 36, p. 255; ch. 64, pp. 484–85.
79. *M*, ch. 11, p. 70; ch. 31, p. 216; ch. 36, p. 258.
80. *M*, ch. 76, p. 557; ch. 81, p. 580.

ing and the terrible burden hidden in the specious dream he brought to his marriage; for him, the poetry of creativity and community is destroyed. Still, through the creation of such a character, George Eliot implicates the reader in the process of adjustment denied to him. She furthers the poetry of community by making the reader care for Lydgate, and she does so without displacing the prose, for it is through his paralytic sense of failure that she generates in the reader feelings of sympathy and tolerance.

At one point in *Middlemarch*, the narrator remarks that "life would be no better than candlelight tinsel and daylight rubbish if our spirits were not touched by what has been, to issues of longing and constancy" (ch. 54, p. 393). Expressing a disaffection with what "is," metaphors such as these appear with great frequency in George Eliot's fiction. Linking the deceptively attractive and the seemingly worthless, they reveal "candlelight tinsel" to be no less tied to prosaic reality than "daylight rubbish." In Lydgate, as we have seen, the former simply disguises the one and contributes to the other. Although Romola makes an accommodation of sorts as the "common deeds of a dusty life" are touched by " 'the glow of a common life,' " the glow is inconstant (ch. 40, p. 352; ch. 61, p. 487). Trying to steady it so as to offset the feelings of despair or resignation she herself felt toward both the speciously poetic and the utterly prosaic, George Eliot often enlists a language of deliverance, for her imagination was haunted not only by the elaborate set of associations she brought to "this working-day world" but also by a desire to escape. Her letters reveal a "dread of coming to swear by my own 'deliverances' "; yet, writing to an admirer, she speaks of "the intense comfort I have found in the response which your mind has given to every 'deliverance' of mine" (*Letters*, 5: 76, 325). Truly comfortable with neither, her uneasiness is reflected in the inflated rhetoric she brings to the instantaneous (and consequently unconvincing) recognitions of fellowship in her fiction, as between Tryan and Janet, Maggie and Dr. Kenn, Romola and Savonarola, Lydgate and Dorothea, Daniel and Mirah, or Daniel and Mordecai. Sometimes the overall dramatic action renders such moments ironical, disclosing them to be brief respites essentially powerless to affect everyday reality, as in Dorothea's momentary rescues of Lydgate and later Rosamond. At other times, the events confirm the deliverance by countering the negations that would otherwise play themselves out. To take a simple instance of this, Deronda literally delivers Mirah from death, and she then becomes so emblematic of community that "a painter," we are told, "need have changed nothing" had he wanted to put her face "in front of the host singing 'peace on earth and goodwill to men'" (ch. 32, p. 418). Even this song, however, is likely to be intricately orchestrated, as may be seen from the portraits of Esther and Gwendolen.

Esther is delivered through her love for Felix, but she becomes an agent of deliverance as well, affecting her audience during her testimony at Felix's trial much as George Eliot would affect the reader. The theme is further complicated when the rescue offered a character is consciously resisted by the author, as in the final scenes between Deronda and Gwendolen. The deliverances of Esther and Gwendolen, moreover, are part of a long and intricate process, beginning with their entrancement within a specious candlelight world, continuing throughout the daylight disenchantments they later experience, and culminating finally in reconciliations (themselves questionable).[81] Each step in this process of entrancement, disenchantment, and deliverance implicates the prose and poetry of community in new and critical ways.

The entrancement with being a "lady" that Esther and Gwendolen feel serves to measure the absence of value in a self-indulgent, upper-class world that is revealed to be no less "middling" than the ordinary world, but a good deal more hypocritical, for its "'niceties'" simply mask the vulgarities they pretend to shut out.[82] Lyon's cluttered study, the Holborn book shop, and the small house at Chelsea where the poor but cultured Meyricks live become the loci of genuine poetry, while the drawing room and country estate, along with all the other scenery associated with "genteel romance," are shown to be imprisoning, holding one "captive by the ordinary wirework of social forms" (*DD*, ch. 6, p. 83). That Esther does not perceive for so long just how ordinary they are reveals only her relatively innocent retreat from reality. Gwendolen's attitudes are more complicated, since she regularly mocks conventional social forms and yet is unable to recognize her own subjection to them.

Esther's "imaginary mansion" collapses, and Gwendolen's conservatory life becomes a "penitentiary," her large drawing room no better than a "painted gilded prison."[83] The disenchantment of

81. Barbara Hardy presents a fine analysis of the "scenes of disenchantment" in *Novels of George Eliot*, pp. 189–200.

82. For examples, see *FH*, ch. 3, p. 102 and *DD*, ch. 4, p. 68; however, these words are used frequently to express Esther's and Gwendolen's contempt for ordinary life.

83. *FH*, ch. 44, p. 550; *DD*, ch. 24, p. 315; ch. 48, p. 651.

Esther is essentially vicarious, experienced through Mrs. Transome, whose "life had been like a spoiled shabby pleasure-day, in which the music and the processions are all missed"; but its very vicariousness provides a paradigm for the reader, who may also, like Esther, "be helped to lead a life of 'vision and of choice.' "[84] Gwendolen's disenchantment is first prompted by her own reflection in the mirror, which reminds her of "the packed-up shows of a departing fair" (*DD*, ch. 23, p. 306). Through both kinds of disenchantments, George Eliot uncovers a consuming selfishness in the false values of a make-believe world that desecrates the everyday one while pretending to ignore or look down on it. In addition, as Barbara Hardy points out, while the scenes of disenchantment suggest a "prosaic present stretching into an unchanging prosaic future . . . each conversion of poetry into prose depends on the dispelling of a dream. . . . It is a test and a prelude to change."[85]

When the dream that has been dispelled is replaced by a form of deliverance, however, the prose again becomes poetry. This final conversion is designed to function as a healing force, but unresolved tensions continue to surface. The poetry Esther had thought to find in Harold Transome turns unambiguously into prose; but the poetry she discovers in Felix, though it allegedly returns her to "that rougher, commoner world where her home had been," merely substitutes one romantic notion for another (ch. 43, p. 526). Felix "is my champagne," Esther declares, as she is urged "towards the life where the draughts of joy sprang from the unchanging fountains of reverence and devout love" (ch. 43, p. 539; ch. 50, p. 597). All signs of her former "sauciness" disappear; "devotion," "perfect love," "inspiration," "consecration," and "ecstasy" appear in its place (ch. 43, pp. 547–51). The settings of the love scenes as well contribute to the displacement of the everyday, since most of them occur in a Sunday, countryside world.

In these ways and others, Esther becomes the "ballad heroine" we are supposed to believe she refuses to be. Still, she is a ballad heroine with a difference—delivered from riches to marry the man she loves.[86] Furthermore, at the trial held after the Election Day riots, her testimony sets Felix free by transforming the disagreement and hostility in the courtroom into cooperation and sympathy. In several ways, this act constitutes something of a model for the

84. *FH*, ch. 1, p. 99; H. S. Kakar, *The Persistent Self*, p. 95.
85. Hardy, *Novels of George Eliot*, pp. 190, 196–98.
86. Lenore Wisney Horowitz discusses the implications of Esther's rejection of the Transome estate in "George Eliot's Vision of Society."

kind of deliverance George Eliot hoped to provide for her readers. Esther's testimony is prompted by the "inward revolution" she has experienced (ch. 49, p. 591). Her effect on her listeners depends on the same kind of "ardour which has flashed out and illuminated all poetry and history" (ch. 46, p. 571). Creating in others a corresponding "state of sympathetic ardour," the impression she makes on their feeling dispels what had been "unmitigated daylight."[87] But while Esther affects the jury as George Eliot wished to affect her audience, the overturning of the verdict nonetheless circumvents the task commonly ascribed to witness and realistic novelist alike. For Esther's power, derived from her "inspired ignorance" and "incongruously simple" testimony, speaks only in the most minimal way to the daylight realities presented throughout the novel (ch. 46, p. 571).

As though further acknowledging the incongruities in *Felix Holt,* George Eliot seems in *Middlemarch* to mock the earlier book, when she says of Lydgate:

> he was beginning now to imagine how two creatures who loved each other, and had a stock of thoughts in common, might laugh over their shabby furniture, and their calculations how far they could afford butter and eggs. But the glimpse of that poetry seemed as far off from him as the carelessness of the golden age.
>
> [ch. 69, p. 514

As we have seen, she denies to Lydgate the reconciliations allowed to Romola and Esther. Returning in Gwendolen to a character similar to Esther, but far more complicated, George Eliot both offers and denies her deliverance. Gwendolen's need for deliverance from Grandcourt is so great that the word appears again and again, in one sentence alone three times:

> The thought that his death was the only possible deliverance for her was one with the thought that deliverance would never come— the double deliverance from the injury with which other beings might reproach her and from the yoke she had brought on her own neck.
>
> [ch. 48, p. 669

But while Gwendolen continues to wear that yoke after Grandcourt's death, and must learn to find her own deliverance by recognizing a world outside of self, still George Eliot attempts once

---

87. *FH*, ch. 47, p. 576; ch. 46, p. 560.

again to affirm the "way our brother may be in the stead of God to us" (ch. 64, p. 833).

The stressfulness of the task makes itself felt in the jagged and unevenly controlled rhythms of the scenes between Deronda and Gwendolen as the novel approaches its close. Repeatedly withdrawing from the deliverance he also offers to Gwendolen, in chapters 56, 57, and 65 (the first two following immediately upon Grandcourt's death and Deronda's discovery of his own Jewish lineage) Deronda is caught between all-absorbing sympathy for Gwendolen and rapt attention to his new life's task. The latter requires him " 'to bind our race together in spite of heresy,' " but his race excludes Gwendolen, and the wavering control in these chapters may very well be related to the heresy this created for George Eliot: not the prejudiced one demonstrated by many of her Victorian readers, but an unorthodoxy in violation of her own credo. Sanctioning Deronda to become the leader of a people he has not yet met, she allows "general doctrine" to take precedence over "direct fellow-feeling with individual fellow-men."[88] George Eliot's uncertain handling of this material is noticeable as well in the inappropriate metaphors she uses, comparing Gwendolen and Deronda, who are suffering the terrors of an adult crisis, to bereft children (ch. 56, p. 755; ch. 65, p. 842). Her uneasiness is suggested also by the protracted amount of time she needed to finish the novel.[89]

In chapter 69, however, when Deronda finally discloses his departure to Gwendolen, though the characters are nervous and their emotions intense, the double recognitions given to each make for a more controlled presentation. While the child images persist, Deronda acknowledges that Gwendolen is "the victim of his happiness," and Gwendolen feels herself

> for the first time being dislodged from her supremacy in her own world, and getting a sense that her horizon was but a dipping onward of an existence with which her own was revolving.

A combined prose and poetry of community is asserted in other ways too: in Gwendolen's feeling herself "solitary and helpless . . . before the bewildering vision of these wide-stretching purposes in which she felt herself reduced to a mere speck"; in the narrator's suggesting the "paradoxical" relation between Deronda's happiness and Gwendolen's sorrow; and in Deronda's tempering the grandeur of restoring a political existence to his people by admit-

88. *DD*, ch. 63, pp. 819–20; *M*, ch. 61, p. 453.
89. Haight, *Biography*, p. 483.

ting the tentativeness of his mission. Voicing a qualification, later picked up in the narrator's description of the mission as "something spiritual and vaguely tremendous," Deronda speaks of perhaps being able to " 'awaken a movement in other minds, such as has been awakened in my own.' "[90]

Still, the stated resolution in the next and concluding chapter goes in another direction: " 'nothing but well and fair' " for Deronda (ch. 70, p. 883); and Gwendolen taking her leave by writing "It is better—it shall be better with me because I have known you" (ch. 70, pp. 882–83). As in *Romola* and *Felix Holt*, the poetry of community emerges as predominant at the close, and again it threatens to displace the prose. At the same time, the more persistent and self-conscious nature of George Eliot's effort to reconcile opposites in *Daniel Deronda* heightens an irony also present, though not as sharp, in these other two novels. Emerging most clearly in *Middlemarch*, it is rooted in a tension between the affirmations of community and the paradoxes that call them into question. Those affirmations depend most of all on the inward modifications individual characters experience. To the extent that they learn to discern between a true and false poetry of community, the affirmations are successful. At the same time, the paradoxes stem from a poetry that fails to do justice to the "hard, unaccommodating Actual" (*DD*, ch. 33, p. 430), in part because George Eliot would counter what her realism of presentation so powerfully accommodates. The major tension then, here as elsewhere, is between her realism of presentation and idealism of conception.

Both are implicit in the holiday-workaday metaphor with which we began this discussion. Over the years, the "naked prose" and "poetry" of her private world became, as it were, socialized and structured. Ceasing to be primarily personal, they embody that correlation between the public and private crucial to the concept of natural history. Structured too through her art, the workaday-holiday images employed in her fiction reveal how closely both the poetry and prose are bound to the idea of community. George Eliot's apprehension of its diminished force and her enduring commitment to its renewal are evident in her use of framing devices, her frequent and varied discriminations between community in the

90. Passages quoted in this paragraph are from *DD*, ch. 69, pp. 868, 875–77. Barbara Hardy points out that Deronda's qualifying statement, absent from the manuscript, was "presumably added in proof in order to make Daniel's statement and political destiny sound more tentative and realistic" (*DD*, Notes, p. 903).

past and community in the present, and the countless connections she establishes between the two.

The positive connections lead regularly to a concept of community that is relational rather than geographical, one based on consciousness far more than on external fact. At its most extreme, the result is a "poetry" of the "mind" allegedly capable of creating a "sense of fellowship which thrills from the near to the distant, and back again from the distant to the near," but actually keeping much that is near at a distance (*DD*, ch. 19, p. 245). Still, this poetry of mind and feeling comes most nearly to define community in the modern world. In George Eliot's fiction, it achieves its fullest and most persuasive dramatic representation when the subject is itself the changes of consciousness her characters experience. However, while their education brings to the discerning of opposite claims a fusion of fact and value, the opposing claims often remain unadjusted.

In George Eliot's fiction, then, as in the writings of the social theorists, the speculative ideal and the factual real, though they are supposed to be mutually supportive, create at best a resistant blend. Her art could not escape, no more than could their science, the constant tensions between the two. While she hoped her fiction could bring together realism and idealism, neutrality and partisanship, Gesellschaft and Gemeinschaft, the prosaic and the poetic, most often it reveals the conflicts that obscure and complicate a vision of fellowship. Nonetheless, the very instabilities contribute in a vital way to the natural history she was creating. By capturing polarities that point to antagonistic values, while evoking through the effort to overcome them a vision of wholeness, she created a body of fiction most compelling when it reveals a double consciousness, moving toward fusion while uncovering conflict as each side implicates the other both affirmatively and negatively. As a result, her most successful reconciliations are those tenuous and makeshift ones that render fragile the very principle of fellowship she struggled to affirm. Powerfully confronting both sides and creating an engaging and embattled middle ground, she held out to her readers an ideal of community while suggesting, sometimes at the same moment, the impossibility of that ideal. For the most part, her readers did not welcome this challenge, preferring instead the comforts of a softened realism, but the record of their responses to her fiction (as we shall see in chapters 6 and 7) reveals how they struggled nevertheless to come to terms with a writer who quietly but strenuously compelled them toward a revolution in thought and sensibility. Yet although George Eliot was painfully aware of the impediments, she would not accept the impossibility of such a revolution. How she strove in still another major way (and one that again has its counterpart in nineteenth-century social theory) to affirm community in a changing world is the subject of the next pair of chapters.

FOUR

◆

Social Organicism

Social Statics

Philosophical and formal realism, at their most consistent, lend authority not to communal but to individualist values. Often highlighting instead of healing the gap between an imagined ideal of community and actual social reality, the theoretic and artistic efforts we have examined thus far have been either fragmentary or inconsistent. But the corrective effort was far more comprehensive than we have yet seen, deriving its essential form from an idea itself representative of wholeness, namely, the concept of organicism.

Organic concepts have long provided metaphors of unification, and the particular analogy at issue here, between the social and the individual organism, dates back at least to Aristotle. Organicism became even more compelling a concept in the nineteenth century as current scientific and sociological thinking promised to make this correspondence not simply a metaphor but a fact. New evolutionary theories shared with earlier organic notions that emphasis on growth and development discussed in the previous chapters and, in addition, incorporated recent advances in biology concerning the structure and purpose of living organisms. Even aesthetics entered the configuration, when, earlier in the century, Coleridge developed organicism as an aesthetic theory. But while he for the most part ignored its social correlative, the writers we are considering addressed this similitude as well. Scientists and artists, it seemed, were beginning to walk hand in hand.

To do so, however, the social theorists had first to restructure the concept of organicism to correspond with their way of looking at social order and social progress. Certain aspects of the inherited definition were basic enough to continue to serve, among them two assumptions fundamental to all organicist thinking: first, that

150

all parts "are in keeping with each other and with the whole"; and
second, that an "alteration of a part will bring with it the alteration
of the whole."[1] George Eliot evokes these assumptions in having
Mordecai measure " 'the ultimate unity of mankind' " according to
whether " 'a part possesses the whole as the whole possesses every
part' " (*DD*, ch. 61, p. 802). Spencer, Comte, and Lewes held these
assumptions as well, but offer them as reasoned conclusions, based
on biological evidence applied to societies and individual organisms alike. In the "organic aggregate" and the "social aggregate,"
Spencer writes, "the changes in the parts are mutually determined,
and the changed actions of the parts are mutually dependent"
(*Principles of Sociology* 1: 439). Deriving his thoughts from Spencer and Comte, Lewes speaks in a similar way. "The Organism,"
he claims, consists of "groups of minor organisms, all sharing in a
common life. . . ; precisely as the great Social Organism is a group
of societies, each of which is a group of families, all sharing in a
common life,—every family having at once its individual independence and its social dependence through connection with every
other" (*Problems* 1: 105).

In addition to the biological claim, this quotation from Lewes
suggests another of the ideas particular to positivistic organicism.
Speaking of "individual independence" as well as "social dependence," Lewes posits a balance between the two, which is typical
of the revised organicism we are defining, but different from most
organic theories of the state, which claim society to be an end in
itself and the individual to exist for the sake of the whole.[2] Even
Comte, who is closest in this respect to the earlier tradition, argues
for a fusion of public and private, or for the "independence of the
individual" and "convergence of the body politic" (*General View
of Positivism*, p. 406). Spencer, as we might expect, mounts the fullest defense of the individual in spite of a theory that characteristically diminished the self. Using principles derived from natural
science, he justifies both individualism and organicism. Maintaining that societies and organisms increase in complexity of structure as they increase in size, and that they undergo simultaneously
a like differentiation of structure and function, he establishes an
evolutionary progression from simple to complex, from general
to specialized, and from homogeneity to heterogeneity. The greater
the complexity the greater the organization and integration into

1. *Dictionary of the History of Ideas*, 1973 ed., s.v. "Organicism," by G. N. G.
Orsini.
2. F. W. Coker, *Organismic Theories of the State*, pp. 27, 193, and passim.

the whole; but at the same time, the greater the diversity, the greater the individuality.[3]

Both Spencer and Lewes join these conclusions with still another argument for equilibrium, one based on the premise of "the
continuous adjustment of internal relations to external relations."[4]
Positing that adaptation, in the realm of the human, is purposeful,
this argument works to counter Darwin's view of adaptation as
largely a matter of chance and accident. The emphasis on the interplay between the external and internal gives great importance to
what Darwin undervalues, namely, the significance of the social
medium both in shaping and in being shaped by individuals. All
these matters are at issue in this account by Lewes:

> Biology furnishes both method and data in the elucidation of the
> relations of the organism and the external medium; and so far as
> Animal Psychology is concerned this is enough. But Human Psy-
> chology has a wider reach, includes another important factor, the
> influence of the social medium. . . . Culture transforms Nature
> physically and morally, fashioning the forest and the swamp into
> garden and meadow-lands, the selfish savage into the sympathetic
> citizen. The organism adjusts itself to the external medium; it cre-
> ates, and is in turn modified by, the social medium, for Society is
> the product of human feelings, and its existence is *pari passu* de-
> veloped with the feelings which in turn it modifies and enlarges at
> each stage.
>
> [*Problems* 4: 71–72[5]

Lewes's thoughts on modification and Spencer's attention to
relations echo our earlier discussion, while the additional terms
introduce a new vocabulary, though one familiar to readers of
George Eliot. The terms *medium, external* and *internal, outward*

3. Spencer, *Social Statics*, pp. 496–97; "The Social Organism"; *Principles of
Sociology* 1: 437–50. These works were familiar to George Eliot (see *Letters*
2: 11, 14; 6: 124; 7: 348). The idea of a progression from homogeneity to
heterogeneity appears in her own writing (see *Essays*, pp. 290, 433). This idea
appears in Comte, too, but for him the movement from simplicity to complexity entails a decrease in individualism (*Polity* 2: 376).

4. Spencer, *Principles of Biology* 1: 462. See also Maurice Mandelbaum,
History, Man, & Reason, p. 231.

5. The fourth volume of *Problems*, published posthumously, was seen
through the press by George Eliot. K. M. Newton's essay "George Eliot, George
Henry Lewes, and Darwinism" draws a valuable contrast between Darwin's
view of the social medium and of "purpose" in evolution, and the views of
Eliot and Lewes (pp. 280–85).

and *inward* mark with significance the many moments in her novels that support or disturb a sense of equilibrium. However strained, the marriage between individualism and organicism in her work speaks to her effort to correct, through a revised organicism, the perils of individualism while yet affirming its value.

Perhaps the most firmly grounded of the arguments for a dependency, not in itself compromising to individuality, rests in another idea particular to nineteenth-century organicism, that of consensus. It promotes, as did earlier organic theories, a belief in the essential interdependence of human beings, and gives scientific grounding to this belief by applying to sociology a term long associated with physiology. *Consensus* "expresses that fact in a complex organism by which no part can suffer increase or diminution without a participation of all other parts in the effect produced & a consequent modification of the organism as a whole." This definition is offered by George Eliot in "Notes on Form in Art" (1868) in answer to the question "what is form?" as applied to all organic bodies (*Essays*, pp. 434–35). *Consensus* is similarly defined by Comte, Spencer, and Mill, each of whom draws from its physiological meaning new support for old assumptions about the interdependence of all social phenomena.[6]

George Eliot further explicates the theory of consensus in using the verb "to suffer" to denote the reciprocity of response that consensus signifies, thereby writing into the physiological meaning a prescription for sympathy. In the particular definition quoted, she does not mention the close link between suffering and sympathy; however, elsewhere in her work, and regularly in Comte, Spencer, Mill, and Lewes, the link between consensus and sympathy is direct. Indeed, consensus means that a disorder in any one part of an organism produces a sympathetic response, or corresponding condition, in the other parts. This effect has special pertinence in the realm of the human:

> the animal . . . has sympathy and is moved by sympathetic impulses, but these are never altruistic; the ends consciously sought are never remote ends. Our moral life [in contrast] is feeling for others, working for others, quite irrespective of any personal good beyond the satisfaction of this social impulse.
>
> [Lewes, *Problems* 4: 140

6. Comte, *Positive Philosophy*, p. 461; Spencer, *Principles of Sociology* 1: 473–75; Mill, *Logic, Collected Works* 8: 899; *Auguste Comte and Positivism*, p. 89.

Sympathy and altruism are thus offshoots of interdependence; each suffers an increase as society becomes more complex. In this way the concept of consensus brings to Gesellschaft the "social force and sympathy" Tönnies too calls "consensus" but assigns only to the prescientific world of Gemeinschaft (G&G, p. 47).

Just how specific consensus becomes to the "state of the Social Organism at the time being" for Comte, Spencer, Mill, and George Eliot is apparent in their definitions of Social Statics. As Mill explains in his book on Comte, in contrast to the evolutionary emphasis of Social Dynamics (the science of progress), Social Statics (the science of order) is "confined to what is common to the progressive and the stationary state. . . . The statics of society is the study of the conditions of existence and permanence of the social state." It is also "the theory of the consensus, or interdependence of social phaenomena."[7] According to Comte, furthermore, not only is consensus an "essentially organic attribute" but "society forms the highest stage of organic evolution" because of consensus.[8]

Treating the science of Social Statics in his own work, Mill coins the term uniformities of coexistence, a concept also at play in the "co-existences" George Eliot mentions in her essay on Lecky.[9] Considering the subject at greater length in her notes on "Historic Guidance," she dwells on these ideas in ways that indicate her preoccupation with Comte as well as Mill. In these notes, she speaks of "Continuity (in human history)," a phrase suggestive of Comte's Social Dynamics, just as the succeeding phrase, "Solidarity (in the members of the race)," is suggestive of Comte's Social Statics. Their "fundamental law" is "the intimate solidarity and the mutual dependence of all social elements, at all the moments of their common evolution,"[10] a concept implicit in George Eliot's definition of "solidarity" as "a mutual determination of each other's life by contemporaries," while her other definitions of the term, by emphasizing "interdependence . . . among co-existent beings," echo both Comte and Mill ("More Leaves," p. 371).

The science of Social Statics had primary importance also for Spencer and Lewes, who along with Comte and Mill granted "succession" and "co-existence," or "continuity" and "solidarity," the status of "laws." According to positivist theory, "laws" refer to per-

7. Mill, Comte, p. 89; Lewes makes the same point, Problems 1: 160.
8. Coker, Organismic Theories, p. 123.
9. Mill, Logic, Collected Works 8: 917; Eliot, Essays, p. 402.
10. L. Lévy-Bruhl, The Philosophy of Auguste Comte, pp. 269–70.

sistent identities of pattern descriptive of the actual nature of the thing, in this case, social progress and social order. George Eliot's meaning is similar when she notes in "Historic Guidance" that "Continuity" and "Solidarity . . . must be taken first as facts quite apart from their entrance into the human consciousness as matter of contemplation" ("More Leaves," p. 371). To bring these facts "into the human consciousness," by observing and describing them, was the task of the new science.

Yet the moral edge carried by a word such as *solidarity* suggests something else as well—"something like a rule of life, something that should embody all the phases of our multiform knowledge," as Frederic Harrison puts it, "and yet slake our thirst for organic order."[11] Social Statics, then, no less than Social Dynamics, was part of the persistent effort to fuse fact and value. Attempting to anchor progressive ideas in moorings at once scientific and elemental, Social Statics tried to find its grounding in positivist method, and its "matter of contemplation" in consensus, solidarity, order, and equilibrium. It, too, participates in the effort to uncover, through the science of Gesellschaft, the stability and unity hitherto associated with Gemeinschaft.

Structure and Telos

The emphasis in Social Statics on existence in the present, however, brings to the forefront questions that tend to be pushed aside by the long evolutionary sweeps characteristic of Social Dynamics. Perhaps the most primary of these questions is whether the guiding principles of Social Statics can be translated into workable institutions. Calling Comte and Mill "the two most eminent propagandists for social science of the first half of the nineteenth century," J. W. Burrow points out that we have in their work "the conceptual basis for the study of societies as working systems." Spencer continues this tradition and extends it, devoting "almost as much attention to structural/functional relations" as to social theory. Yet as Burrow demonstrates, Social Statics—despite the ambitiousness of the undertaking—inhibited far more than it assisted the study of society as a working social system. Burrow explains the failure primarily in terms of a "gap between theory and practice" caused by the theorists' paying too much attention to their " 'speculative' . . . evolutionary preoccupations" and too little to the needs of " 'practical' sociology"; yet he seems to undercut his explanation by mak-

11. Quoted by Tjoa, *George Henry Lewes*, p. 133.

ing a "theoretical framework" essential to those needs. He speaks also of opposing "ethical attitudes"—the " 'practical' students of society" wanted "immediate social amelioration," while the " 'speculative' " thinkers cared far more about ethical and political theory—though elsewhere in his study he makes the ethical concerns of the evolutionary social theorists extremely pressing and immediate.[12]

Whereas Burrow looks to Social Dynamics to explain the failure of Social Statics, it seems instead that both the science of progress and the science of order suffered from a similar failure—a failure caused by the ethical demands. In the case of Social Statics, the ethical demands were themselves conflicted. Committed both to pioneering new modes of social existence and to preserving a social organism based on inviolable laws of nature, Social Statics suffered from a self-contradictory ideal. A piece Lewes wrote for the *Leader* offers a striking example of this dual orientation, for while he insists that "society is a growth, not a transplantation," he also opposes taking this admission to mean "a rigorous abstinence from all radical changes." Separating his views from the "systematic Socialists," he proclaims "not a *system*, but a *doctrine*," whose underlying premise is Comte's belief that new institutions will "arise, without giving room for any serious shock" when a "community of principles" introduces into "existing institutions" new forces and new elements.[13] But faced with having actually to alter existing institutions, Social Statics suffers a form of paralysis. It could not give rise to institutions in harmony with its principles because those principles contained irreconcilable strains. Social Statics was based on so strange a mutation of organic concepts as to inhibit productive change, and its inability to apply social theory to social structure is most apparent when relations between the individual and society are at issue.

The "thirst for organic life" suggests one set of structures or actions; the freedom of the individual another. Each in turn raises questions about the function and purpose of social structure, questions that traditional organismic concepts of the state had no difficulty in answering. Given the traditional assumptions that the individual exists for the sake of the state and that the state itself is the end of its existence, certain structures or actions are necessarily appropriate. But within the far more liberal tradition we

12. Burrow, *Evolution and Society*, pp. 84, 89–93, 193–96.
13. [Lewes], "Socialism," p. 204; *Comte's Philosophy of the Sciences*, p. 14. See also chapter 1 above, pp. 7–8, 16–17.

are defining, such an answer was entirely unsatisfactory to all but Comte.

Yet any new answer had to address the issue of purpose or telos, whatever its metaphysical overtones, and not only because the old answer still carried great weight. As Alfred North Whitehead explains, scientific positivism represents one set of assumptions about the laws of nature; the "speculative extension" characteristic of metaphysical inquiry another. Whereas positivists take law to be "merely Description," metaphysicians regard law as "immanent." Comte, Spencer, and Lewes repudiated "essence," a concept that is central to the doctrine of law as immanent. Yet both doctrines, the metaphysical and the positivist, are at play in their work. As Isaiah Berlin argues, the former includes teleological explanations that are "profoundly anti-empirical," but such explanations are also characteristic of the laws of nature in Social Dynamics and Social Statics. Even in his own time, Comte, the founding father of the new science, was thought to be "a metaphysician in Positivist clothing."[14] The other theorists also exhibited this contradiction, but they were not in agreement about what the proper end or telos should be.

As defined within the traditional context of natural-law doctrine, telos presumes that "every kind of thing or species has its own nature or end and its characteristic excellence is realized in performing whatever conduces to this end."[15] As applied specifically to the natural laws of Comtean Social Statics, for the human species that end is society or community. "The only principle on which Politics can be subordinated to Morals," Comte writes, is "that individuals should be regarded, not as so many distinct beings, but as organs of one Supreme Being" (*General View of Positivism*, pp. 402–3). The moral base explicit in this statement demonstrates how tied Comte remains to traditional natural-law doctrine, just as the appeal to a "Supreme Being" implies corresponding metaphysical assumptions, while the statement as a whole suggests that for him the end of the human organism is membership in the collectivity. That idea in turn sanctions duty and self-renunciation, a principle the positivists popularized with the phrase "*Vivre pour*

14. See Whitehead, *Adventures of Ideas*, pp. 142–47, 164; Berlin, *Historical Inevitability*, pp. 14–19; W. M. Simon, *European Positivism in the Nineteenth Century*, p. 212, n. 36. See also the conclusion to chapter 2 above.

15. *Encyclopedia of Philosophy*, 1972 ed., s.v. "Natural Law," by Richard Wollheim.

autrui." "Live for others," they insisted, "does not mean—Die to self. It means a life of sympathy—happiness sought in a social ideal."[16] Nonetheless, to demand altruism in an age of individualism surely unbalances any easy equation between individual and social ends.

How tipped the scales actually were may be seen by comparing Comte and Spencer. "The only point of community between us," Spencer writes (in a letter to Lewes), is "the notion of a social organism" (*Autobiography* 2: 568), but it is more a vanishing than a meeting point, since they bring that notion to such opposite conclusions. For Comte "the only real life is the collective life of the race; . . . individual life has no existence except as an abstraction" (*General View of Positivism*, p. 404); for Spencer, the reverse:

> The society exists for the benefit of its members; not its members for the benefit of the society. It has ever to be remembered that great as may be the efforts made for the prosperity of the body politic, yet the claims of the body politic are nothing in themselves, and become something only in so far as they embody the claims of its component individuals.
>
> [*Principles of Sociology* 1: 449–50

Defining the end of the social organism in terms of the general good, Comte is consistent in his ideology, at least, if not in his method. In Spencer's case each is conflicted. As Ernest Barker observes, "the living social organism, [Spencer's] inheritance from early idealism, is continually at war with the doctrine of individual natural rights, that inheritance from a still earlier Radicalism."[17] Though Spencer's name is often taken quite simply as a byword for laissez-faire individualism, his adherence to the concept of the social organism complicates the matter considerably. Throughout his career, Spencer was unable to overcome the antagonism between individualism and an organic conception of society. In *Principles of Ethics*, the study that closes the many volumes of *Synthetic Philosophy*, he still asks:

> How then are there to be reconciled the interests of the individual and the interests of the race? This question, which here unavoidably presents itself, is one difficult, if not impossible to answer— perhaps they cannot be reconciled.
>
> [*Principles of Ethics* 1: 553

16. Frederic Harrison, *On Society*, pp. 237–38.
17. Ernest Barker, *Political Thought in England from Herbert Spencer to the Present Day*, pp. 95–96.

Continuing as always to be hot for certainty, he nonetheless answers the question, though in such a way as to contradict the definition of telos in his earlier work:

> One thing, however, is certain. No conclusion can be sustained which does not conform to the ultimate truth that the interests of the race must predominate over the interests of the individual.

[1: 554

To admit the impossibility of answering the questions he poses was extremely rare for Spencer; most often, he engages instead in "equilibration." Lewes, in contrast, though he does not always acknowledge an impasse, nonetheless signals awareness by equivocating. If in his study of Comte's *Philosophy of the Sciences* he turns the question "Is it possible to conceive anything more wonderful than . . . our social organism?" into a lyrical celebration of the relation between the self and society in Comte, still at the close of the volume he judges Comte's "attempts to reorganize society on the basis he lays down" to be "premature," but he also dodges the issue by saying "this is not the place to enter upon so vast a subject" (pp. 263, 339). Similarly, in his revision of *Biographical History*, while he continues to applaud Comte for his "comprehensive Method," again he would "draw the veil . . . over his subsequent efforts to found a social doctrine" (2: 787).

Although Mill did not draw a veil over the subject, he too responded with uncertainty; and the very instability of his views testifies to the intractability of the issues. In his *Autobiography*, Mill labels Comte's *Polity* "a monumental warning to thinkers on society and politics, of what happens when once men lose sight, in their speculations, of the value of Liberty and of Individuality" (pp. 127–28). His criticism becomes even harsher in *On Liberty*, where he faults Comte for trying to establish "a despotism of society over the individual, surpassing anything contemplated in the political ideal of the most rigid disciplinarian among the ancient philosophers" (*Collected Works* 18: 227). Now Comte's social system signifies to Mill "engines of moral repression" (18: 226), though it had once meant organic wholeness. Early in his career, Mill had conceived of society as an organic entity. Like Comte, he had measured "the completeness of the social union" in terms of subordinating one's "selfish . . . propensities" to a "common system of opinions" and one's personal impulses to the aims and ends of society (*Logic, Collected Works* 8: 921, 926). Doubts crept in soon enough, but his response was to separate the method from the application

so as to retain Comte's "theory" but not his "sociological opinions."[18] Yet the two are not really separable, something Mill could
not perhaps afford to admit.

J. M. Robson writes that "it would have been only just of Mill
to acknowledge the insight Comte gave him into the organic workings of social institutions."[19] That Mill did not suggests his own unresolved conflicts. They are evident again if one compares *On
Liberty* (1859) with the still later *Auguste Comte and Positivism*
(1865). Though Mill acknowledges two types of "human excellence" in *On Liberty*—" 'Pagan self-assertion' " and " 'Christian
self-denial' "—his support at this time goes to the first (*Collected
Works* 18: 265–66). Yet, in *Auguste Comte and Positivism*, though
he would not demand that one "live for others," he nonetheless
desires a social ideology that would encourage altruism (pp. 138–
46). In the end, repudiation yields to hedging. "M. Comte has got
hold of half the truth," he now writes, "and the so-called liberal or
revolutionary school possesses the other half" (p. 97). George Eliot
regarded Comte in a similar way, but was even more self-divided
than Mill because the claims of these two rights seemed to her so
equal; she calls Comte "one-sided; but . . . a great thinker, nevertheless" (*Letters* 3: 439).

Whether called "half" or "side," however, these two parts do
not make a whole. Had Comte been right in little else, his charge
that Mill and Lewes disregarded the indivisibility of his system
was well taken. Any organic system requires at least the total integration of parts and whole, and often demands, in addition, that
the whole be more than merely the sum of the parts. The new
social structure posited by Comte met these requirements, but the
others rejected his polity. The criterion of telos thus exposes as
hollow or facile the natural and necessary harmony between the
individual and the social organism that was supposed to be created
simply by locating a center both within and outside of the self.
When put to the test of telos, the most basic assumptions of organismic theory dissolve, and the theorists of positivistic organicism
often disagree or contradict themselves. Trying to affirm two opposing social ideologies—one designating the end of social structure in community, and the other in the freedom of the individual—
they devise conceptual frameworks that cannot be translated into
workable social institutions because they are so self-conflicted.

18. See Mill to Littré, 22 Dec. 1848, Hugh S. R. Elliot, ed., *Letters* 1: 139;
cited by W. M. Simon, *European Positivism*, p. 188.
19. Robson, *Improvement of Mankind*, p. 105.

Contract and "Natural Identity of Interests"

Still, in one important area—having to do with contract in civil and natural law—theory and practice were to some extent joined. Sir Henry Sumner Maine writes in *Ancient Law*, published in 1861:

> There are few general propositions concerning the age to which we belong which seem at first sight likely to be received with readier concurrence than the assertion that the society of our day is mainly distinguished from that of preceding generations by the largeness of the sphere which is occupied in it by Contract.

[p. 295

The movement he describes is from status to contract, or from "forms of reciprocity in rights and duties which have their origin in the Family . . . towards a phase of social order in which all these relations arise from the free agreement of individuals" (p. 163). On this point, Tönnies and others draw extensively upon Maine, but they sometimes forget what he is careful to point out—that the shift had its origins in " 'mixed modes of thought' " concerning natural and civil law, and that the mix, after having been in abeyance for some time, was to be seen again in his "own day" (p. 70).

Maine locates the origins of the mixture in the joining together of *"Jus Naturale"* and *"Jus Gentium"* in Roman law. *Jus gentium*, George Eliot observes (in her chapter-by-chapter summary of Maine's book) was

> in the beginning simply a resource for deciding questions between Romans & Roman denizens from the Italian states, & was arrived at by inquiring which element in the law applicable to a given case was common both to the Roman & the other Italian states. [']"Ius Gentium" was, in fact, the sum of the common ingredients in the customs of the old Italian tribes, for they were *all the nations* whom the Romans had the means of observing."[20]

As her jottings also indicate, this " 'Law common to all Nations' became . . . in the progress of juridicial conception . . . the Law of Nature, Ius naturale" (*"Middlemarch" Notebooks*, p. 203). *Jus Naturale*, Maine points out, derives from the earlier Greek conception of an "ideal and absolutely perfect law" marked by "sim-

---

20. John Clark Pratt and Victor A. Neufeldt, eds., *George Eliot's "Middlemarch" Notebooks: A Transcription*, p. 203. Pratt and Neufeldt note that George Eliot read Maine's *Ancient Law* between 17 November and 1 December 1869 (Introduction, p. xlii).

plicity and symmetry" (p. 75), a point George Eliot highlights by noting the "importance of the conception of Ius Naturale as a type of excellence, a rule of Reform." Immediately following this statement, and still paraphrasing Maine but now also questioning him, George Eliot writes: "The secret of Bentham's influence was his proposal of such a rule in the good of the community?" ("*Middlemarch*" *Notebooks*, p. 204). Maine's study of ancient law was in part an inquiry into conditions in modern England, and George Eliot clearly took a great interest in his work.

The "Roman idea that natural law coexisted with civil law and gradually absorbed it," Maine argues, "conveyed a theory concerning the origin, composition and development of human institutions" (p. 90), and one which had enabled the freedom of the individual and the good of the community to be translated into working institutions. The theory of the social contract developed during the Enlightenment, however, had so limited natural law to individualistic rights derived from a presocial state of nature as to have countermanded the Roman legacy. According to Maine, that inheritance was first reclaimed when the nineteenth-century utilitarians united empirical principles with communitarian ones to affirm values at once individualist and social, and this recovery was being continued by "the science of Political Economy, the only department of moral inquiry which has made any considerable progress in our day" (pp. 75, 296).

Revising social-contract theory to eliminate the idea of metaphysical design and a rationally devised social order, the nineteenth-century practitioners of political economy introduced the theory of the " 'natural identity of interests.' "[21] The latter was a far narrower concept, for it did not require individuals to view their actions in terms of society as a whole but only to act rationally to achieve their own selfish ends. Thus it sanctioned the rational pursuit of self-interest, later called by Tönnies the keystone of Gesellschaft. The theory of the natural identity of interests, however, also affirmed the interdependence of mutually contributing parts, by maintaining that corresponding self-interests, beneficial to each party, are likely to exist between one individual and another. If the balance between "interest" and "natural identity" in Bentham is still heavily weighted on the side of self-interest, the further revision introduced by the theory of consensus brings into the configuration what is absent from Bentham and vital to community:

21. See Burrow, *Evolution and Society*, pp. 104–6.

the doctrine of sympathy. As a result, relationships that had for the last two hundred years been deemed "artificial" now take on organic "natural" attributes.

We see this in Spencer's inversion of the standard order of value. Instead of associating the emergence of an industrial system with the decline of organic community, he observes in modern society the social organism at its highest stage of development. Though individuals pursue their own separate interests, they are knit together in voluntary associations, voicing their consent through contract, itself the rule of industry as well as the principle upon which voluntary cooperation rests. From the increasing division of labor in modern society (the result of progressive differentiation), distinct spheres of interest arise, but they demand cooperation from within. The growing intersection of interests causes people to discover egoistic pleasure in the performance of cooperative and altruistic acts: we promote the welfare of others because their welfare affects our own. The community of mankind advances as egoism becomes compatible with altruism. At the same time, because the state as an organ functions, according to Spencer, as a "joint-stock protection-society" for "mutual" assurance, it makes possible what Tönnies thought impossible: a " 'joint-stock Gemeinschaft.' "[22]

Though Mill is a good deal more tentative than Spencer, he too relies on the theory of a natural identity of interests to posit a coalescence of communal and individualist values. Discussing the subject of contract in *Principles of Political Economy*, he draws attention to the need to extend the "co-operative principle" so as to achieve greater "unity of interest" through the "Laws of Partnership" (*Collected Works* 3: 895–96). Eventually this leads to his "qualified Socialism," as in his endorsement of the cooperative associations formed by workmen in France, as well as in his declaration that the "extension of the co-operative principle in the larger sense of the term, [is] the great economical necessity of modern industry."[23] Addressing far more than the cash nexus, his argument for encouraging workers' cooperatives in England is as much "moral" as "economical":

22. Spencer, *Social Statics*, p. 303; Tönnies, *G&G*, p. 34. Spencer anticipates Durkheim, whose concept of "organic solidarity" is also based on the interdependence of specialized parts.

23. Mill, *Autobiography*, p. 115; *Principles of Political Economy, Collected Works* 2: xciii; 3: 758–96, 895 (phrase "in the larger sense of the term" added 1865).

> It is, above all, with reference to the improvement and elevation of the working classes that complete freedom in the conditions of partnership is indispensable. . . . Associations of workpeople . . . are the most powerful means of effecting the social emancipation of the labourers through their own moral qualities.
>
> [*Political Economy, Collected Works* 3: 903

In their specific recommendations, Spencer and Mill differed considerably. Nonetheless, both refuted the idea that contract led necessarily to the impoverishment of community; indeed, they looked to the laws of contract for its enrichment.[24]

This identification of private with public interests in spite of, and even by way of, self-interest, also appears regularly in George Eliot's work. In *Scenes of Clerical Life,* her first published fiction, the equation is applied to tradesmen and customers to demonstrate how "convenience, that admirable branch system from the main line of self-interest, makes us all fellow-helpers in spite of adverse resolutions" ("Janet's Repentance," ch. 10, p. 317). Similarly, in *Theophrastus Such,* the last work she published, she illustrates by way of a man who "made his fortune in the cotton manufacture," how "the nature of things transmuted his active egoism into a demand for a public benefit" (pp. 136, 139). Again, the "nature of things" means a "natural identity of interests":

> any molecule of the body politic working towards his own interest in an orderly way gets his understanding more or less penetrated with the fact that his interest is included in that of a large number.
>
> [p. 133

In her essays and notes of the 1860s and 70s, George Eliot continues to find in self-interest "a duct for sympathy." She also establishes that "as social & international relations become more manifold & stringent, . . . solidarity, which is a mutual determination of each other's life by contemporaries," exerts increasing "pressure on the egoistic mind."[25]

Yet on the actual matter of contract, her attitudes waver. In her letters, she speaks of the "marriage state" as holding the "highest

24. For an opposing point of view, see N. N. Feltes, "Community and the Limits of Liability in Two Mid-Victorian Novels." Feltes argues that Mill's support of limited liability legislation in *Political Economy* set the tone for proposals that impoverished Victorian concepts of community.

25. *Essays,* p. 402; "More Leaves," pp. 371–73. On the role of self-interest in promoting the social good in *Felix Holt,* see Fred C. Thomson, "Politics and Society in *Felix Holt.*"

possibilities of our mortal lot," but she also favors a property bill (thought radical at the time) giving "married women . . . legal right to their own earnings, as a counteractive to wife-beating and other evils," and she calls "excellent" the chapter of the *Subjection* in which Mill criticizes marriage law for failing to secure for women the rights contract is supposed to ensure.[26] Her criticism of marriage law is evident also in her comments on *Jane Eyre*:

> I have read Jane Eyre, mon ami, and shall be glad to know what you admire in it. All self-sacrifice is good—but one would like it to be in a somewhat nobler cause than that of a diabolical law which chains a man soul and body to a putrefying carcase.
>
> [*Letters* 1: 268

The "mon ami," in this case, is Charles Bray, whose philosophy she criticized on the grounds that he considered "the disregard of individuals as a lofty condition of mind" (*Letters* 2: 403). Her own regard for working men and women is reflected in her support of various cooperative movements, among them one initiated by Leclaire, a house-painter in Paris whom Mill had singled out in *Political Economy* for having, as George Eliot says, "initiated an excellent plan of co-operative sharing for his workmen" (*Letters* 7: 332–33).

But she was also skeptical and uncertain about how much laws of reform could accomplish. Her novels often suggest that private vices make not public virtues but "national vices," while her essays present arguments for "common interest," "fellow-feeling," and the "common good" that regularly express what men "must" but do not yet do. At the same time, in the "Address to Working Men, by Felix Holt," the essay in which all these phrases appear, the invocation of "right remedies" and "right methods" is marked by a vagueness that contrasts sharply with the certainty she brings to the opposite point—that "men . . . have not found out for themselves institutions which express and carry into practise the truth, that the highest interest of mankind must at last be a common and not a divided interest" (*Essays*, p. 420). This contrast of common and divided interests is also rendered equivocal by an opposing proposition (expressed with equal passion in other essays)—that "the strength of a man's intellect, or moral sense, or affection" may bring "him into opposition with the rules which society has sanctioned" (*Essays*, p. 265).

The rhetoric George Eliot uses, furthermore, in the phrases

26. *Letters* 9: 192; 2: 225, 227; 8: 458.

quoted above displays the very opposition between natural and positive law that the fusion of *jus naturale* and *jus gentium* was to heal. This opposition suggests, in addition, how natural law, by ceasing to be positivistic when it affirms norms and rules of excellence, ceases also to lend scientific credence to Social Statics. In "Address . . . by Felix Holt," George Eliot's spokesman asks that we turn over to "those who hold the treasure of knowledge . . . the task of searching for new remedies, and finding the right methods of applying them." The best course is "to get the chief power into the hands of the wisest, which means to get our life regulated according to the truest principles mankind [possesses]" (*Essays*, p. 428). But, as we earlier noted, when it comes to translating abstract principles into specific remedies, the science of Social Statics (and certainly "the wisest" included its practitioners) is disabled by paralysis. The rhetoric George Eliot employs when her subject of discourse is social order inadvertently displays that same paralysis.

Finally, laws of contract, like all the other laws of Social Statics, because they were concerned with social order, neglected Darwin's new body of theory, which challenged traditional concepts of order and changed the shape of scientific knowledge in the second half of the nineteenth century. The revised organicism we have been defining was an effort directed toward preserving the notion of community by absorbing into it a value system and a social structure supporting moral automony and self-development. But the very need to which the organic model was so fully suited—the need to affirm wholeness—also demanded that positivistic organicism gloss over what Darwinian theory proposed, namely, that competition and conflict are the fundamental conditions of existence. Although Spencer coined the phrase "survival of the fittest," unlike Marxian socialists and later Social Darwinists who stressed persistent conflicts arising from the "tense interpenetration of opposed interests," he maintained that competition would eventually lead to a "condition of harmony."[27] To make that argument he had to incorporate into the natural laws of his Social Statics assumptions implicitly metaphysical and moral. Darwin, in contrast, specifically disclaims the laws of nature, as does Huxley, along with the corollary that society is in any scientific sense an organism. "Social progress," Huxley writes, "means a checking of the cosmic process at

27. Don Martindale, *Community, Character, and Civilization*, p. 17; see also his discussion of the differences between the sociological schools of Positivistic Organicism and Conflict Theory, pp. 14–19.

every step and the substitution for it of another, which may be called the ethical process." The "innate tendency to self-assertion was the condition of victory in the struggle for existence"; but "the necessary condition for the origin of human society" is control over "this free play of self-assertion, or natural liberty."[28]

Huxley locates those checks not in law (either natural or contractual) but in culture. The two specific forms of culture he identifies are "the mutual affection of parent and offspring, intensified by the long infancy of the human species," and the great susceptibility of human individuals to public opinion: "It is needful only to look around us," he writes, "to see that the greatest restrainer of the anti-social tendencies of men is fear, not of the law, but of the opinion of their fellows."[29] Thus the checks Huxley finds most essential are central also to positivistic organicism; and their centrality to both systems radically exposes in the latter its tenuous foundation in science, its failure to balance communitarian and individualist values, and its incapacity to effect concrete changes in the working social structure.

The Woman Question

All these disabilities surface perhaps most sharply when the role of women within the newly defined social organism is at issue. Recognizing the importance of the subject, Spencer speaks of how "a people's condition may be judged by the treatment which women receive" under "the laws ... and the public opinion" (*Social Statics*, p. 179); and Comte says, "It is from the feminine aspect only that human life, whether individually or collectively considered, can really be comprehended as a whole" (*General View of Positivism*, p. 4). That "aspect" included marriage—called by Comte "the most elementary," and by Mill "the most fundamental of the social relations."[30] Precisely what the role of woman should be, however, was very much open to question; her nature and telos were the subject of extended debate.

In the 1830s the "woman question," as it was called, became a prominent topic of discussion among social theorists and intellectuals. Among those who were promoting women's rights were many

28. Thomas H. Huxley, *Evolution and Ethics and Other Essays*, pp. 27, 81.
29. Ibid., pp. 28–29. For another perspective on the difference between cultural law and natural law in George Eliot's work, see Elizabeth Ermarth, "Incarnations: George Eliot's Conception of 'Undeviating Law.'"
30. Comte, *General View of Positivism*, p. 260; Mill, *Subjection*, p. 236.

of George Eliot's friends—Barbara Bodichon, Anna Jameson, John
Morley, Harriet Martineau, and Bessie Rayner Parkes. By the
1870s, general interest in the subject was so great that the *Examiner*, a popular weekly, collected and reprinted in a separate volume, titled *The Woman Question*, articles that had appeared in the
periodical, among them "The Education of Women," "The Female Franchise," and "Women and Work." At issue was not only
a woman's appropriate social role but also conventional definitions
of her nature and sphere. As expressed in the *Examiner*,

> The rapid growth of literature on the "woman question" indicates
> a prevailing impression that hitherto society has failed to draw
> from women all the good they are capable of doing, that it leaves
> their powers insufficiently developed.[31]

Although Comte, Spencer, and Mill agreed about the importance
of the social role of women, they differed greatly in their attitudes
toward such key issues as the relation between marriage and vocation, and women's legal and political rights. Still, despite substantial differences among them, and self-contradictions as well, their
desire to affirm values conducive to community caused them to continue, albeit to widely varying degrees, to place constraints on
women that limited the full expression of their energies. The social
organism depended on virtues traditionally designated "feminine":
sympathy, commitment to others, peacefulness, and the capacity to
nurture. These altruistic graces were to counter the aggressive competition, rational calculation, and self-serving individualism of the
marketplace. Regarding women's role, revised organicism thus re-
states the traditional paradox of a telos that is public and social
but a domain that is private and domestic. Instead of assimilating
the individualist critique of community, the role ascribed to wom-
en in Social Statics exemplifies it.

Comte, for instance, in his *Polity*, holds women's nature and telos
to be one. Women's "strongly sympathetic nature," like their special
capacity for love "tends of itself towards the preponderance of social

31. Passage quoted from "Words of Weight," *The Woman Question: Papers
Reprinted from "The Examiner,"* p. 15. John Killham, *Tennyson and "The
Princess": Reflections of an Age*, discusses the importance of the woman ques-
tion in England during the 1830s and 1840s; see especially pp. 17, 88, 110–37.
Bibliographies that list primary sources on the woman question include S.
Barbara Kanner, "The Women of England in a Century of Social Change,
1815–1914," pp. 178–81; J. A. Banks and Olive Banks, Appendix to *Feminism
and Family Planning in Victorian England*, pp. 135–40.

feeling over self-interest"; but "Love cannot govern." Therefore, while Comte regards the "service of women as the basis for the individual of his service to society," and thinks woman "undoubtedly superior to man" because of her "tendency to place social above personal feeling," still in "every phase of human society," he argues, "women's life is essentially domestic, public life being confined to men." For all her "superiority in strength of feeling," since "man excels her in force" and in "mental capacity," she "can never do more than modify the harshness with which men exercise their authority." These are "natural" distinctions, he argues, based on nothing less than the "laws of nature"; but, while they clearly give women a moral superiority over men, still, when the two marry each somehow becomes "necessary to the moral development of the other." Marriage is therefore "the only association in which entire identity of interests is possible."[32]

Defined in this way, marriage becomes the meeting point for two systems of law: women bring to it the moral excellence of *jus naturale*; men, the practical expertise of *jus gentium*. Yet the organic unity Comte would attest to by dividing function according to gender is in many ways specious. His laws of nature are not positivist; his gender distinctions limit consensus and solidarity; his dictum that women are "more especially adapted to . . . *Live for Others*" disturbs mutuality of interdependence as well as balanced independence (*General View of Positivism*, p. 431). The ironies are many, and their sum yields incongruity not unity. Elevating women, he creates a disparity between parts in relation to one another and to the whole. Denying women the public sphere though they excel in social feeling, and making men the governing force both within and outside the home, he turns women's "ideal superiority" into "practical subordination."[33] Taking up this last matter in *The Subjection of Women*, Mill is quick to point out the contradiction:

> As for moral differences, considered as distinguished from intellectual, the distinction commonly drawn is to the advantage of women. They are declared to be better than men; an empty compliment, which must provoke a bitter smile from every woman of

32. Comte summarizes his views on "the Influence of Positivism Upon Women" in the fourth chapter of *A General View of Positivism* (pp. 227–303); passages quoted from *A General View of Positivism*, pp. 234–36, 260–61, 265, 360, and *Polity* 4: 58.

33. Christopher Kent, *Brains and Numbers*, p. 101.

spirit, since there is no other situation in life in which it is the established order, and considered quite natural and suitable, that the better should obey the worse.

[p. 213

The marriage contract, Mill demonstrates, is governed not by "community of interests," but by the "law of the strongest" (pp. 131, 151).

Relegating that law to a passing order, military rather than industrial in nature, Spencer in his *Social Statics* (written nearly twenty years before Mill's *Subjection*), argues for "the rights of women." He unequivocally declares: "Equity knows no difference of sex. . . . The law of equal freedom manifestly applies to the whole race—female as well as male." Advancing his case, he correlates natural, moral, and social law by identifying the "law of equal freedom" with a "principle rooted in the nature of things." Insisting that the rise of peaceful industrialism makes fairly negligible "differences of bodily organization," he argues that neither they, nor "those trifling mental variations which distinguish female from male, should exclude one-half of the race from the benefits of . . . the law of equal freedom." Linking political "tyranny" with "domestic oppression," he maintains that women be given "political privileges" and "political power," while contesting the grounds of the denial:

> We are told . . . that "woman's mission" is a domestic one—that her character and position do not admit of her taking a part in the decision of public questions—that politics are beyond her sphere. But this raises the question—Who shall say what her sphere is? . . . As the usages of mankind vary so much, let us hear how it is to be shown that the sphere *we* assign her is the true one—that the limits *we* have set to female activity are just the proper limits.

From every direction, then, Spencer attacks the "laws . . . and the public opinion of England" for countenancing doctrines that enforce the subjection of women.[34]

Published in 1851, *Social Statics* appeared quite radical in its demands for women's rights, but it is consistent with Spencer's general views on individual rights and organic social evolution. Nearly all such consistency vanishes, however, when in the 1870s Spencer entirely revokes his earlier stand. Though he does not ac-

34. Spencer, "The Rights of Women," *Social Statics*, pp. 173–191; passages quoted from pp. 173–74, 179–80, 188–89, 191.

knowledge his defection, the "differences of constitution" and "mental variations" he had earlier declared insignificant become in *Principles of Sociology* definitive "natural" limitations. This change in his view of woman's nature effects a corresponding change of telos:

> It must be concluded that no considerable alteration in the careers of women in general, can be, or should be, so produced [i.e., by abolishing the hindrances that preclude their pursuing independent careers]; and further, that any extensive change in the education of women, made with the view of fitting them for businesses and professions, would be mischievous. If women comprehended all that is contained in the domestic sphere, they would ask no other.

Political rights, equality in marriage, even "the moral relations of married life," all give way before "the preponderance of power" that "must . . . continue with the man."[35]

In defining women's sphere, Spencer does now what he had earlier derided, thereby exposing a major weakness in his concept of the social organism, for the compensatory role he assigns to women makes clear that the evolutionary struggle for survival brings conflict, not altruism and harmony. Ethics and evolution, as Huxley later points out, do not correspond. Spencer, however, evades the complexities of the issue by creating a simple separation between the "ethics of the Family and the ethics of the State": love and benevolent care reign in the one, since without them children would not survive; struggle and conflict (at least for the time being) rule in the other, for without them society would not progress. As a result, the "status" of women in *Principles of Sociology* (as opposed to their "rights" in *Social Statics*) differs little from their place in Comte's *Polity*, although Spencer does not elevate women by endowing them with moral superiority.[36] Thinking them inferior to men in this area too, he diminishes even the value of the "unqualified generosity" it becomes women's primary function to dispense (*Principles of Sociology* 1: 758). For all his individualism, then, Spencer in his later work sacrifices the freedom of women to what he supposes is the progress of the race.

Mill, in contrast, mounts a steady defense of the rights of women

35. Passages quoted from *Social Statics*, p. 173, and *Principles of Sociology* 1: 755–57. Lorna Duffin discusses Spencer's views on women in "Prisoners of Progress: Women and Evolution."

36. Duffin, "Prisoners of Progress," p. 72.

and rejects the patriarchal politics of Comte's *Polity*. Still, when the family is at issue, his strong liberal feminism becomes divided against itself. The result in *Subjection of Women* is an internal incoherence: his philosophical commitment to formal equality of civil and political rights for women does not inform his practical recommendations for the family as a working institution.[37]

Neither Mill's definition of women's nature, nor his attitude toward legal equality of citizenship, nor even entirely the role he assigns to the family accounts for the contradiction. His repudiation of the "intention of Nature" argument in the first chapter of *Subjection*, on the grounds that woman has been kept in so unnatural a state that we cannot know what her nature is, leads directly to his critique in the second chapter of the legal inequalities enforced by the marriage contract. In all areas of contemporary life but one, Mill argues, the movement from status to contract has engendered the egalitarian tendencies now transforming modern politics and morals. The one exception are the laws annexed to the marriage contract, for they guarantee a "relation of command and obedience" instead of a true "morality of justice" (pp. 151, 173).

The solution he proposes is double-edged. On the one side, he argues not for less contract but more, so that marriage may truly be an equal and voluntary association, as the laws of contract demand. On the other side, he proposes that marriage also be a "sympathetic association; having its root no longer in the instinct of equals for self-protection, but in a cultivated sympathy between them; and no one being now left out, but an equal measure being extended to all" (p. 174). "Sympathetic association" suggests again the moral excellence of *jus naturale*; and "equal association," the legal guarantees of *jus gentium*. But for Mill these divisions are entirely free of gender distinctions.

Yet, when Mill considers the family, this double-edged, unified defense no longer consistently cuts both ways. Up until close to the end of the second chapter his liberal feminism remains consistent; the moral principle of "sympathy in equality" and the social principle of legal equality are regularly joined, achieving their most fully imagined unity in the figure of the family as it "should be." Though the family "as at present constituted . . . is a school of despotism, . . . the family, justly constituted, would be the real school of the virtues of freedom":

37. My discussion of Mill draws substantially upon Richard W. Krouse's "Patriarchal Liberalism and Beyond."

The true virtue of human beings is fitness to live together as equals; claiming nothing for themselves but what they freely concede to every one else; regarding command of any kind as an exceptional necessity, and in all cases a temporary one; and preferring, whenever possible, the society of those with whom leading and following can be alternate and reciprocal. To these virtues, nothing in life as at present constituted gives cultivation by exercise. . . . Citizenship, in free countries, is partly a school of society in equality; but citizenship fills only a small place in modern life, and does not come near the daily habits or inmost sentiments. . . . What is needed is, that it [the family] should be a school of sympathy in equality, of living together in love, without power on one side or obedience on the other.

[*Subjection*, pp. 174–75

This equality of power within the marriage partnership requires, as Mill points out, more than sympathetic and equal association. It requires also, he tells us, that women be fully capable of surviving independently outside the family, for only if they are free to preserve their autonomy are they free to marry on equal terms. Yet when it comes to extending the full logic of this principle to *within* the family, Mill falters.[38] Though he grants in the midst of his argument that the deciding voice in the family is likely to be "on the side, whichever it is, that brings the means of support" (p. 170), at the close of the chapter that voice becomes indisputably masculine. Women should have "the *power* of earning," he grants, but they should not exercise that power:

In an otherwise just state of things, it is not . . . a desirable custom, that the wife should contribute by her labour to the income of the family. . . . Like a man when he chooses a profession, so, when a woman marries, it may in general be understood that she makes choice of the management of a household, and the bringing up of a family, as the first call upon her exertions. . . . The actual exercise, in a habitual or systematic manner, of outdoor occupations, or such as cannot be carried on at home, would by this principle be practically interdicted to the greater number of married women.

[p. 179

Favoring within the family a traditional division of labor, Mill yields to an inequality he is otherwise careful to resist and thus separates what he would unite: the public sphere remains masculine and the private feminine.

38. See Krouse, "Patriarchal Liberalism," pp. 161-65.

Faltering in this way, Mill finally assigns to women a telos not so very different from that prescribed by Comte and Spencer; and he does so for a similar reason. For all three, the safekeeping of a nonpublic sphere, whose center is the family, seemed essential to the preservation of society. Because they each resisted changing that most fundamental of the institutions which shape women's lives, though their definitions of women's role are radically different in degree, they are less so in kind. Further, in rendering the family static, they set their theory of society against itself, separating Social Statics from Social Dynamics, the science of order from the science of progress. Making woman's sphere essentially private, and her telos essentially social, they deny the congruence between inward and outward, public and private, that they thought essential to individual and social harmony. The distinctions they draw between the sexes preclude full mutuality of sympathy and solidarity, and argue against the natural identity of interests they sought to establish. In so many respects, their definition of woman's role ultimately subverts the relation between the individual and the social organism they were trying to affirm.

The irony is that their failure to promote with any consistency changes in the structures regulating the relation between the sexes resulted from the same need that attracted them to the concept of a social organism: the need to justify community. Because a consistent application of their organicism would have threatened social concord, they sought in the family a justification for the status quo. As a result, the application of their theories to working social structures, instead of relieving the pressure to reconcile public and private, communal and individual values, merely transfers to women the constraints. Endorsing the most traditional of social structures, the role they assigned to women, instead of curing the paralysis that was turning Social Statics into social stasis, displays their inability to reform working institutions. The final turn is that the Darwinian concept of conflict as the condition of existence, which they resisted, enters Social Statics by default, for the task it assigned to women was compensatory, promoting precisely those virtues that the competitive market world of struggle and competition excludes.[39]

In George Eliot's discursive remarks about the woman question, these same matters are at issue. Like Mill, she takes the " 'intention

39. For an excellent discussion of the relation between Darwinian determinism and feminist issues, see Gillian Beer's "Beyond Determinism."

of Nature' " argument to be a "pitiable fallacy" and an "odious vulgarity," and she points to the "folly of absolute definitions of woman's nature and absolute demarcations of woman's mission."[40] However, differentiating between "zoological" and "moral evolution," she speaks of "distinction of function" based on gender or "ultimate nature." Like Spencer, she maintains that "zoological evolution" has given to woman "the worse share in existence"; like Comte, she contends that women are morally superior to men (*Letters* 4: 364, 467–68).

Among the many strands in George Eliot's views of women only two are even minimally consistent, one of which is this belief in "woman's peculiar constitution for a special moral influence." Arguing that surface "physical and physiological differences between women and men" create "deep roots of psychological development," she derives from them "that exquisite type of gentleness, tenderness, possible maternity suffusing a woman's being with affectionateness, which makes what we mean by the feminine character" (*Letters* 4: 467–68). Arguing as well that "it is the function of love in the largest sense, to mitigate the harshness of all fatalities," she also finds in the limitations imposed upon women a major source of "the spiritual wealth acquired for mankind" (*Letters* 4: 364, 468). As Patricia Spacks contends, "the most remarkable nineteenth-century woman writers," among them George Eliot, "rebelled in print against the injustices of women's lot," but they also believed "that the limitations imposed on women . . . may provide opportunity rather than impediment in the struggle for moral and emotional fulfillment."[41] George Eliot believed, furthermore, that the large-scale effects of women's moral evolution were enormous in their potential, affecting nothing less than the "effort of growing moral force to lighten the pressure of hard non-moral outward conditions" (*Letters* 4: 365).

But even within the consistency of this position, major contradictions exist. The split between zoological and moral evolution enforces a division between ethics and evolution similar to Huxley's, but fatal to social organicism, because it separates natural from social law. "The animal kingdom," Huxley declares, is "founded on the free development of the principle of non-moral evolution," while the "kingdom of Man [is] governed upon the principle of moral evolution" (*Evolution and Ethics*, p. 205). Ex-

40. *Essays*, p. 203; *Letters* 4: 364, 425.
41. Spacks, *The Female Imagination*, p. 36.

pressing similar sentiments and relating them specifically to the education of women, George Eliot says, "if it were not for the accumulated result of social effort, we should be in the state of wild beasts" (*Letters* 6: 287). But her position has neither the clarity nor the consistency of Huxley's because her Lamarckianism holds moral and zoological evolution to be biological.

In addition, George Eliot both resists and succumbs to the idea promoted by Comte, and widely current in Victorian thought, that women are special vessels of sympathy, and that the emancipation of women will weaken their "moral influence by distracting attention to the outside world or by coarsening the feminine nature."[42] As recent feminist critics have shown, George Eliot identifies "social community and moral intensity with women" while opposing the harshness and sterility of patriarchy by seeking "the promise of spiritual and social evolution in the profound sympathies of the female psyche."[43] But since her emphasis continues to be on the actions of women in the private rather than the public sphere, the effect is not fully to confront the ruling ideology.

At the same time, George Eliot "keenly sympathize[d]" with several of the most important figures in the women's movement, one of whom, Barbara Bodichon, was among her closest friends. With a good many others—Mrs. Peter Alfred Taylor, Mrs. Nassau John Senior, Lady Amberley, Emily Davies, Octavia Hill, Bessie Rayner Parkes, Frederick Denison Maurice—she had extensive and continued correspondence. Advocating property rights for married women, suffrage and "the admission of women to political power," "improvement in female education," and access to "all professions,"[44] they were directly challenging what Comte's and Spencer's Social Statics ultimately sanctioned: the structure of existing social institutions as they apply to women.

About the need to reform one of those institutions George Eliot insisted she had "*no doubt.*" That the system of higher education should be changed to include women was the "one point" of the several within the women question toward which she felt both a

42. Walter E. Houghton, *Victorian Frame of Mind*, p. 352.

43. Sandra M. Gilbert and Susan Gubar, *Madwoman in the Attic*, p. 528; see also pp. 498–99; Elaine Showalter, *A Literature of Their Own*, p. 149.

44. "The Claims of Women" as presented in a lecture Lady Amberley gave in 1870, and subsequently published in the *Fortnightly Review*; passages quoted from pp. 100, 102, 109. Responding to the lecture, George Eliot writes: "Now that I have read it at length I find little of which I cannot say that I both agree and keenly sympathize" (*Letters* 8: 477).

"strong conviction" and an obligation "to act." She wholehearted-
ly endorsed the founding of Girton College, calling it a "great
scheme which is pre-eminently worth trying for," and urging a
large not " 'a small scale' " beginning. She also contributed some
money to the college and advised its chief founder, Emily Davies.
Yet, though her conviction "that women ought to have the same
fund of truth placed within their reach as men have" was entirely
firm, still her expressions of support for women's education are
regularly circumscribed by qualifications and self-doubt.[45]

The qualifications arise from her fear that university education
might possibly weaken in women, as it already had in men, the "high
and generous emotions" nurtured by the strength of "family affection" and the bonds of "human love."[46] Yet she felt also that though
"it is not likely that any perfect plan for educating women can soon
be found, for we are very far from having found a perfect plan for
educating men," still "it will not do to wait for perfection" (*Letters*
5: 58). The self-doubt, reflected in her inability to "trust very con-
fidently to my own impressions on this subject," arises from what
she often referred to as "the peculiarities of my own lot" (*Letters*
4: 364). "She greatly desired," Benjamin Jowett reports, "to write
something for the good of women. But she thought that there were
circumstances in her own life which unfitted her for this task."[47]
Perhaps the pressure of those circumstances caused her to defend the
education of women as beneficial to the marriage relationship. Even
Mill would justify the "good" to be expected "from the changes
proposed in our customs and institutions" in terms of "complete
unity and unanimity" between marriage partners "as to the great
objects of life" (*Subjection*, pp. 216, 233–35). Similarly, George
Eliot (writing to Emily Davies) says:

> The answer to those alarms of men about education is, to admit
> fully that the mutual delight of the sexes in each other must enter
> into the perfection of life, but to point out that complete union
> and sympathy can only come by women having opened to them the
> same store of acquired truth or beliefs as men have, so that their
> grounds of judgment may be as far as possible the same.
> [*Letters* 4: 468

45. *Letters* 4: 399; 8: 409; 5: 58; 4: 401.
46. *Letters* 6: 287; 4: 468. Cross, *George Eliot's Life* 3: 309.
47. Evelyn Abbott and Lewis Campbell, *The Life and Letters of Benjamin
Jowett* 2: 182; see also 274.

In this way, the root of individual "justice" is made one with "community of interest."[48] Where education for women is concerned, defense and qualification join rank.

The issue of working women elicits from her a similar, though not quite as positive, response. On the one hand, she worries that emancipation will hinder rather than further "the great amount of social unproductive labour which needs to be done by women, and which is now either not done at all or done wretchedly"—meaning by such "labour" work that results in social as opposed to material gain (*Letters* 4: 425). On the other hand, she supports friends— Barbara Bodichon, Anna Jameson, Mrs. Peter Alfred Taylor, Edith Simcox, Lady Amberley—who were struggling to secure through legislation and women's trade unions better conditions for working women. The one constant in her attitude toward work, whether performed by women or men, is that it be done well. On these grounds she "venerate[s]" Barbara Bodichon who was "struggling in the thick of the contest" for women's rights. She also admires Mrs. Nassau John Senior, one of the first women to have a job in municipal government, calling her a "clear-eyed ardent practical woman" for her work as a poor-law inspector.[49]

Yet, George Eliot is plagued by doubt on the issue of suffrage. To extend women's participation in government in the most basic of ways, by giving them the right to vote, seems to have been for her the most agonizing issue of all. Opposing the vote in 1853, she writes to Mrs. Peter Taylor:

> "Enfranchisement of women" only makes creeping progress; and that is best, for woman does not yet deserve a much better lot than man gives her.
>
> [*Letters* 2: 86

In this same letter, she admires John J. S. Wharton's *Laws Relating to the Women of England,* a book that reveals many of those laws to be "imperfect and reprehensible," but especially the ones prohibiting women from nearly all kinds of employment and married

48. George Eliot calls "community of interest" the "root of justice" (*Essays,* p. 449). Mill identifies "community of interest" as essential to a full and just marriage relationship throughout the *Subjection.*

49. On George Eliot's support of these figures, see *Letters* 2: 105, 396 (including n. 7); 6: 46, 119, 374–75; 8: xviii–xix, 477. Ray Strachey discusses Mrs. Nassau John Senior's pioneering role in municipal government in *"The Cause,"* pp. 205–8.

women from independent property rights.[50] Still, and despite the "due equality" position Wharton takes on most issues, he too balks at giving women the vote. Since his brief is the moral power of women, his argument is worth quoting at length:

> [T]he acquirement of such a right [to vote] would deprive the fair sex of much, if not all, of that powerful and humanizing influence, which their purely social virtues now so justly command, and would very sensibly detract from that mild majesty of their private life, which contributes more effectually to the increase of refinement and good manners, than all our other social elements combined. This natural empire of woman, without which, indeed, our infancy would be without succour, our manhood without happiness, and our old age without consolation, would be lost, were she to quit the sacred retirement of her undisplayed care and sympathy, and mix in the public arena of angry debate and heartless ambition; her powerful spell would be broken, her worth compromised, her respect decreased, and her unalloyed virtues—the consequences indeed of her domestic life—weakened and debased. Let not, then, her present glorious mission be taken away!
>
> [p. 174

But it is not on these grounds that George Eliot resists, at this point, the enfranchisement of women. The cynical tone of her comment suggests not that political action may interfere with woman's "glorious mission," but that her mission was not being fulfilled. Her tone, however, is by no means stable, and even within this letter, she takes solace in the belief "that the moral tendencies of human nature are yet only in their germ."

While the future she looked forward to in 1853 could hardly have seemed significantly nearer in 1867, by that time, her comments on women's suffrage change considerably. Writing to John Morley about "Female Enfranchisement," she says:

> If I were called on to act in the matter, I would certainly not oppose any plan which held out any reasonable promise of tending to establish as far as possible equivalence of advantages for the two . . sexes, as to education and the possibilities of free development.[51]

This letter is dated 14 May, 1867; that is, in the same month that Mill initiated in the House of Commons the first parliamentary

50. John Jane Smith Wharton, *An Exposition of the Laws Relating to the Women of England*, pp. 257–64, 312–13, 181.
51. *Letters* 8: 402–3. Letter first printed in extract, 4: 364–65.

debate on women's suffrage and two weeks before Morley published in the *Fortnightly Review* an article on women's status in which he expresses views that correspond to George Eliot's.[52] Writing to him to clarify a recent conversation, she opens her letter by saying: "Your attitude in relation to Female Enfranchisement seems to be very nearly mine."

How greatly her attitude had changed since the 1850s is demonstrated by Morley's position. Maintaining, like Mill, that "it is contrary to the whole spirit of modern movement for us to throw ourselves upon some imagined intention or design of nature, and then in obedience to this picture to determine for half of the race what is for their own good to do and what to abstain from," he argues:

> Whatever view we may take of the future destiny of society, it is clear that any measure which, like the proposed enfranchisement of women, is virtually no more than the removal of a restriction or a set of restrictions, must be a preliminary step.

Further, he notes the "wretched dislocation of life and purpose which so constantly marks the ordinary female history, in the avowedly unsatisfactory state of their education, and in their relations to their husbands if they are married, and to the world generally if they are not married," and recommends that "the laws which fix the status of women" be changed and that women "be endowed with enough direct political power to press on such a change."

Additional evidence of George Eliot's shifting position is provided by another letter she wrote in May 1867, again to Mrs. Peter Taylor, to whom she now says:

> On the whole I am inclined to hope for much good from the serious presentation of women's claims before Parliament. I thought Mill's speech sober and judicious from his point of view—Karslake's [in opposition to suffrage] an abomination.
>
> [*Letters* 4: 366

Yet in October 1867, in a letter to her old friend Sara Hennell (who had joined the campaign for women's rights), George Eliot calls women's suffrage "an extremely doubtful good" (*Letters* 4: 390). And in 1869, writing to Mrs. Nassau John Senior, she is as edgy and as negative as she had been in 1853. "There is no subject,"

---

52. John Morley, Review of *The Social and Political Dependence of Women.* Morley's analysis corresponds closely to Mill's speech before Parliament in May 1867.

she says, "on which I am more inclined to hold my peace and learn, than on the 'Woman Question.' It seems to me to overhang abysses, of which even prostitution is not the worst. Conclusions seem easy so long as we keep large blinkers on and look in the direction of our own private path" (*Letters* 5: 58). Her skepticism surfaces even in her letters supporting the suffrage movement, for example, in the many qualifying phrases in the May 1867 letters. Indeed, it is in her letter to Morley that she draws the distinction, mentioned earlier, between zoological and moral evolution; and this, finally, is the crux.

George Eliot's belief "that in the moral evolution we have 'an art which does mend nature'—an art which 'itself is nature,' " made her wary of "political measures for improving society—as leading away from individual efforts to be good."[53] As we have seen in Comte and Wharton, the greater burden of those efforts was assigned to women, with their nature and telos defined accordingly. At the same time, George Eliot and others recognized that such views in effect sanctioned current social institutions and laws that were unfair to women. The former belief allied her with a community of interests defined primarily by men; the latter brought her into an opposing community of interests being forged largely by women. Some men (Mill, Maurice, Morley, Huxley) joined the women; but there was an emerging sense that the "class-weight," or "class-footing," of men and women differed enough as to make members of both groups feel that *women must speak for themselves.*[54] But if Mill's and Huxley's voices carried great authority in nineteenth-century intellectual life, so did Comte's and Spencer's, and their position on women demonstrates a difference of view so great as to signify two opposing communities of interest.

George Eliot identified with both, while recognizing that neither was complete nor even self-consistent and feeling, in addition, extremely defensive about the anomalies in her personal life. She often

---

53. *Letters* 8: 402; 6: 287. See also Cross, *George Eliot's Life* 3: 307–8. Spencer, in the conclusion to *Social Statics* (1850), draws upon the "art . . . nature" passage from *The Winter's Tale* to advance the same Lamarckian argument for moral progress that George Eliot makes in her letter to Morley (8: 402). Spencer, however, makes no gender distinctions (*Social Statics*, pp. 516–17).

54. The phrases quoted are from "Mr. Spencer and the Women," a letter Sara Hennell wrote to the *Examiner*, in which she criticizes Spencer's recent work on women and expresses a "debt of gratitude" to Mill for having "said for us" that *women must speak for themselves.* George Eliot wrote to Sara Hennell that she found the letter to be "much milder than I expected" (*Letters* 6: 15).

equivocated, as in the "limited adherence" she gives to Comte, as well as in the "sympathy" she professes for the women's movement and the "practical adhesion" she opposes.[55] At times her ambivalence gives way to uncontrolled anger and "imperfect . . . sympathy" (*Letters* 5: 58). Far more often, however, equivocation turns into retreat, to wanting to be "delivered," as she puts it, "from any necessity of giving a judgment on the Woman Question."[56] Nonetheless, though she wanted to keep her distance from causes, she also wanted to contribute to "the social right," and she attempts to do both by separating political action from sympathetic belief.

Making this division in her May 1867 letter to Mrs. Peter Taylor, she says:

> I do sympathise with you most emphatically in the desire to see women socially elevated—educated equally with men, and secured as far as possible along with every other breathing creature from suffering the exercise of any unrighteous power. That is a broader ground of sympathy than agreement as to the amount, and kind, of result that may be hoped for from a particular measure.
>
> [*Letters* 4: 366

Once we realize, however, that this "broader ground" is identical with "community of interests," requiring of its tenants an agreement as to the problem but not the solution, "sympathy" too enters into the disagreement. All that is required to erode this "broader ground" is to introduce Comte, who also desires "to see women socially elevated," though he defines their nature, their telos, and their relation to social institutions in severely restrictive ways. To bring into the picture the other figures we have been discussing is to see even more acutely how thought and feeling, instead of being separable from the "particular measures" that regulate social institutions, are inextricably linked to them. The separation, moreover, fails not only on its own ground of sympathetic identification. It also divides what George Eliot thought elsewhere was essential to unite: *jus naturale* and *jus gentium* as well as the public and the private life.

Such fundamental disagreements both within and between identical and opposing communities of interest are no less at issue for

55. Cross, *George Eliot's Life* 3: 302; *Letters* 5: 58.

56. *Letters* 2: 383. The date of this letter is 1857, but the attitudes expressed here span George Eliot's career. When in 1878 Mrs. Taylor "urges" her "to speak for suffrage" (Index to *Letters* 9: 525), she answers, "I thought you understood that I have grave reasons for not speaking on certain public topics" (*Letters* 7: 44).

George Eliot, the artist. In another letter to Mrs. Peter Taylor, this one written in 1878, she declares:

> My function is that of the *aesthetic*, not the doctrinal teacher—the rousing of the nobler emotions, which make mankind desire the social right, not the prescribing of special measures, concerning which the artistic mind, however strongly moved by social sympathy, is often not the best judge.
>
> [*Letters* 7: 44

Again she attempts to separate doctrine and practice from feeling and belief; and again the woman question is central, as the occasion for this letter was Mrs. Taylor's warm request that George Eliot "speak for suffrage."[57] However much George Eliot wished to deny with her aesthetic defense her friend's pragmatic request, "social sympathy" is as much at issue in the one as in the other. Elaine Showalter has commented that to discuss George Eliot's fiction "in terms of its dense and subtle historical context, or its metaphors of vision, system, and community," though valuable, is nonetheless to exclude feminist issues.[58] However, the letter quoted above, together with the occasion that prompted it, reveal the intimate, albeit embattled, connection between George Eliot's social and aesthetic concerns and the nineteenth-century debate on the woman question.

Social and Aesthetic Organicism

The failure of the social theorists to agree on the most fundamental principles which were to govern their science of society seriously impeded the practical application of their theories. Unable to abstract from the study of historical patterns coherent values of community, they could not proceed to translate values into social institutions adequate to an expanding and changing world. George Eliot, however, by choosing to represent such worlds in her fiction, necessarily had to engage in this process of translation. Certainly, the initiating impulse and the shape of her constructs were determined not by a science of society but rather by a social aesthetic; nonetheless, the inability of the theorists to translate social principles into social structures has its counterpart in the narrative structures that shape her fiction.

There is no doubt that in George Eliot's mind an aesthetic of organic form combined with an organic social ideology. Modern

57. Index to *Letters* 9: 525.
58. Elaine Showalter, "The Greening of Sister George," p. 306.

criticism has tended to separate the two, perhaps because aesthetic organicism has been so tied to the idea of the well-wrought urn, or the self-contained, autonomous work of art. As a result, though critics have paid considerable attention to George Eliot's belief that society is an organism, they rarely connect that belief to her aesthetic of organic form.[59] Yet the one is clearly the corollary of the other. This correspondence between organic wholeness in a community and organic structure in a work of art is embedded in the very language of her "Notes on Form in Art."

Sometimes the associations seem private. A seashell analogy, for instance, which she uses in an 1852 letter to describe Nuremberg and the "feeling of brotherhood" it elicits in her, reappears sixteen years later, when she considers in the "Notes" how poetic structures, like natural and social ones, derive their form from the growing life they contain:

> *There* one sees a real mediaeval town, which has grown up with the life of a community as much as the shell of a nautilus has grown with the life of the animal; and the result is just as beautiful. . . . There is no end to the varieties which the vista of every street presents—but it is a variety like Nature's, showing general unity presiding over an endless play of individual variety.
>
> [*Letters* 2: 451–52

> Poetic Form was not begotten by thinking it out or framing it as a shell which should hold emotional expression, any more than the shell of an animal arises before the living creature. . . . Just as the beautiful expanding curves of a bivalve shell are not first made for the reception of the unstable inhabitant, but grow & are limited by the simple rhythmic conditions of its growing life.
>
> [*Essays*, p. 435

59. For discussions of George Eliot's belief in the organic structure of society, see Bernard Paris, *Experiments in Life*, pp. 42–49, 193–204; Robert Colby, *Fiction With a Purpose*, pp. 288–300; Peter Coveney, Introduction to *Felix Holt*, pp. 7–22; K. M. Newton, *George Eliot, Romantic Humanist*, pp. 79–96; David Carroll, "*Felix Holt*."

For a discussion of George Eliot's aesthetic of organic form, see Darrel Mansell, Jr., "George Eliot's Conception of 'Form.'" A few critics relate George Eliot's organic views about society to her concept of form in art. See Michael York Mason, "*Middlemarch* and Science"; J. Hillis Miller, "Narrative and History," and "Optic and Semiotic in *Middlemarch*"; David Carroll, "'Janet's Repentance' and the Myth of the Organic." Mason finds the correspondence between social and aesthetic organicism entirely harmonious. Carroll argues for a dialectical opposition between the two, resolved in the end through synthesis, while Miller finds both deconstructive.

But the contexts of these passages indicate that the analogies and correlations include also a wide frame of reference. The unity-variety motif in the letter suggests the organicism of Comte, Spencer, Mill, and Lewes; and the vocabulary in the "Notes on Form in Art" so echoes Spencer as to make her voice occasionally sound interchangeable with his:

> In the development of a planet, of an organism, of a society, of a science, of an art, the process of integration is seen in a more complete aggregation of each whole and of its constituent parts; but it is also shown in an increasing mutual dependence of the parts.
>
> [Spencer, *First Principles*, p. 211

> As knowledge continues to grow by its alternating processes of distinction & combination, . . . it arrives at the conception of wholes composed of parts more & more multiplied & highly differenced, yet more & more absolutely bound together by various conditions of common likeness or mutual dependence.
>
> [George Eliot, *Essays*, p. 433

The emphasis on development and continuous growth in each of these passages raises in addition the issue of structural complexity. Whereas the description of Nuremberg and the shell analogy emphasize simplicity of structure, the more fully elaborated argument posits a complexity of structure resulting from evolutionary development. Because social development and literary style parallel one another, the movement from homogeneity to heterogeneity applies not only to society but also to works of art. Spencer makes this point as early as 1852 in an essay called "The Philosophy of Style," which he published in the *Westminster Review* when George Eliot was its editor and they were meeting often. He concludes that a truly modern work of art, like "all highly organized products both of man and of nature . . . will be, not a series of like parts simply placed in juxtaposition, but one whole made up of unlike parts that are mutually dependent" (p. 247). This proposition, too, has its counterpart in the "Notes":

> Forms of art can be called higher or lower only on the same principle as that on which we apply these words to organisms; viz. in proportion to the complexity of the parts bound up into one indissoluble whole.
>
> [*Essays*, p. 435

That Lewes also believed in an organic connection between literary form and biological and social structure is evident even from the opening sentences of *The Principles of Success in Literature* (1865):

> In the development of the great series of animal organisms, the Nervous System assumes more and more of an imperial character. . . . In like manner, in the development of the social organism, as the life of nations becomes more complex, Thought assumes a more imperial character; and Literature, in its widest sense, becomes a delicate index of social evolution.
>
> [*Fortnightly Review* 1: 85

Literature is not only an index but also an agent of social evolution. It is language, Lewes argues, that makes "Man" no longer simply "an assemblage of organs, but also . . . an organ in a Collective Organism" (*Problems* 1: 153–54). For Spencer, too, language is the crucial nexus between the individual and the social organism, compensating for nothing less than the one major difference between them. The former, he argues, is composed of proximate parts that form a physical whole; the latter of living units more or less dispersed, but their discreteness is rendered by language into "a living whole" (*Principles of Sociology* 1: 447–48). Bringing full circle the argument for the "Social purpose" of language, Comte claims that "Language . . . cannot be really separated" from "Art" (*Polity* 2: 199–203).

Described in this way, organicist principles in science, society, and art appear to be mutually reinforcing. Since the writing of novels was the one area in which the moral excellence of woman was allowed a public sphere, even George Eliot's choice of profession seems to fit harmoniously into this whole.[60] As recent feminist critics of George Eliot's novels have shown, however, subversion no less than concord is pervasive in her work. In contrast, those critics who focus on George Eliot's organic ideas about society emphasize concord, perhaps because the concept of organicism, by supposing unity and wholeness, predisposes critics to think in terms of harmony and coherence. David Carroll's recent work is to some extent an exception, inasmuch as his discussion of George Eliot's treatment of certain love triangles leads him to conclude that her belief in organic process is "far more precarious than is usually acknowledged." J. Hillis Miller's deconstructionist readings of *Middlemarch* are also an exception, but for him the precariousness is

---

60. Duffin, "Prisoners of Progress," p. 70.

so extreme as to subvert both the concept of organic form in art and of organic wholeness in society.[61]

This sense of precariousness is the subject of the next chapter. Unlike Miller, however, I shall not argue that George Eliot opposes in *Middlemarch* "the notion of a work of art which is an organic unity" (p. 468). Nor shall I argue, as does Carroll, for ultimate reconciliations, at least not in those novels that portray complex as opposed to simple societies. When George Eliot's novels move from Hayslope to St. Ogg's, from Raveloe to Middlemarch, from London to the Continent—a movement that includes for her social, personal, and literary correspondences—her complex fictional structures finally undermine the idea of organic wholeness in society. Arguing for a resolution that is balanced, while yet acknowledging social breakdown and dissolution within, Carroll ascribes to George Eliot the dialectic of Coleridge's aesthetic organicism. But given the correlation between George Eliot's social and aesthetic beliefs, to assign to her an aesthetic that embraces conflict is also to make conflict central to her social views. Yet, positivistic organicism and conflict theories represent decidedly antithetical ways of thinking about society. That the opposition between them is not to be resolved through synthesis is something that Coleridge perhaps foresaw, since his aesthetic organicism remains quite separate from his longings for community.[62]

Within the tradition we have been defining, both are part of the same universe of discourse, but it is not a purposefully dialectical universe. While scientists and artist were walking hand in hand, they were often stumbling. The world we have been describing is consequently messier than Carroll suggests. He speaks of the "myth of the organic," but the figures we have been discussing took the living social organism as their object. Just as any sense of organic harmony dissolves as soon as one closely examines the strange mutations and frequent reversals permeating positivistic organicism—continually separating inward and outward, natural and social, private and public, individual and communal—so does it also dissolve when one analyzes how narrative structure shapes social reality in those novels that George Eliot's Victorian readers took to be her most modern. They are, in addition, the ones which twentieth-

61. Carroll, " 'Janet's Repentance,' " p. 348; Miller, "Narrative and History," pp. 468–71. Miller continues the argument in "Optic and Semiotic."

62. For a discussion of Coleridge's organic theories of art, see Meyer Abrams, *The Mirror and the Lamp*, pp. 124, 174–75, 220–25.

century readers find most engaging. In these novels—*The Mill on the Floss, Middlemarch,* and *Daniel Deronda*—the narrative structures put under significant stress the organic beliefs that inform their author's social aesthetic, and vice versa.

FIVE

◆

Organic Fictions

The Mill on the Floss

In *The Mill on the Floss* George Eliot clearly meant to put organic notions under stress. Narrative statement in the middle of
the novel confirms what the action has dramatized all along—that
"the outward and inward," instead of being in harmony for Maggie, are often in "painful collision."[1] The critical problem posed
by *The Mill on the Floss,* however, concerns not the middle of
the novel, but the reconciliation at the close. Some readers claim
that the end achieves organic unity through a synthesis of the outward and the inward. Others see only disunities, and still others distinguish the unity George Eliot intended from the actual effect she
creates.[2] The last of these positions seems to me the most satisfactory
for reasons advanced by Barbara Hardy, George Levine, and R. H.
Lee, and for other reasons as well. The following discussion presupposes Hardy's attention to autobiography, Levine's to intellectual systems, and Lee's to George Eliot's view of tragedy. Levine's
conclusion that "all the influences so carefully prepared through
the apparently leisurely movement of the early stages of the novel

1. *The Mill on the Floss* (7 books), III, v, 208; IV, ii, 241. To indicate place
within overall structure, citations throughout this chapter are to book part,
chapter, and page. Roman numerals refer to book part only, except in the case
of the *Mill,* where George Eliot used two numbering systems: roman for book,
and for chapters numbered according to book; arabic for chapters numbered
consecutively throughout. Elsewhere, her numbering of chapters is strictly
consecutive.

2. Sara M. Putzell, for instance, argues for synthesis in " 'An Antagonism
of Valid Claims.' " F. R. Leavis is foremost among those who focus on the
novel's disunities; see *The Great Tradition,* pp. 38–47. Among those critics who
argue for an unsatisfactory unity are Barbara Hardy, *"The Mill on the Floss";*
George Levine, "Intelligence as Deception"; and R. H. Lee, "The Unity of
The Mill on the Floss."

come into play in the last book," however, seems overstated to me (p. 406); and Lee's argument that the "comparative failure" of the final two books can be explained by "George Eliot's view of the balance in tragedy of character and circumstance" is, I think, attenuated by the singularity of view he ascribes to her (pp. 50–51). I argue instead that the end both includes and excludes much of the material at the center of the novel and that contradictions in George Eliot's view of tragedy contribute to the forced reconciliations of the close.

In the middle book of *The Mill on the Floss*, the conflict between inward impulse and outward fact brings thirteen-year-old Maggie to a "time of utmost need" (IV, ii, 241). She responds, as this fourth book closes, by rejecting outward things for the new inward life she discovers by reading Thomas à Kempis: " 'Forsake thyself, resign thyself, and thou shalt enjoy much inward peace.' . . . Here, then, was a secret of life that would enable her to renounce all other secrets—here was a sublime height to be reached without the help of outward things" (IV, iii, 254).

The outward causes of this extreme response are presented as both immediate and far-reaching. The immediate ones Maggie understands well enough. They derive from the bankruptcy following her father's lawsuit over water rights for the mill: from conflict, in other words, as opposed to identity of interests. This conflict results in her family's financial ruin, social isolation, and disgrace. While Maggie's father worries that he has "damaged her chance in life" (" 'there'll be nobody to marry her as is fit for her' "), Maggie is most troubled by her family's woes and by having to give up school (IV, iii, 258).

The more general outward facts Maggie apprehends only partially at this time. Her apprehension takes the form of a "peremptory hunger of the soul" and a "blind, unconscious yearning for something that would . . . give her soul a sense of home" (III, v, 208; IV, ii, 241). Trying to satisfy this hunger, she seeks from "masculine wisdom" the "attainments" and "knowledge which made men contented, and even glad to live," but its relation to "this living world" seems so "extremely remote for her" that she is just about to give up the effort when she comes upon Thomas à Kempis (IV, iii, 251–57). The narrator makes clear immediately, however, that the asceticism of à Kempis renders his message no less remote from this living world.

At the same time, the reader is made to confront what Maggie at thirteen cannot possibly understand: how the living world drives her to à Kempis. In a long discursive passage appearing right in the middle of the à Kempis episode, we see that "the root" to which Maggie would "lay the axe" spreads wide indeed. The demands of "good society" lead to organic dysfunction in the "national life"; the form of Maggie's search for belief (or her "emphasis of want") testifies to the fracture by radically separating inward from outward:

In writing the history of unfashionable families, one is apt to fall into a tone of emphasis which is very far from being the tone of good society, where principles and beliefs are not only of an extremely moderate kind, but are always presupposed, no subjects being eligible but such as can be touched with a light and graceful irony. But then, good society has its claret and its velvet-carpets, its dinner-engagements six weeks deep, its opera and its faëry ballrooms; rides off its ennui on thoroughbred horses, lounges at the club, has to keep clear of crinoline vortices, gets its science done by Faraday, and its religion by the superior clergy who are to be met in the best houses: how should it have time or need for belief and emphasis? But good society, floated on gossamer wings of light irony, is of very expensive production; requiring nothing less than a wide and arduous national life condensed in unfragrant deafening factories, cramping itself in mines, sweating at furnaces, grinding, hammering, weaving under more or less oppression of carbonic acid—or else, spread over sheepwalks, and scattered in lonely houses and huts on the clayey or chalky corn-lands, where the rainy days look dreary. This wide national life is based entirely on emphasis —the emphasis of want, which urges it into all the activities necessary for the maintenance of good society and light irony: it spends its heavy years often in a chill, uncarpeted fashion, amidst family discord unsoftened by long corridors. Under such circumstances, there are many among its myriads of souls who have absolutely needed an emphatic belief: life in this unpleasurable shape demanding some solution even to unspeculative minds; just as you inquire into the stuffing of your couch when anything galls you there, whereas eider-down and perfect French springs excite no question. Some have an emphatic belief in alcohol, and seek their *ekstasis* or outside standing-ground in gin; but the rest require something that good society calls "enthusiasm," something that will present motives in an entire absence of high prizes, something that will give patience and feed human love when the limbs ache with weariness, and human looks are hard upon us —something, clearly, that lies outside personal desires, that includes resignation for ourselves and active love for what is not ourselves. Now and then, that sort of enthusiasm finds a far-echoing voice

that comes from an experience springing out of the deepest need.
And it was by being brought within the long lingering vibrations
of such a voice that Maggie, with her girl's face and unnoted sorrows, found an effort and a hope that helped her through years of
loneliness, making out a faith for herself without the aid of established authorities and appointed guides—for they were not at hand,
and her need was pressing.

[IV, iii, 255–56

Though George Eliot writes with brilliance of how "good society"
creates in the nation at large a severe "emphasis of want" and in its
members a need for "emphatic belief," the novel thus far has focused
so exclusively on "unfashionable families" that the evocation of
"good society" is more of an interruption than an explanation. In
the two closing books, however, good society dramatically enters
the novel with the introduction of Stephen Guest. His "diamond
ring, attar of roses, and air of nonchalant leisure, at twelve o'clock
in the day" (VI, i, 316) negatively complement the "light and graceful irony" that accompanies nearly all his remarks during the first
half of Book Six. Ridiculing everyone—Lucy, Maggie, Philip, Dr.
Kenn, Mrs. Tulliver, and his sisters—he is regularly described as
"supercilious," "satirical," "conceited," "saucy, defiant."[3] Playing
the role of " 'Graceful Consort' " (as in the duet by Haydn), he
speaks of Lucy's "faëry touch" and excites in Maggie visions of a
"brighter aërial world," indulging for much of this book in the
"sort of sugared complacency and flattering make-believe" Philip
associates with this music he sings.[4] As another young gentleman
observes, " 'Guest is a great coxcomb, . . . but then he is a privileged person in St Ogg's—he carries all before him: if another
fellow did such things, everybody would say he made a fool of
himself' " (VI, ix, 377). His family is "good society" (VI, vi, 349),
and he is their representative.

This figure Maggie runs off with, then, is presented at first in a
far from flattering way; the correspondences between the images of
good society in Book Four and the portrait of Stephen in the first
half of Book Six are strong. One would expect these correspondences to continue through the novel's conclusion. But let us
examine two critical moments in the closing books, when Maggie
turns once more to à Kempis. The first occurs when she wakes on
the Dutch steamer the morning after she and Stephen have gone
off together. Again there is the sense of homelessness, soul's hunger,

3. *MF*, VI, i, 318; ii, 328; iii, 337; vii, 365–66.
4. *MF*, VI, i, 319–20; iii, 336; xiii, 412.

and utmost need: "Her life with Stephen could have no sacredness: she must for ever sink and wander vaguely, driven by uncertain impulse; for she had let go the clue of life—that clue which once in the far-off years her young need had clutched so strongly. . . . She saw it face to face now—that sad patient loving strength which holds the clue of life—and saw that the thorns were for ever pressing on its brow" (VI, xiv, 413). The thorns, too, connect back to Book Four, one of whose chapters is called "The Torn Nest is Pierced by the Thorns." The second critical moment occurs in the last chapter of the closing book, just after Maggie receives a letter from Stephen imploring her to ask him to " 'Come!' " Recalling à Kempis, she resists the appeal (VII, v, 449–51).

Both of Maggie's returns to à Kempis, like her original discovery of him, are preceded by her feeling "blank," "listless," "paralyzed" —"without active force."[5] In the last book, her need is perhaps greater than it has ever been, her sense of having "no home" and of being a "lonely wanderer" at its most acute (VII, v, 499). But the more substantial difference between Maggie's first turning to à Kempis at thirteen and her returns to him at nineteen is that "good society" is no longer an intangible outward force invoked by the narrator; it is now as palpably present, in the form of Stephen Guest, as is the spiritual emphasis of want that first drove her to à Kempis. Yet, though Maggie's thoughts about à Kempis in Books Six and Seven are clearly prompted by her relation to Stephen, his social status receives almost no attention in these episodes. Perhaps for this reason the strands that connect good society, Stephen Guest, and à Kempis have gone unnoticed.

George Eliot's severance of the correspondence between Stephen and good society begins suddenly in the ninth chapter of Book Six ("Charity in Full-Dress"). Stephen enters this chapter a "coxcomb," but leaves it a figure beset by "moral conflict." For the first time, the narrator defends him:

> The conduct that issues from a moral conflict has often so close a resemblance to vice, that the distinction escapes all outward judgments, founded on a mere comparison of actions. It is clear to you, I hope, that Stephen was not a hypocrite.
>
> [VI, ix, 380

Immediately following this defense, Dr. Kenn first appears in the novel, and his response to Maggie allows the narrator to make of charity, which is the subject of the chapter, an observation that is

5. *MF*, IV, iii, 252–53; VI, xiii, 409; VII, v, 450.

more than ironical: "There is always this possibility of a word or look from a stranger to keep alive the sense of human brotherhood" (382). The theme of brotherhood carries over into the next paragraph, in which Maggie's passion for Stephen—for a "life filled with all luxuries," "adoration," and "all possibilities of culture"— becomes submerged in a different kind of "passion and affection"— consisting of "long deep memories" and of "early claims on her love and pity" (382–84). Those memories and claims include her friend Philip (" 'it would be the best and highest lot for me—to make his life happy' "), but above all her brother Tom (" 'But I can't divide myself from my brother for life' ").

Such motifs, which enter this chapter in a great rush, now become the dominant ones. The image of Stephen as "insolent coxcomb" reappears momentarily, but it is refuted immediately by the image of him as a "hunted" romantic lover beset by devils, whom he tries to resist in the name of "honour and conscience." [6] At the same time, Stephen comes increasingly to epitomize not the shallowness of good society but the "fulness of existence—love, wealth, ease, refinement, all that her nature craved." And Maggie remains desperate to resist her attraction to him because to yield would mean to put "personal enjoyment" above the pity, faith, and sympathy she feels she owes to others (VI, xiii, 402).

This conflict between "two irreconcilable requirements"—one of which speaks to "our individual needs," the other "to the dire necessities of our lot"—is for George Eliot quintessential to tragedy. She writes, "tragedy consists in the terrible difficulty," if not the impossibility, of creating "an adjustment . . . between the individual and the general." [7] The former presupposes a telos focused on the individual; the latter, on society.

The shift in the portrait of Stephen from privileged gentleman to romantic lover enforces this view of tragedy. The more Stephen continues to be merely a coxcomb of good society, the less tenable the idea of a national life that is capable of sustaining a social telos. By minimizing Stephen's social status and emphasizing instead Maggie's inward struggle, George Eliot separates the outward social

6. *MF*, VI, xi, 392; xiii, 401. R. H. Lee presents a valuable analysis of one side of the problem, reasoning that "part of Stephen's dramatic unreality comes from the fact that he stands really for an idea—the idea of romantic love" ("Unity," pp. 49–50).

7. "Notes on *The Spanish Gypsy* and Tragedy in General," in Cross, *George Eliot's Life* 3: 30–35. See also "The Antigone and Its Moral," *Essays*, pp. 264–65.

world from that which is inward or personal, allowing the claims of each to be presented as inviolate. This separation prepares, in turn, for the attempted resolution of the conflict between inward and outward at the close.

In addition to conflict and antithesis, George Eliot's view of tragedy includes two other major principles. One is that "a tragedy has not to expound why the individual must give way to the general; it has to show that it is compelled to give way; the tragedy consisting in the struggle involved, and often in the entirely calamitous issue in spite of a grand submission" (Cross, *George Eliot's Life* 3: 33). The end of the novel and a passage that appears only in the manuscript suggest, however, that while George Eliot thinks Maggie's story tragic, she also retreats from so calamitous a collision.[8] The excised passage, which originally appeared immediately after the first statement contrasting outward and inward, reads: "A girl . . . may still hold forces within her as the living plant-seed does, which will make a way for themselves, often in a shattering, violent manner" (III, v, 208 [n. 7]). The action at the novel's end is "shattering," of course, but Maggie's response is not; no sooner does she know that the flood has come than she feels "a great calm" (VII, v, 451).

This sense of calm is the third aspect of George Eliot's definition of tragedy. Having spoken of how "the individual must give way to the general," she asks, "Now, what is the fact about our individual lots" in the face of "the commonest inherited misfortunes?" Her answer is:

> The utmost approach to well-being that can be made in such a case is through large resignation and acceptance of the inevitable, with as much effort to overcome any disadvantage as good sense will show to be attended with a likelihood of success. Any one may say, that is the dictate of mere rational reflection. But calm can, in hardly any human organism, be attained by rational reflection. Happily, we are not left to that. Love, pity, constituting sympathy, and generous joy with regard to the lot of our fellowmen comes in—has been growing since the beginning—enormously enhanced by wider vision of results, by an imagination actively interested in the lot of mankind generally; and these feelings become piety—*i.e.*, loving, willing submission and heroic Promethean effort towards high possibilities, which may result from our individual life.
>
> [Cross, *George Eliot's Life* 3: 33–34

8. *Letters* 3: 317; 374. See also 3: 269, where Lewes speaks of the "strain of poetry" that "relieve[s] the tragedy" at the close.

The turns and counterturns in this statement, particularly in the light of the preceding comments about "irreparable collision" and "calamitous issue," are dizzying and contradictory. The irreconcilable antitheses George Eliot initially assigns to tragedy are here replaced by a "calm" she associates with "love, pity," and "sympathy . . . with regard to the lot of our fellowmen."

George Eliot's desire to create this kind of affirmation at the close of *The Mill on the Floss* bears directly on the change that occurs in the depiction of Stephen. Whereas the forces that pull Maggie to Stephen are presented as essentially inward, her decision to leave him is presented as satisfying both her inward needs and her sense of duty. Her decision reflects her love for Tom, a family bond, and the love, pity, and sympathy she feels for Lucy and Philip. This union of feelings corresponds to the joining, in the passage above, of the "individual life" and the "lot of our fellowmen." Thus it represents not the single telos that defines her relation to Stephen but one that is double. Had Stephen remained the representative of good society, the indictment of the outward social world would have been so severe as to have made impossible the novel's attempt to affirm a social telos. Society comes off badly enough in the last book because of the behavior of the "world's wife," but Maggie is oblivious to this emblem in a way she could never be to Stephen. Her acceptance of her duty to others depends in part on her paying so little attention to what is said about her: again the affirmation requires evasion.

Maggie's triumph over the world's wife by virtue of her moral superiority participates in this pattern of evasion, for it requires that Stephen continue to be portrayed in a good light. The "heroism of renunciation," George Eliot points out elsewhere, requires "that the thing we renounce is precious."[9] Accordingly, to treat Stephen critically would be to devalue Maggie's renunciation and her moral evolution. The more intense the struggle within each becomes, the less can Stephen be depicted as an "insolent coxcomb." He becomes ardent logician, instead, opposing the love that is "natural" to "unnatural" social bonds. At the same time, as

9. George Eliot is criticizing Geraldine Jewsbury for creating a character who renounced a man " 'not worth the keeping' " (*Essays*, pp. 134–35). Stephen Guest, of course, has been criticized on similar grounds. The most famous attacks are by Leslie Stephen, who emphasizes the early portrait (*George Eliot*, pp. 100–104), and by Leavis, who argues that Stephen is not worthy of Maggie's "spiritual and idealistic nature" though neither character nor author realize it (*Great Tradition*, pp. 43–46).

Maggie matures, love and social bonds become so intertwined within her as to make the one as natural as the other. In the end, it is Stephen's suffering and misery, in fact, that constitute the most "dire . . . temptation to Maggie" (VII, v, 450). In her moral evolution there is " 'an art which does mend nature' "—but not without injuring the art of the novel.

Most readers sense that Maggie's moral evolution is meant to represent that continuous adjustment of external to internal relations essential to social organicism.[10] Nonetheless, the process of adjustment in the closing chapters excludes a good part of what had earlier dissociated the outward from the inward in Maggie's life. In Books Four and Five, Maggie's turning to à Kempis clearly demonstrates that division. His "simple rule" requires the repudiation of earthly good; Maggie, however, initially adopts his rule because of the absence of earthly good from her life. Her longings for this good do not cease; thus, the solace she finds in à Kempis means at best a "negative peace," at worst, continued privation and starvation.[11] When à Kempis is reintroduced in Books Six and Seven, the critique of renunciation and the corresponding critique of society are absent. Renunciation, first presented as shutting out " 'the avenues by which the life of your fellow-men might become known to you' " (V, iii, 286) is now identified with a "new force of unselfish human love" (VII, v, 449). If George Eliot is making a distinction between the "narrow valley of humiliation" of à Kempis's monastic rule and a Feuerbachian or Comtean commitment to sympathy with all that is human as opposed to divine, it is surely a distinction of which Maggie is unaware.

Some years before, in reviewing Mackay's *Progress of the Intellect*, George Eliot spoke of how "religion and philosophy" are "identical . . . when root and branch exhibit the conditions of a healthy and vigorous life" (*Essays*, p. 31). The positive treatment of Maggie's final turning to à Kempis requires this kind of identification, but the repeated images of disease in the novel and the wish for death that accompanies Maggie's final prayer give the lie to "healthy and vigorous" growth. The mending of nature is forced, indeed, when the sense of duty that becomes second nature to Maggie compels a dying to self.

The roots that bind Maggie to family and community blight her life in a similar way; and the elegizing of "roots" and "ties" that takes place nonetheless produces another set of structural discon-

10. See chapter 4 above, pp. 152–53.
11. *MF*, V, iii, 284–88; VI, iii, 336.

tinuities. In the closing book, Maggie's "strong resurgent love towards her brother" is presented as sweeping away "all the later impressions of hard, cruel offence and misunderstanding," leaving "only the deep, underlying, unshakable memories of early union" (VII, v, 453). But as readers have been saying since 1860, their "early union" is filled with sorrow and misunderstanding. The most memorable of the childhood scenes—Maggie driving nails into her doll, chopping off her hair, throwing Lucy in the mud, running away to the gypsies—render the "golden gates of . . . childhood" invoked at the close of the first volume a fantasy (II, vii, 171). This fantasy is repeated in the images that unite Tom and Maggie at the close of each volume even though the two have become progressively more divided from each other.[12]

The "perpetual yearning" in Maggie "that had its root deeper than all change . . . to have no cloud between herself and Tom" stunts and frustrates her equally great yearning for an "intense and varied life."[13] The "roots" and "deep-lying fibres" that bind Maggie to her past are frequently infected by images of organic dysfunction: the rule of à Kempis means laying the " 'axe to the root' " of self, and the "primary natural claim" of family means " 'being benumbed.' " But life with Stephen also means to "be benumbed" by "maiming the faith and sympathy that were the best organs of her soul."[14] Consequently, when Maggie rejects Stephen " 'for the sake of being true to *all* the motives that sanctify our lives, . . . *all* that my past life has made dear and holy to me,' " and when the narrator identifies her "whole soul" (which Maggie had described earlier as divided) with "her mother and brother," the alleged unity fails to confront divisions at the heart of Maggie's life.[15] Such contrived unity is as fatal to the art of the novel as it is to the life of the character.

U. C. Knoepflmacher speaks of the river in *The Mill on the Floss* as a "metaphor for the sweeping progress of history"; and George Eliot views the "historical advance of mankind" as one of the novel's main themes.[16] But the onward evolutionary process George Eliot would affirm is denied by the resolution of the conflict, which depends on the writings of a medieval monk and

12. Important aspects of the "obscuring fantasy" and its relation to George Eliot's life are discussed by Hardy, *"The Mill on the Floss."*

13. *MF*, VI, xii, 398; VI, ii, 326.

14. *MF*, IV, iii, 253; V, iii, 289; V, iv, 293; VI, xiii, 402; VI, xiv, 414.

15. *MF*, VI, xiv, 418–20; VII, v, 453 (italics mine).

16. Knoepflmacher, *Early Novels*, p. 180. *Letters* 8: 465; *MF*, IV, i, 239.

primitive kinship needs. Close to the end of the novel Maggie is pictured seated at a window, "looking blankly at the flowing river, swift with the advancing tide," as described in the manuscript and first edition, but "swift with the backward-rushing tide" in the revised (VII, iv, 445). This telltale change is another indication of how the "onward tendency of things" announced in the middle of the novel gives way to a backward or at best stationary movement. Maggie's blank look reflects the sense of paralysis and numbness she feels at key moments, while the backward rush is the correlative of the structural gaps that lead to the simplistic closing affirmations. Together they undermine all notions of telos and underscore the critical division in positivistic organicism between the ideal of rational progress and the reality (especially for women) of emotional regression.

That the affirmations require Maggie to regress, although she wants so much to grow, is further demonstrated by George Eliot's failure to confront fully the absence of progressive social structures for women; and again we see a corresponding failure of artistic structure. *The Mill on the Floss* provides a "compendium of the handicaps imposed upon women."[17] The ones that most affect Maggie—inequality of education, living " 'in dependence,' " being without power to " 'do something in the world,' " and having no world outside of love—she fights fiercely against.[18] She makes remarkable gains in educating herself and strives to become self-supporting. The novel, moreover, values her independence so greatly as to reverse the usual double standard, by associating her independence with true dignity instead of with immovable and often cruel self-assertion as in the case of Tom, the Dodsons, and the men of St. Ogg's. But George Eliot's recoiling from the Darwinian struggle for predominance causes the novel finally to withdraw from the outward. Wishing to make Maggie's outer life correspond, albeit painfully, to her inward needs, George Eliot evades in the end what she earlier so forcefully confronts: the outer world that frustrates and defeats Maggie's desire for work, attainment, and even marriage. Instead, the concerns of the novel move inward, in part by forgetting how Stephen Guest and the narrow attitudes of good society drove Maggie out of the world altogether into her ultimate emphasis of want.

All this suggests an emphasis of want in George Eliot herself. If it caused her to attempt to unify the separateness she uncovers

17. Patricia Beer, *Reader, I Married Him*, pp. 189–90.
18. *MF*, V, v, 304; VI, vii, 361.

by discovering in Maggie's moral evolution a force of cohesion, it also caused her to turn away from the divisions she so brilliantly dramatizes. While the rhetoric of the ending speaks to Maggie's moral evolution, the climactic action suggests a "difference of view."[19] The former creates a "comfortingly conventional" tone, "barely distinguishable from hundreds of pious exemplary tales," and leads to the view of Maggie as a "heroine" or "angel of renunciation."[20] But the novel's closing action conveys an opposing view as well. If love triumphs over death, so does death triumph over life. Cataclysmic rather than comforting, the ending reveals that a Maggie cut to the pattern is a Maggie cut off from life. Thus the action that is fatal for Tom and Maggie turns out to be vital to the art of the novel, though in ways George Eliot seems not to have intended. Instead of adjustment and organic unity, it dramatizes irreparable collisions and organic dysfunction. Instead of confirming a continuum between natural, moral, and social law, it reinforces the disjunctions between them. George Eliot does not mend nature in this novel; but she does to some degree mend her own art by showing how Maggie's world ravages her nature.

Middlemarch

Commenting on *The Mill* shortly after it was finished, George Eliot admitted to "a want of proportionate fullness in the treatment of the third [volume], which I shall always regret" (*Letters* 3: 317). But while her second novel seemed to her to lack the completeness and balance of *Adam Bede*, she felt *The Mill* had "more thought and a profounder veracity" (*Letters* 3: 374). It was, of course, her first full-fledged attempt to portray a community undergoing industrialization and in the process organic decomposition. Her return in *Silas Marner* to a preindustrial world suggests a shying away from the demands of portraying complex as opposed to simple societies, or perhaps an uncertainty about her ability to create fictional structures adequate to them. Nonetheless, in each of her subsequent novels she set out to confront those demands. Com-

19. The phrase is Virginia Woolf's, from her essay (*Times Literary Supplement*, 20 November 1919) "George Eliot"; reprinted in *The Common Reader*, p. 176. Gillian Beer, too, in "Beyond Determinism," connects the ending of *The Mill* with the "difference of view" Woolf ascribed to Eliot. Her thesis, however, is that "difference of view" manifests itself in "resistance to plot."

20. Miriam Allott, "George Eliot in the 1860's," p. 105; Showalter, *Literature of Their Own*, p. 112; Gilbert and Gubar, *Madwoman*, p. 498.

pleteness and balance, intricacy of thought and greater truth-telling
—she sought somehow to combine them.

After writing *Romola*, she again wonders if she hasn't failed,
thinking this novel too might be "wanting due proportion" (*Letters* 4: 97). Her response, however, is not to return to a simpler
society, but to confront the problems she had left behind in *The
Mill on the Floss*, and to move toward greater complexity of structure and content. Just as "the highest Form . . . is the highest organism," so "forms of art," she proposes, "can be called higher or
lower only on the same principle as that on which we apply these
words to organisms; viz. in proportion to the complexity of the
parts bound up into one indissoluble whole" ("Notes," *Essays*, pp.
433, 435). The "Notes" were written after *Felix Holt* and during
the long period when she was "brooding over her [new] 'English
novel' " while seeming to get nowhere (*Biography*, p. 420). The result, *Middlemarch*, demonstrates that she had indeed been aiming
for the "highest" and for once she seems to have felt, tentatively at
first and then more securely, that perhaps she had succeeded. In
the months following the completion of *Middlemarch*, she speaks
of having made the "work a whole," a "complete organism"; and
she writes in its defense (simultaneously setting the criterion by
which she would have it judged): "It is precisely my ideal—to make
matter and form an inseparable truthfulness" (*Letters* 5: 324, 374).

In recent years, the immense body of criticism devoted to *Middlemarch* has more than vindicated her art. Whatever the aspect
studied—imagery, analogy, allusion, plot, character, narrative
stance—the intricacy of the novel's formal design remains a wonder.
And the "matter" of *Middlemarch* seems unbounded, taking in
feminism as well as determinism, epistemology as well as history,
unified vision as well as separated consciousness, failed aspiration
and art as vocation. Moving far beyond James' pronouncement of
"an indifferent whole" but "a treasure-house of details," most
readers today are meeting George Eliot on her own ground, finding
in the matter and form of *Middlemarch* an inseparable truthfulness. The nature of the bond, however, is still being debated; and
so, consequently, are the truths it contains.

The most radical of the readings supposes the undermining of
all truths, as in J. Hillis Miller's essays on *Middlemarch*, two of
which are here particularly relevant because they concern systems
of unity and totality based on organic assumptions about history,
society, and art.[21] In "Narrative and History," Miller correlates

21. See chapter 4, n. 59.

"formal unity in fiction . . . with the system of concepts making up the Western idea of history." The system he describes is "metaphysical," based on principles that include continuity and organic unity, progress and causality, origin and telos.[22] *Middlemarch*, he argues, seems to assert such a system but actually subverts it. In this essay, Miller presumes George Eliot a conscious participant in this process; however, in "Optic and Semiotic," though he claims to be postponing the issue, his argument supposes her to be affirming unity while unwittingly doing the opposite. Both essays define the relation of parts to whole in *Middlemarch* using the two assumptions common to all organic theories, but in the second essay Miller extends the argument by deducing a family of organic metaphors—web, stream, and parts (often minute) related to wholes. In contrast to these all-encompassing or "totalizing" metaphors, he then defines an opposing family of optic metaphors. The two families, he argues, imply contradictory premises. The former presupposes organic unity, universal laws of human behavior, and an objectively knowable reality; the latter reveals perception to be egocentric, subjective, and projective. This opposition, Miller concludes, undermines entirely the "narrator's effort of totalization" (p. 144), rendering matter and form alike contradictory.

Miller, however, neglects to distinguish between evolutionary and traditional models of history and between revisionary and older concepts of organicism. He also generalizes too broadly about the totalizing metaphors, often claiming that they affirm order and unity when in fact they do not. Among the most famous passages Miller cites is the description of "old provincial society" in chapter 11. Yet even George Eliot's introduction to the passage is ominous and unsettling:

> But any one watching keenly the stealthy convergence of human lots, sees a slow preparation of effects from one life on another, which tells like a calculated irony on the indifference or the frozen stare with which we look at our unintroduced neighbour. Destiny stands by sarcastic with our *dramatis personae* folded in her hand.
>
> [p. 70

While this introductory statement carries a positive warning against neglecting one's neighbor, what it actually describes is "indifference," and a "convergence" dependent on "stealth," "irony," and "sarcasm"; in other words on slyness, incongruity, and discrepancy as opposed to unity—a consensus of coldness not sympa-

22. Miller, "Narrative and History," pp. 459–61, 467.

thy. The first sentence, furthermore, is as much governed by watching and seeing as it is by the totalizing metaphor of converging parts. Similarly, the body of the passage asserts "new consciousness of interdependence" and "fresh threads of connection"; yet the more specifically they are delineated the more ambiguous or negative they become, as in "faultiness of closer acquaintanceship" or "offensive advantage in cunning" (I, 11, 70–71). Again consciousness does not exist apart from but is inherent in the totalizing metaphor. Thus, in this case, as in many of the examples Miller cites, the affirmations and oppositions he construes are actually muted, joined, or treated ironically in the text.

At the same time, metaphors such as these, as Miller observes, are synecdoches. Like so much else in *Middlemarch*, they are parts that represent wholes, and they are also in themselves wholes that represent still smaller parts. Not only are they organic in form, but many are also organic in matter, having as their subject the human and social organism. Whereas Miller finds the synecdoches to be self-defeating because other aspects of the text render their comprehensiveness specious, I find in them a self-questioning that makes for a comprehensiveness beyond the kind he describes. Miller assigns to them the "affirmation of order,"[23] but the totalizing metaphors are often foreboding, critical, skeptical, and even satirical in content and tone.

A close look at a synecdoche that appears at the center of *Middlemarch* and has all these qualities will illustrate that, as Miller holds, the novel radically questions the idea of organic unity in society. However, unlike Miller, I will also argue that *Middlemarch* is aesthetically an organic whole, and that it is unified precisely because it self-consciously questions the idea of organic community. Whatever affirmations take place remain tentative, partial, or incomplete. To put it another way, the novel has structural coherence because (in contrast to *The Mill on the Floss*) George Eliot now makes fragmentation and separateness her abiding subject.

Book Five of *Middlemarch*, in the middle chapter of which Casaubon dies, is titled "The Dead Hand." The book begins just beyond the midpoint of the novel, and it is the first in which all the main strands are not only present, but no longer appear as separate.[24] The "dead hand" refers most directly to Casaubon, standing for his living amputated self and for his attempt to keep Dorothea's hand tied to his even after his death. Regularly, in George

23. Miller, "Optic and Semiotic," p. 138.
24. Jerome Beaty, *"Middlemarch," from Notebook to Novel*, p. 65.

Eliot's fiction, the meeting or joining of hands is emblematic of community, of those acts of sympathy, friendship, and love that unite one individual with another. Here we have a single hand figuratively severed from human relation, as well as a dead hand literally severed from life but trying to enforce relation through death. More generally, then, the dead hand is a synecdoche for organic perversion, for life become moribund. But the "dead hand" applies not only to Dorothea's relation to Casaubon but also, in one way or another, to all the events in Book Five.

The book opens with Dorothea's setting out to see Lydgate in order to find out more about Casaubon's condition (ch. 43). Lydgate is not home, but Dorothea's visit brings her into first contact with Rosamond and allows the reader a first view of Rosamond after her marriage, a glimpse that includes her flirtation with Ladislaw, who is at her house. In the next chapter, Dorothea talks with Lydgate about her husband, and he talks to her about medical reform and about the New Hospital, to which she pledges some money after he describes how the town's hostility to Bulstrode has turned it against the project. Chapter 45, however, demonstrates the hostility to be directed as much toward Lydgate as toward Bulstrode. The struggle in Middlemarch for "another kind of Reform"— political rather than medical—is the subject of chapter 46, in which Brooke and Ladislaw, and then Ladislaw and Lydgate, discuss the pending Reform Bill and the nomination of Brooke for Parliament. Chapter 47 deals with Will's visit to Lowick Church; chapter 48 with the promise Casaubon would exact from Dorothea, the delay in her answer, and the death of Casaubon just moments before she is about to promise; chapters 49 and 50 with the codicil Casaubon attached to his will. The most important event of the book having come to a terminus, the issue of political reform again moves to center stage (ch. 51), this time to put an end to Brooke's political career (and to his use for Will) through the fiasco at the hustings. Finally, chapters 52 and 53 concern the few main strands yet to be included in Book Five, the love story of Fred and Mary and the Raffles-Bulstrode plot.

As even this rough summary indicates, Book Five moves back and forth between two major areas of interest: the love problems to which the title of the previous book refers and the issue of Reform. Though one may seem to be private and the other public, the interweaving of psychological motivation and social situation is so intricate as truly to make the social medium ever-present and ultimately inseparable from the impulses, feelings, and thoughts that prompt a given character to behave in one way or another. But the congruence is hardly harmonious; a persistent sense of actual or impending " 'dead-lock' " pervades Book Five. Lydgate uses this term in chapter 46, applying it to " 'things' " in general, by which he means medical or political reform, for he is still unaware how it has already begun and will come fully to characterize his marriage (p. 341). The "dead hand" of the book's title functions as a synecdoche for all these things, for the sense of deadlock in the everyday lives people lead and in the social institutions surrounding their lives.

Among these institutions, marriage, of course, is traditionally represented as a joining of hands. In Book Five, we see many of its phases: the new marriage of Rosamond and Lydgate beginning to miscarry; the young marriage of Dorothea and Casaubon dead from the start; the childhood sweethearts, Fred and Mary, hoping to turn their umbrella-ring marriage into a reality; the remarried widower, Bulstrode, who has betrayed his first wife. Each of these marriages, moreover, becomes (either now or later and with different consequences) in some way associated with the moribund, and becomes so for reasons inseparable from the institution of marriage.

The economy of George Eliot's presentation is such that no sooner do Lydgate and Rosamond appear as husband and wife than they begin to exhibit those disabilities endemic to the marital roles they unthinkingly play. The couple serves as a living illustration, so to speak, of the kinds of marital disabilities that Mill identifies in the *Subjection* as attesting with particular force to the need to change existing customs and practices. Even within the three short scenes between Rosamond and Lydgate in Book Five, the handicaps become all too apparent. The strategic placement of these scenes at the ends of chapters (43, 45, 46) not only has the advantages of prominence and parallel incremental form but also brings matrimony into proximity with the major Reform issues, thereby making it one of them.

When last seen in Book Four, Rosamond and Lydgate were preparing for their marriage, she by displaying "her quick imitative perception," and he by delighting in "the psychological difference between . . . goose and gander: especially on the innate submissiveness of the goose as beautifully corresponding to the strength of the gander."[25] When the newlyweds first appear in Book Five,

25. IV, 36, 261. George Eliot may well be mocking Darwin's theory of sexual selection. The publication of *The Descent of Man and Selection in Relation to Sex* in 1871 coincides with the writing of *Middlemarch*. Just as Eliot's narra-

Rosamond is already enjoying the "assured subjection" of Lydgate, while deriving great pleasure from discovering "that women, even after marriage, might make conquests and enslave men. . . . How delightful to make captives from the throne of marriage with a husband as crown-prince by your side—himself in fact a subject" (V, 43, 319). As Mill posits in the *Subjection*, not least among the ways in which the predominance assumed by men is damaging to both sexes is that it makes the female, if she too is self-willed, eager to exercise "a counter-tyranny."[26]

The first exchange we witness between the newlyweds introduces the related theme of Lydgate's adoring his wife while neglecting his work and running up bills, and of Rosamond's dissatisfaction with his attention to his work. Their opening comments are playful in tone; yet, Rosamond's "aëry lightness" as she flirts with Will before her husband comes in, and her "playful curiosity" in contemplating "subjection" carry over into this scene, suggesting the costly light irony of good society as well as lighthearted toying. Because Rosamond aspires but does not belong to good society, and because Lydgate does belong but aspires to something more, their lightheartedness furthermore quickly gives way to a serious tone. " 'Haven't you ambition enough to wish that your husband should be something better than a Middlemarch doctor?' " Lydgate asks, "letting his hands fall on to his wife's shoulders, and looking at her with affectionate gravity." And she answers: " 'Of course, I wish you to make discoveries: no one could more wish you to attain a high position in some better place than Middlemarch' " (V, 43, 318–20).

The transposition by which Lydgate would turn his achievement into his wife's ambition, and the tacit understanding of the terms of the marital contract revealed in her reply, brilliantly dramatize a point Mill labors to make in the *Subjection*. Asserting that

---

tor speaks of "goose and gander," so Darwin illustrates human sexual selection by discussing the mating habits of birds. Darwin's female is "passive," but she has "powers of intuition, of rapid perception, and perhaps of imitation," directed toward acquiring "social position and wealth" when she selects a mate—exactly what Rosamond thinks she is doing here. Darwin's male is the epitome of strength. "Man is more powerful in body and mind than woman," Darwin writes. He has "greater intellectual vigour and power of invention," not to mention "size, strength, courage, pugnacity and energy" (*Descent of Man*, pp. 576, 599, 610, 618–19, 629–32).

26. Mill, *Subjection*, pp. 167–68. Some recent feminist studies make a protofeminist of Rosamond (e.g., Gilbert and Gubar, *Madwoman*, pp. 514–16), but the case is a difficult one to support for many reasons, among them her counter-tyranny, for it too is rooted in patriarchal values.

women in the "easy classes" are taught to give primacy to "social consideration" and a "common standard of approbation," he declares a woman's standing to be "inseparably connected with that of her husband." Taking further the case of a man whose talents lead him in an uncommon direction, often at the risk of losing his social or pecuniary standing, Mill concludes, moreover, that unless the man has the unlikely good fortune of a wife whose thoughts and inclinations are as uncommon as his, "he can offer no compensation" (*Subjection*, pp. 228–31). Attempting in this scene to translate his desire for scientific achievement into his wife's desire for social advancement, Lydgate thinks he can offer compensation; and willing enough to trade " 'discoveries' " for " 'high position,' " she accedes to the bargain. That the bargain, however, is doomed to failure, because their situation precludes (as Mill would put it) "real identity of interests," is already forecast when next we see them.

Chapter 45 opens with Lydgate stretched out on the sofa, "his head thrown back, and his hands clasped behind it according to his favourite ruminating attitude." Sensing his self-absorption, Rosamond stops playing the piano. They move closer together, she by "bringing her face nearer to his" and he by placing his hands "gently behind her shoulders." He talks to her of Vesalius, who began a " 'new era in anatomy' " though he had to steal cadavers, contend with great hostility, burn his own books, and suffer the punishment of exile. Still, Vesalius continued his work and finally won recognition, though he died before claiming his honors, as his journey home ended in shipwreck. Bringing his tale to a close, Lydgate says, " 'He died rather miserably' " (V, 45, 334–35).

The response to Lydgate in Middlemarch, dramatized earlier in the chapter, and Lydgate's own comments make clear his identification with Vesalius. Rosamond is quick to pick up the connection: " 'Do you know, Tertius,' " she says, after he finishes his tale, " 'I often wish you had not been a medical man.' " He defends himself and his profession against what he takes to be her denaturing of both, while she continues to persevere quietly in her opinion. The scene closes with Rosamond's teasingly acquiescent promise to dote on all sorts of cadaverous things " 'that end in your dying miserably,' " and with Lydgate's replying, while "petting her resignedly," " 'No, no, not so bad as that' " (V, 45, 335–36).

Before the story of their lives together is finished, however, it will turn out to be at least as bad. The fact that Lydgate dies at exactly the same age as Vesalius, their lives even spanning the same years of their respective centuries, continues the identification between them,[27] but it becomes increasingly more ironical as the novel progresses. In comparison to Vesalius, who pursued his scientific research despite all obstacles and made discoveries that far outlived him, the Finale depicts a Lydgate who "was what is called a successful man," but who "regarded himself as a failure." Believing himself to have been murdered even while alive, Lydgate, in his final image of Rosamond as a "basil plant" flourishing "on a murdered man's brains," bears witness to the uncompensating truth of the vow she had teasingly uttered in the early days of their marriage (Finale, p. 610).

The degeneration of Lydgate and the deterioration of his marriage are not merely the story of this particular husband and wife. Many parallels exist between their case and the broad analysis offered by Mill in the *Subjection*. Just as he writes of how a man keen to achieve great things becomes after a few years of marriage no different "from those who have never had wishes for anything but the common vanities and the common pecuniary objects" (p. 235), so George Eliot tells of how Lydgate comes "to be shapen after the average and fit to be packed by the gross" (II, 15, 107). While Rosamond clearly plays a role in her husband's downfall, the wrong she does just as clearly proceeds in part from her position as a woman.[28] She is undoubtedly, in Mill's terms, "the auxiliary of the common public opinion," operating as a "perpetual dead weight, or, worse than a dead weight, a drag" upon her husband's highest aspirations (p. 228). She is equally, as Lydgate sees her, a "burthen." His "narrowed lot" and "the burthen of her life upon his arms" become one and the same for him: "He must walk as he could, carrying that burthen pitifully" (VIII, 81, 586).

Because Lydgate has not only chosen but also helps to create Rosamond, he too, however, is an auxiliary of the common public opinion. As Mill and George Eliot recognized, both sexes help to perpetuate a system damaging to both. Lydgate's more subtle but no less inescapable complicity is regularly suggested in Book Five by the gestures he makes, in particular his hand movements, both when he would exclude Rosamond from his life (by clasping his hands behind his head) and when he tries to include her (by pressing his hands on her shoulders). Throughout the novel, in fact, his hand movements represent the distance he would place between

27. Robert A. Greenberg points out the connections between Vesalius and Lydgate in "Plexuses and Ganglia," pp. 39–40.

28. See Kathleen Blake, "*Middlemarch* and the Woman Question," p. 302.

her and his masculine world of thought and action, as well as his efforts, coercive even in their gentleness, to force an identity of interests between them, or to pretend to a mastery he does not have (carrying "her life upon his arms").

In the last of the scenes in Book Five between Lydgate and Rosamond, his complicity not only is suggested but also shapes the entire scene. Several times in chapter 46 Rosamond asks Lydgate what is vexing him, and each time, "caressing her penitently," he dodges the question, lastly by lying: " 'Oh, outdoor things—business.' " Bringing the chapter to a close, the narrator adds: "It was really a letter insisting on the payment of a bill for furniture. But Rosamond was expecting to have a baby, and Lydgate wished to save her from any perturbation" (342–43). The scene is as brilliant as it is brief. Within its short space major matrimonial liabilities are portrayed. One is that men teach women to have "no business with things . . . extending beyond the family." Another is that even tenderness and "personal affection," the only "real mitigating causes" which temper the corrupting effects of power, are themselves tainted by inequality. The third (by anticipation) is that women will contrive to get what their subordinate status deprives them of, but covertly because their actual rights are limited and maladroitly because their knowledge and training are scant.[29] All these liabilities help to make the marriage, like the pregnancy Lydgate hopes to protect, miscarry. When Lydgate finally confronts Rosamond with their financial crisis, her refusal to accept responsibility and her inept meddling behind his back fulfill only too well the expectations Lydgate helped to create.

Whether by ironic conjunction or painful disjunction, the relationship between outward and inward in the case of Rosamond and Lydgate is so impaired as to make a mockery of the notion of telos. "Social consideration" does indeed rule in their marriage, but in such a way as to mean not sharing in a wide common life but being held hostage to Mrs. Grundy.[30] In the case of Dorothea, in contrast, social consideration takes the form of an opposing extreme. Thus, when in chapter 48 of Book Five, Dorothea goes out to give Casaubon the promise which would bind her forever to his dead hand, we are told: "Neither law nor the world's opinion compelled her to this . . . only the ideal and not the real yoke of marriage" (V, 48, 353).

29. Mill makes all these points; see *Subjection*, pp. 167–68, 173, 231–32.
30. See Mill, *Subjection*, pp. 229–31. Lee Edwards, too, makes this point in "Women, Energy, and *Middlemarch*," p. 237.

The ideal, however, is shown to be far from perfect. In the passage just quoted, the "ideal" is no less a "yoke" than the "real." Throughout this chapter, moreover, an opposing ideal, one rooted in individual fulfillment and the need for freedom, is repeatedly asserted. To say yes to Casaubon is "to say 'Yes,' " Dorothea herself knows, "to her own doom." In the end deciding to do so, she nonetheless "dreaded going to the spot where she foresaw that she must bind herself to a fellowship from which she shrank." Still, for one moment during this scene, the novel defends the self-sacrificing ideal: "She saw clearly enough the whole situation, yet she was fettered: she could not smite the stricken soul that entreated hers. If that were weakness, Dorothea was weak" (V, 48, 352–53). Yet, if the rhetoric argues for renunciation, the plot, as Gilbert and Gubar argue, promotes freedom: the husband who would keep his wife in painful subjection is fatally smitten just as she is about to submit to his ultimate assertion of power.[31]

But to set the rhetoric against the plot, as Gubar and Gilbert do, is to see the novel as divided against itself. Their argument implies that the plot unwittingly subverts the social telos affirmed by the rhetoric. I am arguing instead that the subversion is self-conscious and that the rhetoric, no less than the plot, puts the social telos under pressure. Even in the "if that were weakness" passage, the rhetoric questions while it defends: "fettered" signifies not sacrifice for a worthy end but freedom constricted and shackled; "could not smite" makes strength a matter of negation; the conditional "if" and the repetition of "weak" render the assertion of strength uncertain. This passage is placed at the moment Dorothea comes closest to complete submission. But elsewhere in the novel, the case for an unqualified rhetoric of submission is far more untenable, and the plot, among other devices, contributes to the qualifications. One could argue that the very death of Casaubon is part of this pattern. Thus the rhetoric and plot, rather than countering one another, work continually together, scrutinizing and interrogating, especially in the case of Dorothea, both the notion of the individual's living for others and of the society's existing for the benefit of the individual.

The doctrine of living for others is examined so thoroughly as to reveal how it miscarries even when one attempts to practice it as an ideal. Just prior to Dorothea's calling at Lydgate's in chapter 43, there is a scene between Dorothea and Casaubon as powerful

31. Gilbert and Gubar, *Madwoman*, pp. 491, 511–13. See also Carol Christ, "Aggression and Providential Death in George Eliot's Fiction."

and important as the one depicting his last wishes and death. The scene occurs at the close of Book Four, in chapter 42, which—unlike the other chapters in Book Four, each related to its immediate predecessor—anticipates the Dorothea-Casaubon chapters (43–44 and 47–50) of Book Five. Indeed, chapter 42 was originally to have opened Book Five.[32] In either case, whether as opening or closing, it prepares for "The Dead Hand."

The most dramatic moments between Dorothea and Casaubon in chapter 42 have their climax in a severing or joining of hands. Going out to comfort her husband just after he has conferred with Lydgate about his health, Dorothea is repulsed by Casaubon with a glance "so chill" as almost to make her retreat; "yet she turned and passed her hand through his arm." His "unresponsive hardness" continues: "Mr. Casaubon kept his hands behind him and allowed her pliant arm to cling with difficulty against his rigid arm." They separate. Left to herself she gives way to "a rebellious anger stronger than any she had felt since her marriage"—so strong it leads to that moment when "in the jar of her whole being, Pity was overthrown." At one moment venting her anger, at another conquering it, she struggles desperately; "but the resolved submission did come." The scene ends with her waiting for her husband. He meets her now with "kind quiet melancholy." Thankful for having "narrowly escaped hurting a lamed creature," Dorothea "put her hand into her husband's, and they went along the broad corridor together" (IV, 42, 312–14). In the next scene between them, however, his "distrust" of "her affection" is as great as ever (V, 44, 322).

Clearly, the sole source of Dorothea's affection for Casaubon is her pity for him. But Casaubon wants far more than her pity:

> She nursed him, she read to him, she anticipated his wants, and was solicitous about his feelings; but there had entered into the husband's mind the certainty that she judged him, and that her wifely devotedness was like a penitential expiation of unbelieving thoughts.
>
> [IV, 42, 306

Showing how Casaubon, debilitated by his jealous pride, "shrank from pity" (305), George Eliot captures with absolute precision the workings of an individual mind; but at the same time she again

---

32. George Eliot, "Quarry for *Middlemarch*," ed. Anna T. Kitchel, p. 630; hereafter referred to as *Quarry*. See also Beaty, *"Middlemarch," from Notebook to Novel*, p. 62.

dramatizes a common form of matrimonial relationship. As Mill puts it, when he considers the case of a woman who tries to meet not Mrs. Grundy's social standard but an exalted "ideal of character," the "masters of women" require "something more from them than actual service. Men do not want solely the obedience of women, they want their sentiments." They desire "not a forced slave but a willing one, not a slave merely, but a favourite. They have therefore put everything in practice to enslave their minds" (*Subjection*, p. 141).

The corresponding ideal of feminine character of which Mill speaks—"to live for others; to make complete abnegation of themselves, and to have no life but in their affections"—corresponds precisely to the " 'characteristic excellences of womanhood' " Casaubon applauds in Dorothea when she agrees to marry him. " 'The great charm of your sex,' " he tells her " 'is its capability of an ardent self-sacrificing affection, and herein we see its fitness to round and complete the existence of our own' " (I, 5, 37). Their marriage demands ever-increasing self-sacrifices of her, but her self-abnegation is accompanied by a growing independence of mind that leads her to judge her husband negatively. She also comes to reprove herself for having been unaware of contributing to his anxieties by constantly pleading for Will (V, 43, 317; 44, 320). But although these negative judgments subsequently dissuade her from pursuing independence—having intensified her pity on her husband and evoked her guilt—her "resolved submission" does not alter Casaubon's estrangement from her. He realizes he has been unable to enslave her mind and senses that her pity represents only a small part of her "sentiments"—a part, moreover, that includes her recognition of his limitations and her suppression of rebellious feelings. Thus he finds in her "self-sacrificing affection" not the completion of his existence but further cause for alienation.

Casaubon's alienation receives its fullest expression in the codicil that seeks to prevent Dorothea from marrying Ladislaw. Like his attempt to keep Dorothea fettered by pledging her to labor in the tombs of his project, this posthumous directive exemplifies the pathological nature of his assertion of power. Even before Dorothea knows of her husband's last wishes, she equates "the perpetual effort demanded by her married life" to living in a "virtual tomb" (V, 43, 348). Casaubon seeks to keep her there, tying her hand to his in death as it has been in life. His attempt to maintain his "cold grasp" over his wife by regulating her property rights employs a legal form characteristic also of the marital contract. Sir Henry

Maine speaks of "the Contract and the Will" as the "two great institutions without which modern society can scarcely be supposed
capable of holding together" (*Ancient Law*, p. 197). George Eliot
also links them together but uncovers in the marital contract and
legal will dangerous instruments of manipulation. When earlier
in the novel Dorothea sought to rectify Casaubon's debt to Ladislaw, she thought of "her husband's will, which had been made at
the time of the marriage."[33] At his death the two are again connected. Contract and will signify for her, as does marriage law in
general for Mill, the yoke in the holding force, not consent and
individual rights.

At the same time, George Eliot's treatment of Dorothea's response to the codicil (in contrast to her closing portrait of Maggie)
openly confronts the disease in "duteous devotion." In chapter 50,
Dorothea is told of the codicil and suffers a "violent shock of
repulsion from her departed husband." For a moment it "terrified
her as if it had been a sin"; but almost immediately his "grasp"
and her guilt "slipped away":

> now her judgment, instead of being controlled by duteous devo-
> tion, was made active by the imbittering discovery that in her past
> union there had lurked the hidden alienation of secrecy and sus-
> picion. The living, suffering man was no longer before her to
> awaken her pity: there remained only the retrospect of painful
> subjection.

Putting pledge and codicil to rest "with the sense that around his
last hard demand and his last injurious assertion of his power, the
silence was unbroken" (V, 50, 360–62), she now comes to see that
the ideal yoke of marriage is the same as the real.[34] The change is
described as "convulsive":

> She might have compared her experience at that moment to the
> vague, alarmed consciousness that her life was taking on a new
> form, that she was undergoing a metamorphosis in which memory
> would not adjust itself to the stirring of new organs. Everything
> was changing its aspect: her husband's conduct, her own duteous

---

33. IV, 34, 273. Will, too, thinks of the Casaubons' marriage in terms of
"legal forms" (II, 21, 155). After discovering the codicil, Dorothea thinks of
"the property" as "the sign of that broken tie" (V, 50, 362).

34. Gilbert and Gubar argue the opposite, maintaining that Eliot "reinforces the lesson of patriarchal morality, for the result of Casaubon's fortuitous
death is Dorothea's guilt" (*Madwoman*, p. 513). Similarly, Christ, in "Aggression
and Providential Death," argues that Eliot prohibits aggression in her characters through a change of heart brought about by the recognition of guilt.

feeling towards him, every struggle between them—and yet more, her whole relation to Will Ladislaw.

[V, 50, 359

Does Dorothea then escape the "dead hand?"

Mill argues that because the laws governing the institution of marriage make the woman's lot so dependent on the treatment she receives from her husband, and because a woman has little choice but to marry, "it is a very cruel aggravation of her fate that she should be allowed to try this chance only once" (*Subjection*, p. 161). Dorothea is saved from this aggravation; she is given a second chance, a second husband who is neither paternal nor despotic. Will Ladislaw, whatever the reader's reservations about him, is among other things a friend to Dorothea, sharing with her "that union of thoughts and inclinations" which Mill, making friendship his model, calls the true "ideal of married life."[35]

To the extent that Dorothea's ideal of marriage both changes and becomes fulfilled when she leaves Middlemarch to live with Will a life of shared emotion and beneficent activity, she escapes from the "dead hand." But her escape does not signify organic recovery. Her second marriage is itself a subversive act, defiant of her husband's will and of her family's values and wishes.[36] Her move to London is an expatriation, not an integrating act so far as the community of Middlemarch is concerned. At the same time, the most essential of the social structures that shape her future life is not new but old in form. Dorothea as the wife of Will Ladislaw remains almost as far from fulfilling her aspirations for a "grand life—here—now—in England" as she had been as the wife of Casaubon (I, 3, 21).

At the start of the Prelude, St. Theresa is pictured as a "little girl walking forth one morning hand-in-hand with her still smaller brother," their hearts "already beating to a national idea; until domestic reality . . . turned them back from their great resolve." Similarly, at key moments during the novel, Dorothea walks forth to give her hand in human fellowship to others—to Casaubon, to Lydgate, to Rosamond; and she also walks hand-in-hand in the end with Will Ladislaw. But while she is sent back, so to speak, only

35. *Subjection*, pp. 231–35. Mary Lyndon Shanley, "Marital Slavery and Friendship," discusses the importance of the idea of marriage as friendship in Mill.

36. Gilbert and Gubar state that Dorothea's marriage to Will is in fact "the most subversive act available to her within the context defined by the author" (*Madwoman*, p. 530).

by Casaubon, hers is far more a static than a forward movement.
"Domestic reality" keeps her in place. Even after Casaubon dies,
she speaks of women's "hands" as "tied" (VI, 54, 393 and 397).

Dorothea exerts a beneficent influence as women characteristically do—through personal influence. Will is in the thick of the
struggle for social reform; she is on the sidelines giving "wifely
help" (Finale, 611). Her situation, in other words, is no different
from that which Mill describes when he speaks of the indirect social
benefit obtained "in many individual cases . . . through the personal influence of individual women over individual men. But these
benefits are partial; their range is extremely circumscribed" (*Subjection*, p. 221). They are as partial and circumscribed as is Dorothea's escape from the dead hand of the social institutions regulating women's lives. The dramatization of Dorothea's life, in
contrast to the treatment Lydgate and Rosamond receive, does not
make telos a travesty, but it does suggest how social customs and
institutions arrest, even if they do not override, individual and
social development. Commenting on the ready-made role Dorothea
ends up playing, the narrator speaks in the Finale of a life filled
with "beneficent activity which she had not the doubtful pains
of discovering and marking out for herself." Such pains would be
doubtful because choice brings burdens and action breeds anxiety;
but doubtful also in the sense of being indefinite and undeter-
mined, having been so little tried.

The novel's mourning of Dorothea's failure to discover and
mark out for herself the life to which she aspired resounds through
Prelude and Finale—through origins and end. The Prelude takes
as a starting point "the indefiniteness" of woman's nature, opposing to it the "limits of variation" commonly ascribed to "the social
lot of women."[37] Dorothea, attempting to break free of those limits,
is like the cygnet of the Prelude—a young swan "reared uneasily
among the ducklings in the brown pond" who "never finds the living stream in fellowship with its own oary-footed kind." The brown
pond is social convention; the cygnet all women who cherish, most
of them silently, high aspirations. In the Finale, the stream of her
life is described as a river, but it is a river whose strength is broken,
spending "itself in channels which had no great name on the

---

37. Mill speaks in *Subjection* of the "extraordinary susceptibility of human
nature to external influences, and the extreme variableness of those of its mani-
festations which are supposed to be most universal and uniform" (p. 149). Just
as Eliot's passage seems to echo Mill, so does it also (as Gillian Beer notes in
"Beyond Determinism") hold out a challenge to Darwin.

earth." It is broken metaphorically by Cyrus, a ruler known to be both a liberator and a conqueror. So marriage for Dorothea, whether to a liberator (Ladislaw) or to an oppressor (Casaubon) diverts the strength of "her full nature" (Finale, p. 613).

Marriage in her world was "technically styled coverture" to signify "that husband and wife are treated at Common Law as one person indivisible, the personal and separate existence of the wife being legally considered as absorbed and consolidated in that of her husband, from which it is judicially indistinguishable, and under whose wing, protection, and cover she acts." The definition, from John J. S. Wharton's *Laws Relating to the Women of England*, makes clear why contract in marriage meant at best not identity but absorption of interests for women. The same point is made by Barbara Bodichon, who writes that the wife's "existence is entirely absorbed in that of her husband," when she explains marriage as coverture. Similarly, George Eliot describes Dorothea as "a creature absorbed into the life of another" even after her marriage to Will.[38]

In addition to these parallels in the use of the word *absorbed*, the river image of the Finale echoes a passage Wharton cites to note the origins of the term *coverture*:

> When a small brooke, or little river, incorporated with Rhodanus, Humber, or the Thames, the poore rivulet loseth her name; it is carried and recarried with the new associate; it beareth no sway, it possesseth nothing during coverture. A woman, as soone as she is married, is called *covert*, in Latine, *nupta*, that is, vailed, as it were, clouded and overshadowed, &c.; she hath lost her streame; she is continually *sub potestate viri*.[39]

Sir Henry Maine as well laments the *"Patria Potestas"* given to husbands by English Common Law with no regard to *jus naturale*:

> Modern jurisprudence, forged in the furnace of barbarian conquest, and formed by the fusion of Roman jurisprudence with patri-

38. Wharton, *Laws*, pp. 311–12; Barbara Leigh Smith Bodichon, *A Brief Summary in Plain Language of the Most Important Laws Concerning Women*, p. 6; *M*, Finale, p. 611. On George Eliot's respect for the work of Bodichon and Wharton, see chapter 4 above, p. 178.

39. Wharton, *Laws*, p. 312, n. (a). The passage is from a seventeenth-century legal text, *The Lawes Resolutions of Womens Rights: Or, The Lawes Provision for Woemen. A Methodicall Collection of such Statutes and Customes, with the Cases, Opinions, Arguments and points of Learning in the Law, as doe properly concerne Women* (London: John More, 1632), pp. 124–25. I am indebted to Thomas E. Foster, LL.B., for locating the source from which Wharton quotes.

archal usage, has absorbed, among its rudiments, much more than usual of those rules concerning the position of women which belong peculiarly to an imperfect civilisation.

[*Ancient Law*, p. 151

Summarizing Maine's point in her notebook, George Eliot wrote simply: "The modern position of woman chiefly determined by barbarian elements" ("*Middlemarch*" *Notebooks*, p. 205). In her novel she transforms Maine's entire argument concerning *jus naturale* and *jus gentium* into terms that summarize the life of Dorothea (née Brooke):

Certainly those determining acts of her life were not ideally beautiful. They were the mixed result of young and noble impulse struggling amidst the conditions of an imperfect social state.

[Finale, p. 612

Given those conditions, the wonder is that Dorothea had any life left to contribute to "the growing good of the world." Dorothea is stymied; and among her neighbors and friends "no one stated exactly what else that was in her power she ought rather to have done." The form George Eliot gives to the formlessness of Dorothea's life brilliantly uncovers the absence of social structures adequate to individual life; it also challenges the reader to halt the arrest.

Of the three love stories central to the novel, one couple does achieve a gratifying marriage. Content to play a traditional role, Fred and Mary find the existing forms adequate though they had not seemed so at the start. In chapter 52 of Book Five, Fred and Mary are still suffering from the dead hand of Featherstone, and again property rights and a despotic will are the disabling force. But even in Book Five, thanks to Farebrother's self-sacrificing intercession, Featherstone's grasp begins to loosen. By the end of the novel, Mary and Fred finally do marry, creating a "solid mutual happiness" (Finale, p. 608). Like Mary's parents, the Garths, the younger couple seem a happy throwback. But just as *Middlemarch* disputes the unifying force of any single system, so its critique of each system carries qualifications. In this case the "limits of variation" include the Freds and Marys, but that they are content with their traditional roles does not mean others can be or should be. The Finale makes this point, too, by way of a few gentle jibes: Mary's *Stories of Great Men* is published by Gripp & Co.; and Letty, her younger sister, is given an entire paragraph to dispute their brother's belief that "girls were good for less than boys." More importantly, within the overall structure of Finale and novel alike, the admonitory stories of the Casaubons and the Lydgates carry far greater force of implication than does the benign accommodation Fred and Mary make.

In the last chapter of Book Five, the dead hand of marriage and property rights returns with a vengeance. Raffles for the first time confronts Bulstrode, making known Bulstrode's wholesale betrayal of his first wife. As the epigraph to the chapter suggests, the perversion of the organic is so great as to make sinister and ironic the process "whereby the belief and the conduct are wrought into mutual sustainment," a union that rests on a "living myriad of hidden suckers." Those suckers become continually more diseased as the novel progresses, culminating in Bulstrode's murder of Raffles. While the second Mrs. Bulstrode remains loyal, she must endure exile and "withering" with him (VIII, 85, 602–3). The reader also discovers in chapter 53 what Bulstrode himself does not yet know: his first wife was Ladislaw's grandmother. With this closing revelation, Book Five is the first to interweave all the major plot strands and to relate virtually all the major characters through kinship.

That the book called "The Dead Hand" reveals these connections suggests how fatal to mutual interest many of them are. Marriage is at their center, as it is throughout the novel, but a good many social issues and institutions are implicated along the way— class, church, property, and progeny, among others. Most often the criticism of these other social forms is perfectly integrated into the marriage theme. Will's anger, for instance, at "those barriers of habitual sentiment which are more fatal to the persistence of mutual interest than all the distance between Rome and Britain" is triggered by the "prejudices about rank and status" that keep him from Dorothea (V, 43, 318); and Mary's attack on men who " 'represent Christianity—as if it were an institution for getting up idiots genteely,' " is motivated by her resistance to Fred's becoming a clergyman (V, 52, 379). Matrimonial government figures as well in the treatment of the two other social issues—medical and political reform—which after marriage are the most important in the fifth book and in the novel. In Lydgate's case, as we have seen, the connection is entirely ironical, effecting a disjunction between inward and outward. At the same time, and again for reasons both public and private, Lydgate's struggle for medical reform works on its own grounds to separate inward from outward.

The major subject of chapters 44 and 45 is the opposition in Middlemarch to Lydgate as medical man set on reforming "doctrine and practice" (V, 44, 321). Lydgate's arrogance, his position as an outsider, and his alliance with Bulstrode make him an easy target. However, when the doctors of Middlemarch join forces against him, creating out of their aversion a community of interests, the personal factors are revealed to be as much an excuse for their animosity as a cause. As the other medical men recognize only too well, Lydgate's fight for reform is a fight against the " '*rationale* of the system.' " For them, Lydgate is far more than a rival. He is a challenge to the prevailing system, a man " 'guilty' " of coming " 'among the members of his profession with innovations which are a libel on their time-honoured procedure.' " His plans for reform—including his medical research, hospital superintendence, and practical criticism (as in his refusal to dispense drugs)—cause his colleagues to charge him with inattention to medical "etiquette" and "breaches of medical propriety." At best, the medical men complain among themselves of an " 'ostentation of reform' " in Lydgate but " 'no real amelioration' " (V, 45, 327–30). At worst, they feed by innuendo the ignorance of the townspeople by encouraging them to think of Lydgate as a "charlatan" engaged in "reckless innovation for the sake of noise" (332).

From both sides, then, from the professional men and from the laity, Lydgate encounters in Middlemarch not the congenial workplace he had hoped to find but the "community of vice" alluded to in the epigraph to chapter 45. "Many different lights" and "every social shade" are brought to bear upon Lydgate in this chapter, but they nearly all serve to confirm "the public sentiment, of which the unanimity at Dollop's was an index" (323–24). That Dollop's, the public house, is located in Slaughter Lane serves nicely to gauge the quality of the public sentiment.

At this point in the novel, Lydgate, taking solace from his identification with Vesalius, is determined to weather the hostility. " 'They will not drive me away,' " he vows. " 'Things can't last as they are: there must be all sorts of reform soon' " (V, 45, 332–33). Things of course don't last as they are, but there is no reform: Lydgate is driven away and things become again as they were. As chapter 45 forewarns, when Farebrother cautions Lydgate not to get "tied" to Bulstrode and not to become hampered by money matters, Lydgate's complicity in his own defeat is great. But so is the town's. When Lydgate's ties subsequently cause him to be implicated in Bulstrode's crime, once again the discussion at Dollop's exemplifies a "type of what was going on in all Middlemarch circles" (*Quarry*, p. 640; VII, 71, 531). Public sentiment leads this time to the town meeting, where discussion of one "sanitary question"—the threat of cholera—quickly gives way to another, the blight of Bulstrode. Lydgate, the man who would be healer, is thought to be part of the disease. If the town's judgment is to some degree sound, the public sentiment is nonetheless tainted. As Lydgate puts it: " 'There is often something poisonous in the air of public rooms' " (VIII, 74, 547). As the entire novel testifies, whenever consensus consists of hostility not sympathy, poison is in the air.

" 'Most people,' " Lydgate complains, " 'never consider that a thing is good to be done unless it is done by their own set' " (V, 44, 321). Ladislaw, for much the same reason, says: " 'If everybody pulled for his own bit against everybody else, the whole question would go to tatters' " (V, 46, 336). The one finds his image of organic wholeness in living tissue, the other in the body politic. Like Lydgate, Ladislaw in Book Five has a certain optimism: " 'Things will grow and ripen as if it were a comet year' " (V, 46, 336). The "things" he has in mind concern the Reform Bill. Because parliamentary legislation is contract writ large, that the question of Reform should be reduced to tatters testifies more directly than do the marital disabilities, or the consensus of hostility suffered by Lydgate, to George Eliot's sense of the precariousness of revisionary social organicism.

Again, the nature of existing institutions is very much at issue. The pending dissolution of Parliament—evidence of a government pulled apart, not together, by the national struggle for Reform—is mentioned so often in Book Five as to become a leitmotif.[40] At the same time, in chapters 46 and 51, the reconstructive effort is closely examined. As Ladislaw tries to teach Brooke, it is the " 'balance of the constitution,' " or the balance of power, that needs to be changed. In good organicist fashion, Ladislaw makes his ideal the balancing of different class interests and claims, but the response he receives suggests how difficult or impossible this will be to achieve. His rival, the editor of the *Trumpet*, attacks him for casting " 'reflections on solid Englishmen generally,' " and for speechifying "by the hour against institutions 'which had existed when he was in his cradle' " (V, 46, 337–39). Partisan newspapers, political parties, geographical situation, social set: all suggest division rather than community of interests.

Chapters 46 and 51 also reveal how Will's ideal itself participates

40. See openings of chapters 46, 50, and 51 in *Middlemarch*, and closings of chapters 47 and 49.

in the haphazard and tentative. He stumbles into his political
career from a desire to be in the neighborhood of Dorothea. The
work turns out to fit: "The easily-stirred rebellion in him helped
the glow of public spirit"; but the congruence is accidental (V,
46, 338). His own attitudes, moreover, are far from stable. He is by
turns ardent, dreamy, skeptical, practical, cynical; doubtful about
whether the "right side" will win, and repelled by the "dirty-
handed" business on both sides (V, 51, 368).

When Ladislaw engages in political debate with Lydgate in
chapter 46, Lydgate charges him with " 'crying up a measure as if
it were a universal cure, and crying up men who are a part of the
very disease that wants curing.' " Pointing to decomposition, not
wholeness, Lydgate adds: " 'You go against rottenness, and there is
nothing more thoroughly rotten than making people believe that
society can be cured by a political hocus-pocus.' " If Lydgate seems
to be accusing Ladislaw of the very charlatanism for which he was
himself being attacked, the two are nonetheless on good terms, in
part because Lydgate is well aware of the parallel obstacles they
face. Ladislaw, furthermore, does not entirely disagree with Lydgate's analysis. What he questions are the conclusions: " 'But your
cure must begin somewhere,' " he tells Lydgate, " 'Put it that a
thousand things which debase a population can never be reformed
without this particular reform to begin with.' " For Ladislaw, the
" 'whole question' " dissolves quickly into parts; for Lydgate it
leads to "seeing himself checkmated" because he too, as he knows,
has nothing to work with but imperfect parts (V, 46, 341).

The immediate undermining of the "whole question" of Reform
is completed in chapter 51. Brooke's buffoonish performance at the
hustings, combined with the "diabolical procedure" set up by the
opposing party, confirms all Lydgate's suspicions and Ladislaw's
worst fears (V, 51, 370). That these events are to be taken as no
chance matter the epigraph to chapter 51 makes clear:

> Party is Nature too, and you shall see
> By force of Logic how they both agree:
> The Many in the One, the One in Many:
> All is not Some, nor Some the same as Any: ...

Just as the ventriloquist turns Brooke's speech to mockery, so the
epigraph takes the language of organicism and turns it to parody.
Like Brooke, the "Many in the One" and the "One in Many" rise
in this novel only in effigy.

Still, "All is not Some." The "some" of the book of "The Dead

Hand" signifies widespread organic dysfunction in individuals and in the institutions regulating their lives. Instead of Statics and Dynamics, the community of Middlemarch exhibits stasis or arrest. But George Eliot's study of provincial life also alludes from Middlemarch to the world beyond. In the closing portions of the Finale, municipality, nation, and world to a large extent supplant the local and the provincial. The standard of value changes along with the geography. Community becomes a matter of consciousness more or less independent of time and place.

The resistance of traditional community to change and the need to break free from provincial boundaries—from hereditary custom, habitual practice, and inherited institutions—are suggested all the way through the novel, in part by locating the desire for reform in characters who are outsiders. Those who most disapprove of present conditions are newcomers: Dorothea objects to woman's lot, Lydgate to the medical system, and Ladislaw to social and political institutions. Their final return to the world beyond Middlemarch speaks to the limits of provincial life, but it carries also some new affirmations.

In the case of Will, the closing makes good to some extent what seemed in Book Five to be merely a fantasy. "Public life" does become "wider and more national" (V, 51, 372). He happily overturns Brooke's wish and prediction: " 'I can't help wishing somebody had a pocket-borough to give you, Ladislaw. You'd never get elected, you know' " (V, 46, 337). But Will would not have gotten elected had he remained in Middlemarch. As if to make this point, the last chapter closes before the first Reform Bill has been passed. By the time of the Finale, however, two Reform bills have become national law. That Will should be returned to Parliament "by a constituency who paid his expenses" anticipates future reforms (Finale, 611). So, in a larger sense, does Will's life in London. Married to Dorothea, and serving as a "public man," he comes closer than any other character to fulfilling a telos that is both individual and social.

Will is himself a reformer, moreover, in still another way. He prides himself on the "sense of belonging to no class" (V, 46, 338). All the characters in the novel who would be reformers are required in some way to break caste, but Will's defection is the most complete. He has, in fact, the marks of being a member of what George Eliot, in her review of Riehl, described as a new Fourth Estate. Composed of "day-labourers with the quill," it seemed to Riehl a quintessential sign of the decomposition of organic society.[41] In *Middlemarch* George Eliot portrays the decomposition even while she begins to reconstruct the parts.

But the parts are at best incomplete. In the novel, dynamic change is initiated by the estranged and the displaced, and the changes themselves call forth reservations. "Will became an ardent public man," the Finale tells us, "working well in those times when reforms were begun with a young hopefulness of immediate good which has been much checked in our days" (610). Legislation, according to revisionary social organicism, is one of the major agencies by which law is brought into harmony with individual needs and society. In *Middlemarch* such harmony is yet to be seen. Will's inadequacies of character—his dilettantism, moments of cruelty, extravagant flights of idealism—speak of a world in which reform and reformer alike are far from perfect or complete. The fragility of George Eliot's affirmation may be seen as well, though probably not by her intention, in the incomplete definition of Will's character. In addition, though Will away from Middlemarch leads a full and fruitful life, for the Bulstrodes expulsion means a life of sad exile, while for Lydgate the diminished life he leads elsewhere comes to much the same result as being swallowed up whole by Middlemarch.

While the Finale's portrait of Will calls attention to national political reform, the farewell to Dorothea celebrates an individual's private contribution to the growing good of the world. Given the structure of values George Eliot brings to the idea of moral evolution, Will's concrete accomplishments can but take second place to Dorothea's "incalculably diffusive" effect. As represented in the novel, the principle of political reform constitutes only a single "channel"; Dorothea's "good," innumerable "channels" (V, 51, 373; Finale, 613). But the price she pays is high—nothing less than the breaking and spending of her nature. Testifying not to organic wholeness, but to the incompleteness of women's lives, qualification and affirmation exist in the Finale, as in Dorothea's telos, side by side.

This incompleteness creates in Dorothea, as it did in Maggie, and in their creator, an emphasis of want. In *Middlemarch*, it takes its most passionate form in Dorothea's visionary yearning for community. "The sense of connection with a manifold pregnant existence had to be kept up painfully as an inward vision, instead of coming from without in claims that would have shaped her ener-

41. See *Essays*, pp. 294–95, and chapter 2 above, p. 37.

gies," we are told at the moment that Dorothea, just returned from her honeymoon with Casaubon, realizes her marriage has brought not liberation from the "gentlewoman's world" but further and more "stifling oppression" (III, 28, 202). In the closing book, Dorothea again rescues herself from intense despair, caused this time by her misapprehension of Will's relation to Rosamond, and does so once more by way of inward vision. A glimpse of distant figures— "a man with a bundle on his back and a woman carrying her baby" —is transformed by her consciousness into an image of "the largeness of the world and the manifold wakings of men to labour and endurance." The transformation represents a great moment of awakening for herself as well:

> She was a part of that involuntary, palpitating life, and could neither look out on it from her luxurious shelter as a mere spectator, nor hide her eyes in selfish complaining.
>
> [VIII, 80, 578

This awakening leads to the "self-subduing act of fellowship" that brings her into communion with Rosamond and Lydgate, leading in turn to the restoration of her faith in Will.

The controlled nature of the affirmation, however, reveals that George Eliot does not yield in *Middlemarch*, as she had in *The Mill*, to her own emphasis of want. But neither, as a result, is she able to affirm organic wholeness through community. Dorothea never finds the comprehensive outward shaping energy she seeks; the "loving heart-beats" of the Prelude's "foundress of nothing" continue to tremble "after an unattained goodness." Her sense of "manifold pregnant existence" is accompanied by the feeling that "all existence seemed to beat with a lower pulse than her own" (III, 28, 202). Only by an abnormally rapid or violent beating of her own heart is she able to bring the outer pulse into any kind of congruence with the inner. The very language of the affirmation—"she was a part of that involuntary *palpitating* life"—incorporates organic dysfunction.

Daniel Deronda

Just as the structural gaps of *The Mill on the Floss* develop from George Eliot's failure to confront the separations she uncovers, so the unity of *Middlemarch* comes from her acceptance of fragmentation. In the one case, the organic unity attributed to life at the novel's close upsets the aesthetic structure; in the other, the artistry of the whole turns the idea of social coherence into a fiction. Both novels make implausible the idea of a healthy and harmonious social organism, though *Middlemarch* does so with far more consistent intent than *The Mill*. In *Daniel Deronda*, this sense of a blighted society becomes greatly intensified. The affliction affects an entire culture, Europe as well as England; the severity and extent of the degenerative disease increase. At the same time, the visionary affirmation of community is in *Daniel Deronda* far more passionately and extensively imagined than in any other novel George Eliot wrote. In both respects—radical disease and radical cure—her last novel is her most extreme. The antithesis is entirely intentional. "I meant everything in the book," she once said, "to be related to everything else there" (*Letters* 6: 290). This desire for comprehensive relationship includes in *Daniel Deronda* a drive for synthesis even while the novel continues to dramatize antithesis. The reach and the limits of the vision, however, cause unintentional structural divisions.

From the moment of publication, readers have pointed to a lack of unity in *Daniel Deronda*. To look at its divisions from the perspective of social organicism is to see George Eliot uncovering increasing brutality and stagnation in the institutions of social life, but also to see her refusing to settle for the vagueness of the solidarity Dorothea apprehends. In *Daniel Deronda*, George Eliot tries to translate an inchoate vision of community into concrete reality. She can do so, however, only by way of transmutation and transplantation, both of which make questionable the organic wholeness she would affirm.

As many critics have observed, George Eliot turns to the visionary in *Daniel Deronda* because she perceives conditions in the present (the novel is set in 1865) to be dire.[42] Again, marriage is central to the degeneration she dramatizes. However much the Casaubons and the Lydgates suffer in marriage, their actions seem almost clean-handed when compared to Grandcourt's treatment of his wife. Because Gwendolen resists marriage in general, as well as marriage to Grandcourt, she is overtly, rather than merely by implication, a woman forced to marry. Books Three and Four are called "Maidens Choosing" and "Gwendolen Gets Her Choice," but the titles turn out to be ironical. The only real alternatives to marriage—teaching or becoming a governess—bring a "sick motive-

42. Among the first modern critics to argue for the importance of the visionary mode in *Daniel Deronda* are Maurice Beebe, "'Visions Are Creators,'" pp. 166–67; and Robert Preyer, "Beyond the Liberal Imagination," pp. 33–54.

lessness" and "world-nausea" upon her (III, 24, 317–18). The one possibility she welcomes, a career on the stage, proves to be chimerical and leaves her feeling lacerated and wounded (III, 23, 305–7). This same sense of a blighted life, described in similar images, marks her response to Grandcourt after the loss of family fortune overpowers her resistance.

As with Dorothea and Rosamond, Gwendolen's case is exemplary; the very language Eliot uses to describe it appears also in John Stuart Mill. When Grandcourt first begins to court Gwendolen, she complains:

> "We women can't go in search of adventures—to find out the North-West Passage or the source of the Nile, or to hunt tigers in the East. We must stay where we grow, or where the gardeners like to transplant us. We are brought up like the flowers, to look as pretty as we can, and be dull without complaining. That is my notion about the plants: they are often bored, and that is the reason why some of them have got poisonous."
>
> [II, 13, 171

The revelations from Mrs. Glasher and the news of financial disaster soon turn the bored, pretty flower into a "parched plant" (III, 27, 341). Both images testify to the "hot-house and stove cultivation" of Mill's *Subjection*: "The result of forced repression in some directions, unnatural stimulation in others," it makes "what is now called the nature of women . . . an eminently artificial thing," one half "kept in a vapour bath and the other half in the snow" (pp. 148–49). Gwendolen " 'stifled' " and Gwendolen " 'frozen' " embody the two extremes.[43]

Grandcourt's wife not only illustrates how women are forced "into marriage by [society's] closing all other doors against them," but also is proof of the cause and effect Mill ascribes to the coercion. The cause is the fear that "all women of spirit and capacity should prefer doing almost anything else, not in their own eyes degrading, rather than marry, when marrying is giving themselves a master" (*Subjection*, p. 156). Mill describes the effect as follows:

> An active and energetic mind, if denied liberty, will seek for power: refused the command of itself, it will assert its personality by attempting to control others. . . . Where liberty cannot be hoped for, and power can, power becomes the grand object of human desire. . . . Where there is least liberty, the passion for power is the most ardent and unscrupulous. The desire of power over others

43. See, for example, III, 26, 340; V, 35, 482.

can only cease to be a depraving agency among mankind, when each of them individually is able to do without it.

[*Subjection*, p. 258

The spirited Gwendolen attempts to subvert the process from the start by marrying a man she believes she can command. Grandcourt is so cunningly the master as to court her by encouraging the deception. Whether Gwendolen is relishing her power of using him as she likes, or whether he is in fact using her as he likes, the delineation of the "depraving agency" is sharp and clear, manifest even in their proposal scene:

At that moment his strongest wish was to be completely master of this creature—this piquant combination of maidenliness and mischief: that she knew things which had made her start away from him, spurred him to triumph over that repugnance; and he was believing that he should triumph. And she—ah, piteous equality in the need to dominate!—she was overcome . . . by the suffused sense that here in this man's homage to her lay the rescue from helpless subjection to an oppressive lot.

[III, 27, 346

Instead of rescue, the marriage brings an oppression so severe as to make Grandcourt's daily pleasure Gwendolen's torture. The forms his power takes correspond to Mill's depiction of a husband as the worst kind of potentate. Just as Mill compares the lot of a wife to that of a "Sultan's favourite slave," so George Eliot alludes sardonically to a "Moslem paradise" when she writes of Gwendolen's imprisonment on her husband's yacht.[44] The novel also demonstrates how Grandcourt keeps Gwendolen in what Mill calls "a chronic state of bribery and intimidation" (p. 137). Holding over her the vow she made to Mrs. Glasher not to marry him, he also conceals what he knows, pretending (as does Gwendolen) that she has no knowledge of his former mistress. As suitor and bridegroom, he uses this secret to heighten the humiliations Gwendolen attempts to hide. As the husband she comes to loathe, he discloses his knowledge to renegotiate the terms of the contract so as to tighten her yoke.

The contractual nature of their marriage is acknowledged by both. "She had no right to complain of her contract, or to withdraw from it," Gwendolen feels, "by saying that there had been a tacit part of the contract on her side—namely, that she meant to

44. *Subjection*, p. 168; VII, 54, 733.

rule and have her own way." Grandcourt thinks likewise: "Her marriage was a contract. . . . He knew quite well that she had not married him—had not overcome her repugnance to certain facts—out of love to him personally; he had won her by the rank and luxuries he had to give her." He now threatens to deprive her of those advantages by changing the terms of his will, naming as his heir the boy he had by Mrs. Glasher should Gwendolen not bear him a son. His intent is entirely clear to Gwendolen: "This question of property and inheritance was meant as a finish to her humiliations and her thraldom."[45]

For Mill, case and judgment would conclude at this point, though the work of reforming the "system" would still remain undone (*Subjection*, p. 137). But George Eliot, whose belief in the moral superiority of women Mill did not share, turns the judgment in a different direction.[46] She makes Grandcourt's moral obtuseness—his inability to understand that Gwendolen's repugnance consists partly of spiritual dread—the cause of his own defeat by showing how his calculations about the will have "an effect the very opposite of what he intended" (VI, 48, 664). While Grandcourt would employ the will to keep his "yoke tightly riveted" on Gwendolen's neck, George Eliot makes the yoke an instrument of her moral regeneration. Grandcourt attempts to increase Gwendolen's thraldom by revising his will; Gwendolen sees in the new arrangement a way of righting the wrong done to Mrs. Glasher. Earlier she asked Deronda how she might make amends. Grandcourt unwittingly provides her with a way of acting on the advice Deronda gave her:

> "That is the bitterest of all—to wear the yoke of our own wrong-doing. But if you submitted to that, as men submit to maiming or a lifelong incurable disease?—and made the unalterable wrong a reason for more effort towards a good that may do something to counterbalance the evil?"
>
> [V, 36, 506

The advice raises questions even as it answers them, just as the later movement of the novel does. The closing affirms Gwendo-

45. VI, 48, 665; VII, 54, 732; VI, 48, 663.

46. For an altogether different estimate of the differences between Eliot and Mill on women, see R. L. P. Jackson, "George Eliot, J. S. Mill and Women's Liberation," pp. 11–33. He takes them to be in every way polar opposites. Seeing Mill exclusively as a proponent of "mechanistic" and "atomistic" individual liberty, Jackson places him entirely on the side of " 'Pagan self-assertion.' " George Eliot he identifies nearly as singularly with " 'Christian self-denial.' "

len's "good," but only tremulously, by projecting a future announced but unseen. Meanwhile, Grandcourt has drowned, and
Gwendolen has confessed how poisonous her thoughts about him
had been. Furthermore, the question of whether Gwendolen could
have saved Grandcourt from drowning is never answered. Although the death of Grandcourt (like the death of Casaubon) gives
a second chance to a wife who had been in thraldom, still Gwendolen's maiming seems lifelong. That part of the disease which
exists within her begins to heal, but she is in the end solitary and
shaken with terror.

At the same time, the sense of atrophy in the social realm decreases only equivocally, if at all. Gwendolen seeks to rectify the
larger injustices her marriage represents, but her weapons signify
barrenness not fertility, subversion rather than reform.[47] Her initial
attempt to defy convention, represented by her desire to marry in
order to command, is itself revealed to be "a sort of subjection" (I,
10, 139). Her second attempt, her acquiescence in making Grandcourt's illegitimate son his heir, turns identity of interests into
travesty. Like so many of her actions, it has more the form of "practical submission" than of "constructive rebellion," more the force
of protest than reform (VI, 48, 667).

Although the criticism of social institutions in *Daniel Deronda*
is vigorous, it has no vent in action where the portrait of English
life is concerned. While the issue of dynamic energy pervades the
novel, the English segments are marked by persistent atrophy and
dissolution. Gwendolen enters the novel with a "dynamic glance";
she leaves with a "withered look of grief." The word *dynamic*,
George Eliot was well aware, means "force producing motion."[48]
Within the actual social world of this novel that force is either
destructive or inert, as in Gwendolen's seeking to "conquer" or

47. Gillian Beer argues in "Beyond Determinism" that Gwendolen's
"triumph is that of barrenness; she does not conceive an heir to Grandcourt"
(pp. 92–93).

48. I, 1, 35; VIII, 69, 878. The word *dynamic* appears in the opening sentence of the novel. When Blackwood sent Eliot the proofs, he commented,
"I remember pausing at the use of the word dynamic in the very first sentence,
and I am not quite sure about it yet as it is a *dictionary* word to so many
people" (*Letters* 6: 183). But she retained the word. Late nineteenth-century
dictionaries label *dynamic* a scientific term, coined earlier in the century,
denoting force producing motion, and the motion of bodies acting mutually
on one another. The psychological dimension George Eliot gives to the word
is an original usage according to the *OED*. Contemporary reviewers pounced
on the word, finding it both unnervingly obscure and portentously scientific.

Gwendolen's suffering "arrest."[49] If Social Statics still signifies co-existence, it is of an especially sinister sort. Again an opening image—so emblematic as not even to refer to specific characters—marks the tone. Commenting on the "varieties of European type" gathered at the gambling hall, "Livonian and Spanish, Graeco-Italian and miscellaneous German, English aristocratic and English plebeian," George Eliot writes:

> Here certainly was a striking admission of human equality. The white bejewelled fingers of an English countess were very near touching a bony, yellow, crab-like hand stretching a bared wrist to clutch a heap of coin—a hand easy to sort with the square, gaunt face, deep-set eyes, grizzled eyebrows, and ill-combed scanty hair which seemed a slight metamorphosis of the vulture.
>
> [I, 1, 36

The theme of dynamic energy, of the driving force behind social order, penetrates the novel in two other important ways, one of which also enters at the start. In contrast to Gwendolen's "dynamic glance," it takes the form of the narrator's and Deronda's ironic gaze. Just as the portrait of Gwendolen's marriage includes an attack on other institutions (among them aristocratic and colonial rule), so Deronda's ironic glance casts an "evil eye" on far more than Gwendolen's ruinous play. The driving force behind Deronda's and the narrator's "measuring gaze" is the radical disjunction the reader must come to perceive between outward conditions and inward vision, material reality and spiritual need.[50] Irony takes disparity as its starting point. To make it a major structural device, as George Eliot does in *Daniel Deronda*, is to take disjunction, not wholeness, as the given. Her irony also exercises a cor-

49. Images of Gwendolen's desire to command appear regularly throughout the first books of the novel. Images of arrest, of Gwendolen as "statue" and "ghost," pervade the second half and the close (e.g., VII, 56, 753; VIII, 65, 841; 69, 876).

50. The first and second chapters are filled with references to Deronda's "smile of irony," "exasperating irony," "measuring . . . ironical gaze," "evil eye," and the like. As later passages reveal, Deronda's ironical glance has a continuing effect on Gwendolen (e.g., III, 24, 316; IV, 29, 375; V, 35, 462). As we shall see shortly, "the irony of earthly mixtures" (V, 43, 606) is at play constantly in the novel in far more comprehensive ways as well. Therefore to locate the novel's "satiric mode" in the Gwendolen (as opposed to the Deronda) plot, and to argue that neither the narrator nor the Jewish segments participate in the novel's "ironic mode," as Cynthia Chase does, seems to me inaccurate. See Chase, "The Decomposition of the Elephants," pp. 215–16.

rective function, leading the reader toward a revolution of consciousness of the sort Gwendolen experiences as a result of heeding Deronda's "evil eye." From this single perspective, Deronda is one tool among many used by the satirist writing *Daniel Deronda*.

The motif of dynamic energy enters the novel also through the visionary theme. Again, the mode of the theme's presentation suggests the nature of the energy. The theme is slowly introduced in chapter 32, tentatively and obliquely, in the form of positive organic images. Deliberately placed, it would seem, by way of flashback in the chapter following Gwendolen's marriage scene, these images prepare for the novel's movement into "the grander orbits of what hath been and shall be" (IV, 32, epigraph). They are furthermore the first positive organic images to appear in the novel. Consonant with the subject of the chapter (Deronda's visit to the Meyricks to inquire after Mirah upon his return to London from Leubronn), the first of these retrospective images speaks of "one fibre" uniting Mirah's whole being (410). The second tells of Deronda's feelings when, during a visit to the Frankfort synagogue, all became momentarily "blent for him as one expression of a binding history" (416–17). The third compares " 'mother's love,' " to a deep-rooted tree " 'that has got all the wood in it, from the very first it made' " (424). In the next chapter, Deronda meets "a man in threadbare clothing, whose age was difficult to guess—from the dead yellowish flatness of the flesh" (IV, 33, 436). Although this first glimpse of Mordecai may seem a return to the theme of disease, it actually initiates an entirely different movement. Like the images in the chapter before, the introduction of Mordecai prefigures an energy that is organic, not literally but metaphorically, not corporeally but spiritually.

Just as the organic is for Modecai far more a vision than a reality, so too Mirah's "one fibre," consisting of her religion, her affections, and memories of her mother, exists in her imagination. So little has she been nourished by the world that she is attempting suicide when we meet her. Deronda's intimations "of a sublimely penetrating life," surfacing from "dust and withered remnants . . . as in the twin green leaves that will become the sheltering tree" during the Frankfort Judengasse retrospect, though they are at this point only stirrings, are similarly imaginative poetic projections. As this scene suggests, he sustains them by neutralizing and transforming the ugliness he meets on his way (IV, 32, 414–15).

The imaginative union in *Daniel Deronda* between the organic and the visionary is as evident in the absence of positive organic images when English life is portrayed as in their presence when Mordecai's voice is heard:

> "I believe in a growth, a passage, and a new unfolding of life whereof the seed is more perfect, more charged with the elements that are pregnant with diviner form."

> "[I] see more and more of the hidden bonds that bind and consecrate change as a dependent growth—yea, consecrate it with kinship."

> "Israel is the heart of mankind, if we mean by heart the core of affection which binds a race and its families in dutiful love."

> "Visions are the creators and feeders of the world. I see, I measure the world as it is, which the vision will create anew."[51]

The last of these quotations signifies that Mordecai's vision, like Deronda's and the narrator's ironical gaze, is a measuring or evaluative device. Each serves to lead the reader to discover how in the absence of spiritual and moral values organic dissolution occurs. George Eliot often combines the two—vision and irony, or spiritual affirmation and parody—into a single satiric tool. Heightening the difference between the world as it is and the world as Mordecai imagines it, the language of vision, for instance, when used by characters other than Mordecai and Daniel, is so perverted as to be parodic.

Playing the courtship game by "dint of divination" and "prevision," Gwendolen jokingly anticipates her first meeting with the much vaunted Grandcourt by devilishly conjuring up the " 'face of a magnified insect.' "[52] The joke turns soon enough to ironical image as Grandcourt the "handsome lizard" turns into "alligator," "serpent," "boa-constrictor."[53] Finding an additional echo in Mordecai's reverberating words, vision and image become ironical in yet another way. If the "men who had the visions" are, as Mordecai believes, "the creators and feeders of the world—moulding and feeding the more passive life which without them would dwindle and shrivel into the narrow tenacity of insects," Grandcourt the "sleepy-eyed animal on the watch for prey" is indeed akin to the

51. Passages quoted from VI, 42, 585, 587, 590; V, 40, 555.
52. I, 9, 128; I, 10, 140.
53. See Hardy, *Novels*, p. 227. These images of Grandcourt appear in II, 13, 174–75; II, 15, 195; V, 35, 477; VII, 54, 735.

"insects."[54] Having "the sensibility which seems like divination" as far as "the gratification of his own will" is concerned, Grandcourt himself, furthermore, makes a mockery of prophecy by divining in order to destroy. Similarly, "second-sight" in Lush means "evil consequences," whereas in Mordecai it means "the passionate current of an ideal life."

Throughout the novel those words most associated with its positive values are rendered chillingly ironical. "Conversion" turns into the coldness of suppressed rage, prophecy to "doom" instead of redemption, "prayers" into murderous wishes and "hidden rites of vengeance," and "metamorphosis" into mutilating or "tragic transformation."[55] This device of overturning the meaning of words that embody spiritual values is used also with Jewish characters. Lapidoth, Mirah's and Mordecai's father, turns religious rites to burlesque and parody simply for the sake of entertainment. Like his son, he too is a man of "strong . . . visions," but the only thing they feed is his appetite for gambling.[56] Sometimes such ironic burlesque is broad, sometimes (as in the following example) oblique. The epigraph to chapter 63, a passage from Heine in German, describes Moses as a great builder of "human [as opposed to granite] pyramids"; the chapter itself compares Mordecai to Moses; a few chapters later, *Pyramids* is the name of the gambling house where Lapidoth loses the little he has (VIII, 66, 844). Given the extensive role of gambling in the novel, the perversion of vision in Lapidoth's passion is far from an isolated matter.

Such parodic images deprecate the actual world and extol Mordecai's vision. But within the novel are other ironic scenes that hold his religious vision up to question. When Deronda at last meets his mother, for instance, the "passionate self-defense" with which she speaks of not having wanted a child makes him feel as if he is witnessing "some strange rite of a religion which gave a sacredness to crime" (VII, 51, 689). Religious rites are subject to a different sort of parody when Jacob (in the chapter in which Mordecai is first revealed to be a visionary) gleefully imitates a mountebank while Mordecai tries to engrave his Hebrew poems on the young boy's

54. VII, 55, 749; V, 35, 465. Succeeding quotations in this paragraph are from VI, 44, 616; IV, 28, 362; V, 38, 531. On Grandcourt's powers of divination, see also VI, 48, 656–58 and 670; for the narrator's meditation on second-sight and its effects on Daniel and Mordecai, see V, 37, 527, and V, 38, 527–31.

55. VI, 48, 656; V, 35, 478; VII, 54, 737–38; IV, 30, 389; VIII, 65, 836.

56. III, 20, 256–57; VIII, 66, 843, 849.

mind (V, 38, 533–37). In both scenes compassion and mockery together enter both the real and imagined worlds. "Mother's love,"
not abstract but concrete, is at issue in the Princess' impassioned
self-defense, which disturbs the definition of woman's maternal
nature in Judaism and organicism alike. Jacob's burlesque as well
opposes abstract to concrete. The poems of fervid vision Mordecai
would "print" in Jacob, hoping thus to have them survive the approaching death of his own diseased body, are for the boy no more
than a "game of imitating unintelligible words." So too when Mordecai meets with friends, among them a number of Jews, at the
Hand and Banner, their response includes compassion (the correlative to Jacob's good humor) but also indifference and mockery.
He is to them, as he is to Jacob, "like a poet among people of a
strange speech" who "have no ear for his cadence" (VI, 42, 588).
They, unlike Jacob, find his words intelligible, but his meaning
seems again entirely divorced from reality.

As we saw earlier, the force of the dynamic in the realm of the
visionary is imaginative and incorporeal. To separate the organic
from the physical and actual, however, is to make the organic entirely metaphorical. The effect is to call seriously into question a
major tenet of revisionary organicism. In *Daniel Deronda*, George
Eliot both goes in this direction and passionately resists it. When
she does not resist, the effect is a double critique. Just as the satire
reveals society, both English and Jewish, to be all body and no
spirit, so does it reveal the visionary world to be all spirit and no
body. One is as organically incomplete as the other. The dynamic
energy the reader must discover, then, involves seeing in the
visionary not a complete but a corrective or admonitory image.

If Mordecai and Deronda were merely fictional devices designed
to achieve this end—tools used by the satirist to expose spiritual
stagnation and social atrophy—then the roundness they are often
faulted for lacking would be a relatively minor flaw. Their very
woodenness would demonstrate that the organic cannot be dynamic
when it lacks physical substantiality any more than can the material
when it lacks spirituality. But George Eliot desires in *Daniel Deronda* to move beyond revolution of consciousness. She attempts
now to resurrect community not on one of its pillars but on all
three.

Crucial to that effort is Deronda's relation to Mordecai. The sick
but spiritually healthy man sheds his "diseased organism" by trans-
mitting the "energetic certitude" of his soul into the spiritually
adrift but physically healthy Deronda. " 'You will be my life: it

will be planted afresh; it will grow,' " Mordecai tells Deronda immediately following their momentous meeting on the bridge. And though he resists at first, Deronda slowly becomes inclined to "receive from Mordecai's mind the complete ideal shape of that personal duty and citizenship which lay in his own thought like sculptured fragments."[57] The fragments are the result of the "revolutionary shock" Deronda experienced when the identity of his parents first began to trouble him as a boy of thirteen. Among the effects are his sense of being physically maimed (as if he had a "deformed foot"), his feeling of psychological distance from the place he knew as home, his morbid sensitivity about his parentage, and his inability to choose a vocation (II, 16). His yearning to shed his "social neutrality" and make himself "an organic part of social life" contends with his perception of himself as a "disembodied spirit, stirred with a vague social passion, but without fixed local habitation to render fellowship real."[58]

Deronda's friendship with Mordecai leads to his finding a "habitation," but his sense of fellowship cannot become "real" in any wide sense until he undergoes a second revolutionary shock, one that restores him to the family and heritage the first had dissolved. The resolution of his natural filial ties is prerequisite to his social reintegration. In this last novel, George Eliot makes the "full guidance of primary [by which she means "family"] duties" essential to the recovery of community (IV, 33, 433). As Deronda tells Mordecai, " 'I am finding the clue of my life in the recognition of my natural parentage,' " a recognition that brings "metamorphosis" and with it "a new sense of fellowship."[59]

The recovery of a geographical " 'organic centre' " follows from the filial ties. " 'Let the unity of Israel which has made the growth and form of its religion be an outward reality,' " Mordecai declares. " 'Looking towards a land and a polity, our dispersed people in all the ends of the earth may share the dignity of a national life which has a voice among the peoples of the East and the West—which will plant the wisdom and skill of our race so that it may be, as of old, a medium of transmission and understanding.' " Above all, he foresees a transmission into community:

> "There is store of wisdom among us to found a new Jewish polity, grand, simple, just, like the old—a republic where there is equality

57. V, 40, 551, 557; VI, 41, 567, 570–71.
58. II, 16, 220; IV, 32, 413.
59. VIII, 63, 821; VII, 55, 747; VIII, 65, 836.

of protection, an equality which shone like a star on the forehead of our ancient community, and gave it more than the brightness of Western freedom amid the despotisms of the East. . . . And the world will gain as Israel gains. For there will be a community in the van of the East which carries the culture and sympathies of every great nation in its bosom."

Its " 'highest transformation' " is world community, but " 'our race' " must first take on again, he argues, " 'the character of a nationality' " (VI, 42, 592–95). Daniel becomes heir to this mission.

When Deronda sets out at the end of the novel to pursue this Zionist dream, all three pillars of community—family, geography, and shared belief and purpose—are in place. He is at last on his way to fulfilling his long quest for a " 'social captainship' " (VIII, 63, 819). So too, through his marriage to Mirah, is he realizing his dream of "blending . . . a complete personal love in one current with a larger duty" (VII, 50, 685). The private and the public come together; his telos seems complete.

Seen in this way, Deronda is less the satirist's tool than a romantic hero undergoing metamorphosis while engaged on a sacred quest. The nature of the quest is both mystical and Comtean, transcendental at first but focused ultimately on social problems, incorporating the visionary and the real, the poetic and the scientific. As William Baker points out, and as Mordecai's allusions to the " 'Cabbala' " and to the Spanish-Jewish mystic poet Jehuda ha-Levi suggest, Kabbalistic mystical doctrine is the source of both the idea of a soul's rebirth within a stronger kindred spirit and the concept of an organic fusion (signified through botanical images) between the "individual and the nation to which he belongs."[60] The Sephardic tradition, to which Deronda's family belongs, is seen furthermore to be " 'a line' " that has " 'borne many students and men of practical power.' " To identify it as such brings Deronda to "one of those rare moments when our yearnings and our acts can be completely one, and the real we behold is our ideal good" (VIII, 63, 817). Providing an answer to the question Comte left unanswered when he argued for the dual presence but institutional separation of spiritual and temporal power, it represents a rare moment in George Eliot's Victorian world as well.

As she explains in her notes on "historic guidance," a "distinction between theory & practice" lies behind the division. If such a

60. V, 38, 534; VI, 43, 599. William Baker, *George Eliot and Judaism*, pp. 157–62, 241.

separation worked in the past, it does not "answer to the demands of the growing world": "Knowledge must become the general inheritance," she states, and "teachers must be had." Rejecting the idea of a "renovated priesthood" in any "literal sense," she proposes "a sort of universal congregationalism" but admits the difficulty of defining its shape. She speaks of the "election of teachers by those who require teaching" while acknowledging the problems this presents; she puts aside the question of institutional organization by calling it a matter "we are not obliged to settle" ("More Leaves," pp. 374–75). Her ideal is to fuse, not distinguish between, priesthood and laity, spiritual and temporal. In the character of Deronda, she tries to give fictional embodiment to that ideal.

Yet there are countless signs in the novel that the ideal, even as dramatized by the Jewish characters, remains incomplete. George Eliot's own sense of the incompleteness is most self-aware concerning the union between the visionary and the real. Throughout the novel, as many readers have noticed, the narrator argues for the ultimate identity of scientific and poetic, empirical and imaginative truth. Many scenes in the novel, however, call that identity into question.[61]

The concept of " 'transmutation of self' " is introduced by Mirah's relating a story about " 'Bouddha giving himself to the famished tigress to save her and her little ones from starving.' " Her tale prompts her listeners to offer a number of responses, most of which separate the imaginative idea from the reality. One of the Meyrick girls responds cynically by questioning the Buddha's motives, and another rationally by questioning the story's truth as well as its beauty. Mirah responds romantically by defending " 'the beauty of the action,' " and Deronda explains her meaning: " 'It is a truth in thought though it may never have been carried out in action. It lives as an idea.' " His very defense, however, separates ideal thought from concrete action. Questioned again by one of the Meyricks, he turns around and defends the myth's everyday reality: " 'It is like a passionate word,' he said; 'the exaggeration

61. Among them is the letter Hans Meyrick wrote to Deronda (VII, 52, 704–9) discussed by Cynthia Chase, "Decomposition of the Elephants." While she sees the irony and parody in the letter as an aberration in the novel, a view at odds with the argument being made here, her point about the "deconstruction of the concept of cause" in *Daniel Deronda* is valuable and valid (p. 217). The prevalence of the ironic mode is one sign of the deconstruction; so are the epigraphs to the closing chapters in each of the last two books. They suggest, however, that George Eliot was trying to make the deconstructive and reconstructive process one.

is a flash of fervour. It is an extreme image of what is happening every day—the transmutation of self.' " Whether George Eliot intended "every day" as an allusion to the biological transmutation of species we cannot know. In any case, when Mirah then offers an illustration of Deronda's meaning, he retracts by saying, " 'But we must not get too far away from practical matters.' " Thus he ends up confirming the separation he first acknowledges and later denies (V, 37, 522–23). This same essential myth of a transmutation of self, we learn in the very next chapter, is central to Mordecai's belief in "transmission."

The issue of concrete embodiment is raised in this scene in another way too, one that suggests George Eliot knew she was having trouble with Deronda as a flesh-and-blood character. No sooner does Mirah finish her story about the Buddha than she says of Deronda: " 'That is what we all imagine of you.' " Repudiating the comparison because it implies he " 'had no wants' " for himself, Deronda replies, " 'Pray don't imagine that.' " Much later in the novel, however, he still seems to the Meyricks so far from down-to-earth that the " 'thought of his marrying,' " or of " 'finding out that he had a tailor's bill, and used boothooks,' " as other men do, is a source of amusement to them.[62] Other scenes and passages make this more than a joking matter.

One such moment occurs immediately upon Deronda's return from Genoa, when he is on his way to visit Mordecai and Mirah to tell them what he has discovered about his birth. This is an especially important occasion, Deronda's first experience of that congruence between private and public for which he has yearned all along:

> The strongest tendencies of his nature were rushing in one current
> —the fervent affectionateness which made him delight in meeting
> the wish of beings near to him, and the imaginative need of some
> far-reaching relation to make the horizon of his immediate, daily
> acts.

The next sentence, however, so punctures this position as to constitute a kind of mock-heroic:

> It has to be admitted that in this classical, romantic, world-historic
> position of his, bringing as it were from its hiding-place his heredi-

62. VII, 52, 719–20. Eliot's awareness of the problem is evident also in the scene at the *Hand and Banner*. Though Deronda does not himself smoke, he carries cigars to offer to others, perhaps because he was "afraid," the narrator says, "of seeming strait-laced, and turning himself into a sort of diagram instead of a growth which can exercise the guiding attraction of fellowship" (VI, 42, 582).

tary armour, he wore—but so, one must suppose, did the most ancient heroes whether Semitic or Japhetic—the summer costume of his contemporaries.

[VIII, 63, 814–15

The second sentence does far more than jest that heroes, despite our romantic notions about them, actually wear the same clothes as everyone else. Mocking the glorious position in which the author has placed her character, the narrator's self-questioning parody raises questions about the character's self-awareness. The "consciously Utopian pictures of his own future" ascribed to Deronda earlier in the novel, along with such things as the Meyricks' laughter at the "knight-errant in his disposition," suggest that he does indeed perceive himself to be occupying the "classical, romantic, world-historic position" the narrator mocks.[63] So does the sentence that follows the two quoted above: "He did not reflect that the drab tints were becoming to him, for he rarely went to the expense of such thinking." If this sentence compliments Deronda for lacking physical vanity, it also criticizes him for failing to pay attention to the physical world. One who would be a " 'greater leader, like Pericles or Washington' " or " 'Moses,' " cannot afford such economies.[64]

Another scene that questions the visionary ideal is one between Mirah and Mordecai in which she labels his repudiation of the material world a " 'fancy' " (VIII, 61, 802–3). Again the context makes the repudiation especially significant, concluding as it does one of the novel's fullest proclamations of organic unity. Anxiously awaiting the return of Deronda from Genoa, Mordecai's exaltation of spirit is at this moment particularly great. Telling Mirah of the " 'divine Unity' " expressed in the *Shemah*, the chief devotional Hebrew prayer, he says:

> this made our religion the fundamental religion for the whole world; for the divine Unity embraced as its consequence the ultimate unity of mankind. See, then—the nation which has been scoffed at for its separateness, has given a binding theory to the human race. Now, in complete unity a part possesses the whole as the whole possesses every part: and in this way human life is tending toward the image of the Supreme Unity: for as our life becomes more spiritual by capacity of thought, and joy therein, pos-

63. IV, 28, 369–70. For Deronda as magical, storybook romantic hero, taken as an object of fun, see also II, 18, 239–40; III, 20, 249, 266.
64. II, 16, 213; VIII, 63, 812, 818.

session tends to become more universal, being independent of gross material contact . . . [and] the creeping paths of the senses.

When Mirah seems not to understand his meaning, he is surprised, for " 'women,' " he says, " 'are specially framed for the love which feels possession in renouncing.' " Trying to clarify his point, he tells her a Hebrew story; and again she rejects his meaning, taking the story to be about jealous " 'human passions' " rather than about losing " 'self in the object of love.' " " 'You can make the story so in your mind,' " she tells her brother, " 'because you are great, and like to fancy the greatest that could be. But I think it was not really like that.' "

This scene occurs in the last book of the novel. In the first, we see Deronda positioned (as Mordecai is here) in a "region outside and above . . . human dross" (I, 1, 38). Central to Deronda's development as a character is the "blent transmission" between himself and Mordecai, but however great the complementarity between them, Deronda's union with this visionary man suggests that the region he inhabits at the end is still "outside and above." Unlike our earlier examples, this last juxtaposition embodies in its rhetoric what the novel at many points attempts to hide. Still, George Eliot struggles strenuously to heal the divide between concrete and abstract in regard to Deronda and Mordecai. However, the novel leaves largely unexplored the implications of the questions it raises in two other important areas: nationalism and the social structures affecting women.

George Eliot would like to make Judaism emblematic of "equality" and of the "unity of mankind." But its doctrines assign to women a role that makes for a subjection at least as great as Comte's. The novel neither entirely evades this fact nor fully comes to terms with it. It is recognized in the "special frame" of women to which Mordecai refers, as well as in what Cohen, the pawnbroker, says: " 'A man is bound to thank God, as we do every Sabbath, that he was not made a woman; but a woman has to thank God that He had made her according to His will. And we all know what He has made her—a child-bearing, tender-hearted thing is the woman of our people.' "[65] The role Judaism allots women is also given a powerful challenge by Deronda's mother in the two scenes in which she reigns. Like the most admirable of the characters in the novel, the

65. VI, 46, 636–37. Actually, a Jewish man is supposed to thank God every day, not once a week, for not having been born a woman. Hardy conjectures in her notes to the Penguin edition that perhaps George Eliot's "feminism worked against her scholarly accuracy here" (p. 899).

Princess' rebellion is motivated by a desire " 'to live a large life' " and inhabit a " 'wide world' " (VII, 51, 693). The ancestral chest that signifies to Deronda the oneness of his origins and telos, however, signifies to his mother " 'things that were thrust on my mind that I might feel them like a wall around my life—my life that was growing like a tree' " (VII, 51, 700). The " 'charter' " her " 'nature' " gave her to be a great actress and singer, her religion denied (VII, 53, 728). What occurs in these scenes takes place nowhere else in the novel: Judaism, instead of feeding organic life, renders it inert.

During one of the most charged moments in the interview between the Princess and Deronda, she says to her son:

> "You are not a woman. You may try—but you can never imagine what it is to have a man's force of genius in you, and yet to suffer the slavery of being a girl. To have a pattern cut out—'this is the Jewish woman; this is what you must be; this is what you are wanted for; a woman's heart must be of such a size and no larger, else it must be pressed small, like Chinese feet.' "

> [VII, 51, 694

Although the specific form of the Princess' oppression is highly relevant to the novel's affirmation of organic unity in Judaism, the issue here involves far more than "the Jewish woman." As Mill described it, using the same image, the issue is all prescribed "rules of conduct" that "endeavour to make every one conform to the approved standard." Such rules, he says, "maim by compression, like a Chinese lady's foot, every part of human nature which stands out prominently."[66] But while everyone suffers from the pressure of approved standards, the restrictions on women were particularly great. As discussed earlier, in the *Subjection* even Mill finally places the needs of the family above those of women. It may be more than circumstantial, then, that the passage just quoted appears not in the *Subjection* but in *On Liberty*, for Mill was no more able than George Eliot to reconcile family demands with women's vocational needs.

Mill acknowledges in the *Subjection*, for instance, that women in the theatrical arts are "confessedly equal, if not superior, to men," and he speaks of "onerous" domestic burdens interfering with the pursuit of their careers (pp. 208–9); yet he still makes the "bringing up of a family" a woman's "first call" (p. 179). Similarly, Deronda, once he recovers from his indignation at having "his pre-

66. Mill, *On Liberty, Collected Works*, 18: 271–72.

conceptions of a mother's tender joy" overturned, acknowledges the Princess' right " 'to be something more than a mere daughter and mother' "; yet he cannot give up urging his mother to consent with her " 'whole soul' " to restoring the family inheritance. She does not yield; she asks him instead to be content that *his* whole soul consents.[67] George Eliot gives great force to the Princess' defense, but the overall movement of the novel participates in Deronda's consent. It can do so, however, only by glossing over the concrete disunities and inequities within the one organic system the novel would affirm.

That affirmation in *Daniel Deronda* suffers from still another strain. Just as the portrait of the Princess undermines the primary pillar of community—the family—so Deronda's setting out for Jerusalem uproots the pillar of place. His mission, furthermore, raises, but does not resolve, the question of nationalism. For all the talk of Jewish separateness leading ultimately to world community, Deronda's task is the forging of an individual nation. The inevitable result is nationalism—analogous in the public realm to self-serving individualism in private life. Deronda's pilgrimage, in addition, runs counter to organicist theory, according to which "society is a growth, not a transplantation."[68] Affirming growth through transplantation, the closing action of George Eliot's last novel nullifies the social whole.

We have seen in the portrait of marriage in this novel a mark of the total absence of organic wholeness in English life. We have seen also how the ironic structure of the novel both criticizes and offers a corrective to social conditions in the present. George Eliot's desire to give that corrective substance—to locate it not only in the mind but also in visible social forms and structures—takes the novel in another direction as well. Her intention is to fuse the various modes—realistic, ironic, visionary, and romantic. The novel aspires to "grand marriages" but in Mordecai's, not Gwendolen's, sense:

> "Our lot is the lot of Israel. The grief and the glory are mingled as the smoke and the flame. . . . These things are wedded for us, as our father was wedded to our mother. . . . 'The Omnipresent,' said a Rabbi, 'is occupied in making marriages.' The levity of the saying lies in the ear of him who hears it; for by marriages the speaker

67. VII, 51, 695; VII, 53, 725–38.
68. See chapter 4 above, p. 156.

meant all the wondrous combinations of the universe whose issue makes our good and evil."

[VIII, 62, 812

Just as this metaphorical marriage collapses under the test of the literal marriages dramatized in the novel, so the organic in *Daniel Deronda* fails to be realized in actual combinations of parts composing either a social or aesthetic whole. Deronda searches for a "local habitation to render fellowship real"; but it is the " 'Omnipresence' " in this novel " 'which is the place and habitation of the world.' " Mordecai says " 'Let the torch of visible community be lit!' "; but it is the torch of invisible community that the novel actually lights.[69] The organic remains an imaginative, not an embodied, ideal.

69. IV, 32, 413; VIII, 63, 818; VI, 42, 596.

❖

SIX

Art and Community:
George Eliot and Her Contemporary Readers

Style and Culture

In chapters 2 and 3, we observed that Social Dynamics, though intended to wed fact and value by bringing Gemeinschaft to Gesellschaft, often uncovered instead separations between the two. The one area in which the fusion seemed to hold—namely, the convergence within the individual consciousness of community of interest and community of feeling—lacked concreteness and wholeness. In chapters 4 and 5, we observed in Social Statics an attempt to overcome these limitations through the restructuring of organicist models. To achieve credibility, the analogy between society, the individual, and organic life had to be given scientific as well as metaphoric definition. To speak to the needs of individuals, the attendant ideology had to be liberalized. The scientific constructs, however, proved to be only partially verifiable. The liberalizing effort was equally vexatious, as public and private, communal and individualist, values seemed more often than not to be at odds.

These conflicts are embodied in the very form and structure of the books that were written in hopes of resolving them. In the works of the social theorists, the discord between method and ideology takes the form of philosophical inconsistencies; in George Eliot's fiction, of aesthetic disjunctions. These intractable oppositions within the formal structures of their works are as significant as the substantive discrepancies. Together they suggest organic connectedness but not entirely of the sort their authors had in mind: the insistent attempts to join opposing tendencies signify the authors' participation in a community of interests they shared with the larger culture, for it too aspired to social wholeness; the persistent divisions within their work testify to antagonistic values within nineteenth-century society that could not be reconciled.

These coexistent predilections demonstrate an organic relation between style and culture, but one whose most characteristic sign is inner contradiction.

Appropriately enough, the idea that style is organically connected to the values of a given culture is essentially, as Raymond Williams points out, "a product of the intellectual history of the nineteenth century."[1] Equally pertinent is Erich Auerbach's thesis that literary structure and style arise in a culture and reflect its ethical and religious values.[2] All the writers we have discussed would have agreed with this proposition. Not only did they find in art an expression of a society's needs and aspirations, but also they would have agreed with Auerbach's complaints against literary styles that separate the "realm of the heroic and sublime from that of the practical and everyday" (p. 106). Even more striking, they, like he, found evidence and arguments for a genuine mixture of styles in the story of Christ, in the writings of Dante, and in the changes brought by the French Revolution.

Works of art that achieve a true mixture of styles, Auerbach argues in *Mimesis*, connect contemporary social circumstances to fictional characters and events, and treat everyday occurrences accurately and seriously. Western art has more frequently exhibited a separation of style, however, ennobling only subjects drawn from high life, and treating those drawn from low life either comically or satirically. This same desire to bring high seriousness to everyday reality and yet accurately reflect ordinary social and historical realities informs Lewes's and George Eliot's arguments for the union of the ideal and the real in art.

George Eliot found in the works of C. C. Hennell and Feuerbach justification for this union. During the 1840s, when she was reading and translating the "higher criticism," she was acutely conscious of the mingling of truth and fiction in the Scriptures, but although she rejected the Bible as divine revelation, she admired its exalted poetry. She valued the work of her friend Hennell because he had done "the utmost that can be done towards obtaining a *real* view of the life and character of Jesus" while "rejecting as little as possible from the Gospels" (*Letters* 1: 237). Hennell's way of treating a great deal of historically inaccurate biblical narrative was to regard it as "fiction." In the Gospel of John, for instance, Hennell finds a dramatist at work on a narrative that is controlled not by the "one-sided or local knowledge which must belong to

1. Williams, *Culture and Society*, p. 130.
2. Auerbach, *Mimesis*; see pp. 63, 161, and 490–91, among others.

an eye-witness," but by "the omniscience of the novelist . . . in accord with the metaphysics of that time."[3] Because "many of the finer thoughts and feelings of mankind find a vent in fiction," Hennell explains, "the perception of historical inaccuracy does not prevent our sharing the thoughts and feelings which have embodied themselves in this manner" (pp. 322–23). He also anticipates Auerbach's contention that "it was the story of Christ, with its ruthless mixture of everyday reality and the highest and most sublime tragedy, which had conquered [for a time] the classical rule of styles" (*Mimesis*, p. 490):

> And in the circumstances attending the death of Jesus, we are forced to see a striking instance of the tendency of the mind to invest ordinary events with a higher beauty and interest than unimpassioned observation alone could discover, and to give to the common places of the world an impress of that higher life and perfection towards which it seems borne by its own nature.
>
> [*Inquiry*, p. 250

Eliot's work on Feuerbach during the early 1850s only would have intensified the secular thrust toward a fusion of style that had its origin in a religious text. In the rallying call that brings *The Essence of Christianity* to a close, Feuerbach urges us to see that "the profoundest secrets lie in common everyday things. . . . It needs only that the ordinary course of things be interrupted in order to vindicate to common things an uncommon significance, *to life, as such, a religious import*" (pp. 276–78). As we noted earlier, Feuerbach would reduce theology to anthropology and constitute humanity in community.

George Eliot responded to his call, attempting in her fiction to bring to "this working-day world" the sense of profundity and seriousness, first brought together, it seemed, in the story of Christ. For her, as for Auerbach, Dante was the writer, at least prior to the nineteenth century, who came closest to achieving such a fusion. Auerbach celebrates "Dante's closeness to the actual in the realm of the sublime," and George Eliot asks us to "witness Dante, who is at once the most precise and homely in his reproduction of actual objects, and the most soaringly at large in his imaginative combinations." Citing canto 15 of *The Inferno*, she contends that:

> powerful imagination is not false outward vision, but intense inward representation, and a creative energy constantly fed by sus-

3. Hennell, *Inquiry Concerning the Origins of Christianity*, p. 294.

ceptibility to the veriest minutiae of experience, which it reproduces and constructs in fresh and fresh wholes; not the habitual
confusion of provable fact with the fictions of fancy and transient
inclination, but a breadth of ideal association.

She concludes that "he is the strongest seer who can support the
stress of creative energy and yet keep that sanity of expectation
which consists in distinguishing, as Dante does, between the *cose
che son vere* outside the individual mind, and the *non falsi errori*
which are the revelations of true imaginative power."[4]

These statements were made at the end of George Eliot's career.
At the start of his, Lewes identified the *cose che son vere*, or the
things that are true outside the individual mind, in the various
elements that constitute the dominant idea or spirit of an age. "Because the poet cannot but see through the medium of his age,"
Lewes tells us, the "dominant Idea" of an epoch is the "key to its
poetry." For his own epoch, it can be found in the French Revolution, inasmuch as

> liberty, equality, humanity (the threefold form of this century's
> mission) . . . express (in the final analysis) the object and faith of
> the crusade in which all Europe is now sensibly or insensibly en-
> gaged, and as they have to complete a great social end, so may
> they be considered as eminently religious.[5]

In this 1842 essay, Lewes was speaking only of poetry and claiming
that " 'the world of art . . . must be the highest, the most ideal.' . . .
It is indeed another world, wherein our own is reflected, but idealized" (p. 53). By the time George Eliot began to write novels, Lewes
was insisting that these two worlds were one. Her own efforts in
fiction contain countless mediations between external reality and
imagined ideals. Like Lewes, she believed furthermore that "the
poet arises to utter the collective creed," and to give expression to

4. Auerbach, *Mimesis*, p. 161; George Eliot, "False Testimonials," *TS*, pp.
236–40. These passages closely correspond with the description in *Middlemarch*
of the ideal Lydgate brings to his scientific pursuits (ch. 16, p. 122), and with
the defense in *Daniel Deronda* of the union between the scientific, the artistic,
and the visionary (ch. 41, p. 572). See also ch. 2 above, pp. 71–79.
5. Alice Kaminsky, ed., *Literary Criticism of George Henry Lewes*, pp. 55–58;
passages quoted appeared originally in Lewes's essay "Hegel's Aesthetics:
Philosophy of Art," *British and Foreign Review* 13 (1842). George Eliot's great
interest in the French Revolution inspired her to plan a Napoleonic novel
during the last years of her life. See William Baker, "George Eliot's Projected
Napoleonic War Novel: An Annotated Reading List."

the "inarticulate yearnings and thoughts" of the people's "common soul."[6]

To judge from contemporary reviews of George Eliot's novels, her readers at least in part confirmed this definition of the artist's task and admired her voicing of their inarticulate yearnings and thoughts. She also, however, challenged as much as uttered the dominant creed, and at times the challenge made her readers so uncomfortable as to cause them to qualify sharply or even withdraw the great praise they otherwise offered. These double responses (often appearing even in the same review) constitute another kind of mirror: the responses of her readers, as well as her novels, reveal the intimate relation between literary style and cultural values.

George Eliot's contemporary readers were very much concerned with the quality of her realism and with the question of unity in her novels. In both these respects, their concerns correspond to matters closely related, as we have seen, to the issue of community in the nineteenth-century world. Her readers were in addition greatly preoccupied with judging the sensibility of the author and her attitude toward the reader, as made known by the narrator's voice. This matter has special importance—narrower but more direct—since it speaks to the immediate effect George Eliot had on her audience. Responses to each of these subjects—realism, unity, and authorial voice—are discussed in the body of this chapter. Authorial voice is also considered in chapter 7, but the focus there is the direct addresses to the reader in her novels.

Realism, Romance, and Fellow-Feeling

The phenomenal success of *Adam Bede* almost immediately created for the unknown George Eliot and the outcast Marian Evans a broad community of readers. Sales alone confirm Lewes's report of the "amazing . . . universal interest" prompted by her first novel:

> We saw people reading it, and heard them talking of it in the remotest parts of North Wales, and at railway stations where only a dozen people were about. The book has found its way to the heart of the people—as it ought.
>
> [*Letters* 3: 152

6. Kaminsky, *Literary Criticism*, p. 58; George Eliot, "The Legend of Jubal," *The Legend of Jubal and Other Poems*, p. 33.

John Forster, writing in the *Edinburgh Review*, concluded that "we, as readers, have every reason to be grateful to the writer for giving us such a book; and he has every reason to feel proud that the universal question in men's mouths in the pause between topics of war and politics, is—'Have you read *Adam Bede?*' "[7] One of those readers even asked George Eliot to " 'perfect and extend' the benefit Adam Bede has 'conferred on society,' by writing a *sequel*" (*Letters* 3: 184). Mapping out the grounds for praise in the *Times* and ranking George Eliot "at once among the masters," E. S. Dallas defined two of the positions that were to become important rallying and battle points throughout George Eliot's career. Together these extremes suggest how much the issue of community was at stake for George Eliot's Victorian readers, and how earnestly as a result they debated the issue of her realism.

Dallas takes as the "first article of belief," in this "first-rate" new novel, the "truism . . . that we are all alike—that the human heart is one." Since this same "grand fact of an underlying unity" is also Thackeray's theme, Dallas proceeds to contrast the two authors.[8] Thackeray, in an effort to make us realize that we had best be charitable because "we are all alike," weak and liable to error, with an "evil corner in our hearts, and little deceitful ways of working," writes the prose of community. But this new author, "Mr. Elliot [*sic*]," captures the poetry of community, telling us "that we have all a remnant of Eden in us, that people are not so bad as is commonly supposed, and that every one has affectionate fibres in his nature—fine, loveable traits, in his character. . . . He is always showing that we are better than we seem, greater than we know, nearer to each other than, perhaps, we would wish." Both writers, with their "broad sympathy and large tolerance," encourage a dem-

7. [John Forster], *Edinburgh Review*, American ed., 110 (1859): 125. Forster's authorship established in *Letters* 3: 148. Michael Wolff notes that *Adam Bede* was reviewed in twenty of the twenty-five mid-Victorian periodicals of "relatively wide circulation" among the "educated" public. The attention *AB* received was unusual not only for a first novel but also because "novels were not widely noticed outside the pages of the literary weeklies." Of the twenty reviews, only two were even "mildly disapproving" (Michael Wolff, "Victorian Reviewers and Cultural Responsibility," pp. 269–89). Wolff offers valuable descriptions of the audiences these journals addressed and an analysis of the mediating role of the reviewers.

8. *CH*, pp. 77–79 (*Times*, 12 April 1859). For articles reprinted in *George Eliot: The Critical Heritage*, ed. David Carroll, the journal, date, and author (if known) follow the *CH* page citations. Reviews cited in text but not reprinted in *CH* are listed at the end of my bibliography.

ocratic cast of mind, but their modes are entirely different. The one is leveling, antiheroic, harsh, and realistic; the other ennobling, celebratory, harmonious, and idealistic (*CH*, pp. 79, 82).

As other Victorian critics took up these distinctions, or made them anew, the issue of realism was referred in a variety of ways to a yearning for solidarity. In their responses to *Adam Bede*, for example, we discover that while certain phrases seem to suggest an appreciation of George Eliot's realism of presentation, the full context of the argument gives the loudest applause to the poetry of the commonplace. In some cases, even in the same review, "natural history," or "a closely true picture of purely rural life," inadvertently vies with the "reign of romance" in a "romantic-looking model parish," or the "fairy realm of Loamshire."[9] Testifying far more often to "ideal association" than to Dantean fusion, the reviews of *Adam Bede* often singled out for praise its realistic "truth to life" and its celebration of our common humanity, but in such a way as to dissociate the two.[10]

Among the occasional exceptions is a review written for the *British Controversialist*, whose subscribers were primarily " 'young men' of the self-educating classes" (laborers, artisans, clerks, shop assistants, small merchants) and the "mutual improvement and discussion societies to which they belonged."[11] The reviewer gives great thanks to George Eliot for having created in the *Scenes* and *Adam Bede* characters who are not "merely ideal, but real." Since Adam, the workingman, is clearly an idealized character, there may be special pleading in the "merely" that devalues the "ideal" in order to elevate the "real." In other respects, however, this review resembles those in the prestigious periodicals, exhibiting the same blurring of real and ideal, despite assertions to the contrary:

> "Adam Bede" belongs strictly to the natural school. Its sketches of nature and character have all the fidelity and exactness of old Dutch paintings. In this respect its author resembles Mr. Thack-

9. *CH*, pp. 86, 97 ([Anne Mozley], *Bentley's Quarterly Review*, July 1859); [W. Lucas Collins], *Blackwood's Magazine* 85 (1859): 491, 502 (authorship identified, *Wellesley Index to Victorian Periodicals, 1824–1900* 1: 108).

10. All the reviews cited in nn. 7–9 illustrate this point. See also [Geraldine Jewsbury], *Athenaeum* (26 February 1859), p. 284; authorship established Geibel, "Annotated Bibliography," p. 75.

11. Michael Wolff, "*The British Controversialist and Impartial Inquirer, 1850–1872*," pp. 369–71. Review of *Adam Bede* in *British Controversialist and Literary Magazine*, 3d ser. 2 (1859): 268–73. I am indebted to Michael Wolff for access to this periodical.

eray. But . . . the country scenes and episodes George Eliot depicts are more healthy and pure than the pictures of London life Mr. Thackeray presents.

[p. 269

An analogous inconsistency is at work in the piece Forster wrote for the *Edinburgh Review*. Typical of many reviews, the praise of the novel's verisimilitude is quickly qualified by an assurance ("Mr. Eliot softens the picture for us") and concludes with a contradiction:

> Mr. Eliot has been compared to Thackeray; but Thackeray's chief power lies in describing the sort of world we live in, and the author of Adam Bede leads us into the world we do not live in.

[pp. 122–23

Charmed by the "poetry" of *Adam Bede*, Forster much prefers Mr. Eliot to Mr. Thackeray. As George Eliot continued to write novels, many of her readers, particularly in response to *The Mill on the Floss* and *Middlemarch*, reveal a similar preference, except that they come to find in her the Thackerayan cynicism Blackwood had warned her against from the very start.

To judge from George Eliot's response to E. S. Dallas's review of *The Mill*, charges of this sort were far more unnerving to her than the tendency to overvalue the ideal. At the close of what is on the whole a favorable review, Dallas worries about the "object" of her second novel:

> that object is, to establish the contrast between a life of utter respectability and a life of stumbling and dubious, but still honest and noble, aspiration. Err as she may, sin as she may, the very faults of Maggie are more to be respected and loved than the hard consistency of her brother Tom and the Pharisaical rigidity of the Dodson family. One must not press the maxim too far, and we protest by anticipation against the novels that are sure to be written on the model of the present one, showing that it is a grand thing to lead a Bohemian life, and that respectability and the payment of one's debts is necessarily mean and uninteresting.

[*CH*, p. 137

Because the review seemed to her to have been "written in a generous spirit, and with so high a degree of intelligence," she felt compelled to respond. She not only defends the collective (or Dodson) creed but also justifies the mediations she had hoped to achieve:

I am so far from hating the Dodsons myself, that I am rather aghast
to find them ticketed with such very ugly adjectives. . . . I am rather
alarmed lest the misapprehensions . . . should be due to my defec-
tive presentation, rather than to any failure on the part of the
critic. I have certainly fulfilled my intention very badly if I have
made the Dodson honesty appear "mean and uninteresting," or
made the payment of one's debts appear a contemptible virtue in
comparison with any sort of "Bohemian" qualities. So far as my
own feeling and intention are concerned, no one class of persons
or form of character is held up to reprobation or to exclusive admiration.

[*Letters* 3: 299

George Eliot was attempting in her second novel, far more than
in her first, to forge a new style by "daring," as she told her friend
D'Albert-Durade, "to be thoroughly familiar" and "intensely col-
loquial." D'Albert-Durade was having difficulty translating *The
Mill*, because he was finding that "certain nuances of style determined by the character and social class of writers [in English]
simply cannot be rendered in French." Urging him to try "to represent in French, at least in some degree, those 'intermédiaires
entre le style commun et le style élégant,' " she explained that "even
in English this daring is far from being general."[12]

The contemporary reception of *The Mill on the Floss* makes
clear that George Eliot's effort to forge an intermediate style was
indeed daring. The reviewers regularly opposed her realism of
presentation to her idealism of conception. The third volume
"aroused the most indignant and sustained opposition George Eliot
had to face in her entire career," largely because of Maggie's fall
from the ideal.[13] Even critics who acknowledged in the novel "a
truth we cannot controvert" felt "there is too much that is painful" and "crude" in the book.[14] A number of reviews, including
one in the *British Controversialist* (June 1860), expressed a lack
of sympathy with virtually everything and everyone in the novel.

Middlemarch, too, is a novel in which the realism of presentation
carries sharp social criticism, but it received a far more favorable

12. *Letters* 3: 374 (part of D'Albert-Durade's letter reprinted in footnote).
I am indebted to Professor John K. Savacool (Department of Romanic Lan-
guages, Williams College) for translating the nuances in this letter.
13. Carroll, Introduction to *CH*, p. 13. The sexual nature of Maggie's fall
contributed greatly to the dismay.
14. *CH*, p. 140 ([John Chapman, prob.], *Westminster Review*, July 1860);
authorship conjectured *Wellesley Index* 3: 630. *CH*, pp. 118–19 (*Saturday
Review*, 14 April 1860). *Athenaeum* (7 April 1860), pp. 467–68.

response than did *The Mill*, in part because of the education George Eliot's readers had by then received from her previous books. Her audience had become extraordinarily responsive to her compassionate realism. It seemed she was indeed having the effect she hoped to have. In one sense, however, her readers had learned their lessons too well. Their response to her later work suggests that the expectations she had created in them caused them to resist new developments in her fiction.

In "Notes on Form in Art," written when she was already thinking about the novel that was to be *Middlemarch*, she worries about the deadening of form:

> A Form being once started . . . is sought after, amplified and elaborated by discrimination of its elements till at last by the abuse of its refinement it preoccupies the room of emotional thinking; & poetry, from being the fullest expression of the human soul, is starved into an ingenious pattern-work, in which tricks with vocables take the place of living words fed with the blood of relevant meaning, & made musical by the continual intercommunication of sensibility & thought.
>
> [*Essays*, p. 436

Later, writing to Blackwood about the new novel she had in mind, she explains that she wants "to show the gradual action of ordinary causes rather than exceptional" and also "to show this in some directions which have not been from time immemorial the beaten path—the Cremorne walks and shows of fiction." She also "fears," however, that she is in "danger of . . . refining when novel readers only think of skipping" (*Letters* 5: 168–69). For all the praise *Middlemarch* received, many readers found in it material they would have preferred to have been omitted. Her study of provincial life seemed to them to make too many new demands on their "sensibility and thought." They complained of its being too scientific and analytical, both in content and method. They found its view of reality too circumstantial and fragmentary, and its tone too bitter and cynical. On all these counts, they sorely missed the geniality they were expecting; they also lamented in *Middlemarch* the absence of a pervasive poetry of community.

The poetry they discovered in *Daniel Deronda*, however, was not what most of them desired. As if to offset the new and different ways in which George Eliot now challenged her contemporaries, they took comfort in Gwendolen's story, finding in it a familiar world treated in a customary way by a favorite author. That the social criticism involved far more than religious or racial prejudice they tended to ignore. Instead, they saw in the novel a dual orientation, with Gwendolen's story realistic and familiar, and Deronda's poetic but remote. George Eliot was herself nervous on both counts. Defending her new novel against Blackwood's "doubtful" response to Mordecai, she explained, it is "just the most difficult thing in art—to give new elements—i.e. elements not already used up—in forms as vivid as those of long familiar types. Doubtless the wider public of novel-readers must feel more interest" in the familiar (*Letters* 6: 223). To a great extent she was right. The innovative form of her last novel was a surprise to everyone and was not well received on the whole, although some critics admired the change. From the contemporary response to *Daniel Deronda*, counter arguments emerge. One endorses the realism of presentation she had taught her readers to value. The other defends an idealism of conception that completes itself not in realism but romance. On each side, the argument about method implicates a projected community of readers.

The critics who favored her realism maintained that fellow-feeling is best nurtured through the portrayal of ordinary experience, or those circumstances, characteristics, and passions "common" to us all. Since readers can "always find excuse" for their own narrower behavior "in the obstinate circumstances of actual life," a character who is exceptional, remarkable, ideal, or rare is less likely to be "a powerful influence in human life." A theme or subject remote from "common life," their argument goes, also lacks "sufficient connexion with broad human feeling."[15] While this standard of judgment may sound democratic, it actually rejects or excludes any themes or characters (the Jews, for example) out of the mainstream. This group of readers seemed content to have the poetry of community be replaced by prose.

An opposing perspective is offered by the critics who approached the novel as romance. They, too, intertwined formal issues with an ideology of community, arguing that our sense of human connection is profoundly enlarged by the ideal or poetical vision that challenges "commonplace and conventional ideas." Romance, then, becomes a way of fighting against the dead level of ordinary experience, affirming the idea of community in "a life of mankind over,

15. *Examiner* 29 (1876): 124–25. *CH*, pp. 361–62 (*Academy*, 5 February 1876). *CH*, p. 374 (George Saintsbury, *Academy*, 9 September 1876). This same standard is invoked in *Athenaeum* (1 July 1876), pp. 14–15, and *Saturday Review* 42 (1876): 356–58.

above, and around the life of the individual man or woman."[16]
This group of readers passionately defended the "Jewish part" of
Daniel Deronda. They admired George Eliot for having the courage
to explore wondrous as well as ordinary combinations, for daring
to fight when she was likely to lose, and for risking an embattled
relation with her readers in the hope of winning them over.

In sum, the Victorians' debate on George Eliot's realism entailed
several arguments concerning community. The truth-to-life standard commonly associated with realism became something of a
middle point in a diverging argument. Readers hailed as salutary
the softened or poetic realism that reflected "genial, all-embracing
charity" (*CH,* p. 222); but they also detected a deviant strain that
carried realism to a self-defeating extreme by calling attention (like
Thackeray) to what was "disagreeable" in human nature and society. By defining her genius in terms of one extreme and criticizing
her work in terms of another, Victorian critics mistook dynamic tensions for static oppositions. But the very contradictions within their
responses reflect the constant cominglings most characteristic of
her work. George Eliot's reversal of method in *Daniel Deronda*
further suggests that she was challenging Victorian notions of community in extremely complicated ways. In the end, the poetry of
community created the greater discomfort. As the response to her
last novel reveals, her idealism of conception was as disturbing as
the realism of presentation that first put some readers on guard.
Her books and the reviewers' judgments of them demonstrate that
she was confirming as well as challenging the collective creed. Fellow-feeling remains the standard of judgment throughout—but a
standard beset by polarities, fusions, contradictions, and tensions.

Organic Unity and Social Order

That George Eliot's readers wanted social unity to be endorsed
is apparent not only in their desire for a softened realism but also
in their evaluation of the unity of her fiction—an issue both less and
more complicated than it has often seemed to be. In his introduction to *George Eliot: The Critical Heritage,* David Carroll con-

16. Joseph Jacobs, *Macmillan's Magazine* 36 (1877): 101–11. *CH,* p. 447
(Edward Dowden, *Contemporary Review,* February 1877). Other reviewers
speak in similar ways of *Daniel Deronda* as a romance. See, for instance, *CH,*
pp. 382–98 (R. E. Francillon, *Gentleman's Magazine,* October 1876); *CH,* pp.
406–16 (James Picciotto, *Gentleman's Magazine,* November 1876). Many
Jewish readers wrote to thank George Eliot for the "heroic vision" of *Daniel
Deronda* (*Biography,* pp. 488–90).

tends that "the majority of reviewers never treated the unity of her novels with the seriousness she intended." She was "anxious . . . for each novel to be read as a complex, unified whole":

> Here, if anywhere, George Eliot is most clearly in advance of her critics. In her critical writings and, of course, in the novels themselves, she reveals a concept of organic form far more subtle and sophisticated than any but the most astute of her reviewers expect to find in fiction. They, for the most part, were distracted from these more formal considerations by the immediate challenge of the novels.
>
> [pp. 5–6

Discussing the Victorian reception of *Middlemarch*, W. J. Harvey argues that "few contemporary reviewers would have understood or shared" our modern concern with the "novel's structural integrity." Most Victorian reviewers, he claims, were "content simply to catalogue various choice items in the 'treasure house of detail.' " Speaking to both George Eliot's extreme sensitivity to "criticisms of the unity of her work" and the critical attitudes prevalent between 1850 and 1870, Richard Stang infers, "there was a very strong demand that all the material included in a single novel be unified, though that unity often eluded strict definition." Kenneth Graham, however, claims the opposite: "the deliberate application of the principle of organic unity," he argues, "is one of the most remarkable and unexpected features in the whole age's criticism of fiction" running counter to the moral thrust of most Victorian literary criticism.[17]

Graham's judgments rest on the notion that "the Master was not really alone in the wilderness" when he proclaimed the novel " 'a living thing, all one and continuous, like every other organism, and in proportion as it lives . . . in each of the parts there is something of each of the other parts' " (p. 113). This standard is the one Percy Lubbock brings to Henry James, or Cleanth Brooks to the well-wrought urn; and certainly twentieth-century critics' focus on the autonomous or organically self-contained work of art enables us to understand better George Eliot's concern with the *whole* question of unity. But such attention to considerations of form is not what Victorian critics meant when talking about unity in a work of art. Unity, for them, had little relation to struc-

17. W. J. Harvey, "Criticism of the Novel," pp. 134–35; Richard Stang, *The Theory of the Novel in England*, 1850–70, pp. 132–34; Kenneth Graham, *English Criticism of the Novel, 1865–1900*, p. 113.

ture as purely a formal matter, and only partial relation to the positivist concept of organic form in art and society. Rather, most nineteenth-century readers held that unity proceeded from the social and religious beliefs informing the work of art. A passage Stang quotes from the *North British Review* implicitly embodies this criterion in linking "unity" to "order . . . 'coherent and vital order' " (p. 134).

The contemporary reviews of George Eliot's fiction amply demonstrate that the order inhering in a novel was thought to be, first and foremost, a matter of social order. Many reviewers of *Middlemarch*, for instance, were not simply content to enjoy the "treasure-house of details," not even Henry James. In the *Nation* and the *Fortnightly Review*, respectively, A. V. Dicey and Sidney Colvin lament the novel's failure to form a whole. The *Athenaeum, Edinburgh Review*, and *Quarterly Review* also bring to the forefront the question of its unity and express confusion, tentativeness, and bafflement; while the *Spectator, British Quarterly Review*, and the *Times* affirm that *Middlemarch* is a "whole" but not "a satisfying imaginative whole," "a perfect work of art" but not "a novel proper." Except for James, who wishes for a central consciousness, and the *Edinburgh Review*, which expresses "gratitude" for the novel's "healthy tone and honest purpose," the reviewers' reservations, confusions, doubts, and qualifications manifest a discomfort with *Middlemarch*'s melancholy social vision, what Sidney Colvin calls the "closer if . . . sadder brotherhood" that binds together the novel, the "human family," and the reader.[18] Thus, while George Eliot sought to integrate form and belief, her Victorian critics assess the beliefs that inform her novelistic structures; her modern critics, the techniques that create fictional forms.

The complicating issue for George Eliot's contemporary readers

18. Passages quoted from starred items. Authorship identified by Carroll (*CH*), Harvey ("Criticism of the Novel"), or Houghton (*Wellesley Index*).
*CH, pp. 353–54 ([Henry James], *Galaxy*, March 1873).
CH, pp. 346–52 ([A. V. Dicey], *Nation*, 30 January 1873).
*CH, pp. 331–38 (Sidney Colvin, *Fortnightly Review*, 19 January 1873).
Athenaeum (7 December 1872), pp. 725–26.
*[Richard Monckton Milnes], *Edinburgh Review*, American ed., 137 (1873): 126–35.
[Robert Laing], *Quarterly Review*, American ed., 134 (1873): 178–95.
CH, pp. 286–314 ([R. H. Hutton], *Spectator*, December 1871–December 1872).
*[Richard Holt Hutton], *British Quarterly Review*, American ed., 57 (1873): 218–29.
*[Frederick Napier Broome], *Times* (7 March 1873), p. 3d–f.

was the value system sustaining the order. Only in *Adam Bede* and
Silas Marner did they perceive the comprehensive "organic" unity
she always meant to bring to the "whole."[19] The simpler, preindustrial settings of these novels in part account for this response.
Equally important was the discovery of George Eliot's true identity.
Before she lost the cover of her pseudonym, the author of the *Scenes*
and *Adam Bede* had been thought by many to be a clerical man.
Once her contemporaries realized that George Eliot was not only
a woman but also the translator of Strauss and Feuerbach, and a
woman living out of wedlock with a man, they knew well enough
of her iconoclastic intellect and behavior but had little sense of
the shape of her new beliefs. *The Mill on the Floss* was the first
book known upon publication to have been written by Marian
Evans, and the negative response it received was undoubtedly
caused in part by its author's identity.

The disclosure brought new confusions. Many critics, for instance, used metaphors of disease to voice their disapproval of *The
Mill*, but no one seems to have noticed, until Ruskin pointed it
out in 1880, that George Eliot purposefully used such metaphors
to depict organic dysfunction in the community of St. Ogg's.[20]
Protecting themselves from the many images of disease, contamina-
tion, and mutilation she employs, her critics were inadvertently
using her own ammunition. At the same time, their failure to see
the affirmation of organic wholeness in the novel speaks not only
to their ignorance of her beliefs but also to failures in the content
and form of *The Mill*.

The more George Eliot's novels affirmed the excellence of the
Christian moral system, the less her readers were reminded that she
had rejected Christianity as divine revelation. To value the one
without the other was the lesson she learned from Hennell. She
could see also from his work the pertinence of this lesson to the
writing of fiction. So long as she did not strenuously question prevailing social morality, her readers accepted her fiction. Whenever

19. See, for instance [John Chapman], *Westminster Review*, American ed.,
71 (1859): 283; authorship identified *Wellesley Index* 3: 629. *CH*, p. 187 (*Westminster Review*, July 1861).

20. *Athenaeum*, 7 April 1860, pp. 467–68. *CH*, p. 130 (*Guardian*, 25 April
1860). [R. H. Hutton], *National Review*, July 1860; reprinted in *George Eliot
and Her Readers: A Selection of Contemporary Reviews*, ed. John Holmstrom
and Laurence Lerner, pp. 37–38; authorship identified *Wellesley Index* 3: 154.
British Quarterly Review 45 (1867): 172. *CH*, p. 165 (Swinburne, *A Note on
Charlotte Brontë*, 1877). *CH*, p. 167 (Ruskin, *Nineteenth Century*, June 1880).

she subjected the "collective creed" to sharp criticism, however, they quickly came to the alert.

A singular review of *Adam Bede* was the first to suggest George Eliot was turning the poetry of religion into fiction. Even more surprising, the reviewer applauds rather than objects. A "genuine catholic spirit," he writes, is "constantly manifested by Mr. Eliot, and especially with reference to religious doctrine." "Hazarding" the following "conjecture," he seems furthermore remarkably astute:

> We think we see indications that he regards the numerous theological creeds, about which the clerical mind has so long disputed, as being only shells of different shape and colour, enclosing the fruit of the religious spirit common to the human race, or as so many mental structures which in less successive metamorphoses man forms and afterwards casts off.

The writer of these comments, however, was engaging in more than conjecture. The review was written by John Chapman, who had pried out of Herbert Spencer the identity of *Adam Bede*'s creator. George Eliot and Lewes were greatly dismayed, not least of all at having been betrayed by friends.[21]

Subsequent responses reveal how hazardous her beliefs were thought to be. In one of the first retrospective reviews of George Eliot, written in October 1860 after *The Mill* appeared, the *London Quarterly Review* warns the reader "that the authoress of these tales is also the translator of Strauss' notorious book." The review, hostile from start to finish, also asks this "distressing question": "Are the various forms under which she has exhibited it [the Gospels] no more for her than the Mahometan and Hindoo systems were for the poet of Thalaba and Kehama?"[22] In another early retrospective essay, less hostile and genuinely astute, Richard Simpson in the *Home and Foreign Review* (October 1863) also takes George Eliot to task for her beliefs (*CH*, pp. 221–50). His starting point, in a sharply formulated and coherent argument designed to reveal the subversive nature of her tolerance, is the "not much regarded," but "true" theory presented earlier by "the critic of the *Westminster Review*."

21. [Chapman], *Westminster Review*, pp. 278, 283. For a discussion of the disclosure of the pseudonym, see Haight, *Biography*, pp. 269–70, 278–79.

22. [James Craigie Robertson], *Quarterly Review*, American ed., 108 (1860): 260; authorship identified *Wellesley Index* 1: 743.

Simpson maintains that George Eliot speaks "as if she had faith," all the while giving form to her own Feuerbachian and positivist beliefs (*CH*, p. 224). His definitions are general enough to be accurate, and his understanding of the role she would play is remarkable. Not only did he see how she attempted to capture through her natural history the forms of belief that characterized past and present communities, but also he realized how she wanted to create through her fiction new forms of belief. But Simpson was distressed by the subterfuge concealed in the tolerance and the debasement (if the truth be known) of traditional religious forms:

> Now here is a dishonesty inseparable from positivist religion, in which religious belief does not correspond to objective truth, but is only an impression on the imagination, useful to excite, direct, and give energy to the feelings . . . . To her mind, the substance of every religion is the same; there is the same meaning at the bottom of all Christian sects, and that one meaning is, love to man. . . . It is indeed a Christian anthropology, without the basis of Christian theology. . . . In reality, the positivist believes in no religion whatever. Belief implies doctrine. To the positivist, however, religious doctrines are only impressions on the imagination, which, though they do not correspond with any reality in the universe, are yet necessary to enable man to turn his feelings into energies— for energy results from the union of belief and feeling. But the imagination is not free; it cannot, without the consciousness of fiction, imagine that to be which it knows not to be.
>
> [*CH*, pp. 231, 247, 224

Simpson grants: "It is no small victory to show that the godless humanitarianism of Strauss and Feuerbach can be made to appear the living centre of all the popular religions" (*CH*, p. 225). He then turns this victory into a defeat for George Eliot that is salutary for the reader. Most readers will fail to perceive, he believes, just how subversive her position is. The pseudonym had allowed her "to gain the public ear as a professedly religious and even clerical author" (*CH*, pp. 222–23). Still, he reasons further, although "the purpose of George Eliot is bad . . . the positive good of her sensible ethics outweighs the negative evil of her atheistic theology; and her books may be read not only with pleasure and profit, but— unless the reader is possessed by squint suspicion—without a conception of the hidden meaning which lies under their plot, their dialogue, and their characters" (*CH*, pp. 249–50).[23]

23. Ruby V. Redinger makes a similar point in *George Eliot: The Emergent Self*, pp. 3–4, 382–92, and passim. Redinger argues that George Eliot's Victorian

I have quoted Simpson at length because he is the first critic to articulate a theme that few others had mentioned, but which became a distinct refrain in the Victorian reviews of George Eliot's fiction.[24] David Carroll remarks that Simpson's "masterly presentation of George Eliot as the anthropologist of Christianity" reveals "the matter" of her fiction to be "so radical that it has to be concealed in a conventional form" (*CH*, pp. 22–23). Simpson's argument and Carroll's comment suggest that the matter and form of George Eliot's novels were indeed at odds so far as "truthfulness" was concerned. Introducing his discussion of her novels by referring to their "machinery," Simpson's vocabulary implies the absence of organic unity in both senses of the term (p. 227).

Even immensely sympathetic readers came to a similar conclusion, though the tone of their remarks was often entirely different. Sidney Colvin concludes, in an essay on *Middlemarch* in the *Fortnightly Review*, that George Eliot has run "the matter into a manner out of direct correspondence with it." His explanation, however, is compassionate and eloquent: "She has walked between two epochs, upon the confines of two worlds. . . . To the old world belong the elements of her experience, to the new world the elements of her reflection on experience" (*CH*, p. 332).

An occasional critic applauded George Eliot for bringing to her fiction a new structure of beliefs. Maintaining that "the moral significance coalesces with the narrative, and lives through the characters," Edward Dowden in the *Contemporary Review* (August 1872) bases his argument for the organic unity of her work on the "complete" moral sensibility of a writer who teaches us that the individual is a part of "collective humanity" and that "to understand

---

readers unknowingly helped the author to free a "second-self" for writing by crowning the pseudonym with respectability and applauding her books, while protecting her private identity by regarding the pseudonym as a separate entity. George Eliot, she concludes, eventually endowed the pseudonym with a personality of its own, accepting and growing into the mask because of the needs it fulfilled (pp. 329–36, and passim).

24. The relation between strategy and structure in George Eliot's novels is first suggested in two reviews of *The Mill on the Floss*: *CH*, pp. 124–31 (*Guardian*, April 1860) and *CH*, pp. 135–37 ([E. S. Dallas], *Times*, May 1860). Beginning with *Romola*, the objections to a lack of unity are too frequent to list. R. H. Hutton and Sidney Colvin grapple persistently and intelligently with the relation between matter and form in George Eliot's fiction; see n. 18 for their *Middlemarch* reviews; *CH*, pp. 365–70 for Hutton's review of *Daniel Deronda*; and *Fortnightly Review*, n.s. 20 (1876): 601–616 for Colvin's. See also Hutton's perceptive analysis of how *Silas Marner* and *Romola* achieve unity of form and belief (*CH*, pp. 175–78; 198–205).

any individual apart from the whole life of the race is impossible."[25]

Dowden's response, however, was exceptional. Far more often reviewers, even those who perceived the larger structure of her beliefs, felt that a doctrine of fellow-feeling, unsupported by Christian theology, was by nature incomplete. Readers doubted the coherence as well as the completeness of her world view. Over and again, George Eliot's Victorian readers scrutinized her theory of consequences. Some pointed to its strictness and others to its arbitrary nature, at one moment finding confirmation of natural, moral, and social law, and at another disturbance. The "inexorable consecutiveness" she would bring to "natural sequence" was often undermined in her novels, they felt, by coincidence and circumstance, especially in their closings.[26] The worlds she created seemed to them sometimes provisional, sometimes providential, escaping consequential morality through the power of circumstance, yet elsewhere so deterministic as to be summoning Nemesis.

Proposing to resolve this dissonance, while trying to avoid strident questioning, one unidentified reviewer writes: "Without wishing the objective vigour of the author's imaginative creations to be clouded by a transparent didactic purpose, her readers may not unnaturally look for an imaged solution of the logical dilemma." Characterizing her fictional worlds, he finds them shaped by a sense that the "experiences of life" are essentially "ephemeral," a matter of accident and yet also determined by a conviction that the "permanent conditions of life," represented through familial, racial, and communal ties, are "a symbol of the strongest bond of human fellowship." Articulating what many readers felt, he detects the root of the dilemma to be the absence of ultimate sanctions that enforce "altruistic as opposed to egoistic impulses."[27] "The logical dilemma" he thereby defines is equally characteristic of revisionary organicism.

Reviewers were rarely so precise about the problem, but the issues of social responsibility and individual telos frequently figure in their comments. George Eliot's readers tended to be uncomfortable when they thought she was blaming society for the failed aspirations of an individual character, but they were equally discom-

25. Edward Dowden, "George Eliot," *Contemporary Review* 20 (1872): 404, 406, 418–20. Both Lewes and George Eliot very much admired Dowden's essay (*Letters* 5: 299–300; 6: 266).

26. Phrases quoted from *CH*, p. 214, but these matters arise frequently in reviews of George Eliot's work.

27. *CH*, pp. 361–62 (*Academy*, 5 February 1876).

forted when they found her relentlessly taking the part "of the species against the individual till we almost feel it is not fair, and want to go over to the other side."[28] Reviewers objected to holding society responsible for the "meanness of opportunity" Dorothea experiences, but they also argued that Gwendolen was held too insistently responsible for her own fate.[29]

As all these remarks indicate, the questions George Eliot's contemporary reviewers raised concerning the unity of her novels were in response to unresolved problems in her fiction—problems inherent as well in the organicist ideology her novels both questioned and affirmed. Challenging the unity she always meant to bring to "the whole," her reviewers were often acute rather than obtuse—but on their own grounds, where the abiding standards were meaning and belief. The stakes at issue are cogently summarized by Lord Acton in *Nineteenth Century* (March 1885):

> If ever science or religion reigns alone over an undivided empire, the books of George Eliot might lose their central and unique importance, but as the emblem of a generation distracted between the intense need of believing and the difficulty of belief, they will live to the last syllable of recorded time.
>
> [*CH*, p. 462

The Aesthetic of Sympathy and the Sensibility of Author and Reader

This "need of believing" was most successfully met by George Eliot when she was able to nourish in her readers the sympathy that "feed[s] . . . faith" by engendering fellow-feeling. From her first novel to her last she thought of *sympathy* as "the one poor word which includes all our best insight and our best love," and of the "want of sympathy" as "[condemning] us to a corresponding stupidity."[30] Regarded as far more than a "poor word," *sympathy* acquired so great an importance during the course of the century that modern critics have identified it with a doctrine or an aesthetic.

28. Sidney Colvin, *Fortnightly Review*, n.s. 20 (1876): 603.

29. The phrase "meanness of opportunity" is from the Prelude to *Middlemarch* (p. 3). As Carroll and Harvey suggest, it is "very probable" that George Eliot revised the Finale for the 1874 book edition in response to the great fuss reviewers made about the severe indictment of "the society into which she [Dorothea] was born" (Introduction, *CH*, p. 29; "Criticism of the Novel," pp. 133–34).

30. *Letters* 4: 119; *AB*, ch. 50, p. 407; *DD*, ch. 48, p. 658.

The doctrine has been defined in various ways, depending on whether scholars look to nineteenth-century fiction, poetry, or prose for its expression. Thomas A. Noble locates the "doctrine of sympathy" in the criticism George Eliot wrote during the 1850s and in her early novels, and ascribes to it a simple credo: "Art has a moral purpose; the purpose is to widen human sympathy; this purpose can be achieved only by giving a true picture of life." Isobel Armstrong derives and defines the doctrine from reviews of poetry written between 1830 and 1870, identifying it as a "great cohesive force" that enlarges and binds together individual sensibilities. George Levine discusses the "anti-romantic and antiheroic" form the "aesthetics of sympathy" takes in prose fiction, in which sympathy is invoked "for the imperfect since imperfection is the condition of this world."[31] Although scholars approach the subject from differing generic perspectives, they agree that sympathy requires seeing other people as we see ourselves, sharing and understanding their situations, and changing places with them in our own imaginations. All these views about the effects of sympathy are present in George Eliot's work. Given her skepticism about the possibility of intellectual agreement, she would have welcomed as well the escape from logical dilemmas offered by a doctrine that emphasizes the affective nature of literature, its power to elicit an emotional as opposed to a reasoned response.

So important was an aesthetic of sympathy to George Eliot that she justified her life and her art according to its ethic. When her first volume of fiction was published, she expressed the hope that "my writing may succeed and so give value to my life—as indications that I can touch the hearts of my fellow men" (*Letters* 2: 416). After her last novel appeared, she continued to feel "there is nothing I should care more to do, if it were possible, than to rouse the imagination of men and women to a vision of human claims," now extending the scope of sympathy to include "those races of their fellow-men who most differ from them in customs and beliefs."[32]

31. Thomas A. Noble, *George Eliot's "Scenes of Clerical Life,"* p. 38; see also chaps. 2–3. Isobel Armstrong, *Victorian Scrutinies: Reviews of Poetry*, pp. 25–26; see also pp. 9, 24, 56–59. George Levine, *The Boundaries of Fiction*, p. 11; see also pp. 8–12. Edward Alexander discusses the high Victorian criterion of "sympathy" in the work of nonfictional prose writers in *Matthew Arnold and John Stuart Mill*, pp. 168–73, 178–79.

32. *Letters* 6: 301–2. Time and again, in letters and essays, George Eliot stresses her belief that "if Art does not enlarge men's sympathies, it does nothing morally." See, for instance, *Letters* 3: 111; 4: 301; *Essays*, pp. 270, 317.

Even these brief comments suggest three matters central to the aesthetic of sympathy: the affective function of literature; the importance of imagination in transforming belief into socially binding action; and the need to engage the reader in a community of feeling with the author and, even more importantly, with the human community at large. These principles speak, however, only to the purpose of the work of art—to enlarging the reader's sensibility to foster social unity—and not to the means of achieving that purpose.

In general, Victorian discussions of sympathy had very little to say about the means the writer was to employ to shape and control the reader's response. One of the few defined means concerned the sensibility of the author. A writer, it was argued, could engage and enlarge the sympathies of the reader only if he or she were sincere. The reader's sympathies were to be aroused by the author's; in the case of a novel, by the novelist's sincere and compassionate attitude toward both fictional world and reader. In addition to sincerity, the criteria included discretion and truthfulness about things genuinely experienced and felt.

Even when Lewes, for instance, concedes that an author must make "his ideas intelligible and attractive," and take into account "what food" is "assimilable," he nonetheless insists that an author should not "write down to the public," but "up to his ideal," always believing in what he writes.[33] Lewes describes the importance of the artist's sincerity and sympathy in fervent language:

> The prophet must be his own disciple, or he will make none. Enthusiasm is contagious: belief creates belief. There is no influence issuing from unbelief or from languid acquiescence. This is peculiarly noticeable in Art, because Art depends on sympathy for its influence, and unless the artist has felt the emotions he depicts we remain unmoved: in proportion to the depth of his feeling is our sympathetic response.
>
> [*Fortnightly Review* 1: 700

George Eliot, too, advocated sincerity in art. She attacked as "deficient in sympathetic emotion" art that "proceeds rather from the poet's perception that it is good for other men to be moral, than from any overflow of moral feeling in himself" (*Essays*, p. 379). She also insisted that the moral effect of her own stories "depends on my power of seeing truly and feeling justly" (*Letters* 2: 362). Like so

33. Lewes, "Principles of Success in Literature," *Fortnightly Review* 1: 92.

many Victorian writers (Carlyle, Ruskin, Arnold), she believed "every great artist is a teacher, . . . giving us his higher sensibility as a medium" (*Essays*, p. 126). Like them, she also thought:

> A nasty mind makes nasty art. . . . And some effect in determining other minds there must be according to the degree of nobleness or meanness in the selection made by the artist's soul.
>
> [*Letters* 5: 391

As this last passage intimates, in practice the relatively simple theory of sympathy contains, proportionately, as many problems as the more complex theories of Social Dynamics and Social Statics. Several examples of these problems are illustrated by George Eliot's own difficulties in acting in accordance with all the precepts derived from sympathy. She felt compelled to assume the disguise of a pseudonym, though the aesthetic principles to which she was committed demanded the reader's conviction of the author's sincerity. Once her identity became known, she could never escape the burden of having to keep proving she did not have a "nasty mind." To write her novels, moreover, she had inevitably to make choices that were as much aesthetic as ideological, whereas the doctrine of sympathy directed the "selection made by the artist's soul" primarily in terms of the latter.

George Eliot adopted the ideological end of extending the readers' sympathies for the sake of moral community. Her means, however, came to include not only leading, guiding, and persuading her readers to sympathetic assent, but also encouraging, perhaps even provoking, them to engage in critical probing and questioning. To inspire her readers to scrutinize conventional and complacent behavior and conduct, she had to risk their antagonism and their dissent. As George Eliot's response to Dallas's review of *The Mill* suggests, she was wary of such risks, for they had the potential to defeat the end she most desired. Thus she had continually to balance criticism that might disturb her readers with reassurances that would elicit their fellow-feeling. Her narrators' provocation of the reader is in this sense part of an elaborate strategy, used not to oppose the aesthetic of sympathy but rather to further its ends. Trying neither to alienate her readers nor make them too comfortable, she sought to unite the conventional idea of sympathy with the uncommon ideal of disturbing discovery.

The use of any such authorial tactics was anathema to the doctrine of sympathy as conventionally defined. While critics did not specify how the writer was to bring about the desired end of social transformation, the principle of sincerity precluded the use of strategy. Thus, the author who was perceived to be a tactician was likely to arouse suspicion. Victorian readers generally assumed that the narrator's attitude toward the fictional world was identical to the author's; indeed, they rarely distinguished between author and narrator. While they were perfectly comfortable with an omniscient author who frequently commented on characters and events in the novel, and even interrupted the story to speak to the reader directly, they wanted their authors to be neither manipulative nor discomforting. Responding to George Eliot, they began to record discomfort with *The Mill on the Floss*, but at that point in her career they were still so preoccupied with the general nature of her realism that they did not often stop to single out the narrower issue of the author's point of view. By the time she published *Middlemarch*, her realism no longer troubled them. Now, for the first time, there was a widespread and anxious concern with the complexity of tone in the author's voice, particularly as directed toward the reader.

In one respect, their suspicions were well-founded. However much George Eliot employed irony, sarcasm, and allied verbal forms as rhetorical devices, still her own attitude toward her audience was mixed. Though she devoted her life to combating "want of sympathy," she was not immune to responding with hostility to a "corresponding stupidity." Her private situation inevitably exacerbated such feelings, as did her substantial self-consciousness. As George Eliot said of herself: "I am rather uncomfortably constituted; for while I am unable to write a sentence for the sake of pleasing other people, I should be unable to write at all without strong proofs that I had touched them" (*Letters* 3: 393). In this case, her uncomfortable constitution served her well. "Proofs" of her having "touched" her audience exist not only in their adoration but also in their distress.

Two critics perceived as early as *The Mill on the Floss* that George Eliot combined remarkable sympathy with complex strategies, and both responded uneasily. Wanting "to speak honestly" himself, the reviewer for the *Guardian* openly acknowledges his reluctance to evaluate this "remarkable" but disturbing novel in which "undeniable imaginative power takes new and very mixed shapes." He refers to the author's "cunning knowledge of the effects of a touch of familiar homeliness or of an allusion to more recondite learning"; to the doubtful "shade . . . of bitterness" in her "profound irony"; and to the "quaint half-smile, and sly taking for

granted of the reader's thoughts, . . . effecting a communication of
sentiment between his greater shrewdness and the narrator's hum-
bler and more simple views of things."[34]

The *Guardian* reviewer's perception of strategy is nervous, but
local, restricted to a few points. In contrast, Dallas's review of *The
Mill on the Floss,* in the *Times,* exhibits a comprehensive sense of
the novelist as strategist. After describing the indictment of the
Dodsons' "vulgar respectability" in the first half of the novel, he
explains how "the author has very cleverly helped herself out of a
difficulty":

> When "George Eliot" got exactly half through her work she fore-
> saw the criticisms which a novel based on such a foundation would
> certainly provoke, and she commenced her fourth book . . . by
> uttering against her story all that the most savage critic can have
> it in his heart to say.

Dallas then summarizes the opening of Book Four, paraphrasing its
three long paragraphs (each consisting of an extended address to
the reader) to drive his point home:

> She says in effect:—"You, reader, are oppressed by all this mean-
> ness—disgusted at all this hardness—perplexed that I should think
> it worthy of your notice. I perfectly agree with you; but such is life,
> and it is in the midst of such a life, the most marked quality of
> which is the utter absence of poetry or religion, that many of us
> grow up—it was in the midst of such a desert that my little heroine,
> Maggie, bloomed into beauty. It is well that these things should be
> impressed upon us, and that we should lay them to heart."
>
> [CH, pp. 135–36

Dallas is the only critic I have come across who recognized, accepted, and admired George Eliot's strategy in *The Mill on the
Floss,* finding in it evidence of her tact. Still, he worried that writers less "sober" would adopt her book as a "model" (*CH,* p. 137).
Far more common were the protests against the model itself. One
reviewer's feelings were so jarred by George Eliot's "interjectional
remarks" that he accused her of sneering and railing "like a sort
of womanly Carlyle at an unreal monster, called by her 'good society.' " Another thought the "offensive . . . intrusion of the writer's
personality" was "intended to have the effect of lofty and subtle
sarcasm."[35]

34. *CH,* pp. 126–29 (*Guardian,* 25 April 1860).
35. *CH,* p. 152 (*Dublin University Magazine,* February 1861). [Robertson],
Quarterly Review, p. 257.

Partly because George Eliot changed her tactics after *The Mill on the Floss*, and partly because the public was generally willing to be deceived (as Simpson had predicted it would be), the clamor subsided in the years following. Until the publication of *Middlemarch*, the question of tone was not generally a matter of controversy. Instead, critics found in her work a salutary adherence to the doctrine of sympathy. There was occasional wariness, as in the warning that follows the praise in the *North British Review*:

> No one would object to the charity which pervades George Eliot's writings. Her wide sympathies, and the generosity with which she appreciates the good in things evil, are great sources of her power, and command hearty admiration.

But the review's conclusion warns, "She owes it to her rare genius to consider well, whether some sobriety . . . would not aid her in the achievement" of her "great ambition." However, a counter warning came from Henry James, who found in her "sagacious tendency to compromise" and "avoid extreme deductions" a "quality of discretion" that is aesthetically self-defeating, even if it engages readers and puts them under her "spell."[36]

No one else seems to have objected to her "discretion." During the middle years of her career, critics gladly perceived her as a writer who participated in and even helped to create the aesthetic of sympathy. For example, John Morley's 1866 review of *Felix Holt* applauds her "enlarged compassion," and the "benign, elevated, and calm spirit which breathes through the authoress's style." His admiration of the absence of that cynicism "which dwarfs us into a swarming tribe of tiny ants" uses an indirect allusion to the Dodsons and Tullivers (called "emmet-like" in *The Mill*) to praise a change for the better in her work.[37]

Another essay Morley wrote in 1866, "George Eliot's Novels," is instructive not only for his remarks but also for George Eliot's response. She did not often express approval of a review, but she seems to have been so pleased by Morley's that she had Lewes "call upon Macmillan [the publisher] to thank him for it."[38] Looking

36. [H. H. Lancaster], "George Eliot's Novels," American ed., *North British Review* 45 (1866): 118, 120; authorship identified *Wellesley Index* 1: 691. James, *CH*, pp. 273–75; review of *Felix Holt* (*Nation*, 16 August 1866).

37. *CH*, pp. 254–55 (*Saturday Review*, June 1866).

38. John Morley, *Macmillan's Magazine* 14 (August 1866): 272–79. *Letters* 4: 309, n. 4. James D. Benson discusses Eliot's "pervasive dissatisfaction with the contemporary reviewing of her novels" as well as "the naiveté of thinking

at Morley's argument, we see how much George Eliot wanted to be perceived as a writer who furthered the general culture by activating not subverting belief. Morley's article reflects, in turn, his interests in literature and society, particularly his desire to translate liberal ideas into politics. At the opening and close of this essay, he explains how literature can revitalize the beliefs that make liberal action possible. He opens by celebrating George Eliot's "expansive energy," that "rare vigour" of mind which is able "to rise to a feeling of the breadth and height and unity of human fortunes." He ends with a fervid appreciation of her unique ability to invigorate in her readers the kind of "belief" that "tends to bring men nearer to one another." During the course of the essay, he praises her "fine artistic moderation, and just completeness, which in art comes of moderation" (p. 276). He also admires her "kindly irony" for being corrective without being harsh or offensive to even "the weakest brother" (pp. 278–79).

In *Middlemarch*, however, she clearly offended a good many people. They took the offense extremely personally. R. H. Hutton, for instance, responded angrily to the sentence in the Finale that begins "But we insignificant people," because he read it to mean "—in other words, we are moulding a bad public opinion about women" *(CH*, p. 307). Like many others, Hutton's dismay at the "biting power" of the "acid criticism" in *Middlemarch* resulted in part from his own commitment to the sympathy George Eliot had led him to expect and value in her *(CH*, p. 290). Many reviewers were disconcerted by the "blending of the author's bitterness with her profound tenderness; the former, they feared would undermine the latter, blocking the "powerful and even flow in every direction [of] the sympathies which bind her to her fellows."[39] The *Athenaeum* and *Academy* critics were among the few who applauded the presence in *Middlemarch* of a narrative tone at once charitable and melancholy, idealistic and accommodating, morally earnest and yet satirical.

---

that George Eliot was unaware of the reception of her work"; see " 'Sympathetic Criticism,' " pp. 428–40.

39. Colvin, *CH*, p. 337; Dowden, "George Eliot," *Contemporary Review*, p. 409. Dowden defines and applauds George Eliot's contribution to the aesthetic of sympathy. Other critics praise her adherence to the doctrine of sympathy in *Middlemarch* but also lament her apostasy. In addition to Colvin, see *CH*, pp. 314–20 (*Saturday Review*, 7 December 1872); *Saturday Review* 34 (21 December 1872): 794–96; Holmstrom and Lerner, p. 78 (*Daily News*, 28 November 1871). See also reviews in *Nation, Quarterly Review, Spectator, British Quarterly Review* cited n. 18 above.

The *Academy* review, written by Edith Simcox, speaks in addition of how the "intricacy" of perception in *Middlemarch* "seems to have an almost oppressive effect on ordinary readers," creating "a feeling of even painful bewilderment." A good many reviews of *Middlemarch* suggest that critics and ordinary readers were having a similar response. As David Carroll explains, "for the first time a majority of critics seem to have become aware of the wide gap separating George Eliot's own beliefs from the beliefs of the world she is presenting. They have been alerted by the persistent irony of the commentary.[40] The critics' polarized responses, many of them individually self-contradictory, reveal in addition great uneasiness with a narrator who both unnerves and comforts the reader. The combination made it impossible for George Eliot's contemporaries to see in *Middlemarch* another *Mill on the Floss*. Now they found not only bitter medicine but also the "glorious Tonics" Blackwood had predicted (*Letters* 5: 199). If they could not stomach the one, neither could they reject the other. The combination was indeed bewildering, causing critics to find the tone of *Middlemarch* both tranquil and distressing, healthy and morbid, majestic and subversive, charming and cynical, constructively reforming the reader by renewing his sympathies but also assaulting him with bitter ironies.

Thus R. H. Hutton asks: Does *Middlemarch* "really add to the happiness of its readers or not?" (*CH*, p. 297). He searches persistently for the answer in the five reviews he wrote while the individual parts were issued, and in two more written after the novel was complete. His two constant themes are the greatness of *Middlemarch* and its harshness. The "acid criticism," the "heavy sarcasms," the "needle-pricks of acrid banter" seemed to him "like broken lancet-points in a living body," altogether out of keeping with her "large friendly way of letting the light fall on human weakness." He focuses so much attention on the "harshly interpolated . . . running comments" that, despite his great admiration for the novel, a "running fire of criticism"—his own and George Eliot's—dominates his reviews.[41] Yet, returning to *Middlemarch* in 1873, he revises his judgment, underplaying the bitterness, the sarcasm, the taunting notes, to emphasize instead the integrity of George Eliot's "painful sincerity." In the end, he seems even to grant that the pain is more his than hers:

40. Simcox, *CH*, pp. 324–25 (*Academy*, 1 January 1873). Carroll, Introduction, *CH*, pp. 30–31.
41. Quotations from *CH*, pp. 289–90, 296, 292, 289, 294.

what she loses in beauty and in grandeur of effect . . . she seems
to gain in ease, and in the obviously greater accordance between
her array of intellectual and moral assumptions, and her artistic
treatment of them.

[*British Quarterly Review*, p. 218

With this reversal, Hutton sets aside the question that haunted
his earlier reviews: Does *Middlemarch* really add to the happiness
of its readers or not? Other critics raised the same question, and
they too leaned toward but resisted a negative answer. Like Hutton,
a number of them found *Middlemarch* left them depressed or defensive. They felt that George Eliot was coercing her readers to
either acknowledge their bond to their fellow-beings or defend
their present ways. The *Saturday Review* pinpointed what was particularly unsettling, the way George Eliot manipulated the reader,
employing her "gifts . . . to betray him into unconscious, and perhaps unwilling, admissions" (*CH*, p. 315). Robert Laing in the
Quarterly Review speaks as well of how the reader finishes *Middlemarch* with a "melancholy and forlorn" sense of "modern society,"
all the while hardly "able to make out to himself how far his hopeless mood had grown directly out of the words of his author or out
of his own musings" (p. 193). Laing's judgment of the novel—that
it "will leave all of us, in greater or less measure, restless and distressed" (p. 191)—is confirmed by Sidney Colvin, who closes his
review with this rueful question:

> Is it that a literature, which confronts all the problems of life and
> the world, and recognises all the springs of action, and all that clogs
> the springs, and all that comes from their smooth or impeded
> working, and all the importance of one life for the mass,—is it that
> such a literature must be like life itself, to leave us sad and hungry?

[*CH*, p. 338

Responding to *Daniel Deronda*, the critics were preoccupied on
the whole with other matters, not with the narrative tone that
seemed to be fairly benign once again, "the cynicism of the inci-
dental irony . . . certainly much less" than in *Middlemarch*, as
Hutton notes, "and the whole spirit of the book . . . wider and
higher."[42] As in *Middlemarch*, they objected again to the author's
scientific language, but they focused primarily, as we noted earlier,

42. *CH*, p. 369 (*Spectator*, 9 September 1876).

on the romance elements. Both traits seemed to her detractors a reflection of her "want of tact" and her hostility to "the 'average man' and the 'dull man,' '' while her advocates saw these traits as signs of her courageous and sincere refusal to put either "her critics" or "her readers at large before the best she could give them."[43]

Even this quick sketch of the aesthetic of sympathy as it relates to George Eliot and her immediate audience illustrates that her readers measured the tone of all her writings according to her "wide sympathy with the heart and life of the people" (*CH*, p. 438). At the beginning of her career, her readers were greatly comforted by the image of underlying social unity E. S. Dallas and others drew from the "broad sympathy and large tolerance" they found in her first novel. At the end of her career, they continued to speak of her "wonderful sympathy with humanity." Such later praise, however, was often accompanied by qualifications. The statement just quoted, for instance, continues: "so far, at least, as it is congenial to the writer."[44] But after *The Mill on the Floss*, her writings were never again dismissed by reviewers as the sneerings of a "womanly Carlyle." Indeed, she came to be so venerated for her "sympathy with humanity" that her readers felt compelled to try to come to grips with her unnerving complexity of tone. More significant than the adjectives they used to characterize that complexity was the challenge—for George Eliot as well as for her readers—of balancing a sympathetic response with a critical one. Over the years that challenge helped to create between author and reader a far more intense and engaged relationship than would have been possible had she remained within the conventional limits of the aesthetic of sympathy. The very contradictions she embraced allowed her to draw into her community of interest a readership "distracted between the intense need of believing and the difficulty of belief." Again the recreation of community comes to rest principally on the relation of artist to reader.

43. *CH*, p. 373 (George Saintsbury, *Academy*, 9 September 1876); *CH*, p. 398 (Francillon, *Gentleman's Magazine*, 1876); *CH*, p. 427 (Henry James, "Daniel Deronda: A Conversation," *Atlantic Monthly*, December 1876). Although James complained in 1866 of her excessive "discretion" (see n. 36), he includes in this piece strong objections to her "want of tact," voiced first by the hostile Pulcheria, and then by Constantius, who picks up the phrase and repeats it five times within three sentences.

44. *CH*, p. 371 (Saintsbury, *Academy*, 1876).

❖

SEVEN

The Author as Citizen

The Omniscient-Author Convention

In the essay "The Novels of George Eliot," written in 1866, Henry James speaks of how the novelist must create his reader:

> In every novel the work is divided between the writer and the reader; but the writer makes the reader very much as he makes his characters. When he makes him ill, that is, makes him indifferent, he does no work; the writer does all. When he makes him well, that is, makes him interested, then the reader does quite half the labor. In making such a deduction as I have just indicated, the reader would be doing but his share of the task; the grand point is to get him to make it. I hold that there is a way. It is perhaps a secret; but until it is found out, I think the art of story-telling cannot be said to have approached perfection.
>
> [p. 485

George Eliot then seemed to him not yet to have discovered that secret. Reviewing *Middlemarch* in 1873, James suggests that she now indeed makes the reader well, exciting interest in Dorothea, whom "we believe in," but he does not explain how:

> By what unerring mechanism this effect is produced—whether by fine strokes or broad ones, by description or by narration, we can hardly say.
>
> [*CH*, p. 354

Rather, it is not worth his while "to say," because he prefers to make the reader in an altogether different way, by suppressing the writer's personality, not by reminding the reader of authorial presence.

George Eliot's narrator is neither removed nor detached, but openly engaged in trying to generate fellow-feeling. As a fiction develops, the reader becomes part of its particularized life and the imagined world connects to a real one outside. Much in George Eliot's fiction contributes to this process, but the reciprocity she wished to create is perhaps most obvious in her narrator's direct addresses to the reader. Passages in which "you," "he," "she," "we," "our," "anyone," or "everyone" are inescapably called upon to respond demonstrate the relationship George Eliot hoped to establish with her audience. Her adherence to the doctrine of sympathy and her belief that the engaged reader and writer must be free to take issue with one another contributed to shaping that relationship.[1] The former creates community of feeling through sympathetic agreement, while the latter brings the reader into a community of interests based far more on awareness than assent. To elicit these kinds of responses, George Eliot used many different rhetorical strategies even within the direct address. The subject of this chapter is the patterns they take.

A number of modern critics have defined significant aspects of George Eliot's authorial voice. In their discussions of Eliot's narrative art, W. J. Harvey, Isobel Armstrong, Karl Kroeber, and Barbara Hardy perform "the labor" James assigns to the well-made reader while removing some of the strictures he would place on the writer. Harvey sets for himself precisely this task when he discusses George Eliot's use of the convention of the omniscient author.[2] Because she "is not aiming at the insulation, the self-sufficiency of the Jamesian novel," she deliberately blurs, Harvey explains, the "boundaries between real and fictional," allowing "us an easy transition from one world to the other" (p. 72). The authorial interventions provide a "bridge or link" between the "fictional microcosm of the characters and the macrocosm of George Eliot and the real world" (p. 71). The kind of fiction she wished to write requires, moreover, that the reader be aware of such links. Yet Harvey also maintains that her fictional world is "surely designed for our contemplation, not for our imaginative participation" (pp. 79–81). In making this distinction, he defends George Eliot from post-Jamesian critical dogmas that often skew our understanding of earlier novelists, but his important corrective work has its own element of distortion. George Eliot was surely working to affect her readers' thoughts *and* feelings; the "mode of contemplation" Harvey defines speaks mainly to their understanding.

Isobel Armstrong's excellent essay on *Middlemarch* argues, in

1. See chapter 1, pp. 11–13, and chapter 6, pp. 263–73.
2. W. J. Harvey, *Art of George Eliot*, chap. 3.

contrast, that George Eliot's narrative commentary "commands the reader's most intense *imaginative* involvement with the world of the novel."[3] Correcting Harvey, Armstrong overstates her case but also supplements his in considering how George Eliot requires from the reader an imaginative participation that depends on feelings and experience, not only understanding:

> Her success depends, I think, upon her capacity to move beyond the moral universe of the novel, turn outwards towards the reader and to invoke a general body of moral and psychological knowledge or, rather, *experience*, which can be the corporate possession of both writer and reader; this shared experience is continually being brought to bear on the novel. She constantly asks for an assent, a corroboration from the reader, before she proceeds. Her way of extending and enlarging the imagination or the "sympathies" of her readers through her art is to move between the known, the common experience, and the unknown, the unique and particular predicaments of the novel.
>
> [pp. 120–21

Describing this outward movement in *Middlemarch*, Armstrong presents a valuable summary of how the reader is directly implicated through the "use of personal pronouns—'we', 'our' " and the generalizing pronoun "one" (p. 124). To Armstrong's analysis we must add two points. First, the formal and impersonal tone of "one" implicates the reader but creates a certain distance between author and reader. Second, the more immediate personal pronouns speak at times only to the inner world of the novel, making claims for its authenticity in terms of what the reader has witnessed ("Maggie, we know," "as you have observed," "as we have seen"). Nonetheless, Armstrong usefully separates the "indirect appeal of proverbial statement" and the "straightforward invoking of the reader," the latter often carefully designed to win the reader's assent (p. 124).

Yet even in reference to *Middlemarch* (the only novel she considers), Armstrong's conclusions about the effects of the narrator's voice are partial. Like Harvey, she finds the narrative tone to be "comfortable" or "comforting," especially as compared to Thackeray, who provokes and makes us " 'uncomfortable' " by playing "ambiguously with our responses" (pp. 122–23). But, as nineteenth-century reviews show, for some Victorian readers George Eliot seemed at times to be alarmingly like Thackeray and on occasion

3. Isobel Armstrong, *"Middlemarch,"* p. 117; italics mine.

even more disturbing.[4] Modern criticism of George Eliot's work, in contrast, is in general marked by the sense of an engagement between author and reader that is expansive and complex but quietly contemplative. A notable exception is the mix of puzzlement, depression, anger, and resistance in some recent feminist responses to George Eliot's fiction.[5] More often, modern critics find in George Eliot's narrators a comforting voice, and they argue that to repel or provoke the reader would have been fatal to the purposes of her art.[6] To look at George Eliot's relationship with her original audience is to uncover elements of disturbance and unease, elements often neglected by twentieth-century critics but vital to her art.

Karl Kroeber sees some of this uneasiness and its uses when he argues that the "pervasiveness of Eliot's authorial presence" should be taken "not as a sign of coziness in her relation to her audience but as a sign of her shrewdness in subverting . . . an original illusion of community between author and reader."[7] Pretending at first to share the readers' attitudes, she lures her audience into participation. Through her "ironic commentaries," she then forces her readers "to reassess the powerful intangibles—public opinion, education, tradition"—bringing them in the end to share her own views. Kroeber too, however, gives undue predominance to one aspect of her authorial point of view. Although he claims that George Eliot "uses this technique in all of her fiction," the illustrations he provides are drawn only from "Janet's Repentance" and *The Mill on the Floss*, works which surely did not have on her immediate readers the full effect he describes. Their response to *The Mill*, as we have seen, reveals that they were resisting rather than sharing her views. Later on, they became adept at detecting subversion, a development for which Kroeber's thesis does not allow. He bases much of his argument, moreover, on supposition. As he himself admits, he does not know whether it is "true" that "some objections to Eliot's 'omniscient' presence in her novels spring from her readers' vague awareness of having been lured into changing their point of view." While his work helps us to see

4. See chapter 6, pp. 249, 251, 255. Comparing Eliot to Thackeray, the *Dublin University Magazine* reviewer writes: "Mr. Thackeray, at least, is too good a workman to draw his characters mostly without a heart" (*CH*, pp. 148–49).

5. See, for instance, Lee Edwards, "Women, Energy, and *Middlemarch*," and Elaine Showalter, "The Greening of Sister George."

6. See, for example, Armstrong, "*Middlemarch*," pp. 122–23; Harvey, *Art of George Eliot*, pp. 80–81, and "Criticism of the Novel," pp. 125–47.

7. Karl Kroeber, *Styles in Fictional Structure*, pp. 48, 50.

how George Eliot would "guide us . . . to a profound understanding from which renewed sympathy for our fellows may flow," his George Eliot (always surreptitious, always condescending) is too subversive (pp. 50–51, 59).

Barbara Hardy's description of a "narrative medium . . . composed of many voices" is more accurate:

> There is the direct speech of the author's pity, both for her own creatures and extending in generalization to lament and admiration for all humanity. There is the more detached voice of irony and analysis. There is the omniscient warning, veiled and unveiled, working in the interests of aesthetic unity and dramatic irony.
>
> [*Novels of George Eliot*, p. 177

Hardy accurately locates a "strong corrective . . . to excessive sympathy and pathos" in the irony and in the "reflective tone" that also characterize the commentary (p. 164). Although George Eliot's direct addresses to the reader are not Hardy's particular concern, all these voices, as well as Harvey's claim for contemplation, Armstrong's for imaginative assent, and Kroeber's for radical reassessment are heard therein.

Face to Face:
George Eliot's Addresses to the Reader

For all their variety, George Eliot's addresses to the reader follow certain patterns. Direct address emerges as a dominant form in *Adam Bede* and reappears in *The Mill on the Floss* but with a radically altered tone. In the middle novels, *Silas Marner*, *Romola*, and *Felix Holt*, George Eliot relies more heavily on the indirect address. The modes typical of the first two novels are combined and expanded in *Middlemarch*, where again the direct address appears with great frequency. *Daniel Deronda* brings further innovations and another retreat.

In all these novels, the narrator tends to turn away from direct appeal when the overt subject matter moves "from the familiar to the strange," the phrase with which the narrator introduces Hetty's long journey in *Adam Bede*, Book Five. Throughout Hetty's search for her lover, during which their baby is delivered and abandoned to its death, the frequency of direct addresses to the reader decreases markedly. Instead, George Eliot relies almost entirely on dramatic representation, as she does in *The Mill on the Floss* when Stephen carries Maggie away in "The Great Temptation," and in *Middlemarch* when Bulstrode is criminally involved with Raffles.[8]

Those novels whose general subject was likely to be thought "disagreeable" by "refined readers" contain a related pattern. Direct address is frequent in *Silas Marner* only when Silas's integration into the community (as opposed to his disinheritance) is at issue. Elsewhere, in *Silas Marner*, and in *Romola, Felix Holt,* and *Daniel Deronda,* indirect generalized statements, authoritative because they sound sagacious, are used more frequently than direct address.[9] Each of these later novels has a risky subject: *Romola* is a historical novel set in Papist times, and Savonarola is an enthusiast as well as a Catholic, both suspect to Victorians; the title *Felix Holt, the Radical* declares the subject matter to be dubious; and *Daniel Deronda* introduces a world foreign to many readers. George Eliot's strategy in these novels is to risk the direct appeal a good deal less frequently than when her subject matter is more conventional or familiar.

Another sign of her awareness of the need for strategic rhetoric is her retreat from the direct address, first in the novels directly following *The Mill on the Floss,* and then again after *Middlemarch*— or after the two books that caused her contemporaries to question her sympathy, suspect her irony, and be wary of her sincerity. Her rhetorical strategies were intended to effect extraordinary acts of balance: to satisfy her readers and challenge them, to arouse their intense sympathy yet allow for dissent, all the while averting their ultimate estrangement.

EARLY NOVELS

Even at its simplest, the pattern of reader address is complex. In *Adam Bede,* a tripartite pattern dominates, involving an appeal

8. One Coventry lady, for instance, was so moved by the dramatic representation of Bulstrode that she could not believe Bulstrode caused Raffles' death. Finding her response amusing, George Eliot reports how the lady lay "awake all night from compassion for Bulstrode" (*Letters* 5: 343). Lewes also describes the lady's response, finding it "strangely significant" in testifying both to "the profoundly real impression the book makes" and to the moral blindness engendered by orthodox religious piety (*Letters* 5: 337); but he was also very pleased when "a West End clergyman alluded . . . in his sermon" to the way " 'that great teacher George Eliot' " has made us shudder " 'at the awful dissection of a guilty conscience' " (*Letters* 5: 333). In contrast, the dramatic representation of Hetty's and Maggie's crises drew both hostile and sympathetic responses.

9. For a discussion of " 'wisdom' " in George Eliot's authorial statements, see Armstrong, "*Middlemarch.*"

to "our" common experience, a plea for a sympathetic response to a fictional character, and a reminder that what "we" are witnessing is authentic. Of course, these three parts are not present in every direct appeal; sometimes one appears alone, and often two of the three are combined.

At best, as in the following example, the direct appeals evolve from the dramatic situation and are reinforced by it. In chapter 5 of *Adam Bede*, as the narrator is about to introduce us to "The Rector," he says:

> Let me take you into that dining-room, and show you the Rev Adolphus Irwine, Rector of Broxton, Vicar of Hayslope, and Vicar of Blythe, a pluralist at whom the severest Church-reformer would have found it difficult to look sour. We will enter very softly.
>
> [p. 47

After we enter, the narrator continues to describe what "you see" and what "we can look" at, lending authenticity to the scene through our presence, and historical veracity through the reference to pluralists and church reformers. At the same time, he begins to solicit our sympathy for Irwine since we are bound to think ourselves more generous than the church reformers. The narrator then describes the elderly and aristocratic Mrs. Irwine, showing us through an exchange between mother and son that the rector deserves our admiration because he has so much sympathy for others. When Irwine is about to go upstairs to visit his invalid sister, though his mother says, " 'It's of no use,' " the narrator again turns back to the reader:

> If you know how much of human speech is mere purposeless impulse or habit, you will not wonder when I tell you that this identical objection had been made, and had received the same kind of answer, many hundred times in the course of the fifteen years that Mr Irwine's sister Anne had been an invalid. Splendid old ladies, who take a long time to dress in the morning, have often slight sympathy with sickly daughters.
>
> [p. 49

The appeal to common experience is carefully modulated, hedged by an "if" that allows the reader an escape, though the narrator validates the observation by testifying to a fifteen-year history, after having already blurred the distinction between the fictional microcosm and the world outside. Subsequent comment on "splendid old ladies" solidifies our alliance with Irwine and elicits our sympathy for invalids. Depending on how attuned the reader is to the irony, it also softens or sharpens the criticism of the old lady.

This scene occurs at the beginning of chapter 5. At its close, long paragraphs directly solicit the reader, making a case for Irwine, despite his lax theological views, because he is "of a sufficiently subtle moral fibre to have an unwearying tenderness for obscure and monotonous suffering, . . . as you have seen" (p. 59). However, since the reader has only just met the Reverend Mr. Irwine, the solicitation is heavier than the scene can successfully bear. Overstatement occurs because the point was so important to George Eliot and because Irwine's ecclesiastical standing was of great concern to her Victorian readers.

All three elements of the pattern are again present in the following passage, giving it eloquence and fullness, but also further demonstrating a tendency to affirm through the authorial voice truths not fully dramatized. The passage appears in the climactic fiftieth chapter, set some eighteen months after Hetty has been convicted of child-murder:

> For Adam, though you see him quite master of himself, working hard and delighting in his work after his inborn inalienable nature, had not outlived his sorrow—had not felt it slip from him as a temporary burthen, and leave him the same man again. Do any of us? God forbid. It would be a poor result of all our anguish and our wrestling, if we won nothing but our old selves at the end of it—if we could return to the same blind loves, the same self-confident blame, the same light thoughts of human suffering, the same frivolous gossip over blighted human lives, the same feeble sense of that Unknown towards which we have sent forth irrepressible cries in our loneliness. Let us rather be thankful that our sorrow lives in us as an indestructible force, only changing its form, as forces do, and passing from pain into sympathy—the one poor word which includes all our best insight and our best love.

[p. 407

The second half of this lengthy address culminates in "the sense of our lives having visible and invisible relations." Thus the transformation of pain into sympathy experienced by one person in response to another becomes an emblem for community. But this appeal seems too diagrammatically conceived a construct. The baptism of suffering, which widens Adam's sympathies, depends on a love for Hetty "so deep," we are told, "that the roots of it would never be torn away" (ch. 54, p. 442). However, Adam's past relation to Hetty and the narrator's responses to her make Adam's love seem more blind than "deep." As a result, the sentiments expressed in this passage seem imposed by the aesthetic of sympathy and the ideology of community rather than prompted by the dramatic action.

For George Eliot's Victorian readers, the sentiment seemed on the whole sufficient, partly because the narrator turns a painful experience into an affirmation. Often in *Adam Bede*, the narrator puts a good light on the common experience so important to the reader address. In her first novel, George Eliot admits to playing the part of the "judicious historian [who] abstains from narrating precisely what ensued. You understand . . ." (ch. 12, p. 109). Yet later in the book, describing Arthur's dilemma, the narrator opposes the "truthful" to the "judicious," disparaging the latter for being merely "a question of tactics" (ch. 28, pp. 258–59). The uneasiness or ambivalence George Eliot felt toward the use of tactics is evident in her portrayal of characters in other novels as well. Philip Wakem's schemes to gain his father's acquiescence are presented as necessary and admirable. The cunning Savonarola displays in his dealings with church and state is viewed sometimes as admirable, sometimes as treacherous. Tito, the ultimate strategist, is revealed to be thoroughly contemptible. Brooke, who maneuvers ineptly, is seen to be quite the fool.

For George Eliot, the writer, the matter of tactics was vexing and vital because it seemed to compromise the sincerity required by the doctrine of sympathy. Even *Adam Bede*, which so convinced her Victorian readers of the author's sincerity, contains hints of the dilemma. The song that opens the novel and introduces the reader to Adam's workshop begins " 'Awake, my soul,' " and ends with an exhortation to sincerity:

> "Let all thy converse be sincere,
> Thy conscience as the noonday clear."
>
> [ch. 1, pp. 5–6

Later, in chapter 17, "in which the story pauses" for the purpose of awakening the reader's soul, the narrator says:

> Human converse, I think some wise man has remarked, is not rigidly sincere. But I herewith discharge my conscience, and declare . . . that human nature is lovable.
>
> [p. 157

Clearly, even at this moment of discharging his conscience, the narrator is at once skeptical and affirmative, coy and sincere.

In *The Mill on the Floss*, George Eliot either misjudged her audience (though I do not think so) or decided to take more risks with sincere human converse. She had the success of *Adam Bede* to encourage her to experiment, and in any case she could no longer hide behind her disguise. While still at work on the first book of *The Mill*, she was forced to reveal her identity after months of gossip that she tried to contradict in order to keep the secret. The gossip may very well have contributed to the hostility toward the public expressed in a good many of the narrative addresses.

In her second novel, George Eliot works to expose a certain superficial refinement exhibited by some women—including, doubtless, some of her female readers—by uncovering the vulgarity and hardness it conceals. When St. Ogg's passes judgment on Maggie, "we" dissolves into the "public opinion, [which] in these cases, is always of the feminine gender" (ch. 55, p. 428). Other comments are specifically addressed to male readers, challenging the rigid, reflexive, morally casual responses to be found among successful civil servants or businessmen. Several times the narrator singles out "a touch of human experience which I flatter myself will come home to the bosoms of not a few substantial or distinguished men."[10] Though the addresses to men are in no single instance as acerbic as the commentary on the "world's wife," their cumulative effect is likely to have been equally striking, if only because unusual in Victorian novels.

While the purpose of the direct address remains the same as in *Adam Bede*—to increase sympathetic response through an appeal to common experience—its general tone in *The Mill on the Floss* is markedly different. At best, and most often, the direct addresses include an appeal to the human fallibilities we all share; at worst they are condescending or sharply recriminatory. The appeal to common experience often contains irony or false testimony:

> Poor relations are undeniably irritating—their existence is so entirely uncalled for on our part, and they are almost always very faulty people.

> [ch. 8, p. 74

10. *MF*, ch. 43, p. 345; see also ch. 7, pp. 59–60; ch. 14, p. 127; ch. 17, p. 156; ch. 46, p. 358.

Whereas *Adam Bede* continually invokes the reader's "best self,"
the self *The Mill on the Floss* most often forces us to confront is
negligent, needy, and unmindful. "We spoil the lives of our neighbours," the narrator says, "without taking . . . much trouble":

> We . . . do it by lazy acquiescence and lazy omission, by trivial
> falsities for which we hardly know a reason, by small frauds neu-
> tralised by small extravagancies, by maladroit flatteries, and clum-
> sily improvised insinuations. We live from hand to mouth, most of
> us, with a small family of immediate desires—we do little else than
> snatch a morsel to satisfy the hungry brood, rarely thinking of
> seed-corn or the next year's crop.
>
> [ch. 3, p. 23

Repeatedly in *The Mill on the Floss*, George Eliot attempts to
force the reader's assent by making emphatic connections, ones
which put pressure on "distinguished men" and "refined" women
to see in their own world the narrow pettiness of St. Ogg's.[11] Her
use of the emphatic or coercive appeal dates back to "Janet's Repentance," as in this bald redress:

> See to it, friend, before you pronounce a too hasty judgement, that
> your own moral sensibilities are not of a hoofed or clawed character.
>
> [*SCL*, ch. 2, p. 324

She uses this mode of address, however, in a more intricate and
sophisticated way in *The Mill*. In *Adam Bede* she avoided caustic
remarks, in part because they had excited Blackwood's worry about
her Thackerayan cynicism. Her return to a sharply critical mode
suggests that the manipulation of tone was self-conscious, the irony
directed at the reader intentionally harsh.

If the coercive appeals in *The Mill* seem at times too severe to
be strategic, still, even the attacks on "good society" (and its "light
irony") show signs of the narrator's effort to exercise discretion.[12]
The "emphasis of want" passage, for instance, begins with an
apology accompanied by an appeal to authenticity:

> In writing the history of unfashionable families, one is apt to
> fall into a tone of emphasis.
>
> [ch. 32, p. 255

11. The appeal to "distinguished men" is from ch. 43, p. 345, but similar
addresses to the male reader appear in ch. 7, pp. 59–60; ch. 14, p. 127; ch. 17,
p. 156; and ch. 46, p. 358. References to "refined" ladies or women appear
throughout.

12. See chapter 5 above, pp. 191–92.

The effort to modulate tone is present both in these lines and those that follow. When the attack is most severe, the narrator substitutes vague noun phrases ("good society," "national life") and indefinite pronouns ("one," "it," "some") for the more directly implicating personal pronouns, restricting the "you" to the trivial but morally neutral act of inquiring "into the stuffing of your couch," and reserving "us" and "ourselves" for the sympathy needed when "human looks are hard upon us," or for calling forth an "active love for what is not ourselves" (pp. 255–56).

Still, as we saw earlier, the novel's strong social criticism and its effort to affirm "wide fellow-feeling with all that is human" are nonetheless dangerously pitched. Positive values are incorporated into the reader addresses principally by expressions of nostalgic reverence for the past and by strong assertions of fellowship.[13] The insistent linking of past and present forces upon the reader affirmations of wholeness and continuity at once organic and Wordsworthian, but the novel also makes clear that such unity exists neither in St. Ogg's nor in the world of George Eliot's contemporary readers. This desire for wholeness and the recognition of its absence often make the addresses that compare past and present unstable and disorienting in their irony. The strong assertions of fellowship, which tend to be made when the dramatic action is suggesting the opposite, are likewise precariously placed. Dr. Kenn, for example, through whom George Eliot attempts "to keep alive the sense of human brotherhood" in Maggie and the reader, is able to counter in only the most limited way the absence of true charity among his parishioners. Thus to say that "most of us . . . would have welcomed a priest of that natural order" speaks far more of wishful desire than to the overriding social realities that produce the extensive ironies of "Charity in Full Dress" (ch. 48, pp. 381–82).

The addresses that mediate most honestly between author and reader, then, are not those that assert all-encompassing fellowship or a beneficent natural order, but rather those that make discriminations between individual human beings and raise questions about order:

13. Auster, *Local Habitations,* discusses the "great store of nostalgic power and ready contrasts with the present" in the novels George Eliot set in the early nineteenth century. He also comments on her interrupting the narration to chide her readers for their ignorance "about the past and casual contempt for it," and to tease them for their "sense of superiority over past crudities" (pp. 57, 166).

But to minds strongly marked by the positive and negative qualities that create severity—strength of will, conscious rectitude of
purpose, narrowness of imagination and intellect, great power of
self-control, and a disposition to exert control over others—prejudices come as the natural food of tendencies which can get no sustenance out of that complex, fragmentary, doubt-provoking knowledge which we call truth. Let a prejudice be bequeathed, . . . however it may come, these minds will give it a habitation. . . . Our good
upright Tom Tulliver's mind was of this class.

[ch. 51, p. 400

In this passage the narrator adroitly separates us from Tom precisely
because "the mysterious complexity of our life is not to be embraced by maxims" or "formulas" (ch. 55, p. 435). That they "re-
press" our "growing insight and sympathy" is dramatized by Tom's
response to Maggie, and by Maggie's great terror of Tom—

afraid with that fear which springs in us when we love one who is
inexorable, unbending, unmodifiable—with a mind that we can
never mould ourselves upon, and yet that we cannot endure to
alienate from us.

[ch. 54, p. 422

The narrator not only makes the reader identify with Maggie's fear
of Tom but also endows Tom with the characteristics of the laws
of nature. "Inexorable, unbending, unmodifiable": they make no
allowance for loving one's neighbor.

MIDDLE NOVELS

Although *The Mill* alienated many readers, George Eliot won
them back with *Silas Marner*, not by molding the narrator to their
tastes and prejudices, but by toning down the "emphasis of want"
and by controlling more carefully the distance between author and
reader. The reader addresses again affirm the values dramatized in
the novel, the simple virtues of the hearth and neighborliness. The
connections between the reader's experiences and occurrences in
the novel are benign and positive, even when the narrator is critical:

I suppose one reason why we are seldom able to comfort our neighbours with our words is that our goodwill gets adulterated, in spite
of ourselves, before it can pass our lips.

[ch. 10, pp. 130–31

Because Silas begins as an outcast and has a "strange history," the
narrator carefully solicits our sympathy for uncommon experience,

but maintains a certain distance between the author and the reader lest the overture become too overbearing. Generally avoiding "we" and "our," the author implicates her readers from the safe remove afforded by references to "people," "a man," "a woman," "all men," "everyone," and "anyone." Such references are especially frequent when Silas is separated from the community of Raveloe and when Godfrey is alienated from himself.

At the same time, George Eliot allows the reader to identify with Godfrey's all-too-human reliance on chance and circumstance. The direct address is used to make this connection, but the move is quite safe. At worst the narrator allows the reader to identify with Godfrey, and he eventually redeems himself. More often, the reader is taken to be at least equal in moral sensibility and superior in general "culture" to the characters in the novel.[14] The contrast to *The Mill on the Floss* is striking. *The Mill*'s narrator alienates the contemporary reader from the familiar; in *Silas Marner* what at first is alien is made familiar. The generalized appeals to common experience benignly enlarge the reader's sympathies, extending his or her understanding without arousing hostility or resentment. Thus the distance works to intensify the sympathetic relation between author and reader.

Romola, too, keeps the reader at a distance, but the tone of the novel is entirely different, and both the historical and narrative distance all too real. A large number of the direct addresses are intended to dissolve the distance between the commercial societies of Renaissance Florence and Victorian England by suggesting that aggressive and destructive self-assertiveness is common to both. At several points the parallels between past and present depend on "our seeing" the Florentine Bardi family as "the Christian Rothschilds of that time" (ch. 5, p. 43). But the analogy is made quietly, so quietly that when reviewers complained it was because they failed to perceive any connection between Renaissance Florence and their own times. Victorian intellectuals appreciated *Romola*, in part because they found the resemblance between past and present finely drawn, but most of her readers thought the book impressively learned and oppressively lifeless.

Yet the relation between the indirect and direct address in *Romola* illustrates a groping movement toward the counterpoised complexity of response characteristic of her later novels. In this middle novel, the indirect address predominates. For the first time it is

14. See, for example, *SM*, ch. 3, pp. 79–80.

regularly sibylline, conveying large generalizations about the human condition:

> The same society has had a gibbet for the murderer and a gibbet for the martyr, an execrating hiss for a dastardly act, and as loud a hiss for many a word of generous truthfulness or just insight: a mixed condition of things which is the sign, not of hopeless confusion, but of struggling order.
>
> [ch. 57, p. 462

To counter the sense of life as thoroughly problematical, the voice of the sibyl speaks with certainty of "struggling order."

In contrast, the authorial voice of the direct address regularly draws the reader into the "helpless confusion" and doubt experienced by the characters. At the moment when Romola, despite her determination to leave Tito, worries nonetheless about "violently rending her life in two," the narrator says to "us":

> This act . . . had a power unexplained to herself, of shaking Romola. It is the way with half the truth amidst which we live, that it only haunts us and makes dull pulsations that are never born into sound.
>
> [ch. 36, p. 313

Similarly, when Savonarola's belief is being severely tested by the demand that he undergo trial by fire, the narrator writes:

> Savonarola could not have explained his conduct satisfactorily to his friends, even if he had been able to explain it thoroughly to himself. And he was not. Our naked feelings make haste to clothe themselves in propositions which lie at hand among our store of opinions, and to give a true account of what passes within us something else is necessary besides sincerity, even when sincerity is unmixed.
>
> [ch. 64, p. 511

The two kinds of solicitation—the unsettling and the reassuring—are at this point still uncomfortably at odds. The fact that the former, now stripped of its intimacy, predominates by way of the indirect address contributes to the lifelessness of the novel. So does the failure to achieve any real integration between the two voices. Attempting affirmations to quiet doubt, George Eliot moves toward and yet resists bringing to the forefront tensions vital to her work.[15]

15. Carole Robinson brings other material to bear on some of the points made here. She argues that "philosophic uncertainty is the keynote of the

Returning in *Felix Holt* to the England of the first Reform Bill, but this time exercising great discretion, George Eliot seems to heed the lessons she learned from the responses to *Adam Bede* and *The Mill on the Floss* and to employ effectively the distancing devices she developed in *Silas Marner* and *Romola*. One sign of the great self-control she characteristically brought to her authorial voice is the disparity between the benign, genial, expansive, and calm spirit reviewers attributed to the author of *Felix Holt*, and the suspicion, despondency, and self-doubt she regularly experienced while writing the novel. In a letter to Blackwood about *Felix Holt*, she speaks of having been frequently tempted by "Despondency":

> The tone of the prevalent literature just now is not encouraging to a writer who at least wishes to be serious and sincere . . . a great deal of this book has been written under so much depression as to its practical effectiveness, that I have sometimes been ready to give it up.
>
> [*Letters* 4: 247–48

However sincere she wished to be, the following three passages offer evidence of the discretion she was actually exercising. The first is from the same letter to Blackwood:

> I took a great deal of pains to get a true idea of the period. My own recollections of it are childish, and of course disjointed, but they help to illuminate my reading. I went through the Times of 1832–33 at the British Museum, to be sure of as many details as I could. It is amazing what strong language was used in those days, especially about the Church. The Times is full of turgid denunciation; "bloated pluralists," "stall-fed dignitaries" etc. are the sort of phrases conspicuous in the leaders. There is one passage of prophecy which I longed to quote, but I thought it wiser to abstain. "Now the beauty of the Reform Bill is, that under its mature operation the people must and will become free agents"—a prophecy which I hope is true, only the maturity of the operation has not arrived yet.

The second passage, from the Epilogue to *Felix Holt*, exemplifies the result of her abstention:

---

novel, and the source of *Romola*'s failure is to be sought not in its moral intentions or its didacticism, but in doubt, and in the novelist's uncertain faith in the affirmations she proposes in her effort to satisfy doubt" ("*Romola*," p. 31).

> Doubtless there is more enlightenment now. Whether the farmers
> are all public-spirited, the shopkeepers nobly independent, the
> Sproxton men entirely sober and judicious, the Dissenters quite
> without narrowness or asperity in religion and politics, and the
> publicans all fit, like Gaius, to be the friends of an apostle—these
> things I have not heard, not having correspondence in those parts.

The third, from chapter 16 of the novel, reveals how carefully she
shaped the materials she researched in the *Times*:

> At that time, when faith in the efficacy of political change was at
> fever-heat in ardent Reformers, many measures which men are
> still discussing with little confidence on either side, were then
> talked about and disposed of like property in near reversion. Cry-
> ing abuses—"bloated paupers," "bloated pluralists," and other cor-
> ruptions hindering men from being wise and happy—had to be
> fought against and slain. Such a time is a time of hope. Afterwards,
> when the corpses of those monsters have been held up to the public
> wonder and abhorrence, and yet wisdom and happiness do not
> follow, but rather a more abundant breeding of the foolish and
> unhappy, comes a time of doubt and despondency. But in the great
> Reform year hope was mighty.
>
> [p. 271

By enclosing the crying abuses in quotation marks, George Eliot
frees the narrator of responsibility for the comments: the judicious
historian simply quotes from the record. But she also silently revises it. Her list of abuses thus includes the rich and the poor, the
disreputable and the established, whereas the denunciation in the
Times speaks only of the upper classes. This trick of singling out
everyone and no one is used also in the Epilogue, where the tone
is mildly playful. In chapter 16, where there is cause for emphasis,
the voice is more meditative than emphatic, the reader present but
never directly addressed.

Throughout *Felix Holt*, elaborate strategems control the severity
of the social criticism, most of them distancing devices: personifi-
cation, chess analogies, large generalizations, deference to authority
(Euripides, Sophocles, Lucretius, the Bible, Dante, a German poet).
This strategy of not directly applying "the lash" becomes the subject of a long meditation at the end of chapter 42, one prompted by
the cutting and unquestionably sincere words spoken by Mrs. Transome in a confrontation with Jermyn. After it is over, the narrator
comments:

Men do not become penitent and learn to abhor themselves by having their backs cut open with the lash; rather, they learn to abhor the lash.

[p. 520

Again, the narrator refers to "men," and immediately before to "human beings," avoiding the direct solicitation except to refer at the end to "a touch of something that makes us all akin" (pp. 519–21).

In the passage on the "great Reform year," quoted earlier, the only strident notes sounded by the narrator occur in the sentence that speaks of "corpses" and "abundant breeding," words themselves related to the organic ideology of the novel. Throughout *Felix Holt*, organic beliefs permeate the direct addresses to the reader. The first extended direct address appears in this now famous passage:

These social changes in Treby parish are comparatively public matters, and this history is chiefly concerned with the private lot of a few men and women; but there is no private life which has not been determined by a wider public life.

The indirect opening turns soon enough into the direct solicitation of "lives we are about to look back upon," implicating us in the "mutual influence of dissimilar destinies which we shall see gradually unfolding itself" (ch. 3, p. 129). Regularly in the novel, almost everything negative, if not either distanced or mitigated by pity, is incorporated into the novel's essentially positive organic ideology.

MIDDLEMARCH

The direct addresses of *Middlemarch* employ with great frequency all the devices of the earlier novels, including the strategies of *The Mill on the Floss*. The result is not only astonishing complexity of tone but also continual confrontation with the author. The omnipresent solicitations are so adroitly handled as to make the constant interplay between narrator and reader extremely various as well. The boldest demand a pause; the subtlest leave the reader scarcely aware of having been drawn in. The passage depicting the "stealthy convergence of human lots," for instance, makes the reader stop short; one reviewer found it so arresting that he accused George Eliot of performing "the part of the 'destiny which stands by sarcastic.' "[16]

16. *M*, ch. 11, p. 70; *CH*, p. 348 ([A. V. Dicey], *Nation*, January 1873).

Other passages are shaped by an extraordinarily subtle movement between fictional character, narrator, and reader, creating an
interaction especially appropriate to a novel in which the reader is
required to feel and think from a number of different centers of
self. This movement, in turn, mirrors and extends the multiple
perspectives the narrator brings to the characters. Unlike "the
majority of us," the narrator says of Farebrother, for example, "he
could excuse others for thinking slightly of him, and could judge
impartially of their conduct even when it told against him." As a
result, however,

> The Vicar's talk was not always inspiriting: he had escaped being a
> Pharisee, but he had not escaped that low estimate of possibilities
> which we rather hastily arrive at as an inference from our own fail-
> ure. Lydgate thought that there was a pitiable infirmity of will in
> Mr. Farebrother.
>
> [ch. 18, p. 139

In contrast, we see that Dorothea, during the early days of her marriage to Casaubon,

> was as blind to his inward troubles as he to hers: she had not yet
> learned those hidden conflicts in her husband which claim our
> pity.
>
> [ch. 20, p. 148

As Jerome Beaty's conclusions about the nature of the revisions
in *Middlemarch* indicate, George Eliot often deliberately adjusted
the distance between omniscient author and a given character by
modulating the tone and emphasis.[17] His observations may be extended to the relation between author and reader. The dominant
forms of direct address in *Middlemarch*—their combinations and
relations to the earlier novels—suggest how self-consciously they
too had been shaped.

Unlike *Romola*, *Middlemarch* confronts the doubts it raises. A
comprehensive sense of human difficulty and complexity informs
one of the dominant patterns of direct address, bringing the reader
to the middle point of unresolved conflict that also characterizes
much of the novel's dramatic action. Often the novel disparages the
singularity of vision to which we are all liable (as in the Farebrother and Dorothea passages), or simultaneously affirms and questions

17. Beaty, *"Middlemarch," from Notebook to Novel*, pp. 112–117, and "The
Text of the Novel," pp. 43–45.

organic connectedness (as in the "stealthy convergence" passage).

The reader is also made to participate in such complexity through the extensive use of direct questions and through the numerous parentheses, which contain an overflow of unsuspected analogies and unexpected relations.[18] Both the Prelude and the Finale, for example, open with direct questions. George Eliot's earlier novels often use questions to bring the reader into the mind of a character, but in *Middlemarch* the direct question serves other purposes as well. The narrator frequently asks the reader a simple question and then provides an unsettling answer, or asks an unsettling question and confirms the disturbance in the answer:

> Will not a tiny speck very close to our vision blot out the glory of the world, and leave only a margin by which we see the blot? I know no speck so troublesome as self.
>
> [ch. 42, p. 307

In addition, the narrator often states a fact and then upends it with a question:

> The younger [Celia] had always worn a yoke; but is there any yoked creature without its private opinions?
>
> [ch. 1, p. 11

Intricate and inquiring, this mode of reader address is often attended by another. The second mode includes the appeal to common experience, but combines the negative summonings of *The Mill on the Floss* with the sympathetic identifications of *Adam Bede* and *Silas Marner*. The result is a gentle but persistent refusal to allow the reader to feel superior to a character. "We" are likely to be implicated even when the implied judgment is negative:

> In his closest meditations the life-long habit of Mr. Bulstrode's mind clad his most egoistic terrors in doctrinal reference to superhuman ends. But even while we are talking and meditating about the earth's orbit and the solar system, what we feel and adjust our movements to is the stable earth and the changing day. And now within all the automatic succession of theoretic phrases—distinct and inmost as the shiver and the ache of oncoming fever when we are discussing abstract pain, was the forecast of disgrace in the presence of his neighbours and of his own wife.
>
> [ch. 53, pp. 385–86

18. For a discussion of how the analogical correspondences make innovative use of the Comparative Method, see chapter 2 above, pp. 47, 67–69.

The first-person singular is also used more extensively in *Middle-march* than in any of the other novels, creating a third mode of reader address. The use of the intimate "I," by giving particularity to the hopes, fears, reflections, difficulties, and uncertainties of the narrator, suggests an effort (not always successful) to avoid the estranging tone of condescension common in *The Mill on the Floss* and to reduce the distance between author and reader. In *Middle-march*, the first-person commentary defines the way of the world or individual frailties but in a tone so modulated as even to be playful at times. Cautioning us, for instance, against the "too hasty judgment" of Casaubon made by Celia, Mr. Brooke, Mrs. Cadwallader, and Sir James, the narrator says:

> I protest against any absolute conclusion. . . . I am not sure that the greatest man of his age, if ever that solitary superlative existed, could escape these unfavourable reflections of himself in various small mirrors; and even Milton, looking for his portrait in a spoon, must submit to have the facial angle of a bumpkin.
>
> [ch. 10, p. 62

Often these three forms of direct address appear in a single passage; they also frequently incorporate the indirect address. Isolating Lydgate's "spots of commonness," the narrator says:

> The faults will not, I hope, be a reason for the withdrawal of your interest in him. Among our valued friends is there not some one or other who is a little too self-confident and disdainful; whose distinguished mind is a little spotted with commonness; who is a little pinched here and protuberant there with native prejudices; or whose better energies are liable to lapse down the wrong channel under the influence of transient solicitations? All these things might be alleged against Lydgate, but then, they are the periphrases of a polite preacher, who talks of Adam, and would not like to mention anything painful to the pew-renters.
>
> [ch. 15, p. 111

The "I" who solicits interest for a flawed character gives way to the "our" of common experience, negative but worthy of sympathy; the succeeding question affirms a disturbing truth. Then, incorporating the indirect address, the narrator refuses the role of the "polite preacher" who avoids what is "painful to the pew-renters." The narrator thus prepares for the particularized anatomy of Lydgate about to follow and hints that the reader will be sitting in the pew throughout the novel. But the passage's sharpness is also dulled in several ways: by moving away from "our valued friends";

by keeping in check the criticism of both the fictional character and the reader; by mocking the circumlocutions or "periphrases" of the narrator who nonetheless continues to use them in the next sentences:

> The particular faults from which these delicate generalities are distilled have distinguishable physiognomies, diction, accent, and grimaces; filling up parts in very various dramas. Our vanities differ as our noses do: all conceit is not the same conceit, but varies in correspondence with the minutiae of mental make in which one of us differs from another.

Employing highly formal scientific language, while deflating it by making "our noses" the measure of "our vanities," the narrator directs the irony against herself. As W. J. Harvey observes, "self-inclusive . . . irony" is a "device new to George Eliot's art," derived from the "stability of the author-novel relationship."[19]

The very poise of *Middlemarch*, however, upset the balance of the author-reader relationship for George Eliot's contemporaries. Central to that relationship is the coming together in this novel of the ideal of sympathy and the challenge of discomforting discovery. As a result, *Middlemarch* contains a fusion of the benign solicitations her readers welcomed in *Adam Bede* and the tense exhortations they resisted in *The Mill on the Floss*. The deliberateness of George Eliot's effort to create a blend that would be critical and corrective, without being offensive, may be seen in her revisions of the Finale's penultimate paragraph.

Common to all three versions is the direct address at the paragraph's close:

> But we insignificant people with our daily words and acts are preparing the lives of many Dorotheas, some of which may present a far sadder sacrifice than that of the Dorothea whose story we know.

This sentence exemplifies five characteristics typical of George Eliot's direct addresses: the appeal to common experience of the communalizing "we"; sharp criticism of the reader through "our daily words and acts"; sympathy for the character's sad "sacrifice"; identification with a world outside; and verification of the authenticity of the life dramatized within. At the same time, the tone of the entire paragraph is controlled by the preceding sentences, which in the two earlier versions contain a long indirect address. Its absence from the final version clearly softens the criticism of

19. Harvey, *Art of George Eliot*, pp. 88–89.

the reader; yet George Eliot resists substantive compromise even while working to modulate the tone. The three versions, with brackets added to mark the sections excised from the final text, read as follows.[20]

Manuscript (October 1872): Certainly those determining acts of her life were not ideally beautiful. They were the mixed result of young and noble impulse struggling [with imperfect conditions. Among the many criticisms which passed on her first marriage nobody remarked that it could not have happened if she had not been born into a society which smiled on propositions of marriage from a sickly man to a girl less than half his own age, and, in general, encouraged the view that to renounce an advantage to oneself which might be got from the folly or ignorance of others is a sign of mental weakness. While this tone of opinion is part of the social medium in which young creatures begin to breathe, there will be collisions such as those in Dorothea's life, where] great feelings will take the aspect of error, and great faith the aspect of illusion. For there is no creature whose inward being is so strong that it is not greatly determined by what lies outside it. [It is not likely that] a new Theresa will have the opportunity of reforming a conventual life. . . .

First Edition (December 1872, part-publication of Book Eight): Certainly those determining acts of her life were not ideally beautiful. They were the mixed result of young and noble impulse struggling [under prosaic conditions. Among the many remarks passed on her mistakes, it was never said in the neighbourhood of Middlemarch that such mistakes could not have happened if the society into which she was born had not smiled on propositions of marriage from a sickly man to a girl less than half his own age— on modes of education which make a woman's knowledge another name for motley ignorance—on rules of conduct which are in flat contradiction with its own loudly-asserted beliefs. While this is the social air in which mortals begin to breathe, there will be collisions such as those in Dorothea's life, where] great feelings will take the aspect of illusion. For there is no creature whose inward being is so strong that it is not greatly determined by what lies outside it. A new Theresa will hardly have the opportunity of reforming a conventual life. . . .

1874 Edition (final revision for book publication): Certainly those determining acts of her life were not ideally beautiful. They were

20. Jerome Beaty prints these three versions in "The Text of the Novel," pp. 59–60.

the mixed result of young and noble impulse struggling amidst the conditions of an imperfect social state, in which great feelings will often take the aspect of error, and great faith the aspect of illusion. For there is no creature whose inward being is so strong that it is not greatly determined by what lies outside it. A new Theresa will hardly have the opportunity of reforming a conventual life. . . .

While the second version is clearly more linguistically adroit than the first, the changes in content tend to be self-canceling. Whereas the manuscript version offers "nobody remarked," which the reader might have to regard as self-inclusive, the first edition restricts itself to those who live "in the neighbourhood of Middlemarch." Similarly, the "criticisms" in the manuscript are in the first edition softened to "remarks." But a reverse pattern, intensifying the indictment of society, is also present in the first edition: "her first marriage" is replaced by "mistakes" caused by outward conditions, and those conditions are more sharply and specifically delineated as the passage continues. Yet, though the criticism is in these respects more pointed, its very directness suggests, through the reference to "modes of education," a possibility for concrete institutional reform absent from the manuscript version.

As we noted earlier, the final alterations were most likely prompted by objections reviewers raised. Often in *Middlemarch*, when the criticism is severe, the narrator's "I" is absorbed into the "we," as in the "you and me" of the last sentence of the novel. However, in the first two versions of the penultimate paragraph, the "we"—followed as it is by "insignificant people" and preceded by a long, severe indirect address—seems to exclude the "I." To judge from the first responses, by the time the passage culminates in "we," the distance between author and reader was perceived to be complete.

The passage in the 1874 edition is somewhat softer and more balanced in its criticism. For those readers most in need of changing their ways, the attack becomes less alienating. Moving away from particularities and toward generalization, which nonetheless achieves something of a focus in the closing appeal for change, the emphasis now is on the narrator's wisdom. In keeping with the endless complexities explored in the novel, the stress falls on "the mixed result," when the specific charges go unmentioned. Then, too, the qualifying "often" lends more accuracy to the account. Changes such as these seem intended to answer the charge some critics made that George Eliot was oversimplifying in the end the complexities they had struggled to comprehend in the novel as a whole.

All these deletions and substitutions work to adjust the tone of the entire passage, in effect altering the import of the crucial last sentence, although its wording remains unchanged. Despite the trimming, a resistance to bending accompanies George Eliot's painstaking effort to moderate tone. A comparison of the three versions reveals a quiet return to sincere severity in the last. Replacing the "imperfect conditions" and "prosaic conditions" of the first two versions with "the conditions of an imperfect social state," George Eliot gently returns to society the blame the excised lines contain. If the measure of George Eliot's encounters with her readers is the extent to which she made them aware of the perplexing but vital connection between her charitable and critical voice—between the need for sympathy and for discriminating analysis—then she did indeed make her readers well in *Middlemarch*—so well, it seems, as even to have created a collaboration of sorts.

DANIEL DERONDA

In *Daniel Deronda*, George Eliot once again changed her tactics, bringing new devices to bear on the community of interests and feelings she wished to create. As always when her subject matter is the unusual rather than the ordinary, she relies less frequently on the direct address. Yet when she uses it, employing what by now is a panoply of familiar devices, she also focuses the reader address anew.

The theme of complexity, which characterized a dominant mode of reader address in *Middlemarch*, is given new emphasis. Now the stress falls on the difficulty of making connections but the need to make them nevertheless. The narrator's appeals to the reader dwell on comparison, difference, and combination—both valid and false —and on the need to discern their validity. The thematic connections we are asked to make include relations between past and present, general and particular, deeds and consequences, action and belief, life and art, science and poetry, the organic and the prophetic, working-day reality and the poetry of vision, sexual roles and morality. The forceful critique of single vision in *Middlemarch* becomes in *Daniel Deronda* an overt plea for perceiving wider relations. In *Middlemarch*, the addresses to the reader mediate and create tension, leading at most to nervous resolutions. In *Daniel*

Deronda, the attention to comparison and difference leads to arduous affirmations.

On one hand, the narrator speaks ironically of how "ignorance gives one a large range of probabilities" (ch. 13, p. 174); and sardonically of how "the truth is something different from the habitual lazy combinations begotten by our wishes" (ch. 22, p. 280). On the other hand, she warns the reader to "beware of arriving at conclusions without comparison" (ch. 4, p. 71), and demonstrates the power of comparison to correct:

> But a little comparison will often diminish our surprise and disgust at the aberrations of Jews and other dissidents whose lives do not offer a consistent or lovely pattern of their creed; and this evening Deronda, becoming more conscious that he was falling into unfairness and ridiculous exaggeration, began to use that corrective comparison.
>
> [ch. 32, p. 415

Simultaneously, the addresses to the reader regularly call attention to difference, to how "one man differs from another, as we all differ from the Bosjesman, in a sensibility to checks, that come from variety of needs, spiritual or other."[21] Difference too, the narrator points out, works as a corrective, making known things "which to you are imperceptible" (ch. 28, p. 370). Together, comparison and contrast extend the limits of the conceivable.

Extending those limits still further in *Daniel Deronda* is a new mode of reader address consisting of an often repeated imperative to "imagine." The narrator implores the reader to imagine a great many things about a good many characters. "Imagine a rambling, patchy house," she says, to open the chapter that describes Mrs. Glasher hidden away at Gadsmere. "Imagine," she says again a few pages later, as she brings Mrs. Glasher face to face with Grandcourt, "the difference in rate of emotion between this woman whom the years had worn to a more conscious dependence and sharper eagerness, and this man whom they were dulling into a more and more neutral obstinacy" (ch. 30, pp. 384, 391). We are asked also to "imagine" the condition of Gwendolen upon finding herself "disthroned" (ch. 26, p. 334). Later in the novel, when Gwendolen confesses to Deronda the guilt she feels after Grandcourt's death, the

---

21. *DD,* ch. 28, p. 370. The reference to the Bosjesman, the bushman of South Africa, further evidences George Eliot's interest in the Comparative Method of Social Dynamics (see n. 18 above).

narrator implores the reader to "imagine the conflict of feeling" her confessor felt (ch. 56, p. 754). The Princess' interview with Deronda offers a variation on this theme, as the question of what can be imagined becomes itself an issue. We move from sympathy to countercharge to mystery as the focus shifts from Deronda to the Princess to the reader.[22] In each of these instances, the power to imagine is brought to bear primarily on the lot of women, and in such a way as to make understanding the characters' feelings far more important than judging their failings. Given the severity of the charges that might be leveled against them (child-deserter, adulteress and kept-woman, perhaps even murderer), the pleas to imagine the plight of the Princess, Mrs. Glasher, and Gwendolen make daring claims on the sympathies of the reader.

Still, such claims are more an extension of old boundaries than a new departure. When the call to imagine combines with the need to compare, a more thorough innovation occurs. As noted earlier, some of the addresses in *The Mill on the Floss* are directed toward female readers, others toward males. In *Daniel Deronda*, the narrator's commentary often compares men and women but in such a way as to make the reader discount or disapprove of the conventional double standard. Referring to Gwendolen, the narrator says:

> To be a queen disthroned is not so hard as some other down-stepping: imagine one who had been made to believe in his own divinity finding all homage withdrawn, and himself unable to perform a miracle that would recall the homage and restore his own confidence. Something akin to this illusion and this helplessness had befallen the poor spoiled child.
>
> [ch. 26, p. 334

The substitution of "his" and "himself," in place of the female pronouns one would expect after "queen," is quiet here. Elsewhere, the double standard is more clearly a subject, as in this passage from the chapter that asks the reader to imagine Mrs. Glasher at Gadsmere:

> No one talked of Mrs. Glasher now, any more than they talked of the victim in a trial for manslaughter ten years before: she was a lost vessel after whom nobody would send out an expedition

---

22. As usual when the unconventional is at issue, the narrator maintains a distance. The question of what Deronda and his mother can imagine is presented in a dramatized scene (ch. 51, p. 694). When the reader is later invoked, George Eliot uses the conditional "you might have imagined" (ch. 53, p. 723).

of search; but Grandcourt was seen in harbour with his colours flying, registered as seaworthy as ever.

[ch. 30, p. 386

At the same time, the narrator exercises discretion by referring to "they" and "nobody" rather than "we," thus distancing the criticism. A similar modulation of tone, achieved by way of indirect address, a mode that includes generalized analytic commentary on human behavior, occurs in the following passage:

Lapidoth counted on the fascination of his cleverness—an old habit of mind which early experience had sanctioned; and it is not only women who are unaware of their diminished charm, or imagine that they can feign not to be worn out.

[ch. 66, p. 844

Another such passage opens with Gwendolen, and again renders what is imagined ironical to point out frailties both sexes share:

She was not without enjoyment in this occasion of going to Brackenshaw Castle with her new dignities upon her, as men whose affairs are sadly involved will enjoy dining out among persons likely to be under a pleasant mistake about them.

[ch. 35, p. 480[23]

The most radical and sustained of the appeals to imagine, however, originate in Deronda's relation to Mordecai. The most prominent of these appears in the chapter immediately following the meeting on the bridge at the close of Book Five. Its placement at the opening of Book Six is striking. "Imagine," the book begins, "the conflict in a mind like Deronda's, given not only to feel strongly but to question actively, on the evening after that interview with Mordecai" (ch. 41, p. 567). The entire chapter is devoted to Deronda's meditation on their meeting, a rumination that begins with Deronda's alarm at having been so stirred by Mordecai. Deronda then imagines Mordecai as Sir Hugo would describe him, "a consumptive Jew, possessed by a fanaticism," a judgment that expresses antagonisms the reader may at first be likely to share. Here and throughout the reader is required to participate in Deronda's imag-

23. This last example deals with imagination only by implication. There are also in *Daniel Deronda* direct addresses, which do not include an appeal to imagine, yet compare male and female models of behavior to negate the differences between the sexes enforced by the usual double standard. See, for instance, the long closing paragraphs in ch. 4 (p. 71) and ch. 14 (p. 193), the opening of ch. 15 (pp. 193–94), and the penultimate paragraph of ch. 24 (pp. 320–21).

inings in a sequence constructed so as to mediate between visionary enthusiasm and worldly response. At one extreme is Mordecai, whose "enthusiasm" makes him the "antipole" to what is "called 'a man of the world.'" At the other extreme is the "man of the world," who, knowing always "what to think beforehand," finds Mordecai a figure to ridicule. Daniel bears the accouterments of such a man; like him, he is a "white-handed gentleman" who "dressed for dinner" and "wore a white tie." But unlike his counterparts, among them the benign Sir Hugo and readers of the novel, he takes Mordecai seriously. As his meditation continues, the object of ridicule is reversed: ultimately the charge of vulgarity is laid not to the "poor Jewish workman" but to the "white-handed gentleman."[24] This strategy is used often in the novel, functioning elsewhere as it does here, first to indulge common biases and then to counterpoint or reverse the target of the parody or ridicule.[25]

Simultaneously in this chapter, several other kinds of mediation between inspired, passionate belief and conventional judgment are taking place. The appeal to imagine Deronda's conflict becomes an admonition against "dulness of imagination":

> If the influence he imagined himself submitting to had been that of some honoured professor, some authority in a seat of learning, some philosopher who had been accepted as a voice of the age, would a thorough receptiveness towards direction have been ridiculed? . . . Poverty and poor clothes are no sign of inspiration, said Deronda to his inward objector, but they have gone with it in some remarkable cases. And to regard discipleship as out of the question because of them, would be mere dulness of imagination.
>
> [ch. 41, p. 571

The effect is to separate Deronda from the reader, and yet to suggest connections, while affirming the standard of value toward which the reader should aspire:

> Our consciences are not all of the same pattern, an inner deliverance of fixed laws: they are the voice of sensibilities as various as our memories (which also have their kinship and likeness). And Deronda's conscience included sensibilities beyond the common, enlarged by his early habit of thinking himself imaginatively into the experience of others.
>
> [ch. 41, p. 570

24. Ch. 40, p. 552; ch. 41, pp. 567–68, 571.
25. See, for instance, ch. 42, p. 582; ch. 43, p. 604.

As Deronda's meditation unfolds, the power of imagination becomes synonymous with the strength to discover in all spheres of life:

> Columbus had some impressions about himself which we call superstitions, and used some arguments which we disapprove; but he had also some true physical conceptions, and he had the passionate patience of genius to make them tell on mankind. The world has made up its mind rather contemptuously about those who were deaf to Columbus.
>
> [ch. 41, pp. 572–73

The defense of imagination in chapter 41 is at the same time part of a larger argument about the relation between artistic representation and social value. We see Deronda grappling with the recognition that the heroic does not exist apart from but within the encumbrances of daily life. Regularly in *Daniel Deronda*, commonplace concerns and unseemly outward conditions accompany images of inner heroic life. At another such moment, George Eliot writes:

> Such is the irony of earthly mixtures, that the heroes have not always had carpets and tea-cups of their own; and, seen through the open window by the mackerel-vendor, may have been invited with some hopefulness to pay three hundred per cent in the form of fourpence.
>
> [ch. 43, p. 606

Such is the irony that even Deronda on occasion succumbs to "putting the lower effect for the higher."[26]

In this last novel, however, George Eliot often excludes the "irony of earthly mixtures" from the plea to imagine because of her own desire to affirm. She writes of Deronda, for instance, after he discovers his parentage:

> Imagine the difference in Deronda's state of mind when he left England and when he returned to it. He had set out for Genoa in total uncertainty how far the actual bent of his wishes and affections would be encouraged—how far the claims revealed to him might draw him into new paths, far away from the tracks his thoughts had lately been pursuing with a consent of desire which uncertainty made dangerous. He came back with something like a discovered charter warranting the inherited right that his ambition had begun to yearn for.
>
> [ch. 63, pp. 812–13

26. Ch. 41, pp. 567, 571; ch. 43, p. 606; ch. 47, p. 639. See also ch. 33, pp. 430–31 and the entry "Historic Imagination" in "More Leaves," pp. 355–56.

Still, the singularity of this affirmation is soon enough undercut by the mock heroic description of his "classical, romantic, world-historic position."[27] The earliest of the appeals to imagine associated with the Jewish theme offers a far more extreme example of George Eliot's tendency to omit from *Daniel Deronda* elements vital to her art. As might be expected, the summons is made in behalf of Mirah, surely the weakest character in the novel:

> Imagine her—it is always good to imagine a human creature in whom bodily loveliness seems as properly one with the entire being as the bodily loveliness of those wondrous transparent orbs of life that we find in the sea—imagine her with her dark hair brushed from her temples, but yet showing certain tiny rings. . . .
>
> [ch. 32, pp. 421–22

Another of the appeals to imagine, different because it is mischievous, occurs as Hans teasingly withholds from Mrs. Meyrick and Mirah the news from Italy.

> Imagine how some of us feel and behave when an event, not disagreeable, seems to be confirming and carrying out our private constructions. We say, "What do you think?" in a pregnant tone to some innocent person who has not embarked his wisdom in the same boat with ours, and finds our information flat.
>
> [ch. 61, p. 794

Hans, we are told a few pages later, "was given to a form of experiment on live animals which consisted in irritating his friends playfully" (p. 797). One wonders if George Eliot were not also being a bit mischievous at her own expense here—prompted, however, more by anxiety than playfulness. She knew full well that the experiment in which she was engaged was likely to be irritating to many. Worse yet, it might fall flat.

More typical of the appeals to imagine is this summons in behalf of Mordecai:

> Imagine—we all of us can—the pathetic stamp of consumption with its brilliancy of glance to which the sharply-defined structure of features, reminding one of a forsaken temple, give already a far-off look as of one getting unwillingly out of reach; and imagine it on a Jewish face. . . .
>
> [ch. 40, p. 552

27. Ch. 63, p. 815; see the discussion of *Daniel Deronda* in chapter 5, pp. 238–39.

A few sentences earlier Deronda and Mordecai turn "face to face . . . as if they had been two undeclared lovers." At the opening of the chapter, however, when Deronda thought to keep his distance from Mordecai, George Eliot writes:

> And yet it might be that he had neared and parted as one can imagine two ships doing, each freighted with an exile who would have recognised the other if the two could have looked out face to face.
>
> [ch. 40, p. 549

Not only does the novel bring face to face several individuals who are seeking community even while they are experiencing exile, but also, imploring her readers to imagine new possibilities, George Eliot looks out face to face.

For some of her readers the novel undoubtedly fell flat. Many others returned a hostile or troubled glance. Even if she did not win the assent of the latter, however, she was unquestionably still furthering her purposes. The language of Sidney Colvin's judgment eloquently testifies to the kind of community of interests she created, one free from the need for assent:

> Since the beginning of this year, Daniel Deronda and those about him . . . have been among the public personages whose doings and motives have been most warmly canvassed in newspapers and in common talk. . . . We have all had our say, and if to many the book has seemed not easy, and to some not agreeable, the interest of all is the great tribute to its power; find what faults we please, it is certain that no other writer living is able thus to arrest, occupy, and nourish our thoughts.
>
> [*Fortnightly Review*, p. 601

Daniel Deronda "is in everybody's hands," George Saintsbury wrote; and another reviewer insisted that George Eliot "has accomplished more for the cause of toleration and enlightenment than could have been achieved by any amount of legislation."[28] According to E. P. Whipple, her community of readers extended even to America:

> "Daniel Deronda" has been, during the past season, the one book which has attracted all classes of readers, which has been the subject of general comment, and which has elicited criticisms as diverse as the different points of view from which it has been surveyed. . . . To judge from the tone of the disputants, he [Deronda]

28. Saintsbury, *CH*, pp. 371–72.

appeared to be a much more real personage to them than Mr.
Tilden or Mr. Hayes.

[*North American Review* 124 (1877): 31

Writer as Citizen

"We have among us physicians, geometers, chemists, astrono-
mers, poets, musicians and painters, but we have no citizens."[29] So
Rousseau wrote in his *Discours sur les Sciences et les Arts* (1750).
The efforts of George Eliot and the Victorian social scientists to
further a revolution of consciousness made them citizens. Just as
Rousseau exemplified for George Eliot the role of artist as citizen
by awakening in her a "fresh world of thought and feeling," so she
came to have over her readers a similar kind of power (*Letters* 1:
277). He influenced her not by winning her assent but by arousing
new perceptions; she generated in her readers the same kind of
response. They often withheld consent, but their very resistance
contributed to the growing good of her fiction by helping to maintain the tensions characteristic of her best work, among them that
nervous belief in community she shared with such writers as Lewes
and Mill.

Sometimes her readers were slow to respond. "It takes the public
a long time," John Blackwood said, "to digest and fully appreciate
the value of such food and talk to their neighbors about it as we
found with Middlemarch" (*Letters* 6: 186). Eventually, however,
"the 'Great Teacher' that readers discovered in *Middlemarch*
brought George Eliot more letters than any other aspect of the
book." During the last years of her life, "scores of letters from unknown admirers poured into the Priory from all over the world."[30]
A few decades later the illustrious eleventh edition of the *Encyclopaedia Britannica* testified to George Eliot's "ever-growing army of
readers."[31] She had become an international figure, but the English
laid claim to her, declaring a "national calamity" when she temporarily stopped writing fiction, proclaiming a "national blessing"
when she promised them a new novel.[32] Her community of readers
considered her to possess the distinctive genius she revered in Rousseau, George Sand, Carlyle, and Ruskin: she had become the quint-

29. Jean-Jacques Rousseau, *Discours sur les Sciences et les Arts*, p. 150; my
translation.
30. Haight, *Biography*, pp. 451, 492.
31. *Encyclopaedia Britannica*, [1910] 11th ed., s.v. "George Eliot" by P. M. T.
C[raigie].
32. *London Quarterly and Holborn Review* 40 (1873): 99. *Letters* 6: 91.

essential "artist who rouses, and fires, and attaches her multitudinous readers."[33]

But while the community of interests and feelings she created among her readers transcended to some extent the tensions of her fiction, the embattled idealism that marked her career from beginning to end still shaped her authorial voice. Reflecting on the loss of social engagement in much of twentieth-century fiction, John Updike has observed that Faulkner was the last great example of a writer who could "draw tales from a community of neighbors":

> An instinctive, respectful identification with the people of one's locale comes hard now, in the menacing cities or disposable suburbs, yet without it a genuine belief in the significance of humanity, in humane significances, comes not at all.

George Eliot surely belonged to Updike's "vanishing breed—the writer as citizen";[34] yet a sense of community clearly came hard even to her.

Although she identified with the people of the Midlands—where she grew up and where most of her novels are set—the oppressive narrowness she knew existed there qualified her respect. Her own past, in turn, conditioned her attitudes toward community in the present. The retrospective point of view she employs in nearly all her fiction reveals how the past creates and coexists with the present: the Gemeinschafts of traditional community and Gesellschafts of modern society interpenetrate in her fiction, and within each an obdurate workaday world regularly contends with a poetic ideal of community. The continuing Gemeinschaft ideal of fruitful kinship ties, dignifying work, mutuality of obligation, social sympathy, and love is regularly disturbed, whether by narrow custom, class prejudice, or religious intolerance in traditional Gemeinschaft, or by contract and social convention in the marketplace world of Gesellschaft. Consequently community becomes for George Eliot, her characters, and readers a matter of consciousness, of discovering an interior poetry of community through self-awareness and social understanding. But this poetry often recoils from the empirical and concrete.

Similar in effect to the uneasy relation between George Eliot's prose and poetry of community is the relation her fiction establishes between the social organism as metaphor and as fact. When George Eliot resists taking the figurative for the literal, as she does in *Mid-*

---

33. *London Quarterly and Holborn Review* 40 (1873): 102.
34. John Updike, *Picked-up Pieces* (New York: Knopf, 1975), p. 489.

dlemarch, she writes a brilliant novel, but one that puts under severe stress the organic concepts she elsewhere attempts regularly to affirm. The affirmations, moreover, testify for the most part not to biological and sociological entities but rather to a myth or vision of organic unity.

Such confrontations between community as fact and community as consciousness are as important to George Eliot's addresses to the reader as they are to her natural history and organic fictions. She desired above all to generate change by transforming the perceptions of her readers, but her attitudes toward this surrogate "community of neighbors" were understandably mixed. "All originality is estrangement," Lewes once wrote; however, neither he nor George Eliot would resign themselves to this rueful fact. "The great thinker," they believed, had also to be "the secretary of his age":

> If his quick-glancing mind outrun the swiftest of his contemporaries, he will not be listened to; the prophet must find disciples. If he outrun the majority of his contemporaries, he will have but a small circle of influence.
>
> [*Problems* 1: 160–61

The day before the publication of the novel that became her first extraordinary success, George Eliot expressed both her fear of outstripping her readers and her desire for a wide circle of influence. Her comments on *Adam Bede* also suggest that the community of feeling she wished to create had by necessity to include herself. Writing to her publisher (who knew nothing about her), she remarks on "the depressing influences to which I am peculiarly sensitive," before saying: "I perceive I have not the characteristics of the 'popular author,' and yet I am much in need of the warmly expressed sympathy which only popularity can win" (*Letters* 3: 6). Over the years she spoke often of finding her "most precious encouragements" in letters from individual readers. Responding to one, she writes, "Indeed, after my husband's sympathy letters from those personally unknown to me are the only testimonies to the effect of my writing on which I thoroughly rely" (*Letters* 5: 373). She claimed especially to need "the support of sympathy and approval from those [few] who are capable of understanding" her aims, but her letters indicate how much she also wanted "to be read by the many." "My books," she once commented, "are written out of my deepest belief, and as well as I can, for the great public."[35]

35. *Letters* 4: 300; 3: 373, 405.

However, her beliefs and theirs were often at odds, which exerted a painful pressure, made all the more keen by her "disbelief in my own $\begin{cases} \text{duty} \\ \text{right} \end{cases}$ to speak to the public, which is apt with me to make all beginnings of work like a rowing against tide" (*Letters* 6: 387).

"She complained of being troubled by a double consciousness," Herbert Spencer reports, a split most obvious in Marian Evans's reentering society and winning social acceptance under a masculine pseudonym.[36] The Princess in *Daniel Deronda* also suffers from a "double consciousness" (ch. 51, p. 691). For the Alcharisi its source is creative achievement in conflict with traditional models of female identity, a tension felt also by her creator. Unlike the Princess, however, George Eliot achieves a compromise by appropriating into her work Victorian beliefs concerning woman's mission. But if her narrative voice is nurturing, kindly, and sympathetic, it is also skeptical and coolly analytic.

George Eliot strove continually to reconcile antitheses, to balance opposing forces, to discover integral truths concerning not only matters of gender but also of fact and value, sympathy and criticism, ideality and the hard, unaccommodating actual. She created her art from urgent needs, intellectual, spiritual, and emotional. Her own development confirms the belief she shared with the social theorists that "Art is in a state of perpetual evolution, new forms arise under new conditions."[37] Making the same point later, Tönnies identifies art with the recovery of community, insisting that the "artistic spirit . . . develops itself by absorbing new contents, which it reproduces in new forms." "All creative, formative, and contributive activity," he claims, "is akin to art and . . . an organic process by which human will flows into the alien matter and gives form to it."[38] At the same time, the characteristic forms and devices of literary works seem inevitably to express what Raymond Williams calls "the deadlocks and unsolved problems of the society."[39]

Everywhere in this study we have come upon deadlocks, finding theorists and novelist alike responding to the erosions of coherent social faiths and orders. Exploring the past, they might at least understand the relationship between communal and traditional values. They could be objective and tolerant when describing or dramatizing historical practices that appeared to them outmoded.

36. Spencer, *Autobiography* 1: 459.
37. Lewes, "Causeries," *Fortnightly Review* 6 (1866): 760.
38. *G&G*, pp. 148, 80.
39. Williams, *Long Revolution*, p. 69.

But they could not resist transferring their own needs to their idea of what community might be. Trying to replace religious with social belief, they held to an attenuated ideal of perfection, one that excluded the celestial city but embraced a secularized ideal of brotherhood—at the price, however, of compromising empiricism in philosophy and realism in art. The solutions they proposed were often frail, and many of the correctives to which they turned evaded concrete issues at hand. The role assigned to women in the revised organicism, for example, underscores rather than eliminates the deadlock. Another sign of stasis and paralysis is their failure to translate theory into practice, to effect changes in the visible structure of social institutions. Many of the characteristic forms and devices of George Eliot's art—patterns of imagery, character development, overall structure—reflect these problems. Her addresses to the reader suggest too how sympathy and public opinion were being asked to correct more than they possibly could.

Aware of inner oppositions, George Eliot and the social theorists always strove for fusions that involved integrating concepts and methods traditionally kept apart. Yet the desire to balance opposite claims had its own limitations. They attempted to be both attuned to gradual outward change and equipped for mental revolution, but while they understood the close relation between the public and the private, they did not consider fully enough how differences between the two might impede the transformation of each, nor did they take the similarities far enough. Their stress on revolution of consciousness speaks far more fully to individual dilemmas than to the transformation of public life. Their stress on organic wholeness and equilibrium entails a retreat from conflict and a failure to confront adequately the presence of violent self-assertion and uncontrollable aggression. In contrast, modern artists and social theorists often dramatize and explore an immersion in the destructive element that reveals savage, irreconcilable antagonisms within and between individuals and nations at every level of social development. Interdependence, instead of confirming organic wholeness, makes human needs and vulnerability more extreme—a paradox George Eliot recognized, although she and the others did not foresee some of the murderous movements of modern history.

But in many respects the divergence between what these Victorians were able to imagine and what they could accomplish defines the scope and limits of community in ways that speak as much to our world as to theirs. The concept of community continues to be both descriptive of social life and expressive of an ideal that might satisfy "our vague yearnings for a commonality of desire, a communion with those around us, an extension of the bonds of kin and friend to all those who share a common fate with us."[40] For us as well as for the Victorian writers, this ideal is beset by disparities between dream and actuality, fact and value. Both in their century and in ours, awareness of the need for reform has been far greater than the ability to restructure society, at least in the West. The crisis of belief experienced by many Victorians is if anything more pertinent to our times than to theirs, and many among us have responded as they did, by turning old answers into new questions, and acknowledging that our aims are unlikely to be realized, but yet refusing to give up.[41] They and we would have concurred with the second-century rabbi who said "it is not for you to finish the work, but neither are you free to desist from it." Implicit in much of the material explored in this study is a question still being asked today: Is there a way of understanding community that might enable the freedom of the individual and the fraternity of the community meaningfully to coexist? As did the Victorians, we attempt to preserve and strengthen the notion of community by incorporating into it the values of liberal theory—freedom, self-direction, autonomy. The effort to reformulate community still engages those who refuse to see the loss of community as a "necessary condition of the emancipation of the self-conscious, self-directing individual."[42]

For us and many of George Eliot's contemporaries, her genius resides not in resolving conflicts but rather in creating dramas that powerfully convey the difficulty of reconciling visionary and practical, individual and social values. The constant qualifications and persistent affirmations in her fiction together make known her "genuine belief in the significance of humanity, in humane significances." Questioning community at the same time she celebrated it, George Eliot established her citizenship in her own time and ours.

40. David W. Minar and Scott Greer, *Concept of Community*, p. ix. See also Raymond Plant, *Community and Ideology*, pp. 41–42; Jessie Bernard, *Sociology of Community*, pp. 3–5, 106–7, 180; Joseph R. Gusfield, *Community*, p. xvi; Dennis E. Poplin, *Communities*, pp. 7, 25.

41. See, for instance, the closing chapter of Irving Howe's *A Margin of Hope: An Intellectual Autobiography* (New York: Harcourt Brace Jovanovich, 1982).

42. Plant, *Community and Ideology*, p. 31; see also pp. 30, 32–34, 42, 51; Bernard, *Sociology of Community*, p. 30.

Selected Bibliography

Contemporary—frequently unsigned—reviews of George Eliot's work not included in *George Eliot: The Critical Heritage,* ed. David Carroll, are listed separately at the end of this bibliography.

Abbott, Evelyn, and Campbell, Lewis. *The Life and Letters of Benjamin Jowett.* 2 vols. London: John Murray, 1897.

Abrams, M. H. *The Mirror and the Lamp: Romantic Theory and the Critical Tradition.* New York: W. W. Norton & Co., 1958.

Alexander, Edward. *Matthew Arnold and John Stuart Mill.* New York: Columbia University Press, 1965.

Allott, Miriam. "George Eliot in the 1860's." *Victorian Studies* 5 (1961): 93–108.

Amberley, [Lady] K[atherine]. "The Claims of Women." *Fortnightly Review,* n.s. 9 (1871): 95–110.

Anderson, Quentin. "George Eliot in *Middlemarch.*" In *The Pelican Guide to English Literature.* Vol. 6. *From Dickens to Hardy,* edited by Boris Ford, pp. 274–93. Harmondsworth, England: Penguin Books, 1958.

Armstrong, Isobel. "*Middlemarch*: A Note on George Eliot's 'Wisdom.'" In *Critical Essays on George Eliot,* edited by Barbara Hardy, pp. 116–32. New York: Barnes & Noble, 1970.

———. *Victorian Scrutinies: Reviews of Poetry, 1830–1870.* London: Athlone Press, 1972.

Auerbach, Erich. *Mimesis: The Representation of Reality in Western Literature.* Translated by Willard Trask. Garden City, N.Y.: Doubleday Anchor Books, 1957.

Auster, Henry. *Local Habitations: Regionalism in the Early Novels of George Eliot.* Cambridge, Mass.: Harvard University Press, 1970.

Baker, William. *George Eliot and Judaism.* Salzburg: Institut für Englische Sprache und Literatur, Universität Salzburg, 1975.

————. "George Eliot's Projected Napoleonic War Novel: An Unnoted Reading List." *Nineteenth-Century Fiction* 29 (1975): 453–60.

Banks, J. A., and Banks, Olive. *Feminism and Family Planning in Victorian England.* New York: Schocken Books, 1964.

Barker, Ernest. *Political Thought in England from Herbert Spencer to the Present Day.* New York: Henry Holt & Co., [1915?].

Barth, Karl. Introduction to *The Essence of Christianity,* by Ludwig Feuerbach. New York: Harper Torchbooks, 1957.

Beaty, Jerome. *"Middlemarch," from Notebook to Novel: A Study of George Eliot's Creative Method.* Illinois Studies in Language and Literature, vol. 47. Urbana: University of Illinois Press, 1960.

————. "The Text of the Novel, A Study of the Proof." In *"Middlemarch": Critical Approaches to the Novel,* edited by Barbara Hardy, pp. 38–62. London: Athlone Press, 1967.

Bedient, Calvin. *Architects of the Self: George Eliot, D. H. Lawrence, E. M. Forster.* Berkeley: University of California Press, 1972.

Beebe, Maurice. " 'Visions Are Creators': The Unity of *Daniel Deronda.*" *Boston University Studies in English* 1 (1955): 166–77.

Beer, Gillian. "Beyond Determinism: George Eliot and Virginia Woolf." In *Women Writing and Writing about Women,* edited by Mary Jacobus, pp. 80–99. New York: Barnes & Noble, 1979.

Beer, Patricia. *Reader, I Married Him: A Study of the Women Characters of Jane Austen, Charlotte Brontë, Elizabeth Gaskell, and George Eliot.* New York: Barnes & Noble, 1974.

Bender, Thomas. *Community and Social Change.* New Brunswick, N.J.: Rutgers University Press, 1978.

Benson, James D. " 'Sympathetic' Criticism: George Eliot's Response to Contemporary Reviewing." *Nineteenth-Century Fiction* 29 (1975): 428–40.

Berlin, Isaiah. *Historical Inevitability.* London and New York: Oxford University Press, 1955.

Bernard, Jessie. *The Sociology of Community.* Glenview, Ill.: Scott, Foresman & Co., 1973.

Bissell, Claude. "Social Analysis in the Novels of George Eliot." *English Literary History* 18 (1951): 221–239.

Blake, Kathleen. "*Middlemarch* and the Woman Question." *Nineteenth-Century Fiction* 31 (1976): 285–312.

Bodichon, Barbara Leigh Smith. *A Brief Summary in Plain Language of the Most Important Laws Concerning Women; Together with a Few Observations Thereon.* 1854. Reprinted in part in *Victorian Women: A Documentary Account of Women's Lives in Nineteenth-Century England, France, and the United States,* edited by Erna Olafson Hellerstein, Leslie Parker Hume, and Karen M. Offen, p. 164. Stanford: Stanford University Press, 1981.

Bourl'honne, P. *George Eliot: Essai de biographie intellectuelle et morale, 1819–1854; influences anglaises et etrangères*. 1933. Reprint. New York: AMS Press, 1973.

Bray, Charles. *The Philosophy of Necessity; or, The Law of Consequences: as Applicable to Mental, Moral, and Social Science*. London: Longman, Orme, Browne, Green, and Longmans, 1841.

Brown, John Crombie. *The Ethics of George Eliot's Works*. 1879. Reprint. Port Washington, N.Y.: Kennikat Press, 1969.

Bryson, Gladys. *Man and Society: The Scottish Inquiry of the Eighteenth Century*. Princeton: Princeton University Press, 1945.

Bullen, J. B. "George Eliot's *Romola* as a Positivist Allegory." *Review of English Studies*, n.s. 26 (1975): 425–35.

Burrow, J. W. *Evolution and Society: A Study in Victorian Social Theory*. London: Cambridge University Press, 1966.

Cahnman, Werner J. "Tönnies and Marx: Evaluation and Excerpts." In *Ferdinand Tönnies: A New Evaluation. Essays and Documents*, edited by Werner J. Cahnman, pp. 219–38. Leiden: E. J. Brill, 1973.
———. "Tönnies and Social Change." In *Ferdinand Tönnies: A New Evaluation. Essays and Documents*, edited by Werner J. Cahnman, pp. 101–24. Leiden: E. J. Brill, 1973.

Cahnman, Werner J., and Heberle, Rudolf. Introduction to *On Sociology: Pure, Applied, and Empirical. Selected Writings*, by Ferdinand Toennies, edited by Werner J. Cahnman and Rudolph Heberle. Chicago and London: University of Chicago Press, 1971.

[Call, Wathen Mark Wilks, and Chapman, John.] "The Religion of Positivism." *Westminster Review*, American ed., 69 (1858): 167–92.

Carroll, David. "*Felix Holt*: Society As Protagonist," *Nineteenth-Century Fiction* 17 (1962): 237–52.
———. Introduction to *George Eliot: The Critical Heritage*, edited by David Carroll. London: Routledge & Kegan Paul, 1971.
———. " 'Janet's Repentance' and the Myth of the Organic." *Nineteenth-Century Fiction* 35 (1980): 331–48.
———. "Unity Through Analogy: An Interpretation of *Middlemarch*." *Victorian Studies* 2 (1959): 305–16.

Chase, Cynthia. "The Decomposition of the Elephants: Double-Reading *Daniel Deronda*," *PMLA* 93 (1978): 215–25.

Christ, Carol. "Aggression and Providential Death in George Eliot's Fiction." *Novel* 9 (1976): 130–40.

Coker, F. W. *Organismic Theories of the State: Nineteenth Century Interpretations of the State as Organism or as Person*. New York: Longmans, Green & Co., 1910.

Colby, Robert A. *Fiction with a Purpose: Major and Minor Nineteenth-Century Novels*. Bloomington: Indiana University Press, 1967.

Collins, K. K. "Questions of Method: Some Unpublished Late Essays." *Nineteenth-Century Fiction* 35 (1980): 385–405.

Comte, Auguste. *A General View of Positivism.* [*Discours sur l'ensemble du positivism,* 1848; incorporated into *Système de politique positive,* vol. 1, 1851.] Translated by J. H. Bridges. n.d. 1st ed., 1865; 2nd ed., 1880. Reprint. New York: Robert Speller & Sons, 1957.

————. *The Positive Philosophy.* [*Cours de philosophie positive,* 1830–42.] Freely translated and condensed by Harriet Martineau. [1853]. New York: Calvin Blanchard, 1855.

————. *System of Positive Polity.* [*Système de politique positive,* 1851–54.] 4 vols. Translated by John Henry Bridges, Frederic Harrison, Richard Congreve, et al. London: Longmans, Green & Co., 1875–77.

Congreve, Richard. "Mr. Huxley on M. Comte." *Fortnightly Review,* n.s. 5 (1869): 407–18.

Cooke, George Willis. *George Eliot: A Critical Study of Her Life, Writings and Philosophy.* Boston and New York: Houghton Mifflin Co., 1883.

Coveney, Peter. Introduction to *Felix Holt, The Radical,* by George Eliot. Harmondsworth, England: Penguin Books, 1972.

Cox, C. B. *The Free Spirit: A Study of Liberal Humanism in the Novels of George Eliot, Henry James, E. M. Forster, Virginia Woolf, and Angus Wilson.* London: Oxford University Press, 1963.

Cross, J. W., ed. *George Eliot's Life as Related in Her Letters and Journals.* 3 vols. New York: Harper & Brothers, 1885.

Darwin, Charles. *The Descent of Man and Selection in Relation to Sex.* [1871.] 2nd ed., rev. and enl. New York: D. Appleton & Co., 1898.

Dictionary of the History of Ideas, 1973 ed. S.v. "Organicism," by G. N. G. Orsini.

Duffin, Lorna. "Prisoners of Progress: Women and Evolution." In *The Nineteenth-Century Woman: Her Culture and Physical World,* edited by Sara Delamont and Lorna Duffin, pp. 57–91. New York: Barnes & Noble, 1978.

Duncan, David. *Life and Letters of Herbert Spencer.* 2 vols. New York: D. Appleton & Co., 1908.

Edwards, Lee. "Women, Energy, and *Middlemarch.*" *Massachusetts Review* 13 (1972): 223–38.

Eliot, George. *Adam Bede.* 1859. Reprint. Edited by John Paterson. Boston: Houghton Mifflin Co., 1968.

[————.] "Art and Belles Lettres." *Westminster Review,* American ed., 65 (1856): 343–56.

[————.] "Belles Lettres." *Westminster Review,* American ed., 64 (1855): 312–21.

[————.] "Belles Lettres." *Westminster Review,* American ed., 65 (1856): 160–72.

[————.] "Belles Lettres." *Westminster Review,* American ed., 66 (1856): 311–19.

————. *Daniel Deronda*. 1876. Reprint. Edited by Barbara Hardy. Harmondsworth, England: Penguin Books, 1967.

————. *Essays of George Eliot*. [1846–79?] Edited by Thomas Pinney. New York: Columbia University Press, 1963.

————. *Felix Holt, the Radical*. 1866. Reprint. Edited by Peter Coveney. Harmondsworth, England: Penguin Books, 1972.

————. *The George Eliot Letters* [1836–1881]. 9 vols. Edited by Gordon S. Haight. New Haven: Yale University Press, 1954–78.

————. *George Eliot's "Middlemarch" Notebooks* [1868–71]: *A Transcription*. Edited with an introduction by John Clark Pratt and Victor A. Neufeldt. Berkeley and Los Angeles: University of California Press, 1979.

————. *Impressions of Theophrastus Such*. Cabinet ed. Edinburgh and London: William Blackwood & Sons, 1879.

————. *The Legend of Jubal and Other Poems*. Author's ed. Boston: James Osgood & Co., 1874.

[————.] "Memoirs of the Court of Austria." *Westminster Review*, American ed., 63 (1855): 159–76.

————. *Middlemarch*. 1871–72. Reprint. Edited by Gordon S. Haight. Boston: Houghton Mifflin Co., 1956.

————. *The Mill on the Floss*. 1860. Reprint. Edited by Gordon S. Haight. Boston: Houghton Mifflin Co., 1961.

————. "More Leaves from George Eliot's Notebook." [1872–79?] Edited by Thomas Pinney. *Huntington Library Quarterly* 29 (1966): 353–76.

————. *Quarry for "Middlemarch."* [1868–72.] Edited by Anna T. Kitchel. In *"Middlemarch": An Authoritative Text, Background, Reviews, Criticism*, edited by Bert G. Hornback, pp. 607–42. New York: W. W. Norton & Co., 1977.

————. *Romola*. 1863. Reprint. Everyman's Library. London: Dent, 1968.

————. *Scenes of Clerical Life*. 1858. Reprint. Edited by David Lodge. Harmondsworth, England: Penguin Books, 1973.

————. *Silas Marner*. 1861. Reprint. Edited by Q. D. Leavis. Harmondsworth, England: Penguin Books, 1967.

Encyclopaedia Britannica, 11th ed. S.v. "George Eliot," by P. M. T. C[raigie].

Encyclopedia of Philosophy, 1972 ed. S.v. "Natural Law," by Richard Wollheim.

Ermarth, Elizabeth. "Incarnations: George Eliot's Conception of 'Undeviating Law.'" *Nineteenth-Century Fiction* 29 (1974): 273–86.

Feltes, N. N. "Community and the Limits of Liability in Two Mid-Victorian Novels." *Victorian Studies* 17 (1974): 355–69.

Feuerbach, Ludwig. *The Essence of Christianity*. Translated by George

Eliot [from 2nd German ed., 1843]. 1854. Reprint. New York: Harper Torchbooks, 1957.

Fricke, Douglas C. "Art and Artists in *Daniel Deronda*." *Studies in the Novel* 5 (1973): 220–28.

Geibel, James Wayne. "An Annotated Bibliography of British Criticism of George Eliot, 1858–1900." Ph.D. dissertation, Ohio State University, 1969.

Gilbert, Sandra M., and Gubar, Susan. *The Madwoman in the Attic: The Woman Writer and the Nineteenth-Century Literary Imagination*. New Haven and London: Yale University Press, 1979.

Gooch, G. P. *History and Historians in the Nineteenth Century*. 2nd ed. London: Longmans, Green, & Co., 1913.

Graham, Kenneth. *English Criticism of the Novel, 1865–1900*. Oxford: Clarendon Press, 1965.

Greenberg, Robert A. "Plexuses and Ganglia: Scientific Allusion in *Middlemarch*." *Nineteenth-Century Fiction* 30 (1975): 33–52.

Gusfield, Joseph R. *Community: A Critical Response*. New York: Harper & Row, 1975.

Haight, Gordon S. *George Eliot: A Biography*. New York: Oxford University Press, 1968.

————, ed. *The George Eliot Letters* [1836–1881]. 9 vols. New Haven: Yale University Press, 1954–78.

Hardy, Barbara. Introduction and Notes to *Daniel Deronda*, by George Eliot. Harmondsworth, England: Penguin Books, 1967.

————. "*The Mill on the Floss*." In *Critical Essays on George Eliot*, edited by Barbara Hardy, pp. 42–58. New York: Barnes & Noble, 1970.

————. *The Novels of George Eliot: A Study in Form*. London: Athlone Press, 1959.

————. *Rituals and Feeling in the Novels of George Eliot*. Swansea, Wales: University College of Swansea, 1973.

Harrison, Frederic. *On Society*. London: Macmillan & Co., 1918.

Harvey, W. J. *The Art of George Eliot*. New York: Oxford University Press, 1962.

————. "Criticism of the Novel: Contemporary Reception." In *"Middlemarch": Critical Approaches to the Novel*, edited by Barbara Hardy, pp. 125–41. London: Athlone Press, 1967.

————. "George Eliot." In *Victorian Fiction: A Guide to Research*, edited by Lionel Stevenson, pp. 294–323. Cambridge, Mass.: Harvard University Press, 1966.

————. "Idea and Image in the Novels Of George Eliot." In *Critical Essays on George Eliot*, edited by Barbara Hardy, pp. 151–98. New York: Barnes & Noble, 1970.

Heberle, Rudolf. Introduction to *Custom: An Essay on Social Codes*, by Ferdinand Tönnies. Gateway Edition. Chicago: Henry Regnery Co., 1961.

————. "The Sociological System of Ferdinand Tönnies: An Introduction." In *Ferdinand Tönnies: A New Evaluation. Essays and Documents*, edited by Werner J. Cahnman, pp. 47–69. Leiden: E. J. Brill, 1973.

Hennell, Charles Christian. *An Inquiry Concerning the Origins of Christianity*. [1838.] 2nd ed. London: T. Allman, 1841.

Hennell, Sara S. "Mr. Spencer and the Women." Letter to *Examiner*, 7 February 1874, p. 135.

Holmstrom, John, and Lerner, Laurence, eds. *George Eliot and Her Readers: A Selection of Contemporary Reviews*. New York: Barnes & Noble, 1966.

Horowitz, Lenore Wisney. "George Eliot's Vision of Society in *Felix Holt, the Radical*." *Texas Studies in Literature and Language* 17 (1975): 175–91.

Houghton, Walter E. *The Victorian Frame of Mind, 1830–1870*. New Haven: Yale University Press, 1957.

————, ed. *The Wellesley Index to Victorian Periodicals, 1824–1900*. 3 vols. to date. Toronto: University of Toronto Press, 1966–.

Huxley, Thomas Henry. *Evolution and Ethics and Other Essays*. New York: D. Appleton & Co., 1897.

————. "A Liberal Education; and Where to Find It." [1868.] In *Lay Sermons, Addresses, and Reviews*, pp. 31–59. London: Macmillan & Co., 1870.

————. "On the Physical Basis of Life." *Fortnightly Review*, n.s. 5 (1869): 129–45.

————. "The Scientific Aspects of Positivism." *Fortnightly Review*, n.s. 5 (1869): 653–70.

International Encyclopedia of the Social Sciences, 1968 ed. S.v. "Community-Society Continua," by Horace M. Miner.

Jackson, R. L. P. "George Eliot, J. S. Mill and Women's Liberation." *Quadrant* 94 (1975): 11–33.

[James, Henry.] "The Novels of George Eliot." *Atlantic Monthly* 18 (1866): 479–92.

Kakar, H. S. *The Persistent Self: An Approach to "Middlemarch."* Delhi: Doaba House, 1977.

Kaminsky, Alice R., ed. *Literary Criticism of George Henry Lewes*. Lincoln: University of Nebraska Press, 1964.

Kanner, S. Barbara. "The Women of England in a Century of Social Change, 1815–1914: A Select Bibliography." In *Suffer and Be Still: Women in the Victorian Age*, edited by Martha Vicinus, pp. 173–206. Bloomington & London: Indiana University Press, 1972.

Kent, Christopher. *Brains and Numbers: Elitism, Comtism, and Democracy in Mid-Victorian England.* Toronto: University of Toronto Press, 1978.

Killham, John. "The Idea of Community in the English Novel." *Nineteenth-Century Fiction* 31 (1977): 379–96.

———. *Tennyson and "The Princess": Reflections of an Age.* London: Athlone Press, 1958.

Kingsley, Charles. "Robert Owen's First Principle." Letter to *Leader* 1 (1850): 613–14.

Kitchel, Anna, ed. *"Quarry for 'Middlemarch'* by George Eliot." In *"Middlemarch": An Authoritative Text, Background, Reviews, Criticism,* edited by Bert G. Hornback, pp. 607–42. New York: W. W. Norton & Co., 1977.

Knoepflmacher, U. C. "George Eliot." In *Victorian Fiction: A Second Guide to Research,* edited by George H. Ford, pp. 234–73. New York: Modern Language Association of America, 1978.

———. *George Eliot's Early Novels: The Limits of Realism.* Berkeley and Los Angeles: University of California Press, 1968.

———. *Religious Humanism and the Victorian Novel: George Eliot, Walter Pater, and Samuel Butler.* Princeton: Princeton University Press, 1965.

Kroeber, Karl. *Styles in Fictional Structure: The Art of Jane Austen, Charlotte Brontë, George Eliot.* Princeton: Princeton University Press, 1971.

Krouse, Richard W. "Patriarchal Liberalism and Beyond: From John Stuart Mill to Harriet Taylor." In *The Family in Political Thought: Past and Present,* edited by Jean Bethke Elshtain, pp. 145–72. Amherst: University of Massachusetts Press, 1982.

Leavis, F. R. *The Great Tradition: George Eliot, Henry James, Joseph Conrad.* London: Chatto & Windus, 1950.

Leavis, Q. D. Introduction to *Silas Marner,* by George Eliot. Harmondsworth, England: Penguin Books, 1967.

Lee, R. H. "The Unity of *The Mill on the Floss.*" *English Studies in Africa* 7 (1964): 34–53.

Levine, George. *The Boundaries of Fiction: Carlyle, Macaulay, Newman.* Princeton: Princeton University Press, 1968.

———. "Determinism and Responsibility in the Works of George Eliot." *PMLA* 77 (1962): 268–79.

———. "George Eliot's Hypothesis of Reality." *Nineteenth-Century Fiction* 35 (1980): 1–28.

———. "Intelligence as Deception: *The Mill on the Floss.*" *PMLA* 80 (1965): 402–9.

———. *The Realistic Imagination: English Fiction from Frankenstein to Lady Chatterley.* Chicago: University of Chicago Press, 1981.

Lévy-Bruhl, L. *The Philosophy of Auguste Comte.* 1903. Reprint. Clifton, N.J.: Augustus M. Kelley, 1973.

[Lewes, George Henry.] "The Art of History—Macaulay." *British Quarterly Review* 23 (1856): 297–325.

————. "Auguste Comte." *Fortnightly Review* 3 (1866): 385–410.

————. *The Biographical History of Philosophy: From Its Origin in Greece Down to the Present Day.* [1845–46.] 2 vols., rev. and enl. Library ed. [1857]. New York: D. Appleton & Co., 1881.

[————.] "Buchez and Daunou on the Science of History." *Foreign Quarterly Review*, American ed., 32 (1844): 176–88.

————. "Causeries." *Fortnightly Review* 6 (1866): 757–62.

————. "Communism as an Ideal." *Leader* 1 (1850): 733–34.

————. "Comte and Mill." *Fortnightly Review* 6 (1866): 385–406.

————. *Comte's Philosophy of the Sciences: Being an Exposition of the Principles of the "Cours de Philosophie Positive" of Auguste Comte.* [1852–53.] London: George Bell & Sons, 1883.

————. "Dickens in Relation to Criticism." *Fortnightly Review*, n.s. 11 (1872): 141–54.

[————.] "History by Modern Frenchmen." *British Quarterly Review* 14 (1851): 405–37.

[————.] "Mrs. Grundy and the Public Press." *Leader* 1 (1850): 36.

————. *The Principles of Success in Literature.* In *Fortnightly Review* 1 (1865): 85–95, 185–96, 572–89, 697–709; *Fortnightly Review* 2 (1865): 257–68, 689–710.

————. *Problems of Life and Mind.* 5 vols. 1874–79. Vols. 1–2. *The Foundations of a Creed.* Boston: James R. Osgood & Co., 1874–75. Vol. 4. *The Study of Psychology: Its Object, Scope, and Method.* London: Trübner & Co., 1879.

[————.] "Realism in Art: Recent German Fiction." *Westminster Review*, American ed., 70 (1858): 271–87.

[————.] "Sidney Smith's Mother Country." *Leader* 1 (1850): 663.

[————.] "Socialism." *Leader* 1 (1850): 204.

[————.] "The State of Historical Science in France." *British and Foreign Review* 31 (1844): 72–118.

[————.] "The Thirty Years' Peace." *British Quarterly Review* 11 (1850): 355–71.

Loomis, Charles P., and McKinney, John C. Introduction to *Community and Society (Gemeinschaft und Gesellschaft)*, by Ferdinand Tönnies. Translated and edited by Charles P. Loomis. New York: Harper & Row, 1963.

Maine, Sir Henry Sumner. *Ancient Law: Its Connection with the Early History of Society and its Relation to Modern Ideas.* [1861.] New York: Henry Holt & Co., 1906.

Mandelbaum, Maurice. *History, Man, & Reason: A Study in Nineteenth-*

Century Thought. Baltimore and London: Johns Hopkins Press, 1971.

Mansell, Darrel, Jr. "George Eliot's Conception of 'Form.'" *Studies in English Literature* 5 (1965): 651–62.

Marcus, Steven. "Literature and Social Theory: Starting In with George Eliot." In *Representations: Essays on Literature and Society*, pp. 183–213. New York: Random House, 1975.

Martin, Graham. "*Daniel Deronda*: George Eliot and Political Change." In *Critical Essays on George Eliot*, edited by Barbara Hardy, pp. 133–50. New York: Barnes & Noble, 1970.

Martindale, Don. *Community, Character, and Civilization: Studies in Social Behaviorism*. Glencoe, Ill.: Free Press of Glencoe, 1963.

Marx, Karl, and Engels, Frederick. *Collected Works*. 17 vols. to date. New York: International Publishers, 1975–. Vol. 5, *Marx and Engels, 1845–1847*, Karl Marx ["Theses on Feuerbach"], pp. 3–5, 1976.

Mason, Michael York. "*Middlemarch* and Science: Problems of Life and Mind." *Review of English Studies*, n.s. 22 (1971): 151–69.

Mill, John Stuart. *Auguste Comte and Positivism*. London: N. Trübner & Co., 1865.

———. *Autobiography*. [1873.] Edited by Jack Stillinger. Boston: Houghton Mifflin Co., 1969.

———. *Collected Works of John Stuart Mill*. J. M. Robson, General Editor. 19 vols. to date. Toronto and London: University of Toronto Press and Routledge & Kegan Paul, 1963–. Vols. 2–3, *Principles of Political Economy with Some of Their Applications to Social Philosophy* [1848], edited by J. M. Robson, 1965. Vols. 7–8, *A System of Logic Ratiocinative and Inductive* [1843], edited by J. M. Robson, 1973. Vol. 18, *Essays on Politics and Society, On Liberty* [1859], edited by J. M. Robson, pp. 213–310, 1977.

———. *Dissertations and Discussions: Political, Philosophical, and Historical*. 3 vols. Boston: William V. Spencer, 1865. Vol. 1. "Thoughts on Poetry and Its Varieties," pp. 89–120.

———. *The Subjection of Women*. [1869.] Reprinted in *Essays on Sex Equality: John Stuart Mill and Harriet Taylor Mill*, edited by Alice S. Rossi, pp. 125–242. Chicago and London: University of Chicago Press, 1970.

Miller, J. Hillis. "Narrative and History." *English Literary History* 41 (1974): 455–73.

———. "Optic and Semiotic in *Middlemarch*." In *The Worlds of Victorian Fiction*, edited by Jerome Buckley, pp. 125–45. Harvard English Studies 6. Cambridge, Mass.: Harvard University Press, 1975.

Milner, Ian. *The Structure of Values in George Eliot*. Acta Universitatis Carolinae Philologica, Monographia 23. Prague: Universita Karlova, 1968.

Minar, David W. and Greer, Scott, eds. *The Concept of Community: Readings with Interpretations*. Chicago: Aldine Publishing Co., 1969.

Mintz, Alan. *George Eliot and the Novel of Vocation*. Cambridge, Mass.: Harvard University Press, 1978.

Morley, John. Review of *The Social and Political Dependence of Women*. *Fortnightly Review*, n.s. 1 (1867): 764–65.

Murphy, Howard R. "The Ethical Revolt against Christian Orthodoxy in Early Victorian England." *American Historical Review* 60 (1955): 800–17.

Myers, William. "George Eliot: Politics and Personality." In *Literature and Politics in the Nineteenth Century*, edited by John Lucas, pp. 105–129. London: Methuen & Co., 1971.

Newton, K. M. "George Eliot, George Henry Lewes, and Darwinism." *Durham University Journal*, n.s. 35 (1974): 278–93.

———. *George Eliot, Romantic Humanist: A Study of the Philosophical Structure of Her Novels*. Totowa, N.J.: Barnes & Noble, 1981.

Nisbet, Robert A. *History of the Idea of Progress*. New York: Basic Books, 1980.

———. *Social Change and History: Aspects of the Western Theory of Development*. New York: Oxford University Press, 1969.

———. *The Social Philosophers: Community and Conflict in Western Thought*. New York: Thomas Y. Crowell Co., 1973.

———. *The Sociological Tradition*. New York: Basic Books, 1966.

Noble, Thomas A. *George Eliot's "Scenes of Clerical Life."* New Haven: Yale University Press, 1965.

Pappenheim, Fritz. *The Alienation of Modern Man: An Interpretation Based on Marx and Tönnies*. New York and London: Modern Reader Paperbacks, 1959.

Paris, Bernard J. *Experiments in Life: George Eliot's Quest for Values*. Detroit: Wayne State University Press, 1965.

Pinney, Thomas. "The Authority of the Past in George Eliot's Novels." *Nineteenth-Century Fiction* 21 (1966): 131–47.

———, ed. *Essays of George Eliot*. New York: Columbia University Press, 1963.

———, ed. "More Leaves from George Eliot's Notebook." *Huntington Library Quarterly* 29 (1966): 353–76.

Plant, Raymond. *Community and Ideology: An Essay in Applied Social Philosophy*. London and Boston: Routledge & Kegan Paul, 1974.

Poplin, Dennis E. *Communities: A Survey of Theories and Methods of Research*. New York: Macmillan Co., 1972.

Popper, Karl R. *The Poverty of Historicism*. Boston: Beacon Press, 1957.

Pratt, John Clark, and Neufeldt, Victor A., eds. *George Eliot's "Middle-*

march" Notebooks: A Transcription. Berkeley and Los Angeles: University of California Press, 1979.

Preyer, Robert. "Beyond the Liberal Imagination: Vision and Unreality in *Daniel Deronda*." *Victorian Studies* 4 (1960): 33–54.

Putzell, Sara M. " 'An Antagonism of Valid Claims': The Dynamics of *The Mill on the Floss*." *Studies in the Novel* 7 (1975): 227–44.

Redinger, Ruby V. *George Eliot: The Emergent Self*. New York: Alfred A. Knopf, 1975.

Riehl, W. H. *Die bürgerliche Gesellschaft* [1851.] 8th ed. Stuttgart: Verlag der J. G. Gotta'schen Buchhandlung, 1885.

———. *Land und Leute*. [1853.] 8th ed. Stuttgart: Verlag der J. G. Gotta'schen Buchhandlung, 1883.

Roberts, Neil. *George Eliot: Her Beliefs and Her Art*. N.p., University of Pittsburgh Press, 1975.

Robinson, Carole. "*Romola*: A Reading of the Novel." *Victorian Studies* 6 (1962): 29–42.

Robson, John M. *The Improvement of Mankind: The Social and Political Thought of John Stuart Mill*. London: Routledge & Kegan Paul, 1968.

Rousseau, Jean-Jacques. *Discours sur les Sciences et les Arts*. [1750.] Edited by George R. Havens. New York: Modern Language Association of America, 1946.

Rumney, Jay. *Herbert Spencer's Sociology: A Study in the History of Social Theory*. 1937. Reprint. New York: Atherton Press, 1966.

Salomon, Albert. "In Memoriam Ferdinand Tönnies." In *Ferdinand Tönnies: A New Evaluation. Essays and Documents*, edited by Werner J. Cahnman, pp. 33–46. Leiden: E. J. Brill, 1973.

Sambrook, A. J. "The Natural Historian of Our Social Classes." *English* 14 (1963): 130–34.

Scott, James F. "George Eliot, Positivism, and the Social Vision of *Middlemarch*." *Victorian Studies* 16 (1972): 59–76.

Shanley, Mary Lyndon. "Marital Slavery and Friendship: John Stuart Mill's *The Subjection of Women*." *Political Theory* 9 (1981): 229–47.

Showalter, Elaine. "The Greening of Sister George." *Nineteenth-Century Fiction* 35 (1980): 292–311.

———. *A Literature of Their Own: British Women Novelists from Brontë to Lessing*. Princeton: Princeton University Press, 1977.

Simon, W. M. *European Positivism in the Nineteenth Century: An Essay in Intellectual History*. Ithaca: Cornell University Press, 1963.

Smelser, Neil J., ed. *Sociology: An Introduction*. 2nd ed. New York: John Wiley & Sons, 1973.

Spacks, Patricia Meyer. *The Female Imagination*. New York: Alfred A. Knopf, 1975.

Spencer, Herbert. *An Autobiography.* 2 vols. New York: D. Appleton and Co., 1904.

————. "Bain on the Emotions and the Will." [1860.] In Herbert Spencer, *Illustrations of Universal Progress,* pp. 288–312. New York: D. Appleton & Co., 1880.

————. "The Development Hypothesis." [1852.] In *Illustrations of Universal Progress,* pp. 365–71. New York: D. Appleton & Co., 1880.

————. *First Principles.* New York: D. Appleton & Co., 1862.

[————.] "Manners and Fashion." *Westminster Review,* American ed., 61 (1854): 189–208.

[————.] "The Philosophy of Style." *Westminster Review,* American ed., 58 (1852): 234–47.

————. *Principles of Biology.* [1864–67.] 2 vols. American ed. New York: D. Appleton & Co., 1896.

————. *Principles of Ethics.* [1879–93.] 2 vols. Westminster ed. New York: D. Appleton & Co., 1892–93.

————. *Principles of Sociology.* [1876–96; incorporates *The Study of Sociology,* 1873–78.] 3rd ed., rev. and enl. New York: D. Appleton & Co., 1888.

————. *Principles of Psychology.* [1855.] 2 vols. 3rd ed. New York: D. Appleton & Co., 1897.

[————.] "Progress: Its Law and Cause." *Westminster Review,* American ed., 67 (1857): 244–67.

————. *"Reasons for Dissenting From the Philosophy of M. Comte,"* and Other Essays. 1864–76. Reprint. Berkeley: The Glendessary Press, 1968.

[————.] "The Social Organism." *Westminster Review,* American ed., 73 (1860): 51–68.

————. *Social Statics; or, The Conditions Essential to Human Happiness.* [1850.] American ed. New York: D. Appleton & Co., 1865.

[————.] "A Theory of Population, Deduced from the General Law of Animal Fertility." *Westminster Review,* American ed., 57 (1852): 250–68.

[————.] "The Universal Postulate." *Westminster Review,* American ed., 60 (1853): 269–88.

————. "The Use of Anthropomorphism." [1853.] In *Illustrations of Universal Progress,* pp. 428–34. New York: D. Appleton & Co., 1880.

Squires, Michael. *The Pastoral Novel: Studies in George Eliot, Thomas Hardy, and D. H. Lawrence.* Charlottesville: University of Virginia Press, 1974.

Stang, Richard. *The Theory of the Novel in England, 1850–70.* London: Routledge & Kegan Paul, 1959.

Stephen, Leslie. *George Eliot.* New York: Macmillan Co., 1902.

Strachey, Ray. *"The Cause": A Short History of the Women's Move-*

ment in Great Britain. 1928. Reprint. Port Washington, N.Y.: Kennikat Press, 1969.

Strauss, David Friedrich. *The Life of Jesus, Critically Examined.* 3 vols. Translated by [George Eliot] from 4th German ed. [1840]. London: Chapman Brothers, 1846.

——. *A New Life of Jesus.* [1864.] 2 vols. Authorized translation. 2nd ed. London: Williams and Norgate, 1879.

Stump, Reva. *Movement and Vision in George Eliot's Novels.* Seattle: University of Washington Press, 1959.

Teggart, Frederick J. *Theory and Processes of History.* 1918 and 1925. Reprint. Berkeley and Los Angeles: University of California Press, 1960.

Thomson, Fred C. "The Legal Plot in *Felix Holt.*" *Studies in English Literature* 7 (1967): 691–704.

——. "Politics and Society in *Felix Holt.*" In *The Classic British Novel,* edited by Howard M. Harper, Jr. and Charles Edge, pp. 103–120. Athens: University of Georgia Press, 1972.

Tjoa, Hock Guan. *George Henry Lewes: A Victorian Mind.* Cambridge, Mass.: Harvard University Press, 1977.

Tönnies, Ferdinand. *Community and Society (Gemeinschaft und Gesellschaft).* [1887.] Translated and edited by Charles P. Loomis. New York: Harper & Row, 1963.

——. *Custom: An Essay on Social Codes.* [1909.] Translated by A. Farrell Borenstein. Chicago: Free Press, 1961.

——. *On Sociology: Pure, Applied, and Empirical. Selected Writings.* [1887–1935.] Edited by Werner J. Cahnman and Rudolf Heberle. Chicago and London: University of Chicago Press, 1971.

Watt, Ian. *The Rise of the Novel: Studies in Defoe, Richardson, and Fielding.* Berkeley and Los Angeles: University of California Press, 1959.

Wharton, John Jane Smith. *An Exposition of the Laws Relating to the Women of England.* London: Longman, Brown, Green and Longmans, 1853.

Whitehead, Alfred North. *Adventures of Ideas.* New York: Macmillan Co., 1933.

Wiesenfarth, Joseph. *George Eliot's Mythmaking.* Heidelberg: Carl Winter Universitätsverlag, 1977.

Willey, Basil. *Nineteenth Century Studies.* New York: Columbia University Press, 1949.

Williams, Raymond. *The Country and the City.* New York: Oxford University Press, 1973.

——. *Culture and Society: 1780–1950.* [1958.] New York: Harper & Row, 1966.

————. *The English Novel from Dickens to Lawrence.* New York: Oxford University Press, 1970.

————. *The Long Revolution.* New York: Columbia University Press, 1961.

Witemeyer, Hugh. *George Eliot and the Visual Arts.* New Haven and London: Yale University Press, 1979.

Wolff, Michael. "Marian Evans to George Eliot: The Moral and Intellectual Foundations of Her Career." Ph.D. dissertation, Princeton University, 1958.

————. *"The British Controversialist and Impartial Inquirer,* 1850–1872: A Pearl from the Golden Stream." In *The Victorian Periodical Press: Samplings and Soundings,* edited by Joanne Shattock and Michael Wolff, pp. 367–92. Leicester: Leicester University Press, 1982.

————. "Victorian Reviewers and Cultural Responsibility." In *1859: Entering an Age of Crisis,* edited by Philip Appleman, William A. Madden, and Michael Wolff, pp. 269–89. Bloomington: Indiana University Press, 1959.

The Woman Question: Papers Reprinted From "The Examiner." London: R. H. Lapham, 1872.

Woolf, Virginia. "George Eliot." [*Times Literary Supplement,* 20 November 1919.] In *The Common Reader,* pp. 166–76. New York: Harcourt, Brace & World, 1925.

Contemporary Reviews

Academy 18 (1880): 460.
Athenaeum, 26 February 1859, p. 284. [Geraldine Jewsbury.]
————, 7 April 1860, pp. 467–68.
————, 7 December 1872, pp. 725–26.
————, 1 July 1876, pp. 14–15.
Atlantic Monthly 18 (1866): 479–92. [Henry James.]
Blackwood's Edinburgh Magazine 85 (1859): 490–504. [W. Lucas Collins.]
British Controversialist and Literary Magazine, 3d ser. 2 (1859): 268–73.
————, 3d ser. 3 (1860): 412–16.
British Quarterly Review 45 (1867): 141–78.
————, American ed., 57 (1873): 218–29. [Richard Holt Hutton.]
Contemporary Review 20 (1872): 403–22. Edward Dowden.
Daily News, 28 November 1871, p. 5.
Edinburgh Review, American ed., 110 (1859): 114–25. [John Forster.]
————, American ed., 137 (1873): 126–35. [Richard Monckton Milnes.]
Examiner, 29 January 1876, pp. 124–25.
Fortnightly Review, n.s. 20 (1876): 601–16. Sidney Colvin.
London Quarterly and Holborn Review 40 (1873): 99–110.

Macmillan's Magazine 14 (1866): 272–79. John Morley.
—— 36 (1877): 101–11. Joseph Jacobs.
National Review 11 (1860): 191–219. [Richard Holt Hutton.]
North American Review 124 (1877): 31–52. Edwin P. Whipple.
North British Review, American ed., 45 (1866): 103–20. [H. H. Lancaster.]
Quarterly Review, American ed., 108 (1860): 245–60. [James Craigie Robertson.]
——, American ed., 134 (1873): 178–95. [Rev. Robert Laing.]
Saint Paul's Magazine 12 (1873): 592–616. George Barnett Smith.
Saturday Review 34 (1872): 733–34; 794–96.
—— 42 (1876): 356–58.
Standard [London], 24 December 1880, p. 3.
The Times, 7 March 1873, pp. 3d–f. [Frederick Napier Broome.]
Westminster Review, American ed., 71 (1859): 269–83. [John Chapman.]

Index

ology of, 18, 45, 71–72, 155, 157–59; and Mill, 72, 163–64; and organicism, 42, 151–59, 163, 166, 170, 185–86; on progress, 46, 51, 57, 171, 181n; on religion, 4, 53, 56; and Social Dynamics, 45–46, 61, 64–65; and Social Statics, 45, 152–55, 167, 170–71, 174, 176; and Tönnies, 15–16, 31, 51; and woman question, 167–68, 170–71, 174–76, 181

Spinoza, Baruch de, 53n

Squires, Michael, 21–22, 24, 102, 107, 130

Stang, Richard, 256–57

Stephen, Leslie, 196n

Stowe, Harriet Beecher, 49–50

Strauss, David Friedrich: on Christianity, 3–4, 53–54, 56–57, 59–60; and Eliot, 3–4, 53–54, 57, 59–60, 76, 259–60; importance of, 3–4; methodology of, 45, 60; and myth, 60, 76; and Religion of Humanity, 57, 76, 260; anticipated Tönnies, 15

Stump, Reva, 138n

Taylor, Clementia Doughty (Mrs. Peter Alfred), 176, 178, 180, 182–83

Teggart, Frederick J., 40, 43n

Thackeray, William Makepeace, 12, 249, 251, 255, 276, 277n, 284

Theophrastus Such, Impressions of, 58, 68, 77, 137, 164, 247

Thomson, Fred C., 164n

Tjoa, Hock Guan, 72n, 73, 155n

Tönnies, Ferdinand: on art, 15, 17, 77, 118, 309; compared with other theorists, 15–18, 31, 41, 48, 66; and Comte, 15–16, 31; on consensus, 154; on custom, 51, 96, 127, 132; and Eliot (*see* Eliot, George, relation to social theorists; Gemeinschaft, and fiction of Eliot; Gesellschaft, and fiction of Eliot); Gemeinschaft/Gesellschaft typology of, 14, 24, 30–31,

109, 115, 124 (*see also* Gemeinschaft; Gesellschaft); on human nature, 15–16, 115; importance of, 14–17, 23–26; J. Killham on, 23; and Maine, 15–16, 51, 161; and Marx, 16–17; methodology of, 17–18; nostalgia of, 16–17, 37; and Riehl, 30–31, 37, 51; on socialism, 16–17; and Spencer, 15–16, 31, 51; on status and contract, 51, 161

Tradition: decline of, 3, 51; Eliot on, 52; Eliot's treatment of, 15, 21, 49, 94–96, 99–101, 136n, 277 (*see also individual titles of novels*, custom in); as pillar of community, 31, 35

Tylor, E. B., 5

Updike, John, 307

Utilitarianism, 162

Watt, Ian, 77–79

Wharton, John J. S., 178–79, 181, 216

Whipple, E. P., 305–6

Whitehead, Alfred North, 157

Wiesenfarth, Joseph, 60, 94n

Willey, Basil, 4n, 45n, 57n

Williams, Raymond, 18–25, 52, 102, 244, 309

Witemeyer, Hugh, 119n

Wolff, Michael, 5n, 249n, 250n

Woman question: and *DD*, 225–29, 240–42, 300–301; Eliot on, 174–83, 217; and *M*, 141, 205–18, 222–24; and J. S. Mill, 167–75, 177, 179–81, 205–9, 212–15, 226–28, 241; and *MF*, 199–200, 283, 300; Victorian debate on, 167–83, 205–6n, 215–17, 310

Woolf, Virginia, 200n

Wordsworth, William, 11–12, 77, 101–2, 285

Working classes: and concept of community, 19–20, 22; Eliot on, 39, 165; Eliot's treatment of, 19–20, 116, 134–35; Mill on, 163–64, 165

Designer: Marilyn Perry
Compositor: Heritage Printers, Inc.
Text: Linotype Baskerville
Display: Foundry Baskerville
Printer: Heritage Printers, Inc.
Binder: The Delmar Company